PRAISE FOR

THE KING OF VODKA

WINNER OF THE WILLIAM SAROYAN
INTERNATIONAL PRIZE FOR WRITING, NONFICTION

JAMES BEARD AWARD NOMINEE

A *BUSINESSWEEK* BEST BUSINESS BOOK OF 2009

SILVER MEDAL WINNER AXIOM BUSINESS BOOK AWARDS

A *SAN FRANCISCO CHRONICLE* NOTABLE BOOK

A 2010 INTERNATIONAL ASSOCIATION OF CULINARY
PROFESSIONALS (IACP) AWARDS FINALIST

"A colorful chronicle of the rise of a business. Ms. Himelstein, a veteran journalist, keeps her narrative moving neatly along, distilling complex matters of commerce into a clear and readable form."
—*Wall Street Journal*

"Himelstein makes Russian history and even current politics come alive."
—*USA Today*

"The tale of Pyotr Smirnov . . . reads more like a vivid cinematic script than meticulously researched nonfiction."
—*San Jose Mercury News*

"Himelstein brings thorough research and strong writing to bear on a fascinating subject."
—*BusinessWeek*

"The book is an impressive feat of research, told swiftly and enthusiastically."
—*San Francisco Chronicle*

"An astonishing tale."   —*Miami Herald*

"While the dozens of obstacles, including the closure of the Imperial Archives and a dearth of information about Smirnov's years of serfdom, might have deterred lesser researchers, Himelstein has triumphed with a timeless book that entertains, informs, and inspires any would-be entrepreneur to chase his dreams."
                                                          —*Publishers Weekly*

"In *The King of Vodka*, journalist Linda Himelstein delivers the intriguing back story of how the international swig of choice came into being."   —*Daily News* (New York)

"He didn't have Twitter, Facebook, or even television, but Pyotr Smirnov still built his vodka into the dominant brand in Russia. Linda Himelstein tells how he did it, overcoming his serf status and lack of education. His story includes plenty of colorful characters, including one Leo Tolstoy, temperance leader, and tells what life was like in nineteenth and early-twentieth-century Russia."
                                                          —*Kansas City Star*

"Himelstein's extensive research renders an interesting tale packed with history, struggle, and success amid political upheaval that might inspire readers to do some research of their own."
                                                          —*Denver Times*

"Had Pyotr Smirnov (1831–98) been literary-minded, he might have entitled a memoir *Up from Serfdom*. But he was all business, as recounted in this history of the famous vodka brand. Recalling the entrepreneurial milieu in which Smirnov distilled and marketed his way to success, Himelstein points to the Muscovite uncle in the vodka trade who provided her provincial protagonist's toehold in the world of commerce. Capping the saga with the legal survival of the Smirnov trademarks, Himelstein's storytelling success distills diligent research into something appealing to popular tastes for family and Russian history alike."   —*Booklist*

"The story of the Smirnov family is an operatic tour de force, and Linda Himelstein tells it with grace and passion."

—Tilar J. Mazzeo, author of *The Widow Clicquot*

"Through impressive research and gifted narration, Himelstein unearths and polishes the Dickensian story of Pyotr Smirnov, a strong-willed Russian entrepreneur whose wily maneuverings created the eponymous brand that remains a household name. The intriguing twists and turns of Smirnov's life will appeal even to readers who don't care for Bloody Marys. Himelstein's grasp of the intertwining of politics and business also yields a parallel story: how Russia's nineteenth-century experiment with capitalism contributed to the country's transition from an oppressive yet orderly tsarist social order into a nation battered by chaos and revolution."

—Alice Schroeder, author of
The Snowball: Warren Buffet and the Business of Life

"Russia is a land of epic struggle, and vodka is the spirit of its tormented soul. Pyotr Smirnov and his extended family provide Linda Himelstein with a cast of unforgettable characters and a vivid narrative that embodies and explains Russia's hundred-year journey from tsarism to Bolshevism. I can think of no better way to bring this wrenching story to life. *The King of Vodka* is a triumph."

—Tom Gjelten, author of *Bacardi and the Long Fight for Cuba*

THE
KING of VODKA

The Cast

Main Family Characters

Pyotr Arsenievich Smirnov *The King of Vodka*

Mariya Nikolayevna Smirnova *Smirnov's third wife*

Arseniy Smirnov *Smirnov's father*

Grigoriy Smirnov *Smirnov's uncle*

Ivan Smirnov *Smirnov's uncle*

Pyotr Petrovich Smirnov *Smirnov's eldest son*

Nikolay Petrovich Smirnov *Smirnov's second-eldest son*

Vladimir Petrovich Smirnov *Smirnov's third-eldest son*

Sergey Petrovich Smirnov *Smirnov's fourth-eldest son*

Aleksey Petrovich Smirnov *Smirnov's youngest son*

Aleksandra Petrovna Smirnova *Smirnov's youngest daughter*

Supporting Family Characters and Others Connected to Them

Matryona Smirnova *Smirnov's mother*

Venedikt Smirnov *Smirnov's uncle*

Eugeniya Ilyinichna Smirnova *Pyotr Petrovich's wife*

Aleksandra Pavlovna Smirnova *Vladimir Petrovich's second wife, mother of his son*

Tatiana Smirnova-Maksheyeva *Vladimir Petrovich's third wife and memoirist*

Valentina Piontkovskaya *Operetta star and Vladimir's lover*

Martemyan Borisovskiy *Aleksandra Smirnova's lover, later husband*

Konstantin Petrovich Bakhrushin *Smirnov's son-in-law*

Arseniy Petrovich Smirnov *Smirnov's grandson born to Pyotr*

Vladimir Vladimirovich Smirnov *Smirnov's grandson born to Vladimir*

Nikolay Venediktovich Smirnov *Smirnov's cousin and vodka factory director*

Oleg Smirnov *Smirnov's grandson born to Sergey*

Boris Smirnov *Smirnov's great-great-grandson, through Aleksey's line*

Smirnov's Vodka Producing Rivals

Aleksander Shtriter
Kamill Deprés
M. A. Popov
Nikolay Shustov
Emile Rouget
Keller & Co.

Key Members of the Russian Bureaucracy

Tsar Aleksander II *Known by some as the Great Reformer*

Tsar Aleksander III *Proponent of the vodka monopoly*

Tsar Nikolay II *Last Russian tsar*

Ivan Vyshnegradskiy *Minister of Finance 1887–1892*

Sergey Witte *Minister of Finance 1892–1903*

Revolutionaries

Vladimir Lenin *Leader of the Bolshevik Party*

Leon Trotskiy *Lenin's number two and Commander of the Red Army*

Josef Stalin *Future leader of the Soviet Union*

Key Literary Figures

Lev Tolstoy *Outspoken temperance advocate*

Anton Chekhov *Critic of Smirnov and other vodka makers*

Maxim Gorkiy *Chronicled the Russian Revolution*

Fyodor Dostoevskiy *Anti-alcohol, anti-merchant advocate*

Aleksander Ostrovskiy *Playwright, outspoken critic of merchants*

THE KING OF VODKA

The Story of Pyotr Smirnov and the Upheaval of an Empire

Linda Himelstein

HARPER ● PERENNIAL

NEW YORK • LONDON • TORONTO • SYDNEY • NEW DELHI • AUCKLAND

HARPER ● PERENNIAL

A hardcover edition of this book was published in 2009 by HarperCollins Publishers.

P.S.™ is a trademark of HarperCollins Publishers.

THE KING OF VODKA. Copyright © 2009 by Linda Himelstein. All rights reserved. Printed in the United States of America. No part of this book may be used or reproduced in any manner whatsoever without written permission except in the case of brief quotations embodied in critical articles and reviews. For information address HarperCollins Publishers, 10 East 53rd Street, New York, NY 10022.

HarperCollins books may be purchased for educational, business, or sales promotional use. For information please write: Special Markets Department, HarperCollins Publishers, 10 East 53rd Street, New York, NY 10022.

FIRST HARPER PERENNIAL EDITION PUBLISHED 2010.

Designed by Renato Stanisic

The Library of Congress has catalogued the hardcover edition as follows:

Himelstein, Linda.
     The King of Vodka : the Story of Pyotr Smirnov and the upheaval of an empire / Linda Himelstein.
          p. cm.
     Includes bibliographical references and index.
     ISBN 978-0-06-085589-5
     1.   Smirnov, P. A. (Petr Arsen'evich) 2.   Smirnov (Firm)   3. Distillers–Russia–Biography.   4. Vodka industry–Russia–History.   I. Title.
     TP591.S64H56 2009
     338.7'6635–dc22
     [B]

10 11 12 13 14   OV/RRD   10 9 8 7 6 5 4 3 2 1

ISBN 978-0-06-085591-8 (pbk.)

To my family, the best there is

Contents

PART TWO

A man comes from the dust and in the dust he will end—
and in the meantime, it is good to drink a sip of vodka.

—OLD PROVERB

Author's Note

This historical narrative account is based on exhaustive research conducted over more than four years in the United States and Russia. Information included in the book was gleaned from over 500 archival documents, approximately 250 articles from periodicals and newspapers, more than 900 books, and interviews with a dozen or more leading experts in related fields. In some instances, primary sources could not be found at all, were incomplete, or in conflict with other sources. In these cases, available documentation and relevant historical context were relied upon to provide likely accounts of events. In other circumstances, corroborating evidence supporting personal recollections or viewpoints could not be found. For example, some of Vladimir Smirnov's many remembrances, recorded by his third wife, could not be verified. Notations have been included throughout the book to alert readers to these occasions wherever possible.

Citations, both in English and Russian, are extensive, though they do not include references for facts that are

widely known or accepted. And unless otherwise noted, transla-
tions of Russian documents were provided by Tatiana Glezer.
Names in the book are transliterated into a hybrid of Russian
and English spellings to retain their Russian feel but make them
easier to read. In addition, Russia followed the Julian calendar
until January 31, 1918. Thus, all dates prior to that time are given
according to the Julian, not Gregorian, calendar. Finally, con-
verting nineteenth- and early twentieth-century Russian rubles
into today's dollar equivalents proved to be a particularly daunting challenge. An elaborate three-step process was developed
to make this calculation with the help of Sofya Alekseyevna
Salomatina, coordinator of the Center for Economic History
at Moscow State University, and an indispensable resource by
Samuel Williamson titled *Six Ways to Compute the Relative Value
of a U.S. Dollar Amount, 1774 to Present.*

Prologue: Good-bye

The smell of mud and wet stone hung in the air. Moscow had been in the midst of an unusually warm spell. It was already late November, yet dandelions and daisies were poking out of the earth, nurtured by a steady balmy drizzle. The few flakes of snow that had fallen had quickly vanished, leaving cobblestones glistening on the ground. As the springlike days wore on, it seemed like winter might never come.

But it did, finally. As December 1898 arrived, a chill snuck up on Moscow like an invading army. Snow began to fall before daybreak and continued without interruption. Soon, a thick coat of white buried the city. Sledges, large wooden carriages that glided around town on metal runners, took the place of clumsier wheeled vehicles. Within a day, temperatures dropped another fifteen degrees, leaving Russia's then second-largest city in its more typical seasonal state: gray and frigid.

Little else, however, was typical that December day, particularly at the corner of Pyatnitskaya Street just past the

Cast Iron Bridge, a pathway that led directly to Red Square and the Kremlin. Since 8 AM, crowds had flowed into this neighborhood, known as a hub for Moscow's flourishing merchant class. Wealthy businessmen arrived with their elegant wives; important government officials and religious leaders left behind other pressing matters to make an appearance. Workers and peasants showed up in droves, spilling out into the street leading to St. John the Baptist Church. The crush was so dense that movement became almost impossible. Horse-drawn trams that usually seesawed through the center of Pyatnitskaya were forced to stop running as long lines of mourning carriages surrounded the block.[1]

At 9 AM, the bell rang out, snapping the masses to attention. All eyes turned toward a majestic funeral chariot outfitted with a canopy of rich silver brocade.[2] It was parked before the grandest residence on the block, a three-story-high mansion that was a testament to the architectural beauty cropping up all over Russia. The home's sheer size—with thirty-one street-facing windows—would have been enough to stop even the most refined passersby. But this structure also looked something like a museum. Ornate carvings of flowers, leaves, lions, and two-headed eagles were etched into the outer façade. A cast-iron balcony adorned the corner of the third floor along with glorious artisan porches. At the main entrance, an elaborate, black-iron archway marked the home's stately gateway. Viewing the home at its cornermost point from across the Moscow River, it resembled a small luxury liner heading out to sea.

The heavy wooden doors parted and the archdeacon from St. John the Baptist Church emerged, softly reciting prayers. A group carrying a coffin cover decorated with a wreath made of natural flowers fell into line after him. A choir came out then, singing the Holy God prayer, followed by a dozen workers. Each carried a pillow with sacred medals and honors earned by the deceased during an extraordinary life. Other church elders and dignitaries followed next, including ten priests wearing shimmering robes.

At last, a coffin emerged, draped in a sumptuous fabric made of golden brocade and raspberry velvet.

It was the second day of December, and this eloquent tribute was not for a tsar or a high-ranking minister or a military chief. The man inside the long oak box was Pyotr Arsenievich Smirnov, arguably the most famous vodka maker in the world.

That such a spectacle would be held for a man like Smirnov would have been unthinkable in 1831 when he was born at the family home in Kayurovo, a small farming village roughly 170 miles due north from Moscow. His parents were poor, barely literate, and most telling, they were serfs, part of Russia's legally bound underclass. They were essentially slaves, owned by the proprietors of the land on which they lived and worked. All that they earned was shared with their landowners, who had control over what they did, where they went, and how they survived.

This commoner background, in tandem with Smirnov's ultimate notoriety as a leading purveyor of liquors, was not a life that typically beat a path to prominence. Moreover, for the last decade of his life, alcoholism was raging throughout society and calls for increased controls on spirits producers were rampant. Still, when Smirnov died at age sixty-seven of heart failure, newspapers treated the event as a national tragedy. Descriptions like "distinguished," "exemplary," and "a giant of Russian industry" appeared in news stories. Smirnov's passing shared the front page with the weightiest developments of the day— from the United States's intention to sell the Philippines, to the controversial and scandalous Dreyfus Affair. Alfred Dreyfus, a Jewish artillery officer was serving time on Devil's Island for allegedly passing military secrets to Germany. But supporters, including writer Émile Zola who published his renowned *J'accuse* letter, successfully proved that anti-Semites had framed Dreyfus. Ten months after Smirnov's death, Dreyfus was pardoned, later becoming a knight in the French Legion of Honor.

From a certain perspective, Smirnov was a lot like Dreyfus.

They were both underdogs, born into positions that were neither of their own making nor choosing. Dreyfus, a Jew; Smirnov, a serf—yet neither man let the disadvantage of their labels dictate their life choices. Smirnov had to overcome both his lowly status and a thoroughly unsophisticated, rudimentary makeup. Life in rural Russia was remote and plebeian, and as a serf Smirnov's main occupations as a young boy likely would have been helping his mother care for younger siblings, lending a hand with the livestock and crops, and picking wild mushrooms and berries. He could not have attended school even if he had wanted to as none existed where he lived. When he did venture beyond his home village, the journey was fraught with peril—particularly at night. Smirnov would have had to carry metal sticks with him, banging them together or against trees to scare off hungry, wild wolves that lurked nearby. Young Pyotr was surely better off at home, tending to the family's most immediate needs.*

Young Smirnov, always obedient, did as he was told. But beneath his outwardly quiet and reserved demeanor, he must have been restless, internally agitated, a racehorse at the starting gate. It wasn't as if he knew where he was going. Rather, he was someone who made where he was the very place to be. He devoured his surroundings, taking in seemingly inconsequential events and details and spitting them out as life-altering encounters. This was how he came to vodka.

IN RUSSIA, VODKA was as fundamental to daily life as food and the wintry chill. Around 1500, it is believed that monks were distilling the liquid in their monasteries, isolated hillside retreats where chemical experiments and scientific discoveries

---

* Little independent or primary evidence exists detailing Smirnov's early childhood. This reconstruction is drawn from available data on serfs and information provided by Vladimir Grechukhin, the director of the Folk Ethnographic Museum in Myshkin, which houses a small museum devoted to Smirnov.

were routinely made. Surpluses of grain made production relatively easy—and cheap. Monks used primitive stills, producing liquor that often had a greenish blue tinge to it caused by traces of copper sulfate from the copper fermentation vessels—and a foul smell.[3] In those days vodka wasn't merely consumed for pleasure, it was a medicinal product. It could be a powerful disinfectant for wounds or a soothing, warm balm massaged into the back and chest. Its uses changed quickly, of course, becoming Russia's beverage of choice when distilling methods were improved and medicinal additives were replaced with sweet aromas and tasty spices.

Almost overnight, vodka, whose name is derived from the Russian word *voda*, meaning water, became a focal point for a variety of rituals. A practice known as "wetting the bargain" used vodka as an inducement to bring communities together to build a church, bring in a harvest, or construct a bridge. A job well done meant that vodka would flow freely. Vodka drinking was also a favorite pastime of Peter the Great, who instituted the "penalty shot" during his reign from 1682 to 1725. It purportedly forced anyone late for a meeting or gathering to pay either a fine or drink a large cup of vodka. Over the years, vodka was used as payment in lieu of money, as a bribe, and as encouragement for soldiers on the front lines. The so-called drink of life was even fed to women in labor and to newborn babies when other remedies failed to calm them. The tsarist government, which maintained firm control over the vodka economy, sanctioned and encouraged these practices. Increased consumption of vodka was an easy way to pump up state coffers.

By the time Smirnov came around, vodka was an entrenched national habit. More than that it was big business, having surpassed salt to become the dominant source of revenue for the government. Taxes on vodka covered one-third of the state's ordinary expenses and generated enough to pay for all of Russia's peacetime defense.[4]

Pyotr Smirnov saw how powerful vodka could be. His uncle Grigoriy operated hotels and pubs in Uglich,[5] a town best known as the home base of Ivan the Terrible's son in the sixteenth century. Grigoriy also ran a brewery and at least one wine cellar.[6] As a young boy, Smirnov worked for his uncle. He washed dishes, mopped floors, waited tables, and tended bar. He must have observed how the men drank, how their teeth unclenched and their faces smoothed as soon as the drink passed their lips. He would have seen that the mere act of drinking, of swallowing, brought a pleasure rarely found within a Russian peasant's arduous life. And he surely would have understood that vodka meant money—good money. The pubs, inns, and wine business had made Grigoriy, also a serf, wealthy enough to buy his freedom. He became a successful and admired businessman in his community, and young Smirnov yearned for that himself—and more.

In truth, Pyotr probably would have preferred a more outwardly honorable, less controversial vocation. He was a devout Orthodox Christian all his life, presumably attending confessions from the time he was seven. He was a collector of religious icons and a churchwarden of two Kremlin Court cathedrals, which were much-revered positions.[7] As for liquor, he did not much care for it personally. He drank minimally, mainly to taste his own concoctions, join celebrations, or avoid insulting a thirsty guest. He rather despised the loud drunks who swallowed away what little money they had and made nuisances of themselves.

But those feelings were quietly set aside. More than anything, Smirnov was an opportunist and a capitalist. Liquor was what he knew—and he made the most of it. When Pyotr Smirnov died, he was the country's leading producer of vodka, the chief of a business worth an estimated 20 million rubles (about $265 million today).[8] He was one of the largest retailers of liquor in Russia—the purveyor to the tsar and Imperial Court—and his bottles were on the tables of royalty from Sweden to Spain. His personal fortune, including two immense homes, two vacation compounds, one factory and numerous shops, warehouses and cellars, topped 10 million rubles (roughly $132.7 million), making him one of the wealthiest men in all of Russia.[9] In 1886 he even captured one of the most elusive awards when he earned the title of hereditary honored citizen, an extraordinary accomplishment for an ex-serf and an honor that was bestowed on only the most deserving citizens.

It was an unexpected life, to be sure, built on sheer determination and an unwavering sense of purpose. Smirnov, a tall dashing man with a commanding presence, never had much use for the shades of gray that inhabited most people's lives—tell him something couldn't be done and he would do it twice just to make a point. It was a quality that brought out fear in some and great admiration in others. However it affected those around him, they knew they were in the presence of a man who would not be bound by normal constraints.

Perhaps that is why so many had turned out that bitter December day to stand in the cold and watch a funeral march by. The solemn, black-clothed crowd followed the slow procession, their footsteps crackling as they crunched through the freshly fallen snow. St. John the Baptist Church, one of Russia's most ancient houses of worship, never looked more beautiful. Its three-tiered belfry, which towered above all else on this section of Pyatnitskaya Street, served as a beacon to Russians passing by that day. Tropical plants and brilliantly colored flowers framed both sides of the church; a walkway before the entrance was layered in black cloth. At the helm of the ceremony stood the highest ranked member of the Russian clergy, the Metropolitan Vladimir. He presided over official events for Russia's tsars, and his presence alone left no doubt about the importance of Smirnov's death.

Candles lit the way to the raised platform in the church where Smirnov's body lay. A collection of sterling silver wreaths adorned the coffin. One wreath from his three older sons was inscribed: "To the unforgettable parent from his heartily loving children, Pyotr, Nikolay, and Vladimir Smirnov." Another from Smirnov's wife read: "To a dear, unforgettable husband from his loving wife."[10] Other wreaths from friends, workers, and admirers were piled onto the coffin as well.

The cold had crept into the church, but those who managed to make it through the doorway seemed not to notice. Heat coming from their bodies and breath offered enough warmth, especially as the voices in the choir began to rise. The liturgy lasted a full two hours, followed by an hour-long burial service.

The lengthy journey to Smirnov's ultimate resting place began as his coffin was loaded onto a luxuriously adorned barrow. Three carts bursting with wreaths came next, followed immediately by the funeral chariot. Then, some one hundred carriages lined up to make the four-mile trip to the cemetery. The commoners would walk the route, which took them over the Cast Iron Bridge, past the Kremlin, and through Red Square. When they arrived at their destination, it was 3 PM. Daylight would last only another twenty-eight minutes.

Smirnov's body was placed in the ground just before darkness fell and covered with stones and fresh dirt. A simple metal cross was erected, and then, it was over. Or was it? Smirnov was not a man to leave his final destiny to chance. He had requested in writing that prayers be said in at least forty churches for forty days after his death. His belief, which followed Russian Orthodox doctrines, was that it would take those forty days to determine whether his soul was bound for heaven or hell. He had instructed those around him to pray that his sins be forgiven and a place be made for him in paradise.

Was Smirnov afraid of what the afterlife might have in store for him? It's not hard to imagine. More than a decade before Smirnov's death, the stigma attached to alcohol—and alcoholism—was intensifying. The topic had been debated for many years. A handful of temperance societies had been founded.

Writers had portrayed foul drunkards in their literature. They were always the lost, weak souls who could do little more than inspire pity and wreak havoc. Fyodor Dostoevskiy, for instance, whose own father was a cruel drunk, wrote passionately about the perils of alcoholism: "The consumption of alcoholic beverages brutalizes and makes a man savage, hardens him, distracts him from bright thoughts, blunts all good propaganda and above all else weakens the will, and in general uproots any kind of humanity."[11] These eloquent rants were certainly thought provoking, but they did not inspire a call to action, nor did they give anyone reason enough to take on a government addicted to its annual vodka windfalls.

At the height of Smirnov's popularity in the 1880s, Russia's anti-alcohol movement began a slow progression. More organizations touting sobriety popped up. More books described the harmful effects of alcohol. Writers, clergy, and doctors took up the cause. Apart from basic information on health, temperance leaders also had the sad state of the vodka industry on their side. At the time, hundreds of rogue distillers and corrupt tavern owners were operating throughout Russia. They cared little about the quality of their often dirty, bitter swill, which was routinely diluted with water, lime, or sandalwood. It had even been known to poison some unlucky imbibers.

All that mattered to these renegade producers was quantity. Their primary objective was to claim as many rubles as possible. They attacked one another, taking on leading producers of the day, such as Smirnov, Popov, and Shustov. They peddled counterfeit vodkas, including Smirnov's, and some rivals even hired scientists to test vodkas made by the largest distillers—and then declared them rotten or impure.

The stoic Smirnov was incensed. He had spent his life cultivating an image of respect and morality that was beyond reproach. Smirnov fought back with full-page ads defending his vodkas and slamming his critics. He developed branded corks, hoping to trip up his rivals. The battles and Smirnov's countermeasures riveted many observers, but to famed playwright Anton Chekhov, they were abhorrent—and examples of the worst of Russia. Long before he penned *Uncle Vanya* and *The Cherry Orchard*, Chekhov, a physician by training, chronicled in 1885 what he dubbed a "war" among vodka producers. He wrote about the peddlers of "satan's blood," the evil vodka makers who he predicted one day would destroy one another. In a column he wrote for *Shards* magazine in St. Petersburg, Chekhov singled out Smirnov as one of the chief offenders. "Each enemy, trying to prove that the vodka of his competitor is worthless, sends torpedoes, sinks ships, and exasperates with politics. What *isn't* done in order to sprinkle pepper in the nose of the sleeping enemy? . . . In all likelihood, the war will end with the producers suing each other. . . . Fighting spiders eat each other so that in the end, only the legs are left."[12]

These public tongue-lashings pressured the tsar and his government, which finally determined that something needed to be done. In 1886, a law was passed making it a crime for employers to continue their common practice of substituting vodka or anything else for wages. All salaries were to be paid in cash. Pubs were banished. These laws, however, did little to sober up Russians—or the workplace. But they did embolden other anti-alcohol crusaders, the most celebrated one being Count Lev Nikolaevich Tolstoy.

Tolstoy had been a world-class carouser as a young man, despite his somewhat awkward and reserved nature. He spent much of his early adulthood living in the heart of a war that made no sense to him. He hid his misgivings under a mountain of cigarettes, loose women, and gambling binges. Never an ardent tippler, Tolstoy nonetheless found that moderate imbibing enabled him to slip into situations he otherwise would have never dared to enter. After a religious crisis following the great success of

Anna Karenina, Tolstoy admitted, with horror, to his transgressions in *Confessions*, a moralistic tome that first appeared in 1879. "I killed people in war; summoned others to duels in order to kill them, gambled at cards; I devoured the fruits of the peasants' labor and punished them; I fornicated and practiced deceit. Lying, thieving, promiscuity of all kinds, drunkenness, violence, murder—there was not a crime I did not commit."[13]

Now Tolstoy devoted himself to evangelizing abstinence. His reputation enabled him to reach vast numbers of people. For the next three decades, he wrote regularly about the perils of drinking, which he considered the root of all evil. In an 1886 comedic play titled *The First Distiller*, for instance, Tolstoy invented his own vodka concoction. The ingredients: blood of a fox, a wolf, and a pig. He also founded a publishing house to disseminate moralistic literature, and he enlisted his friend, noted artist Ilya Repin, to illustrate some of his writings. In 1887, he founded the Union Against Drunkenness, a grassroots temperance society.

Early one morning that year, Tolstoy called the people in his village of Yasnaya Polyana together. A table and bench were placed before the communal house near his estate. Tolstoy reached into his pocket, pulled out a piece of paper, and placed it on the table next to a bottle of ink and a pen. He then spoke passionately about the curses of tobacco and vodka. He entreated every man to sign the paper, a pledge to drink no more. Once they did, many at the urgings of their wives and children, Tolstoy asked them to dig a ditch. It was quickly filled with cigarettes, cigars, jars of tobacco, pipes, and cigar cases.[14]

Smirnov was undoubtedly aware of Tolstoy's high-profile campaign, and he probably resented his life's work being characterized as amoral or anti-Christian. After all, Smirnov saw himself quite the opposite. He rose from modest means to become a respected business leader, the proud patriarch of an empire that provided jobs to five thousand Russians and funneled millions of rubles to the tsar's treasury.[15] What's more, Smirnov believed he had turned vodka making into a kind of art form. He cared deeply about the quality and purity of his pristine formulas, and he claimed that his ingredients were the best, his vodkas the finest.

Ultimately, though, vodka itself was blamed. Tsar Aleksander III could no longer ignore the problem of alcoholism in his country. In 1895, three years before Smirnov's death, the tsar established the State Vodka Monopoly in order to control the amount, and ensure the quality, of alcohol sold to the public. After that, vodka could be sold only in state-run stores, crippling independent distillers like Smirnov. His company managed to remain profitable, switching much of its vodka operation to other products and spirits, such as wine and Cognac. But Smirnov's output eventually shriveled to a fraction of what it had been before the monopoly. No longer did some two hundred horse-drawn lorries bring barrels of liquor from the railroad to Smirnov's warehouses. No longer was Smirnov's factory able to produce his most famous drink, Table Wine No. 21 (vodka), or an array of his other original recipes.

As the signs of a more treacherous business environment rose, his health grew precarious, too. Smirnov began to plan for death. His goal was to craft an uncontestable will. He wanted no ambiguity about his desire. Smirnov had reason for concern. He had had three wives in his lifetime, only one of whom was still living, and ten surviving children. His family had managed to function much like a wheel. Smirnov served as the central hub, keeping the spokes connected—but at a reasonable, workable distance. Like so many others born into privilege, some of Smirnov's children were cavalier about work, responsibility, or morality. Two of his sons, Nikolay and Vladimir, were notorious playboys. They gambled to excess and spent money indifferently, to the delight of proprietors of Moscow's toniest shops.

Smirnov's eldest son, Pyotr, was more business minded. But his ideas for running the vodka empire may have differed greatly from those of his siblings or stepmother, Smirnov's third wife, Mariya Nikolayevna Smirnova. A genteel beauty twenty-seven years younger than her husband, Mariya had less concern for the futures of Smirnov's oldest sons, who were already grown.* She focused on Vladimir and her two youngest sons, Sergey and Aleksey, who were just thirteen and nine, respectively, when their father died. The family schisms likely worried Smirnov. He understood that without him to keep the assemblage intact, it could disintegrate, taking his legacy and cherished empire down with it.

In the days after Smirnov's death and his funeral, it seemed that his fears were on their way to becoming reality. Fights were brewing over how to run the business, who should manage the company, and how Smirnov's considerable assets would be disbursed. Smirnov's five daughters took no part in the discussion since each of them was allotted a flat 30,000 rubles (nearly $400,000). The rest of the estate was to be divided equally between Mariya and the Smirnov boys.[16]

Pyotr Arsenievich Smirnov was dead now. A calmness enveloped Moscow late that cold Wednesday in 1898. As the mourners scattered, more than one thousand of the poorest in attendance were treated to free dinners provided by the Smirnovs and their friends. It was a grand gesture, a civility that would too soon be replaced with jealousy, anger, resentment, and ultimately, chaos.

---

* Mariya's age is calculated by church records at the time of her death. No birth records for her could be found.

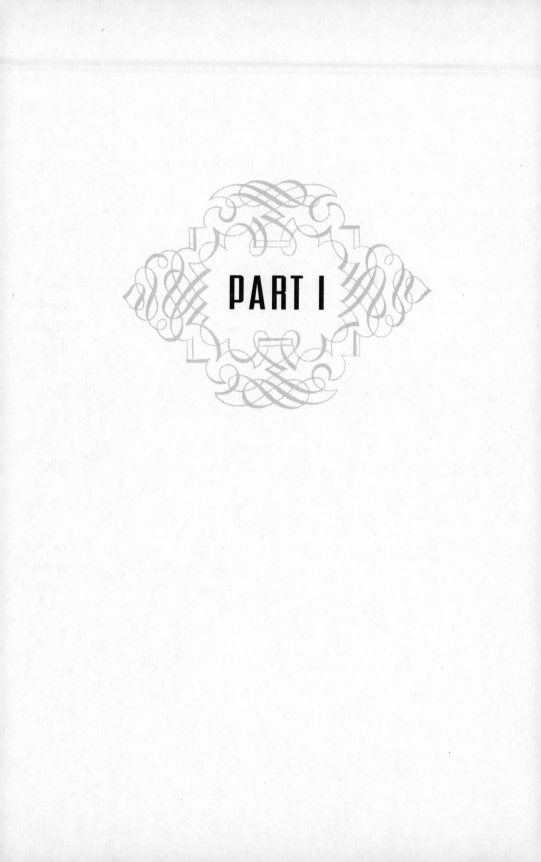

PART I

Chapter 1

Hello

Carts hauling withered bodies bumped along the dirt roads. Arms dangled off the sides of the wooden flatbeds like overgrown weeds. Victims, young and old, rich and poor, lay like toppled dominos, one after another. As they passed, making their way from the villages, cities, and towns to the freshly stirred ground in the forested countryside, pedestrians watched anxiously, covering their faces with cloth. The stench was worse now that summer was in full swing. Cholera had come to Russia.

The disease first appeared in 1823, coming ashore in the southernmost regions of Russia. At first, it looked to be little more than an isolated disturbance. Cases were reported sporadically but no one, including Tsar Nikolay I, seemed alarmed. A few extra doctors were dispatched and data collected about those infected and those who died. Then . . . nothing. For six years, Russia remained cholera free. Not until the summer of 1830 did Russia's government and population recognize they were on the brink of a nationwide calamity.

2 THE KING OF VODKA

Sickness quickly permeated the whole of Russia, wearing it down like a shark devours its prey, one deadly tear at a time. Scores of citizens fell ill after drinking water contaminated with the cholera bacteria or by coming in contact with untreated sewage. They suffered from a variety of intestinal ailments and severe cramping, which often led to crippling dehydration, shock, and then death. The outbreak had returned in July to Astrakhan, an important waterside trading hub in southern Russia near the Caspian Sea. Within six weeks, nearly three thousand residents died, or about 8 percent of the city's total population.[1] A gathering terror settled within Russia's borders as cholera made its way north, loosely tracking the path of the Volga River.

The tsar acted quickly, imposing quarantines wherever cases were reported. Anyone wishing to leave sequestered communities had to endure observation periods that could last anywhere from eight days to two weeks. Those detained had to wash themselves daily with a chlorine-lime solution.[2] Their luggage was repeatedly fumigated. Once outside the quarantined zone, travelers had to get through military-enforced cordons. Of the eighteen entrances leading to Moscow eight were shuttered, slowing trade and sharply restricting movement. Guards were ordered to shoot anyone who tried to break through the barriers.[3]

Other cleansing measures were just as onerous. Walls and floors in the homes of the infected were sprinkled with chlorine. Clothes and sheets were either rigorously washed in chlorine or simply burned. All water was boiled and the eating of apples, prunes, melons, and cucumbers was forbidden. Garlic, a natural disinfectant, became part of people's diets as the government doled out daily rations.

The tsar's containment policies applied to everyone, regardless of social position or stature. In September 1830, the poet Aleksander Pushkin had planned a short trip to his family's estate in Boldino. He ended up staying there, under virtual house arrest, for three months. This period, nonetheless, turned out to be one of the most prolific in the writer's life. Among other works, he came close to completing his most famous, *Eugene Onegin*, while under quarantine.[4]

But most others were not as fortunate. Mass hysteria overtook many who spread ugly rumors that cholera was the weapon chosen by Jews, foreigners, government officials, and aristocrats to rid the nation of its niggling underclass. People charged that wells were deliberately poisoned.[5] The absurd talk inflamed the already suspicious masses. They were fed up with a string of seemingly endless regulations and began to speak of being heard, of fighting back, of murder. The talk soon escalated into violence.

In November 1830 the first cholera riot exploded in Tambov, three hundred miles southeast of Moscow. Mobs raided hospitals and police departments; they captured Tambov's governor and killed doctors and officers suspected of mistreating or torturing patients. Rebels overtook the streets and broke into quarantined homes, liberating those who they said had been confined too long. The rebellion, finally suppressed by the Russian military after two violent days, caused serious damage. Some two hundred people in Tambov lost their lives and countless others suffered injuries.

Other riots sprouted throughout Russia, with one of the most serious erupting in St. Petersburg seven months after Tambov. Nearly six hundred people died every day as the situation disintegrated in the nation's capital. Arrests were common during the first ten days of the epidemic. Typically humdrum behaviors, from eating vegetables to drinking water from canals, became criminal acts. Everyone was under suspicion and frustration gave way to anger. Citizens assembled near the cholera hospital in Sennaya Square, ambushing ambulances carrying infected residents. They threw stones at hospitals, smashing windows, then rushed the hospital itself, beating doctors and attendants who stood in the way. One doctor, a German, was discovered while treating a patient. Within moments, his body was left pummeled to death on the floor. The army fought furiously to subdue the angry crowds and restore peace. But it could not soothe their troubled souls.[6]

That task was left to the tsar, who came out of seclusion at his summer palace in Peterhof to address his subjects. His personal appearance and arrival at Sennaya Square in an open carriage, with no military escort, was highly unusual. Tsars typically limited their interactions with their subjects, believing too much direct contact could undermine their prestige and authority. But this time, Nikolay I determined that the dire circumstances demanded his personal touch.

More than five thousand people gathered around the tsar, who rose in his carriage and crossed himself after seeing the destruction around him. He wore his military best, a crisp black double-breasted coat with gold buttons, which fit tightly around the tsar's slim waistline before dropping loosely to just below his knees. Bright golden epaulettes surrounded by gold tassels adorned his shoulders, providing Nikolay I with the regal, authoritarian look this moment demanded.

The tsar stood, then commanded his people to kneel. "A great burden has been given us by God: a plague. We must take measures to stop its progress. All these measures have been taken by my orders. Therefore it is against me that you complain—Me! And I order obedience! . . . If you have offended me by your disobedience, you have offended God still more by a crime: A murder has been committed! Innocent blood has been spilled. Pray God that he forgive you."[7]

By the time cholera ran its course, Russia lost more than 243,000 of its citizens.[8] It had also gained one infant boy, born in the midst of the epidemic and its mayhem.

PYOTR ARSENIEVICH SMIRNOV began life on Friday, January 9, 1831, at his home in Kayurovo, a village just sixty miles east of a quarantine district. The day was cloudy, dark, and cold. The home, known in Russian as an *izba*, like most others occupied by peasants in the area, was thoroughly modest. It was made of round pine logs, which sometimes had to be dragged for miles, and it had a slanted roof. The few windows were small, the distance between the end of a person's fingertips and elbow. Each was covered with the dried bladder of a bull, which did not do nearly enough to keep out the cold but was useful in letting in some natural light. The typical structure, at just 420 square feet, offered little privacy for the multiple generations who routinely lived together.*

Delivering babies in a small village like Kayurovo was treated like any other task on the farm. Pyotr's mother, Matryona, was likely placed on a plank bed near the oven in the middle of the room. The huge oven was the focal point of peasant home life. In those days, the oven had a large hole so people could climb inside, sit down, and wash themselves in relative warmth and comfort. Elder family members slept on a flat surface on top of the oven. The oven was also where most of the cooking took place, and where young calves, lambs, and pigs were kept to protect them from the harsh conditions outdoors. The heavy odor here, as if fused into the walls and floors, was a peculiar mixture of boiled potatoes, meats, soups, and animal fur. That day, however, only the laboring mother and a local midwife occupied the coveted spot.

Few details of Smirnov's birth are known. The simple four-line birth record, typical for serfs, listed first the name of the landowner for whom the family worked. It then listed the village name, the father's name, the godfather's name, and the baby's gender. Last came the child's given name: Pyotr.[9] No surname was provided as most serfs did not have one. It was unnecessary, primarily because serfs rarely traveled outside their

---

* Details of Smirnov's village life are drawn from regional museums and archives with the help of Vladimir Grechukhin. They reflect the most pervasive local customs at the time.

small communities. Exactly when Pyotr did gain a surname is not clear, though most likely it was more than two decades later. Smirnov was a common last name in the region and a derivative of *smirnoy*, meaning quiet and law abiding. Today, 2.7 million Russians call themselves Smirnov, making it the most common name in the nation.[10]

It can be assumed that Pyotr was born hearty. The infant mortality rate in Russia was among the highest in nineteenth-century Europe. Indeed, one out of every four babies born died before they reached their first year of life. The Smirnovs themselves lost three infant girls of their own, two from epilepsy and one from measles.[11] But Pyotr, the third out of four surviving children and the second son, was a standout from the start.

Much like his adult years, Pyotr's boyhood was dominated by three primary concerns: work, religion, and family. A seemingly incongruent hodgepodge of allegiances, these devotions were complimentary in practice, providing the foundation for Smirnov's willingness—even eagerness—to do whatever was required of him, checked by an ever-bending conscience born out of rigid Christian orthodoxy.

Smirnov's days, alongside his older brother, Yakov, were crammed with farm work, feeding the animals, hauling firewood, gardening, and cultivating the land. Serfs were required to tend their master's fields—often using their own equipment—to provide for everyone who lived in the community. In Smirnov's province, agriculture was dominated by flax, potato, rye, and wheat. The work was difficult, tedious, and long, particularly for a young child. Pyotr did as he was told, perhaps because he had no other choice.

Many serfs were viewed by their masters as "baptized property," according to Aleksander Gertsen, a Russian social activist. Most masters made little distinction between the people who plowed their fields and the horses that pulled the plows. Like merchandise at the community market, they could be bought, sold, or presented as gifts, almost on a whim. Those who stepped out of line or didn't pull their weight could find themselves shipped off to a new home or an entirely new town—sometimes without their families.

The Smirnovs did not have to worry about such penalties. Diligent workers who made no trouble pleased their owners. Unlike the stereotypical serfs, whom the nobility routinely dismissed as ignorant and uncultured, Pyotr's family was industrious and opportunistic. When Pyotr and his siblings were not consumed by chores, they received rudimentary lessons in reading, writing, math, and religion from their parents. Since just 1 percent of serfs were literate at the time, even this superficial education set the family apart from the some 551,000 serfs living in their local province of Yaroslavl. It also made them more valuable. Literate serfs could fetch a purchase price of 300 rubles each compared to just 200 rubles for those who lacked basic reading skills.[12]

Clearly, the Smirnovs' owners, first the Skripitsyns and later the Demidovs, both descendants of wealthy aristocratic dynasties, appreciated their more capable serfs. The Smirnov's home, though small, was likely larger than any other occupied by serfs in the village. Family members were also given more entrusted positions. Pyotr's father, Arseniy, was handpicked by Nadezhda Stepanovna Skripitsyna out of dozens of serfs to represent her interests when land was distributed between members of the nobility. This responsibility made him a manager of sorts, someone who commanded a degree of respect and authority. Arseniy's younger brother, Ivan, was a house serf. He was one of a handful of serfs permitted to work in the master's lavish estate, to receive meals there, and to organize the affairs of the house. This role exempted Ivan from the hard manual labor others endured daily, though his job was not considered a particularly privileged one. House serfs did not get to share in the bounty of the land, had to live in small *izbas* behind or near the master's home, and were viewed as even lower on the social ladder than ordinary serfs.

Still, life inside the master's home was more than comfortable. A typical estate consisted of multiple buildings, including a palatial main residence full of lavish imported furnishings and a large two-floored, stone outhouse. These dwellings were often surrounded by wooden garagelike structures to house carriages, stone or wood stables for the horses, a greenhouse, a bowling alley, various sheds to hold hay and grains, and a special structure for summertime activities and entertainment.

The Smirnovs maintained amicable relations with their masters and made the best of their provincial circumstances. Village life could be pleasant—and stable. But it was hardly the most desirable situation, nor was it profitable. The soil, overrun with dense forests, swamps, and ravines, was not particularly fertile. Difficult agricultural conditions presented a tough hurdle for serfs who ached to earn enough money to buy their freedom. At that time, peasants could ransom themselves by paying their masters an agreed-upon sum. In the Smirnov's region of Yaroslavl, the average price of freedom in the early nineteenth century was between 219 and 266 rubles, the equivalent of about $39 to $48 then.* Though it was no more than the cost of about twenty horses[13], it was as far out of reach for the ordinary serf as a private conversation with the tsar. To narrow the gap, serfs often sought permission from their landowners to venture beyond their small surroundings and seek jobs in larger towns and cities. They could make considerably more money— as much as 100 rubles in one winter—that then would have to be divided with their masters. This seasonal migration, a relatively common practice, was primarily meant for men and their sons. Women and girls often remained behind to maintain the homestead and do the hard work necessary to create their dowries,

---

* The value of a ruble in 1821 was about twenty-one cents.

which often included home-sown bed linens, towels, napkins, and tablecloths.

Naturally, the Smirnovs yearned for freedom. The first to go after it was Grigoriy, Pyotr's uncle and one of his father's younger brothers. Pyotr was still a toddler when his uncle packed up his meager belongings in 1835 and made for the twenty-five-mile dirt road that led from his village to the bustling town of Uglich. The walk was long and tedious, but Grigoriy would have kept himself occupied, meeting up with caravans heading here or there and stopping at the homes of acquaintances for rest and nourishment. Mostly, though, he probably thought about his future. At age twenty-six, Grigoriy had big plans.

GRIGORIY HAD CERTAINLY been to Uglich before. It was a busy trading stop for people en route to St. Petersburg, Moscow, and other important cities. Although the town had only nine thousand permanent inhabitants, its ranks swelled throughout the week as transients stopped to barter goods, purchase supplies, and rest. Grigoriy, enterprising and resourceful, figured that Uglich could improve its local economy if it gave visitors a good enough reason to hang around longer. The best way to do that, he surmised, was to offer comfortable accommodations, decent food, and plenty of liquor. And that's what he told his master's brother, Mikhail Skripitsyn.

Skripitsyn must have seen something special in Grigoriy. He wasted no time at all scribbling out the legal document required for a serf to travel and work away from home. Skripitsyn likely figured that if Grigoriy was as successful as he suspected he would be, a big payday would be in the offing. Grigoriy might have carried the letter, which attested to his integrity and moral character, inside the folds of his heavy coat. It would have rested against his breast like a priceless treasure map. When Grigoriy took it out to present to officials in Uglich, seeking permission to open his first inn, he did so with confidence. The document was dated December 10, 1835, and stated:

> This certificate is provided by the landowner, the Titular Advisor and Cavalier Mikhail Stepanov Skripitsyn, to the peasant Grigoriy Aleksiyev Smirnov from the Yaroslavl province, who has been in my possession. The certificate gives him the right to run hotels and any such establishment in the town of Uglich. I know that his behavior is good and irreproachable and that he has not been involved in any suspicious activities. He has never been fined or sued and therefore can be permitted to engage in the mentioned hotel. I confirm this by my personal signature.[14]

It was as if Grigoriy had been reborn. No longer just a village serf, he was now a "trading peasant, fourth class."[15] Though still a world away from the upper crust, his new status nonetheless gave him ample opportunity to make the acquaintance of one of Uglich's most prominent families, the Zimins. They owned tanneries and linen factories, and produced supplies for Russia's armies. More importantly, the family was into local real estate. Grigoriy leased a house from the Zimins. Its location in the center of town was perfect for the hotel and restaurant he planned to put there. The building was spacious and loaded with such modern conveniences as glass windows.[16] Grigoriy transformed the property into a welcoming inn, restaurant, and drinking establishment. He had gained permission from local authorities to rent out rooms and serve a variety of food and beverages, including tea, hot chocolate, beer, and rum. He could also offer sweet drinks made with vodka. Homemade or counterfeit vodkas, as well as pure vodkas, were forbidden. No matter: Grigoriy, who took on the Smirnov name almost at random when he left his village, was peddling vodka for his own account—the first Smirnov to do so.

The establishment was an instant hit. In less than a year,

Grigoriy earned enough money to buy his freedom. It was a momentous occasion for the entire Smirnov family. Grigoriy's emancipation brought hope that all of its members might one day leave their peasant roots behind to become part of a burgeoning class of merchants.

Opportunity that had long evaded Russia's lower classes was not as elusive as it had been in previous years. In the nineteenth century, Russia's tsars allowed for more free enterprise than virtually any generation since Peter the Great. A newfangled brand of capitalism and entrepreneurship blossomed, beginning with the reign of Alexander I, in large part due to the demands of industrialization. The state could not single-handedly manage all that was needed to jumpstart economic development, from building railroads to modernizing arcane industries to establishing banking centers. Necessity, in its purest form, opened the door to dozens of ambitious go-getters—especially those involved in less capital-intensive enterprises.[17] Grigoriy, and later Pyotr, were just two of the thousands who seized the moment.

Grigoriy led the way, powering ahead in Uglich. Within five years, he owned three hotels and several wine cellars—and he was also making his own beer.* The former village serf was managing a rapidly increasing portfolio. Grigoriy's new status intoxicated Pyotr especially, though his father and older brother certainly took note. Together, around 1840, they left their village for Uglich to get a closer look at the face of prosperity.†

THE TRIO ARRIVED full of anticipation. It must have been eye-opening for young Pyotr and Yakov, to see their uncle now mingling with his well-heeled neighbors. He opened his wallet

---

* Grigoriy's business history is culled from pages in the Uglich government archives.

† A local listing of businesses confirms that Arseniy came to Uglich to work with Grigoriy. It is presumed that Pyotr and his brother did as well since boys typically stayed with their fathers.

nearly as easily as they did. As the business grew, Grigoriy installed Arseniy as manager of the front desk in one of his hotels. The boys, alongside Grigoriy's own sons, took on whatever menial tasks came their way—from serving drinks to cleaning up the foul smells left by men too drunk to see their way clear to the outhouse.

Pyotr and Yakov had been around burly, hard-drinking men before. Every village, including the Smirnovs', had at least one family designated to make moonshine. Usually a couple of miles outside the main residences, a little wooden house was erected for the sole purpose of producing alcohol made from fermented bread. They used a rudimentary system, which often created liquor with pieces of bread still swimming on top. The drink was cheap, plentiful, and popular. For many, it was a breakfast staple, a warming agent to combat frosty dawns before the workday began.

Village moonshine, though, was nothing compared to the drinks at Uncle Grigoriy's taverns. They were a substantial cut above the boys' previous, comparatively primitive experiences. But that was not what most fascinated them about their new surroundings. More enticing was the actual running of a business. The boys had never seen such an operation in action before, and Pyotr must have been mesmerized. He soon began approaching his menial job like a boy at school, observing everything, studying everyone. Grigoriy, a beloved uncle and shrewd entrepreneur, became his mentor. Pyotr, a doting nephew, enthusiastically slipped into the role of pupil.

The education of Pyotr Smirnov had begun. The subtle—and not so subtle—lessons he picked up from Grigoriy would later prove essential to Pyotr's own success. Indeed, many of them served as roadmaps for how Pyotr launched and grew his businesses. He learned how vital it was to be fearless, expeditious, and innovative. Grigoriy, for instance, was a location mastermind. All three of his hotels were situated in central areas with high foot traffic. It was ideal for drawing in the greatest number of walk-in customers and for building name recognition from passersby. He also never hesitated to expand his business, more fearful of complacency than of risk taking; he elbowed out competitors vying for coveted rental spaces and business licenses. Grigoriy was also an innovator. He was the first proprietor in town to seek permission to open up at seven o'clock in the morning. He argued before local officials that "crowds of people," mostly peasants, began forming as early as five o'clock because, unlike the more well-to-do residents and visitors, they had nowhere to go to escape the bitter cold.[18] They could not warm themselves with a cup of tea because only taverns could provide tea for "gray people," slang for commoners.* These travelers had no access to the more upscale watering holes. Grigoriy got his wish, endearing himself to throngs of new paying customers passing through Uglich. Soon, everyone was open early. But again, Grigoriy was there first.

At his uncle's knee, Pyotr's business instincts and quiet intelligence were sharpened well beyond his years. But Pyotr's time in Uglich was coming to an end, although he didn't know it quite yet. In 1843 Pyotr's grandfather, still at home in the village, took ill and died. The sad event forced Arseniy, the most unencumbered of the Smirnov men of his generation, to return to his village immediately to help manage the property and console family members. The big question: What to do with the boys? Pyotr, just twelve years old, was maturing quickly, but he still had much to learn from his uncle, something Arseniy may have instinctively understood. He agreed to let Pyotr remain in Uglich—at least for the time being. He could continue to earn money and still be close enough to home if Arseniy needed his help. Yakov, however, was almost

---

* The expression "gray people" has two meanings. Here it is derived from the Russian term *"Seriy lyud,"* which was used in the letter written by Grigoriy.

seventeen, having grown into a tall, robust young man. The family needed to increase its income to have any hope of gaining its freedom, and Yakov could do better in Moscow than in Uglich, earning twice as much money there, even by washing dishes.

Already a growing number of peasants from the Yaroslavl province, about 9 percent, were leaving for seasonal work. Most went to St. Petersburg, the capital. But increasingly, they were also heading to Moscow, where communities of immigrant serfs were settling in small pockets throughout the growing city. Arseniy's brother, Ivan, belonged to this group. He had been going to Moscow for seasonal work since the age of ten.[19] He would pick up odd jobs here and there, mostly in wine cellars and pubs. Yaroslavl peasants were well represented in Moscow's liquor industry; indeed, one-third of them found jobs in the shops, cellars, or pubs.

Ivan had been more successful than most. About the same time Grigoriy launched his business in Uglich, Ivan landed a plum job working for Aleksander Yakovlev, a wine merchant in Moscow.* As Yakovlev's right-hand man, he helped manage the former peasant's wine cellar and retail outlets. The work was a natural fit for Ivan—and fruitful. When Yakovlev died suddenly in 1839, Ivan took over the business. Within one year, he had earned enough to be the second Smirnov to pay off his ransom and, in 1840, gain his freedom. Within another year, Ivan was firmly established as a merchant of the "third guild," the lowest rung in the hierarchy of Moscow merchants. But it was a solid step toward independence and respectability.

Thinking about his son, Arseniy made the most practical choice: Yakov must go to Moscow. There, under Ivan's watchful eye, he might earn enough money to hasten the family's quest for liberty.

---

* The timing of Ivan's arrival in Moscow is derived from his death notice.

Pyotr may well have envied Yakov. He knew most Muscovites would have looked on him as a country bumpkin. He was uneducated and uncultured, but Pyotr had grown into a determined adolescent while in Uglich. He had tasted freedom and scratched up against success; he had seen one of his own climb from the bottom of the social order to a position of respect. Staying behind in this relative speck of a town, while his brother got to experience the great metropolis, may have seemed unfair. Why should he remain glued to his humble birthplace, close to his parents, while others were migrating, progressing, and succeeding?

His situation darkened even more when Grigoriy died unexpectedly in 1844 from edema. Time did not just seem to stop after that; it appeared to move backward. Little of the details are known about what exactly happened to Grigoriy's dreamed-about hotel empire, but it seems as if it vanished as quickly as it had appeared. The family, too, appeared to stall. It did not take long for Grigoriy's wife and sons to fall from the merchant class into the petite bourgeoisie, a rung just above peasant status.

This episode, then, became another valuable lesson for Pyotr: Success was not tangible or guaranteed. It could be there one moment, gone the next.

Now Pyotr saw his time in Uglich disappear. In less than a day, he was back where he started, but Pyotr was not the same little boy who had left his village four years earlier. To him, what had once been a comfortable, beloved home, a place full of belonging, felt worn. It was as if life in the village suddenly came into focus, and the picture was dull, as flat as the land surrounding the Yaroslavl province.

Pyotr probably never said a word to his family about his wanderlust. Ever the dutiful son, he had learned not to question his father. Arseniy, a rational, calculating man who did things for a reason, must have had a plan for Pyotr. So Pyotr waited. For almost two years, he went about his business on the farm, performing all the usual tasks.

Arseniy could see that his son was restless and ready to move on—*needed* to move on, so perhaps it was time. His brother, Ivan, seemed to be gaining both financially and in stature with every passing week. His son, Yakov, gone nearly four years, was thriving, too. He came home from time to time, full of stories about the rush of Moscow, the thrill that permeated the city and created opportunities for anyone sharp enough to find them.

It was time, Arseniy concluded. Pyotr would go to Moscow.

Chapter 2

MOSCOW

P yotr probably was up before the sun. So were his parents, who gathered around him. They prayed together as a family, asking for safe travels. His bag was packed. It contained clothes, bread, cheese, water, and small gifts for friends. Pyotr also brought an extra pair of shoes. The walk from his small village would be a long 170 mile journey.*

In his jacket Pyotr carried the obligatory passport. It was a permission slip, of sorts, which allowed him to be away from his village and landowner. It listed the usual facts—name, age, physical description, religion, and residence. It also included details about his owner. Pyotr would need this document, purchased for a few rubles, in order to enter Moscow and navigate his way around the city. Anyone caught without a properly issued passport could be severely punished, even exiled to Siberia.

With everything in hand, Pyotr hitched his bag over

---

* The journey to Moscow has been re-created from available records and from typical stories of serfs going to Moscow for seasonal work.

his shoulder and kissed his family good-bye. Pyotr most likely hooked up with his father's brother, Uncle Venedikt, for this journey: according to church confession books, they were together in their village and then in Moscow at the same time. The duo made for the dirt road, worn by trading carts that delivered sugar, wheat, and other necessities to Russia's countryside, that would take them to their first stop. Pyotr and Venedikt likely hopped aboard one of these carts, saving their legs for less well-traveled portions of their journey. They no doubt passed by their friends and acquaintances. Travelers to and from the cities and towns were so plentiful that each village had a person specifically designated to welcome them with tea, food, and shelter.

This road was familiar to the fifteen-year-old Smirnov. It was the same one he had traveled en route to Uglich. So he moved with a confidence not expected of a boy embarking on his first expedition so far from home. He stopped with his uncle for some tea at a nearby village before continuing on the twenty-two-mile stretch that would take him back to Uglich. The trip was straightforward—except when the couple arrived at the Volga River, which they had to cross to get to Uglich. There were no bridges or makeshift paths to follow, so they had to find a ferryman willing to take them along for the ten-minute ride.

Pyotr basked in those moments. Beyond the water, Uglich looked beautiful, just as Pyotr remembered it. He could see the golden domes from the churches in the distance as well as the former residence of Ivan the Terrible's son, Dmitriy. He also heard a chorus of bells coming from the cathedrals as worshipers entered for their late afternoon prayers. The melody comforted Pyotr. Yet he practically flew off the ferry as it connected with the shore, so anxious was he to get on with his journey.

Once on the other side, he made his way with Venedikt to the center of town, where they sought out Pyotr's older sister, Glafira, who had married the son of a beer factory owner in Uglich. They would stay with her for the night.

The next day was much the same, beginning with a prayer followed by long stretches of walking. Every now and then, Pyotr and Venedikt would climb aboard a passing dray. Often, the draymen would sing old Russian tunes. Pyotr listened to the music from his childhood while he studied the dense forests and ravines going by. The leaves had begun to turn bright shades of red and gold even though it was not yet autumn. The days still had the feel of summer in them.

The nights were getting cooler, though, and they came too quickly for Pyotr. The darkness slowed the uncle and nephew down, forcing them to find a patch of grass or a room in a friendly shelter. Pyotr would have preferred to have kept moving, anxious to get to Moscow. In his brief life, he had always had his father to guide him and instruct him. He was the obedient son, never questioning his elders' wishes. But now, even with Venedikt at his side, Pyotr felt as if he were on his own, able to choose when to stop for bread and where he would rest. It brought out powerful feelings inside him, urges that he had not really understood were there before. At first, he tried to suppress them, thinking it unbecoming of a Christian boy in a staunchly patriarchal society to embrace so fully the idea of independence or of self. But Pyotr could not deny the truth—he liked navigating his own way.

And he was good at it. Pyotr and Venedikt made superb time. By the seventh day, they were closing in on Sergiyev Posad, perhaps the holiest site in all of Russia since its founding in 1340. They could see the fortress monastery in the distance, surrounded by dark pine forests. The trees framed the church's blue and gold domes, which shot bright reflections into the light blue sky. Pyotr sat in awe as he looked out at the horizon. He had heard about this place, and now, seeing it in the distance, he felt a sense of deep spirituality. He quickened his step, anxious to get a closer look.

The road had swelled suddenly with a crush of people. Most,

like Pyotr, were traveling by foot. But the more well-to-do came by stage coaches usually pulled by a team of four horses. France's Alexandre Dumas came to Sergiyev Posad some years later by this kind of coach. However people arrived, many were unified by their motivations to be at this sacred place—to pray for whatever their lives lacked. More specifically, they had come to kiss the bones of St. Sergiy, a famous Russian saint.

The bones were kept in a small white chapel inside the vast compound. Pyotr and Venedikt threaded themselves through small openings in the crowd. A monk marked the doorway, guiding them and others through a narrow entrance surrounded by dimly lit candles. The saint's bones, set in the center of the room, high atop a long table, were covered with a pink shroud. Finally it was Pyotr's turn. He followed the lead of others, bending down and kissing the embroidered cross on the pink covering and then backing away. He crossed himself in the elongated Russian Orthodox manner with his right hand and turned to exit, allowing the waiting masses to inch closer to the holy relics.

Once back outside, Pyotr took in the grandness of it all. A new world lay ahead of him.

MOSCOW WAS STILL forty-five miles away so the duo needed to get another early start the next morning. If they could keep up their pace, they thought they might reach Moscow within three days. The road stretched out before them, lined with pine forests and more fields of rye. Before long, the scenery changed to birch groves and ravines. If they listened closely, they could hear the two-note calls of the cuckoos.

The next two days passed slowly. On day ten of the journey, the paths closer to Moscow ceased to be flat and silent. They almost heaved, so intense was the motion. The noise was just as fierce, buzzing softly one moment and then almost booming the next, as people flowed to and fro. The commotion hypnotized the village boy. Travelers darted about him as well as peasants who made their living catering to Moscow's comings and goings. They lived along the road, between the numerous pubs and teahouses, selling random goods. They traded religious trinkets, tobacco, and food. Here, customers were plentiful. Scores of Muscovites joined the transients by riding outside the city's boundaries to buy cheaper vodka at the border pubs.

Pyotr had to be careful to avoid getting trampled by the carriages and coaches that thundered by. He stayed close to the road's edge, keeping his eyes fixed in the direction of Moscow. He thought about his mother and father and the life that had been. More often, though, the serf from Kayurovo dreamed of the life still yet to be discovered. Now, he could even smell it.

Factory chimneys set up outside the city skirts of Moscow burped black smoke. This scent was mixed with the odors coming from the blacksmith shops, where coal gas burned constantly. And then there was the most powerful stench: sewage. The city's population had exploded in the last three decades adding some eighty thousand new residents and countless other migrants. By the 1840s, 300,000 people lived in Moscow, forcing the city to cope with a sea of new bodies and their refuse.[1] Strings of these sewage-laden carts lined the streets, hauling away what they could. Uncovered, their contents often spilled out onto the uneven dirt roads, forming pools of waste. Some pedestrians wore rubber boots to wade through these cesspools. A local newspaper remarked on the situation: "Moscow is filled up in the inside and covered from the outside with sewage."[2]

The sour air did little to hamper Pyotr's enthusiasm. Just ahead of him was one of eighteen gates marking the official entrances to Moscow. He and Venedikt would pass through the *Krestovskaya Zastava* gates, joining the more than five thousand others who came through them daily in summer. Initially, the gates had been erected to collect custom taxes and register visitors. But the tax function ended in 1754, and it no longer made sense to log everybody coming through. Many travelers offered fake names or counterfeit passports anyway, making it almost impossible to verify identities. Officials, then, did a mere visual check of a person's credentials.

In the distance, Pyotr would have spied the two stone obelisks that framed the city's gate—each about the height of three grown men. Atop both obelisks perched a two-headed eagle, the state emblem. A stone fence continued out from the obelisks, encasing two yellow houses. A booth sat nearby, too, the place for officers, soldiers, or guardians to mind the gate. Supposedly no one could pass through without one of the officials lifting a black-and-white wooden stick that ran the length of the obelisks, but of course, anyone could get by if they really wanted to. The stick was easily bypassed and the guards often too preoccupied with playing cards or chewing tobacco to notice someone slipping through.

Pyotr had no intention of slipping through. He had no need. A typical exchange between guards and new entrants was perfunctory, nonthreatening. Few words were uttered, as a guard usually inquired of a newcomer like Pyotr: "Who are you?" Obediently, Pyotr would have presented his passport and replied: "I am Pyotr Smirnov, a peasant from Yaroslavl." It probably took less than twenty seconds from the time Pyotr met the guard to the time he and Venedikt passed through the gates and into Moscow.

They headed directly to Varvarka Street, the home of his uncle Ivan, brother Yakov, and a handful of cousins and other relatives. They would not have wanted to dally, for although Moscow was beginning to change, to modernize, it was still a place of strict laws and rules. A general-governor, appointed by the tsar, controlled the city; his henchmen enforced a seemingly endless list of arbitrary prohibitions, including smoking on the streets, beards or mustaches worn by government officials, and long hair on male students. The long hair was considered revolutionary, something only done by "free thinkers" who opposed the existing social and political order. Failure to comply with any of these so-called laws, which varied somewhat from city to city, could result in severe penalties.

Pyotr was probably unfamiliar with Moscow's rigid customs. And although Venedikt had been to the big city before, they likely decided to get to Ivan's place quickly. They did not want to get caught in Moscow's nighttime. Street lighting, what little there was, was primitive. Lamps illuminated with naphtha, a colorless liquid derived from petroleum, were fixed atop clumsy, gray-colored wooden pillars that appeared sporadically on the streets, offering only a dim light. Once the sun went down, pockets of the city were shrouded in a dense, ominous darkness.

Varvarka was a snake of a street. It was one of three that began to unwind just beyond the Moscow River and to the east of Red Square. It was sandwiched between a bustling and important trading center, Gostiniy Dvor, and one of Moscow's crammed Jewish hubs, *Zaryadye*. Gostiniy Dvor, meaning Guest Yard, featured a three-floored building containing warehouses and almost eight hundred small shops. Thousands of buyers and sellers came here daily to trade goods, wandering the long, narrow trading aisles, each dedicated to product lines ranging from saddles to cloth to religious icons. On the other side, *Zaryadye* ("behind the rows") was thick with crowds of Orthodox Jews wandering around its narrow, curved lanes. The segregated neighborhood was considered a slum, low and gray, and the people who lived there, it was rumored, mainly traded stolen goods.

In the middle of this eclectic setting was bustling Varvarka, a dirt-covered street. Varvarka, which was named after a cathedral built to honor St. Varvara, was ancient, almost medieval. Five churches, marked by golden domes and tall belfries, dominated the landscape of the street as well as its tenor. The neighborhood was a haven for Russia's entrenched religious traditions and old beliefs. Residents here, many of whom were serfs, ex-serfs, merchants, or artisans, prayed daily and led simple, devout lives. Their homes, scattered between shops that sold groceries, spices, and wax, were unadorned and made of stone. Their clothes were plain; many men wore long black kaftans and beards instead of more stylish European garments of the more progressive, clean-shaven, educated classes.

There were two exceptions to the street's modesty. The first was located at No. 10 Varvarka Street.* In the sixteenth century, the building had belonged to the grandfather of Russia's first Romanov tsar. The house, or palace, had been restored two centuries later and turned into a museum devoted to the Romanov Boyars.† Ivan's home was just a few paces from it. The second, even more notable exception, was the litter of cellars and shops making or peddling grape wines, beer, and vodka. These establishments, including the one Ivan operated, were generally situated directly under or next to Orthodox churches. Ivan's wine cellar butted up against the small parish church of St. Maksim the Confessor. The church, as it turned out, was also Ivan's landlord. The resident clergy, along with his family, were his housemates.

This arrangement was more than peculiar, it was illegal. Russian law prohibited any liquor establishment to exist closer than 280 feet from a church entrance. Restrictions of this kind first appeared in 1806 in St. Petersburg and in 1821 in Moscow after the clergy, moralists, and temperance leaders complained bitterly about the abuses of alcohol throughout society. Church leaders worried that some members of their congregation were getting too drunk, either immediately before or after services, to remain spiritual and devout. There was also the fear that alcoholism was chipping away at the moral values they preached to parishioners.

---

* The modern address is given here. It was different in the nineteenth century.

† Boyar is an old term referring to a member of the Russian aristocracy.

Enforcement of the law was, however, difficult. Indeed, it was almost nonexistent. Like so many other clashes of conscience in Russia, this one proved easy to overlook—as long as certain financial arrangements were made. Ivan, for instance, was a chief benefactor at St. Maksim's. He contributed funds to renovate the church, and cultivated good relations with local officials, working for a time with the police as chief of a neighborhood watch group whose job it was to report on suspicious or illegal activities by local merchants. This relationship, which likely included financial payoffs or offerings of free liquor, ensured that Ivan received preferential treatment when it came to his own business dealings.

Varvarka Street, it turns out, was the epitome of contradictions. But so, too, was Pyotr. The street and the young man were unusual mixtures of devout religion, ferocious merchantry, and incessant booze making. They made a perfect couple. Pyotr had found his launching pad.

HE AND VENEDIKT made their way to the fourth block of Varvarka where Ivan lived. His uncle, brother, and cousins lived together—eleven of them—in Ivan's humble but ample home. The upstairs served as the living quarters while the street level and basement worked as a wine cellar and shop. Here customers could buy and drink wine and other spirits, including vodka. In those days, vodka was sold by the pail, bottle, or *shtof*, which equaled about one-tenth of a pail or 1.2 liters. Prices varied, of course, depending on the quality and way in which the drink was sold. But generally, a shtof could be had for as little as sixty cents and as much as $1.50. Ivan sold only drinks in his establishment. He did not have a license to sell food.*

---

* Pubs, taverns, wine cellars, and other liquor outlets had to follow strict rules. Taverns, for instance, were allowed to serve food along with liquor to customers while many wine cellars could not. Some shops could serve only take-out drinks while others were allowed to serve drinks on their premises.

This house/bar/shop was to be Pyotr's home. He settled in and got to work. Having made it to Moscow without incident, he was eager to show Ivan that he was no ordinary teenager. Pyotr, when it came to the ins and outs of tavern life, was an old pro—Grigoriy had taught him well. He served drinks, washed glasses, and mopped floors. He hauled whatever needed haul- ing. Pyotr proved his worth—and potential—in no time. Ivan, sensing his nephew's drive and quick mind, also put him to work in his shop in Gostiniy Dvor. The shop was more like a small room or stall, and it was filed between hundreds of others in Gostiniy Dvor's mall-like setup. Ivan sold liquor, to be sure, but he also likely sold tobacco and kefir, a distinctly Russian drink made of sour milk. He did not trade goods at Red Square. In the nineteenth century, the cobblestoned square was the purview of food peddlers, those who mainly sold cakes and sweets. It was also a gathering place for large celebrations and feasts. Alcohol was not a welcome commodity there.

Pyotr's natural intensity, ambition, and focus seemed to thrive in Moscow. He noted how goods were priced, how they were marketed, why people bought what they did. He paid atten- tion to it all, including Uncle Ivan's penchant for vodka—even though it, like so many other things, was specifically forbidden.

Since the time of Catherine the Great in the eighteenth cen- tury, only state-owned distilleries and the gentry could produce vodka legally. The land-owning nobility received this privilege in 1765, which included a pass on taxes that accompanied liquor production. The law, eventually repealed in 1863, rarely stopped anyone from partaking in Russia's great pastime. Villagers made their own home brews. And city businessmen, intent on earning a decent living, could find no better place to apply their entre- preneurial zeal than the nation's pervasive vodka culture.

Villagers and businessmen alike got away with this criminal behavior, for the most part, because it was simply too difficult— and too unpopular—to stop the vodka traffic. Officials happily accepted favors from the would-be felons. Peasants and the bourgeoisie frequented unsanctioned shops and pubs, hoping to buy better, cheaper vodka. And the tsar, who did not want to anger the lower classes by cutting off liquor sources, was willing to let things be.

The situation, complex and corrupt, was one of many that paved the way for some of the most capitalistic advancements the nation had seen. Ivan, by now a well-respected, even prominent businessman, was only too happy to take advantage of the moment, bringing his sons and nephews along with him for the lucrative ride.

PYOTR WAS GAINING valuable experience and earning more money than he had ever had. He was moving quickly through boyhood, maturing into a dashing, lanky man, with eyes that seemed to reach into the soul of anyone who could sustain his penetrating gaze. The fuzz on his face turned brittle, offering up the seeds for the dark, well-cropped beard that Pyotr would wear throughout most of his adult life. Within the community of serfs and beyond, Pyotr presented an attractive package. He was smart, ambitious, and determined. More than that, he could read, even write, albeit not well, according to his signed documents. This outside persona, combined with the fiercely private and reserved side of Pyotr Smirnov, made for a clean canvas on which people could sketch their own portraits of the man behind the handsome, serious face.

Perhaps that is what attracted Nadezhda Yegorova to him when they met during one of Pyotr's routine visits back home. Like so many other migrants, Pyotr regularly appeared in his village during the harvest and planting seasons. On these visits, he would carry back his earnings and present them to his father, Arseniy. As head of the family, he kept the Smirnov accounts, dividing the money as needed, always saving with an eye toward freedom.

It was likely during one of these visits that Pyotr met Nadezhda. Not much is known about her other than she was the daughter of a church deacon from a large nearby village and a couple of years older than Pyotr. Nadezhda was also not a serf. As part of the clergy class, she sat above Pyotr's station: Clergy maintained more comfortable lifestyles, in general, than those of peasants. Pyotr and Nadezhda married on May 21, 1850, when Pyotr was just nineteen years old.

The marriage, like most at the time, was probably arranged by the family's patriarchs. They would have deemed the union a win for both sides. The Smirnovs could attach themselves to a socially superior family while the Yegorovs gained ties to people with a foothold in Moscow and with promising economic prospects. Nonetheless, this marriage was still far from traditional.

In nineteenth-century Russia, the mixing of classes was about as popular as the mixing of vodka. It simply was not done. And when it *was* done, the unions were fraught with risk. They could even be scandalous. That the Smirnovs would snub convention suggests that they were more progressive than most other peasants, at least when it furthered their own aspirations.

The same could have been said about Count Nikolay Petrovich Sheremetev, whose romance with one of his serfs is perhaps the most infamous account of a mismatched coupling and its tragic ramifications. As the son and grandson of great men who were part of the inner circle of Russian royalty from Peter the Great to Catherine the Great, Nikolay was the epitome of high society. The Sheremetevs were the largest landowners in Russia, except for the tsar, and they had an army of more than 200,000 serfs. Their palaces were legendary and opulent, full of the finest European furnishings and the grandest artworks.

Nikolay carried on the family's noble tradition. He held the titles of count, senator, and marshal at various stages in his life. He was also a personal friend of Tsar Pavel I, dating back to their childhoods. Like his father, Nikolay was a leading patron of the arts, building opera houses, establishing theaters and troupes, and launching special drama schools aimed at educating serf children.

Privately, Nikolay was every bit as notorious a playboy as some of his aristocratic brethren. He maintained a harem of serfs, women who often traveled with him and serviced him in any way he chose. Nikolay, short and thick-bodied but exceedingly charming, would peruse the rooms of his favored serf girls while they were working and drop a white handkerchief through the window of whomever he wanted to see that evening. He would then return to the room at night, satisfy his sexual desires and, before leaving, ask that his handkerchief be returned.[3]

Nikolay's promiscuity was nothing unusual for a noble, but his relationship with Praskovya was. She had come to sing for Nikolay when she was just seven years old. He was twenty-four. Nikolay was mesmerized by the girl's melodious voice and delicate features, never mind that she was the daughter of a serf blacksmith. Sheremetev wanted to transform this child into a world-class actress and operatic diva. First, as he did with all his favorite serf actresses, Sheremetev changed Praskovya's surname. He always preferred to call his starlets by names derived from precious stones. So Kovalyova became Zhemchugova, a name derived from *zhemchug*, meaning pearl. Nikolay saw to it that his jewel was educated by the best teachers money could buy. It did not take long for the girl to become one of the most beloved sopranos in all of Russia and a favorite of the emperor.

Praskovya matured into an enchanting young woman. She was a natural beauty, with dark hair and milky white skin. It is not clear when Nikolay's admiration for her artistic talents bloomed into a deep love, but that is what happened. The two had a tortured, secret affair, forbidden to show the true passion between them. It was not until Praskovya fell ill with tuberculosis that Nikolay overcame his devotion to society's mores. He freed his serf and then, in secret, married her on November 6, 1801.

Sadly, the union was brief. Praskovya died from tuberculosis just two years later—three weeks after giving birth to the couple's only child, a son named Dmitriy.

Sheremetev shocked Russian society by disclosing the marriage in a letter to the tsar after his wife's death and asking that his son be recognized as his rightful heir. He also claimed that his wife had been a descendant of Polish nobility, a fiction he hoped would soften the blows he suspected might follow as the news of his marriage became public. It did not. Abandoned by his upper-crust friends, with few attending his wife's funeral or expressing condolences, Nikolay died lonely and bitter in 1809. He summed up his anguish, writing "I thought I had friends who loved me, respected me, and shared my pleasures. But when my wife's death put me in an almost desperate state, I found few people to comfort me and share my sorrow."[4]

The match between Pyotr and Nadezhda, was not nearly as controversial as some more famous love stories, but it was, nonetheless, unconventional. They were from distinctly different classes—and she was the older of the two. It is possible that they married simply because it was what their families ordered them to do. But it is also possible that Pyotr and Nadezhda shared a deep passion and love.

For whatever reason, they carried on, like so many others, at a distance. Women often remained in the villages while their husbands worked in larger towns and cities. In Moscow, men outnumbered women by almost two to one. Still, Pyotr and Nadezhda were together enough to produce their first child, a boy named Nikolay, on December 4, 1852. He died more than two months later from epilepsy, as church records show, a common affliction and cause of infant deaths at the time. Nadezhda was particularly shaken by the loss. She never got pregnant again and succumbed to a sudden fever just three years later.

Pyotr, at only twenty-four, had buried a son and a wife. He

threw himself into work, drowning his sorrows in the constant motions of daily living. He also stayed abreast of another politically pressing matter—the Crimean War. It was a devastating conflict that pitted Russia against a coalition comprised of the United Kingdom, France, the Ottoman Empire, and the Kingdom of Sardinia. The dispute stemmed from unresolved issues in the Middle East, including the question of who would control some of the region's holiest places. The consequences of this war, which produced one of Russia's worst military defeats, would prove pivotal to the future of Russia—and to the Smirnovs as well.

RUSSIA WAS DEVASTATED in the three-year Crimean battle. It lost 259,000 people to a better-financed, more sophisticated, well-trained enemy. While Russia still used flinty smooth-bore muskets, its rivals fired the latest long-range rifled muskets. While Russia relied on a fleet of sailing vessels, its opposition sent a squadron of the more-modern screw-propelled warships. While the coalition was made up of skilled military leaders and loyal, well-trained foot soldiers, the Russian Army consisted largely of peasants and serfs called up to serve just as war broke out. They often fought for days without proper supplies or reinforcements because the country lacked a rail system that connected the economic and population centers with the battlefields.

The famous 349-day siege of Sevastopol in 1854–55, in which a young Tolstoy fought, was a crushing blow to Russia's esteem and international reputation—even though Russian soldiers held the city for nearly a year. In that battle, the Russians were overwhelmed; the technical shortcomings of the armory and national infrastructure were no longer a subject of wonder, they were an internally recognized fact. By the end of the Crimean War in 1856, the military powers of the Allies (British, French,

Turkish) had humiliated Russia's antiquated force—and bank-rupted its treasury.

Tsar Nikolay I had not prepared his nation for the con-frontation. He had been too preoccupied with maintaining his military, monitoring an array of international conflicts, and at-tending to the inner workings of his own bulging government. The Russian bureaucracy swelled by some 40,000 people during his reign. So the tsar never fully grasped the idea that his coun-try, still dominated by an agrarian economy, had fallen behind the rest of the world. The Crimean War made it impossible to overlook any longer.

That realization, coupled with a regime change at the end of the war, offered the masses their first real hope of reform. Aleksander II, at age thirty-six, took control of Russia from his father in 1855. He was an educated, sensitive man who under-stood his country in a way Nikolay had not. He saw compla-cency among the gentry; he recognized an inadequate education system. He even observed the inability of millions of serfs to im-prove their own well-being—or the nation's—under the status quo. Indeed, the restlessness of the underclasses had already bubbled to the surface, led by peasants who had volunteered for the army with the understanding that they would be granted freedom when the battles ended. When this did not happen, people took to the streets, and protests against the tsar and aris-tocracy erupted after the war.[5] They demanded better treatment and screamed for freedom.

Industrialization topped the state's agenda, along with another crucial matter: the abolition of serfdom. The tsar ac-knowledged his intentions when he spoke passionately to a lead-ing group of the aristocracy in Moscow on March 30, 1856. He hoped to win the nobility's approval and support by famously stating the inevitable: "It is much better to abolish serfdom from above than to wait for the time when it will begin to abolish itself from below." Freedom, finally, was in the air.

All of this had been on the mind of Pyotr's father, Arseniy.
It had been some time since he had amassed enough reserves
to pay off his master, but he had hesitated. Although Arseniy
lacked the keen business mind that had served his brothers so
well, he understood the art of good timing. Arseniy enjoyed a
decent, productive relationship with his landowners and found
little reason to uproot what remained of his family without a
clear purpose. For him, as for many of the older generation,
living under a master was secure and uncomplicated.

Patience served Arseniy well. His sons were flourishing in
Moscow, and the money they contributed to the family coffers
made it possible, now, for Arseniy to be free. He could pay off his
master, go to Moscow, and still have enough money left to join
the merchant ranks himself. Plus, his landowner, wary of the
government's reformist tendencies, was in the mood to pocket a
payout from his serfs before the tsar could impose restrictions.

In 1857 Arseniy dipped into his savings, paid off his ransom,
and said goodbye to the lands of Yaroslavl. The Smirnovs were
free, now no longer anybody's property. And soon, thanks to
the new tsar's enlightened agenda and the Smirnovs' own tenac-
ity, they would be much more than that.

Chapter 3

The Land of Darkness

A rseniy could hardly wait to get a taste of the merchant life. He was a proud man who surely had felt more than a twinge of jealousy that his younger brothers had prospered years before him as free men while he, at age fifty-eight, was only now leaving behind his provincial roots and the burdens of serfdom.

The first order of business for Arseniy was to prove to officials in Moscow, beyond a doubt, his devotion to Christian Orthodoxy. It was a requirement for becoming a merchant. This would not be difficult since Arseniy had attended church throughout his life, according to historical church records, confessing his sins and taking communion as often as his religion demanded. He socialized with local clergy, maintaining close ties to them even after leaving his village. And he dressed and acted the part of a conservative, pious Christian. Arseniy always embraced traditional Russian thinking and adhered to the church's interpretations of societal norms, while maintaining patriarchal communities. He, like many others, shunned the blasphemous influences blowing in from Western and Central Europe to modernize.

In the cool spring of 1858, Arseniy most likely headed to the parish his sons and brother Ivan attended on Varvarka Street to obtain a letter from the resident priest that would demonstrate his devotion. Perhaps he brought with him a succinct letter from his own village clergy, attesting to his allegiances. Among other things, it made clear that Arseniy would have no trouble swearing, in writing, that he was neither Jew nor eunuch nor a member of a variety of other "insidious" religious sects, as the law required.[1]

Arseniy had not expected the church to be a stumbling block, but it was an entrenched institution and a notorious bureaucracy. Whether it would be weeks or months to process his request, nobody knows. But any delay must have weighed heavily on Arseniy. He was no longer a young man. True, he was in good health and had easily surpassed his country's life expectancy for men of forty-four years, but he still had so much to do.

Arseniy was worried about Pyotr. His other children were well down the road toward comfortable, pleasant lives. Yakov was entrenched in Uncle Ivan's business, happily married, already the father of three daughters. Arseniy's daughter Glafira had married well and presented no concerns. Although little is known about Aleksandra, his other daughter, it appears that she was also married and focused on her own family. But Pyotr was another matter. He had always adapted to his environment. Silently, however, he was never altogether comfortable. He kept waiting for something to happen, like a runner at the starting line listening for the one unmistakable pop that would thrust him into the race. Pyotr seemed to be simply biding his time, listening. Arseniy fervently hoped he could hasten the quest.

By late April, the days had grown longer and warmer, typical for that time of year. Neither too hot nor too cold, the air was dry, the sky clear. It was during one of those tranquil days that he finally collected the church's recommendation. Now came the most challenging tasks.

Becoming a merchant was arduous, almost Byzantine: The procedure itself dated back to the reign of Catherine the Great. Three guilds had been set up in 1775 and they were structured, like everything else in Russia, by class. Merchants were ranked from the wealthiest and most influential to the poorest and least consequential. Members of the prestigious, tightly knit first guild received special privileges and titles while those in the second and third guilds were restricted in which businesses they could enter and in the number of employees they could hire. Only first-guild merchants, for instance, could work in banking, export to foreign countries, and trade without limit with the Russian government. By contrast, third-guild merchants could not enter finance or heavy industry and had to limit the size of their companies to no more than thirty-two workers.[2]

The strict three-guild hierarchy also allowed the state treasury to tax merchants according to their incomes and resources. When applying to one of the guilds, merchants were required to disclose their capital. Applicants routinely underreported what they had in order to pay the minimum tax. In addition, merchants were strongly encouraged to contribute to a fund purportedly dedicated to helping the poor. The idea was to absolve decent merchants of the guilt they harbored for being so rich, and, hopefully, improve their standing throughout society.

It did not work. Merchants were Russia's pariahs, a largely mistrusted class. Russian playwright Aleksander Ostrovskiy described the world merchants inhabited as "the land of darkness." Ostrovskiy, a child of one of Moscow's main business districts, believed that cultural ignorance, limitless greed, immoral conduct, and sheer stupidity ruled the entire class. He wrote about it repeatedly in his plays, beginning in 1849 with *It's A Family Affair*, a tale of Bolshov the merchant, who pretends to be bankrupt to escape his sizable debts. He transfers his assets to his daughter and son-in-law only to have them run off with the money. The betrayal leaves Bolshov penniless and ultimately in "the pit" or debtors' prison, which the writer contends, is exactly where such cheats belong.

Literary giants from Tolstoy to Nikolay Gogol to Anton Chekhov to Ivan Turgenev joined Ostrovskiy in his ridicule. They, too, created the shadiest of characters out of rotten merchant cloth. Fyodor Dostoevskiy wrote: "A merchant is ready to join any Jew, to betray everyone and everything, for the sake of income."[3]

Russia's general contempt for its merchantry echoed similar though less strident sentiments from other parts of Europe. But it was in Moscow, more than any other place, that the antagonism worked like a translucent fence, isolating the country's future business leaders. This fledgling community occupied a veritable no-man's land, cloistered behind heavy walls and bolted gates that were more like fortresses than homes. For the most part, merchants avoided social gatherings and public events that took them away from their routines and insular lives. They had no place in the schools and little involvement in civic affairs. Even peasants considered them baldly corrupt, happy to have them confined to their capitalist ghettos. "A merchant in Russia occupied a rather low rank in the social hierarchy," explained Dostoevskiy. "And, being frank, he didn't deserve more."[4]

Nor did the merchants seem to want more—at least not yet. They were not particularly interested in challenging the gentry, whom they dubbed lazy and unjustifiably snobbish. Years later, many of the wealthiest and most successful merchants concluded that it was the merchants—not the nobility—who represented the future pinnacle of society. Pavel Tretyakov, one of Moscow's premiere textile merchants and a leading philanthropist for whom the Tretyakov Museum in Moscow is named, strongly opposed his daughter Vera's marriage to pianist—and nobleman—Aleksander Ziloti. Tretyakov objected to Ziloti's frivolous artistic profession, convinced that the musician was after his money. He would have much preferred his daughter to choose a fellow merchant—aristocrat or not. Tretyakov failed to dissuade his daughter from her choice, but he did structure her wedding settlement in a way that prevented anyone he found "distasteful" from getting it. Tretyakov's contemporaries seemed to have come to the same conclusions. "Have you heard that this young boy, Ziloti, already a bright pianist . . . made a brilliant match in the sense of fortune: 400,000 rubles in her dowry?" composer Pyotr Tchaikovskiy was asked in a letter.[5] Tchaikovskiy, a distant relative by marriage, attended Vera's wedding.

To Arseniy, though, becoming a merchant had nothing to do with politics or class warfare. It was about liberty and free enterprise. It was, quite unashamedly, about Pyotr.

Arseniy, the aging ex-serf, set out early on April 30, 1858, hoping to beat the long lines he expected to encounter on the way to obtaining his merchant license.* Pyotr, sensing the import of his father's mission, joined him. They both wore long, dark frock coats atop trousers tucked into long boots, aiming to look decent and traditional. The duo made small talk as they walked. Even though they were both giddy about their business prospects, neither spoke a word about it. Like so many others in Russia, they were superstitious and did not want to jinx their prospects.

It was just a fifteen-minute walk from Ivan's home, down noisy Varvarka and through Red Square to the Moscow State Chamber. There Arseniy would proclaim his finances, pay his taxes, and buy the necessary licenses and tickets required to operate a business. The building was a maze of bureaucratic agencies. It housed the state treasury department, tax collection agen-

---

* This is a reconstruction based on the available evidence.

cies, and some military offices. Arseniy headed to the "Second Census Department," which handled merchant affairs.

Despite its important official functions, nothing about the building was plain or governmental. The Moscow State Chamber was located in a grand classical mansion that once belonged, ironically, to a wealthy noble family. The rooms still dripped with the riches usually reserved for the highest echelon of the upper crust; there were ornate marble interiors and extravagantly painted ceilings. Pushkin and other leading intellectuals had visited there before the home was sold to the state in 1845.

Now Arseniy and Pyotr stood inside, awed by the building's majesty. Little else, however, felt intimidating. Low-level civil servants scurried from office to office like the cogs they were. Peasants, merchants, and aristocrats with various matters that needed attending shuffled about, rarely taking the time to ingest their impressive surroundings. For Arseniy, this moment was a means to an end: He needed the proof that he paid city and social taxes; he needed certificates that would allow him to open a wine shop. And he also needed a few extra rubles to "tip" the men as he made his way through the bureaucracy. The entire process took the better part of a day, but Arseniy got what he came for.

Things were not as easy two weeks later when Arseniy made his way to the Moscow City Society's house—the Merchant Department. This organization managed the merchant guilds themselves. It was an excessive, hierarchical bureaucracy, which operated more like an exclusive country club than a professional organization—and not just anyone could become a member.

Arseniy got an early start again on May 14. The sky was clear and it was already warm by the time he walked down Varvarka Street toward the Moscow City Society. It took Arseniy only about seven minutes to reach Yushkov Lane, a nondescript speck of a street with little to boast about except for a rather lovely church that stood directly in front of the municipal building.

Arseniy, walking alone this time as Pyotr needed to work, instinctively paused before this church, crossed himself and softly mumbled a prayer that God would help him succeed on this momentous day. Then he walked through the iron gates and entered the building.

Arseniy needed an officially stamped application, the guild certificate, to obtain a merchant license. He cleared his throat, stood up as straight as a pencil, and made the inquiry. The man behind the wooden counter looked every bit the part of the clerical worker he was, hair slightly disheveled, eyes bloodshot from too much booze, and a face like a road map. Menial pay and sheer boredom had turned him indifferent to his job and to the people he addressed. The clerk looked up, almost sneering. *Great*, he thought, wiping the beads of sweat from his brow with a dingy kerchief, *another village nobody come to Moscow to seek his fortune.**

It was indeed a trend. The number of serfs and ex-serfs filing into Moscow had grown exponentially after the end of the Crimean War. Some, like Arseniy, were looking to jumpstart the freedoms they saw unfolding. Others sought better seasonal work in the factories and industries that had begun to sprout up all over Russia.

That will be 1.80 rubles, the gatekeeper said.† Arseniy was ready. The application was supposed to cost 90 kopecks—the sign said as much. But everyone knew you had to pay double, and no one ever asked where the money went or why. Arseniy tugged at his wallet and handed over the money; in return, he received the application. Arseniy smiled and nodded his thanks. The man pointed up and Arseniy headed to the second floor.

Unlike the décor of the Moscow State Chamber, the cast-

---

* The dialogue and scene have been created to demonstrate a typical exchange during Smirnov's time.

† $1.30 in 1858 ($36 today).

iron stairs and the iron railing looked overused. Everything in the building did, including the people. Arseniy, however, boyish in his quest, was the exception. He climbed the stairs, turned the corner, and walked into a waiting area outside the chancellery. Arseniy's fate would be determined here.

He took a seat on a worn bench against the wall, glad to sit down and rest his legs. He did not even bother to try to fill out his application in his rudimentary scratch, preferring like everyone else in the room to rely on officials to do the writing.

The chancellery was decidedly more pleasant than the downstairs had been. The room was quite large with wood floors and wooden tables covered by nondescript broadcloth. On the walls hung several portraits of unnamed officials in gilded frames. Five immense windows sucked in the outside breeze.

Arseniy had to wait his turn to see the most senior official here, known as a table head, a common title that stemmed from the fact that he literally sat at the head of a table. This man was clean-shaven, according to the law, and wore the state uniform. He commanded authority within the small army of bureaucrats that pecked away around him. This man could single-handedly determine how pleasant—or unpleasant—to make the day's procedures. His decisions were often sound and reasonable, but they could also seem arbitrary and casual.

As each man made his way to the front of the line, the table head dictated his answers and then signed his name at the bottom of the application. In this way, Arseniy was no different from the others that day, putting his barely legible signature to paper when it was his turn. But he did have an edge over the other men because he had important family ties to the guilds. By this time, Ivan was one of only 1,916 merchants in the first guild and knew exactly how to work the system. He had revealed everything to Arseniy.

The table head looked closely at Arseniy's application, checking for any inaccuracies or opportunities that might yield a few extra rubles from the applicant's pocket. Arseniy, knowing better than to take a chance with his future, did not let the man wait for long. Nonchalantly, he had hidden a little something for him between his documents.

The official found everything in order. He waited for Arseniy to unveil his purpose and justify his intent. He had heard so many stories from the never-ending stream of merchant wannabes who darkened his doorway. This one, he yawned, would be the same as all the others. Still, toying with these poor, ex-serfs could be amusing. Arseniy would have presented an ideal target. The exchange might have gone something like this: *Why do you wish to be a merchant? Isn't it a bit late for you?* the official would ask, smirking as he eyed Arseniy's mostly gray beard and lined, sagging face.

Like my brother Ivan Smirnov before me, I was once a serf. Now I am my own man. I look to create a better life for myself, for my family, and for my community, Arseniy would have replied in his well-rehearsed imagined exchange.

And how will you make such a change? Going to shave that beard of yours? the man might mockingly inquire.

Arseniy would have shown no emotion. He had expected as much from his inquisitor. *I will do what my family does best: I will sell wine. I will sell tobacco. I will sell kefir. My brother Ivan has done this for more than two decades. My brother Grigoriy did it as well. I believe I can do it as well. I believe it is in my blood.*

The table head would be skeptical. He had heard this kind of answer so many times before—outsized ambition trounced by ineptitude. He stared at Arseniy. This one seemed sane enough; he did not look stupid; he was clean and respectful; he was even a bit literate. Arseniy had also understood how to play the game. The table head tucked his ten-ruble tip deeper into his pocket.

Everything seems to be in order, the table head would declare, signing his name to Arseniy's application. *Go pay your fees and I will see that you get your guild certificate.*

Arseniy moved quickly through the chancellery into another room where officials sat, collecting fees and registering capital announcements. Arseniy settled his accounts there and proclaimed his capital to be 2,400 rubles, or roughly $1,800 in 1858, the minimum allowed to enter the merchant estate at the time.* He was then encouraged to contribute to the "poor fund." Arseniy threw in several kopeks to satisfy the officer, who then handed him a certificate. It was Arseniy's ticket, the one that would set him on the path already crossed by his brothers.

Arseniy returned to the chancellery. The last paper Arseniy signed that day was an oath. "I, Arseniy Aleksiyev, a peasant freed by Lady Demidova, added to the Moscow Merchants third guild, put my signature in the house of the Moscow City Society which obliges me to pay all the state and city taxes without delay. I pledge not to do anything that may bring harm to my rank. My family and I are of the Russian Orthodox faith. We're neither eunuchs, nor dukhobors, nor molokans,† nor Jews nor any other especially insidious sect. Furthermore, I will bear responsibility if this should prove false."[6]

The Smirnov men, all of whom were covered by Arseniy's application, could now cast off their serf history like a heavy coat in summer. They had become Russian merchants.

BACK AT ONE of Ivan's shops where Pyotr was working, the conversation flowed. Indeed, it overflowed. In all likelihood, Arseniy and his son rambled on about finding just the right spot from which to peddle wines. They batted around ideas for running the business, what exactly they would sell, and how they would

---

* About $46,768 today.

† Dukhobors were a religious sect that did not accept churches as places for prayer. They were supported by Tolstoy at the end of the nineteenth century. Molokans were a religious sect opposed to the Russian Orthodox Church and its rituals.

sell it. They even discussed the possibility of distilling their own vodka. The Smirnovs were now poised to enter the vodka fray. And the vodka industry was getting ready for them, too.

Problems in the vodka business had been bubbling for some time. It was a complicated—and especially corrupt—aspect of Russian life. The government relied on revenue from vodka sales. By the late 1850s, an eye-popping 46 percent of the state's budget came from taxes on vodka.[7] This revenue gave the tsar and his top lieutenants every incentive to encourage drinking. The more the people drank, the more the state collected.

The nobility, which enjoyed the exclusive right to produce grain alcohol, had no reason to quarrel with the state's position. They too benefited from prolific drinkers. Then there were the tax farmers. In Russia, these were the two hundred or so enterprising entrepreneurs, often merchants, nobles, or members of the petite bourgeoisie, who paid the government for the rights to distribute vodka within specific regions. They bid on these rights at auctions held every four years. The winner received the vodka, at a fixed price, and a license that allowed them to trade it and collect taxes. It was risky for the licensees because they had to buy their entire lot of vodka and hope to sell it all.

Still, the contracts were as precious for the state as they were for the tax farmers. Demand for vodka was endless while supply could be controlled. Given the stakes, would-be distributors would do almost anything to win the auction, including bribery. It was estimated that successful tax farmers paid off as many as 90 percent of the officials in the vodka trading chain of command. The costs of these payoffs by just one farmer to local officials, according to a study published by the minister of finance, amounted to more than 17,000 rubles a year.[8]

It was clearly worth the extra payoff since anything a tax farmer collected above his contract went directly into his own account. One estimate put the annual income of tax farmers in the 1850s at 800 million rubles.[9] The system practically invited criminal activity, which the government tended to ignore as long as revenue continued to flow its way.

One of the most harmful consequences of the tax farming system was the production of dirty, diluted alcohol. To increase supplies and bounty, tax farmers would water down the vodka they sold and use an array of foul additives, from soap to copper to the toxic jimsonweed, to keep the liquor from tasting too bland. This practice not only sickened (and in some cases killed) tipplers but also compelled them to buy more of the bad booze to achieve the desired goal of drunkenness. Making matters worse, the government increased taxes on vodka while farmers routinely charged customers significantly more than the legal, state-mandated price. By the late 1850s, many Russian peasants were paying more than ten rubles for a bucket of vodka—or more than three times the established rate.[10]

The situation was not sustainable and something had to be done. By the end of 1858, just months after Arseniy's triumph at the merchant's department, something was done. Outraged peasants, who paid the dearest price for the vodka trade's corrupt practices, fought back. They began to take oaths of sobriety. Entire communities collectively vowed abstinence. In the southern town of Balashov, for example, townspeople gathered in the main square and prayed on their knees. "With tears of repentance and joy, repenting of the great sin of drunkenness, they then took an oath of sobriety, after which guards were posted at all the taverns, and punishments were established for those who broke the oath."[11]

The protest, of course, did not stem from any moral awakening that liquor was bad. Rather it grew simply out of a desire to force tax farmers to sell better—and cheaper—vodka. As one observer explained: "Vodka in itself is alright. . . . The real harm is done when it is costly, and of poor quality, when in order to get 'carried away' you've got to give the tavern keeper your overcoat, hat, axe, and cart as security, and the vodka itself is such that it only makes you feel bad, like a poison. This is what the people could not bear. This is why they boycotted vodka."[12]

The movement, which soon spread to thirty-two provinces throughout Russia, tore at the foundation of the country. Newspapers reported about it in a special section titled "The Spread of Sobriety." The state, tax farmers, grain harvesters, and tavern owners fretted about what to do. Some tax farmers relented, lowering the price of vodka and improving its overall quality. It was an important first step, albeit a small one, in the direction of a more open, market-driven vodka economy. But it was not enough to overcome the people's growing unrest—and raw bitterness.

In May 1859 the vodka boycott turned violent. People attacked and destroyed drinking houses, smashing bottles of liquor and furniture, and beating up police and state officials. In just one three-day period, sixty-one pubs in the southeast province of Penza were crushed. That was just the beginning. The riots spread quickly, unleashing a torrent of pent-up anger to some thirty-eight different regions or districts in Russia. By the end of that year, 260 liquor establishments had been attacked in two hundred different communities. Nearly eight hundred people were arrested and prosecuted for their participation in the violence, as the government and its army moved in and, eventually, brutally suppressed the offensive.[13]

But the point had been made. The antiquated, thoroughly corrupt system that had ruled vodka commerce in Russia for more than one hundred years was broken, a crippled reminder that reforms were well past due. Like serfdom, tax farming had to go.

WHILE TSAR ALEKSANDER II formulated what later became known as "the great reforms," Pyotr and his father prepared for the coming change. Pyotr had stopped working for his uncle in 1859 and was spending his time making plans with Arseniy.

They had limited capital and were restricted in the scope of their merchant license. But nothing could quell the enthusiasm shared by the two men. It was a happy time for them. And Pyotr had a new woman in his life.

Her name was Nataliya Tarakanova. She had much in common with Pyotr, according to local records. She, too, was a former serf from the Yaroslavl region, having been ransomed from her landowner in 1853. Her father, like Pyotr, had come to Moscow to pursue the merchant life. Shortly after joining the guild in 1853, Nataliya's father died, leaving her and her mother to tend the family's affairs. For her time, she was an able businesswoman, competent and serious. This ability must have been appealing to Pyotr, now eager to find a partner who could understand, support, and promote his ambitions.

He may also have liked Nataliya's appearance. She was young and innocent, probably no more than nineteen years of age when they met (Pyotr was twenty-seven). Her exact features are unknown because no photographs, drawings, or paintings of her exist. More than pleasant looks, though, Nataliya offered a winning combination of intelligence and gentleness. For Pyotr, she would make the perfect spouse—and mother of their children.

The two married in either late 1858 or early 1859. Pyotr could now truly separate from his Uncle Ivan—and wasted no time doing so. The couple rented space from a wealthy merchant who owned several homes, according to real estate records. It was right next to the home Pyotr would eventually buy and inhabit for the rest of his life. The living quarters were in a pale yellow, two-story building that the Smirnovs shared with a spice-cake shop. The smell of these glazed cookies, a kind of national sweet, permeated the entire neighborhood. It did not take long for Nataliya to become pregnant, as her belly swelled by the middle of 1859. She delivered Pyotr's his first daughter, Aleksandra, at their home in December 1859.[14]

Aleksandra did not survive for long, dying six months later

from measles. The death of his second child must have left Pyotr distraught and Nataliya inconsolable—a state that prompted the couple to move again. This time, Pyotr and his wife sought solace and comfort. They found it in the home of the sexton for St. John the Baptist Church, the same place that would host Pyotr's funeral years later. It was located in the Zamoskvorechye district, a hub for merchants in general and immigrants from Yaroslavl in particular. Their street was not the bustling thoroughfare of Varvarka. But it was an up-and-coming trading center, ideal for newly minted merchants.

Pyotr felt at home there. It was as close to village life as he was going to get in Moscow. Familiar faces, similar values, sympathetic, devout neighbors. It was also only a five-minute walk to the infancy of an empire.

ARSENIY OPENED HIS first wine cellar in a house in the Pyatnitskaya district. The business was known as a *renskoviy pogreb*, meaning "the Rhine cellar." The Rhine valley in Germany was the region from which much of the wine in Russia during the eighteenth century had come. In Smirnov's time, wine came from all over, but the term "Rhine cellar" was still used, generically, to refer to any place selling alcoholic drinks. The street-facing entrance to Smirnov's shop was marked by an oil lantern and a green sign inscribed with gold letters that read: RHINE CELLAR OF ARSENIY SMIRNOV. Though the business carried Arseniy's name—and he was the official owner, he handed over much of its operation to Pyotr and his wife.

Arseniy knew comparatively little about the backbone of the spirits industry—its suppliers, pricing, manufacturing. Pyotr, by contrast, knew it all. Years under his uncles' tutelage had taught Pyotr such essentials as where to find the best liquor and to how profit from it. He had contacts all the way north to Uglich as well as right in the heart of Moscow.

The father and son began small—as they had to. Legally, they couldn't distill their own spirits or serve hot meals in their establishment. The Smirnov *renskoviy pogreb* likely sold grape wines by the glass and in bulk, which patrons could choose to drink on the premises or to carry out. They sold vodka, too, produced elsewhere. Wishing to solidify ties to their community, they allowed customers to linger in their small, smoky cellar. But Pyotr was careful not to allow his thirsty customers to drink too much. Unlike some other establishments, his was to be respectable. He nursed his reputation, wanting to be known as someone who cared as much about his patrons as he did about racking up sales. It was an early and unusual commitment to responsible drinking—and the beginnings of a highly cultivated image Pyotr would nurture throughout his career.

Within months, Arseniy and Pyotr added tobacco and kefir to their product line. And by 1861 they opened two trading shops and one cellar, which sold these items, along with liquor for takeout.[15] They worked diligently and prospered more than most, considering the constraints of their time.

Historically, the tsarist regime had always had trouble loosening its tight grip on the economy. Availability of capital was a problem, and incentives for entrepreneurship were almost nonexistent. In addition, foreign investment was scarce. Labor lacked basic protections, benefits, or productivity models. And no real rule of law was in place to govern free enterprise. In that environment, few corporations had been founded—just sixty-eight existed in all of Russia in 1847[16]—and even fewer survived for long, particularly in the government-controlled areas of manufacturing, heavy industry, and transportation.

The tsar knew this scenario could not continue if Russia were to flourish. He had to find a way to jumpstart the nation's most enterprising citizens, to give them incentives to create businesses and work harder. On February 19, 1861, six years after his coronation and after a great deal of discussion, Aleksander II, later known as the great reformer, locked himself alone in his office and signed the manifesto abolishing serfdom. Some 22.5 million serfs, or 40 percent of the nation's population, were granted some civil rights, a structure to own their own land, and the ability to engage freely in any gainful employment they chose.* At about the same time, the government announced that the production, distillation, and wholesale and retail sale of vodka and other spirits would be open to all. The tax farm system would be no more, replaced within two years by an excise tax system. The idea was to end the corruption that had raged among vodka makers and sellers for years while, at the same time, growing government revenues through hefty taxes.

These two gigantic reforms had an extraordinary effect on Russia—and on Pyotr Smirnov. Within months of the tsar's proclamation, signs of progress, modernization, westernization, were everywhere. Memoirs of Muscovites at the time describe a city that transformed from a drab backwater into a hot spot. Old-fashioned carriages disappeared, replaced by sleeker models with coach boxes. Gas was pumped into private homes by huge gas-transporting vans that seemed almost American. Schools for women opened, as higher education came into vogue. Even the press had more freedom. "Something new was in everything," recalled one Moscow resident. "The streets and buildings were the same. But there was no sign of former Moscow. The features of the sleeping kingdom had disappeared."[17]

In its place, liberalized citizens smoked on the streets and wore long, rebellious hairstyles. Men traded in their stodgy top boots for imported low boots. Women donned European fashions purchased from elegant shops that opened on Tverskaya Street. Crowds, once fearful of Moscow's darkness, came out into the night, as new kerosene lamps brightened the city's squares.

---

* Serfs still faced difficulty leaving their villages and often could not afford to buy land offered them because of steep costs.

It was an environment and mind-set that exhilarated most Russians. The effect on merchants, like the Smirnovs, was palpable. Although they were still discriminated against, their status and self-image improved. Pavel Buryshkin, a well-known Russian merchant who chronicled Moscow's nineteenth-century merchant estate, wrote: "Beginning in the 1860s, every day life of [the merchant districts] shifted. Children started receiving education. Young merchants studied not only in the commercial academy but in the university as well. Merchants' daughters started to speak English and play Chopin nocturnes. Stubborn, dumb despots were reborn into businessmen who realized their material power."[18]

It was as if hope had seeped into the water supply, showering an entire population with the promise of better days. Pyotr Smirnov drowned himself in the mood. In Russia's quest to modernize and industrialize, he saw opportunity for himself and his family. In the tsar's acknowledgment that merchants had key roles to play in Russia's economic rebirth, Smirnov might have believed the emperor spoke directly to him. In the call for entrepreneurship, Smirnov did not hesitate.

He marched down to the Moscow City Society, filed his papers with the officials, announced his capital, and walked out with his own merchant license. He joined his father as a member of the merchant's third guild. Unlike his time in Yaroslavl, Smirnov was now completely untethered, ready to mold his own future.

It was 1862 and Pyotr Smirnov had heard the unmistakable pop. For the first time in his life, he seemed to believe that anything was possible. Now he set out to prove it.

Chapter 4

The Vodka Maker

It did not take long for the real Pyotr Smirnov to emerge. A man transfixed by opportunity, as tireless and determined as a missionary, Smirnov was making up for lost time.

Life was a veritable frenzy of activity. Smirnov had taken over almost every aspect of the business from his father. Arseniy was likely so convinced that his boy was on the way to a fruitful future that he gave up his status as a merchant and moved down a rung on the social ladder to the petite bourgeoisie class. He saw no reason to maintain appearances—or continue paying dues to the guild or taxes to the state. Pyotr could take on those responsibilities for the family as it was he who truly reveled in his rapidly improving position. He was consumed by running the three alcohol-trading outlets the family now operated, and he made plans for expansion. At the time, according to a profile compiled for a commercial exhibition, the business employed nine workers, including Pyotr, Nataliya, and Arseniy. But Pyotr could see it would not be long before this small group would be overwhelmed by more and more business.

The spirits industry was booming. After emancipation and the end of tax farming, prices of vodka dropped by 65 percent, from as much as twenty-five rubles per pail to eight rubles sixty kopeks. The intoxicating liquid was then commonly referred to by consumers and in the media as the "cheap stuff."[1] Quality was up, too, as incentives to water down or dirty-up the booze fell away. Consumption skyrocketed: Russians soaked up every drop of alcohol produced and came back for more. They spent 300 million rubles more on alcohol in 1863 than they had in 1862.[2] "It became the conventional wisdom that the reform had led to an orgy of drunkenness," wrote David Christian, a contemporary Russian historian.[3]

Part of the torrid tippling could be explained by the sheer availability of liquor. In the same year, from 1862 to 1863, the number of drinking spots in Moscow alone swelled from 371 to 3,168.[4] These dingy watering holes could be found everywhere—near monasteries, hospitals, cemeteries, and schools. Indeed, there were more pubs per person than doctors. The same was true for all of Russia, which went from having 78,000 pubs before emancipation to more than 265,000 by the end of 1863. The reason was simple: Licenses to operate cellars and pubs had gotten cheap, creating a quick, easy way for the lower classes to upgrade their standard of living. The price to peddle grape wines, for example, was the equivalent of a paltry $27.

Russia suffered under the ill effects of drinking, to be sure. Alcohol-related arrests in Moscow swelled, from about 7,000 in 1842 to almost 12,000 in 1863. Health concerns grew, too. According to official records and historians in 1863, deaths from alcohol poisoning and other liquor-induced diseases were so numerous as to be "too hard to count."[5]

Still, these negative by-products were easily swept aside. It was the euphoria emanating from Tsar Aleksander's II's series of liberalizing reforms that commanded people's attention. In addition to emancipation and the abolition of tax farming, the tsar introduced a form of local self-government known as the *zemstvo*. These civic organizations, which primarily addressed local economic and cultural issues, brought together citizens from across the societal food chain. This spectrum included the gentry, clergy, merchants, and peasants. The *zemstvo* had no real authority and was dubbed by contemporaries as "a building without a foundation or a roof."[6] But at first, it gave many people a sense of empowerment, a feeling that their country might be moving to a more constitutional, democratic model.

In 1864 a set of judicial reforms, including the creation of public jury trials, replaced the old feudal system. The move brought together people from across the economic spectrum to pass judgment on other citizens, helping establish at least the appearance of a rule of law that treated people—and businesses—evenhandedly. The nobility no longer held all the advantages. Other reforms followed in the ensuing years, including decreased censorship, military overhauls, and the establishment of decentralized governmental bodies that included representatives from all classes.

The period of the so-called Great Reforms, which lasted from 1861 to 1874, offered up a special moment for Russians. The era saw the greatest number of corporations ever chartered by the tsarist regime, as well as a commercial banking boom. Technological advancements, a central part of the effort, were made at lightning pace. Perhaps most noteworthy was how much the reforms helped spur the Russian spirit of entrepreneurship and enthusiasm for strong economic development. If the nation had not run headfirst into the litany of domestic problems that later fueled the Bolshevik Revolution, some contemporary historians concluded that Russia might have stayed on a capitalist course, perhaps surpassing leading economies in the West.

It is unlikely that Smirnov understood how these political

and social dynamics affected his immediate circumstances. Nonetheless, he capitalized on them.

IN SOME WAYS, Smirnov's boyhood had been a never-ending series of acting lessons. Outwardly, he had to appear respectful and earnest, a standard bearer for the unquestioned obedience and diplomacy expected of a proper peasant's son. Inwardly, though, Smirnov was reeling, quietly plotting for what might come next. Now in his thirties, Smirnov was repeating the pattern.

He was a small-time liquor peddler, a man doling out an assortment of drinks plus sauerkraut and pickled cucumbers to a group of mostly middle- and lower-class customers. But he ached for much more. Smirnov wanted to join the small but growing list of ex-serfs who relied on innate intelligence and business savvy, rather than birthright, to become some of Russia's most prominent self-made moguls. The names were well known to most Russians, including textile baron and financier Morozov, chocolate maker Abrikosov, and textile manufacturer Konovalov. These people had tucked away their humble beginnings like old photographs, never looking back at the fading images. They had stumbled on good fortune and made the most of it, launching their enterprises at a moment when the state needed them and few competitors existed.

The successes of these moguls could indeed have been the model for Smirnov. They chose to enter industries that were in demand. They grew these businesses by relying on family and friends—and to a lesser extent the state, for manpower, money, and advice. They also invested in and utilized cutting-edge technologies, such as rapid transportation and updated machinery. And last, Smirnov probably noted, they maintained high-profile positions in charitable and religious groups to soften their rich public images and strengthen ties with influential city leaders and aristocrats.

In evaluating the triumphs of these other ex-serfs, Smirnov might have realized the sweet position in which he now found himself. Demand for liquor, specifically vodka, was a bottomless pit. Competition was weak: There were roughly a dozen vodka producers in Moscow in 1864, most with fewer than ten employees. And the price of entry, both in terms of money and human capital, was within his reach.

Smirnov knew that to replicate the prestige and power of men like Morozov or Konovalov he had to think bigger than small pubs and wine cellars. He would have to take on the greedy middlemen who supplied the liquor he sold. Smirnov had plenty of connections to produce his own stuff—a route that would enable him to control his vodka's taste and quality. He could also sell to other pub owners, increasing his revenues and profits. Eventually, he could export to other Russian territories, too. Moscow was at the center of the country's developing railroad hub, making it an ideal location from which to ship products.

Smirnov embraced the obvious: It was time to start making vodka. The year was 1864, the same year that Smirnov's future nemesis, Tolstoy, was writing his epic masterpiece, *War and Peace*.

SMIRNOV SCOUTED THE perfect spot for a vodka distillery in the dwelling of fellow merchant Aleksey Shekhobalov. The location was near Smirnov's home at the time, between Malaya Ordynka and Pyatnitskaya streets. The cramped, dank space was already set up to produce alcohol. A metal still was there, along with a steam boiler and a storage area. It was perfect for making wines, vodka, liqueurs, and sweet *nalivkas*, the fruity vodka mixes for which Smirnov would later became famous.

Smirnov did not manufacture his own pure-grain alcohol, known then as bread wine. That was the job of distillers, who took raw materials, such as wheat, rye, or potatoes, to make spirits. Smirnov would buy this base alcohol directly from select suppliers he knew, then concentrate instead on the more profit-able end of the business, that of mixing the alcohol with water, fruits, and other additives to create the tastiest, most flavorful vodkas money could buy.

Smirnov's entry into the world of vodka making came natu-rally. He had no need to hire a master brewer. Pyotr, with the support of Nataliya, Arseniy, and a handful of other workers, as-sumed the role. He was already well-skilled in the art of distilla-tion. Besides, it was not going to take much to produce the small amounts needed at first: approximately twenty pails-worth of vodka at a time, an amount just large enough to fill an average-sized bathtub.

The process was straightforward. First, Smirnov put on a long white apron and gloves. He then tested the vodka he bought from his suppliers. The strength of the liquid was often variable depending on the temperatures used to produce it—and because distillers often fibbed about the quality of their liquor. He used a common but complex spirit-measurement instrument, known as a hydrometer, to calibrate the percent of alcohol by volume in the spirit. Smirnov relied on this information to determine how much water needed to be added or subtracted from the liquid to achieve whatever strength of alcohol he deemed suitable, usually 38 percent for pure vodka and far less, about 20 percent, for his signature flavored vodkas.* Once finished, Smirnov followed a simple recipe, producing a wide array of flavored vodka drinks.

One of the most common flavors in the 1860s was anise vodka. For this variety, Smirnov would have needed one-half pound of fresh anise, which was ground into a powder. The powder was put into a vat and mixed with nine *shtofs*, or 10.8 liters, of spirit. The liquid would then be poured into a large glass container and allowed to sit idle for nine days. On the tenth day, Smirnov

---

* Russia uses a different way of measuring alcohol content than the United States. Degrees and percents are equivalent, but an alcohol's proof value is different.

would transfer the liquid into a metal still and heat it under a slow fire until it was fully distilled. What was left was nearly five *shtofs*, or six liters, of a highly pungent alcohol. But the taste still needed refining. Sugar and more fresh water were added to the liquid, giving it a slightly milky hue. An egg white was folded into the mixture as well, after which the liquid would be run through a charcoal filter and then stored in a bottle for sale.[7]

This kind of vodka was but one of many offerings from Russia's nineteenth-century vodka makers. Smirnov's must have been at least as good as anyone else's out in the market, for his business took off. Demand outstripped supply—especially for the liquor Smirnov was making. Word had begun to seep out among locals that Pyotr Smirnov cared about the taste and the purity of his drinks. Stories surfaced that he selected the purest water, finest spirits, and freshest ingredients for his mixtures. Smirnov exploited these stories, suggesting to his mostly lower-class customers that he alone was devoted to making high-quality, affordable liquor.

Whether these were mere rumors hatched by Smirnov himself, nobody knows. But the result was the same: Smirnov's business—and financial well-being—swelled far beyond expectations. More wine cellars opened, and by 1867, within three years of opening his vodka factory, Smirnov had enough money to purchase a two-story stone house on the corner of Pyatnitskaya Street near the embankment of the Moscow River. The house was a mansion with a spacious backyard. It was somewhat worn at the time and displayed few of the trappings of wealth that would later stop pedestrians in mid-stride.

The house was large enough for the controlling Smirnov to maintain a constant eye on every aspect of his expanding business empire, which now employed roughly twenty-five people. The first floor of the home worked as a cellar and retail outlet. The second floor, spacious as it was, proved ideal for Smirnov's private office and the living quarters for his brood, which now included four young daughters. The backyard, which featured an uninhabited structure, could be used for everything from storage to housing workers. There was also a deep basement, ideal for preserving wine and liquor.

The location of the house, too, was superb. It was across from the Kremlin and stood at a well-traveled intersection that exposed any passersby to the vodka maker's name, which he proudly displayed above the corner entrance to his shop.

Smirnov's expansion and growing business platform mirrored what was happening all over Moscow. The city had become the heart of Russia's industrial revolution. Factories were sprouting up everywhere. Food producers—from makers of sausage to chocolate to spaghetti—set up shop throughout the city, establishing Moscow as the food-industry capital of Russia. Textile and paper manufacturers flourished, too, attracting capital and laborers in unprecedented waves. Railroad construction was almost constant. Even private banks opened for business, marking the first time the state encouraged independent financial investment in Russian industry. The Merchant Bank, for example, was launched in Moscow in 1866 with a stated mission to create "an establishment promoting industry and trade."[8] The vodka industry was growing more intense, too. Within four years of Smirnov launching his factory, the number of producers in Moscow had tripled.

According to one writer, "Capitalism changed Moscow in those years much more strongly than it changed any other Russian city, including St. Petersburg. In St. Petersburg, the court, officials, and military men still defined the main atmosphere of the city. Moscow, on the contrary, was regenerating from a noble city into a capitalist one."[9] This new money also fed the beginnings of a cultural renaissance. St. Petersburg dominated Russia's artistic scene; nobles and state officials patronized a litany of unparalleled cultural offerings there. But the capital city was tied to traditional values and more conventional thinking about what constituted art. Moscow, with its influx of the newly wealthy and transient multiclass workers, was developing a more liberal attitude about literature, theater, and other artistic endeavors. A genre known as agricultural poetry, for instance, written by peasants and migrants, surfaced in Moscow in the 1860s. New theaters opened, welcoming avant-garde productions. The Moscow Conservatory, which attracted such giants as Pyotr Tchaikovskiy, was founded in 1866 by pianist and composer Nikolay Rubinstein. Its sole mission was to promote greater musical education to the populace. New publications emerged as outlets for some of Russia's most prominent writers, including Tolstoy, Dostoevskiy, and Turgenev.

Moscow's nascent artistic scene was notable, though invisible to many Muscovites, including Smirnov. He had no use for these perceived frivolities, these impractical distractions promoted by the gentry, at the time. Besides, art had nothing to do with religion or with business—the two things that preoccupied the myopic vodka maker and many of his merchant neighbors. "There are entire areas for which the theater just doesn't exist, where inhabitants treat theater performances as devil's mummery. The area of Zamoskvorechye [where Smirnov lived] is one such area," wrote one historian.[10]

One thing that did capture Smirnov's attention, apart from his incessant work, was the birth of his first son. On January 26, 1868, Pyotr Petrovich Smirnov was born. His birth, like Smirnov's death, was recorded at the church of St. John the Baptist farther down Pyatnitskaya Street. The naming of the boy's godfather was a symbolic, telling gesture. He was Nikolay Smirnov, Smirnov's cousin and the son of Smirnov's mentor, Uncle Grigoriy. Few other details about the baby were provided in the church record.

The event was probably momentous to the young Smirnov family. In Russia, family dynasties, most descending from nobility, dominated business. Some, however, were self made.

These families harbored an inherent mistrust of the state and a foreboding sense that individual wealth was a rare, often fleeting privilege that had to be safeguarded. The sentiment forced these merchants to rely on heirs to protect their hard-won positions and financial stature. Smirnov, the former serf and peasant, understood the fragility of his newfound affluence.

With the birth and subsequent survival of this infant son, Smirnov could glimpse how his growing empire might have a long-term future. The appearance of the boy put him on track to emulate the successes of other family dynasties—from the Morozov to the Gubonins to the Tretyakovs. Like them, Smirnov now had the chance to craft a legacy, one that might endure far beyond his own lifetime. Neither he nor his descendants would ever have to fear poverty or hardship again—or so it seemed.

Perhaps inspired by such grandeur, Smirnov thought of little else but how to outproduce, outsell, and outmaneuver his growing list of competitors. Smirnov was already one kind of a success. His neighbors knew him. Peasants from Yaroslavl supported him. Family members and their contacts promoted him. Local restaurants and watering spots served his drinks. But outside this well-defined group, Smirnov was a respectable no-name, no more recognizable than the local blacksmith or butcher.

To the ambitious Smirnov, this lack of far-flung notoriety would not do. He wanted to be acknowledged for his up-from-the-bootstraps achievements. He wanted his vodka to sit on the tables of all Russians. He especially wanted the tsar to know his name and drink his concoctions. In 1869 then, Smirnov, likely with the help of a secretary or personal assistant, took the bold step of petitioning the Imperial Court.

This move was extraordinarily gutsy. Providing *anything* for the High Court was the highest of honors. Over the years, according to imperial archives, many world famous manufacturers and artists enjoyed the title of Purveyor to the Court. Tiffany and Co. and Peter Carl Fabergé were among the tsar's jewelers. Steinway and Sons provided the court with grand pianos. Singer was the imperial sewing machine supplier. The Daimler Motor Company manufactured the court's automobiles. Lesser-known purveyors provided everything from soap to furs to wood to saddles. There was even a royal leech man in the 1850s by the name of Stepan Gorbachevskiy.[11]

That Smirnov would place himself among these and other purveyors, after less than five years as a vodka maker, demonstrates his rising impatience and his inflamed ambitions. Had he bothered to investigate the criteria required to be a purveyor to the court, he would have realized he had no chance. Among other things, no one could be granted the title without having provided services or products to the court for at least eight years. A special note issued in 1866 by the Chancellery of the Office of the Ministry of the Imperial Court explained it all.

> The title of Court Purveyor or Commissioner, and the attending right to depict the imperial coat of arms, is to be bestowed only to those individuals who either supplied certain goods for a significant sum of money to the Imperial Court, or in general have fulfilled some kind of work for the Imperial Court over the course of eight to ten consecutive years. This privilege may not be transferred by inheritance or by any other means from one individual to another. This title is granted to a person who has proven conscientiousness, industriousness, and ability over at least an eight-year period. The title is given only for the time of supply.[12]

Smirnov, unfortunately, had no relationship with the Imperial Court. What's more, he had no prestigious honors, awards, or positions to buttress his case. The one thing Smirnov might have had in his favor was his nationality. At the time, amazingly, just one of the tsar's vodka purveyors, Popov, was Russian born. Two of them hailed from France—Kamill Deprés and Emile Rouget—while a third, Aleksander Shtriter, came from Germany. Although they had factories in Moscow or St. Petersburg, their origins were foreign.

To the tsar and his aristocratic friends, the foreign roots of his vodka purveyors might have been their greatest appeal. Russian vodka had always been associated with homemade simplicity, a drink more suitable for the lowly masses than a royal, sophisticated consumer. Products coming from France, by contrast, were considered particularly refined, stylish, and high class. Indeed, Russians adored and celebrated everything French—be it fashion, food, or literature. Even the language was a status symbol, a sign of good breeding. Russian nobles routinely spoke French when servants were around in order to preserve their privacy.

Undeterred, Smirnov made his case in an application to the minister of the Imperial Court, dated February 20, 1869. According to his application, he emphasized the scope of his business—producing foreign and Russian grape wines, liqueurs, fruit liqueurs, and vodkas. He then tried to sell the court. "Specialists recall finding in my wines workmanship of such a degree that they do not in the least pale in comparison to well-known factories in St. Petersburg and Moscow. I am taking the courage to request before Your Highness about permission for the highest honor to me—to be named purveyor."[13]

The reply, perfunctory and unequivocal, came one month later. Written by an official from the Moscow court office to the minister of the Imperial Court, it stated that Smirnov's request "cannot be complied with since, by existing rules in this ministry, similar advantages are granted only to persons who, for a period of not less than eight years without a break, supply their products to the Royal Court. The applicant, as it has turned out, according to my personal records, has never been a supplier of wine to the Court."

It is uncertain what else Smirnov could have expected. Likely, he hoped for a shortcut to greatness. If he could promote himself as the royal vodka maker, the tsar's chosen supplier, then all other Russians and Europeans would know Smirnov's vodka was the finest. Smirnov's ascent until that point had been as miraculous as it had been efficient. He had experienced one uninterrupted triumph after another and had emerged as a flourishing business upstart. Smirnov now had two choices. He could lick his wounds and go on peddling vodka in the same manner he always had. Or he could craft an inspired plan, one that would assure him of the royal title he so desperately desired. It was a turning point for the vodka maker. The tsar's refusal, rather than deflating Smirnov's outsized ambition, emboldened it. It aroused something deep inside the man, a creative spark that transformed Smirnov from a competent businessman into one of the most ingenious marketers of his time.

Chapter 5

"Demand Smirnov Vodka"

S mirnov had come to a critical realization in the wake of the tsar's refusal. While he had succeeded in his business ventures, he lacked the panache of a royal purveyor. Russia was a country governed by arcane rules, established traditions, and an entrenched hierarchy. Perception mattered as much as reality.

Viewing the situation from this perspective, Smirnov recognized that he had little to recommend himself. He had indeed achieved some measure of refinement in the last few years and had also shed some of the more visible accoutrements from his village days. He no longer wore a long caftan or frock coat with wide dark trousers tucked into high boots, the uniform of lower-class men. He wore instead finely tailored dark or black suits, always cut to the prevailing European fashion. A polished gold pocket watch clung to his waistcoat by a thick chain. His dark beard was closely cropped, according to photos, and he used a pomade to slick back his black hair.

He knew, though, that Russia's ruling elite cared little

about these superficial adjustments. It cared more about position, stature, and demonstrated virtue. In this regard, Smirnov was unformed. He held no leadership role in the merchant guild's administration nor had he pursed any alliances with civic or charitable organizations. His cultural intelligence or aptitude was limited. His reading and writing skills were childlike, lacking the sophistication of an educated, well-bred person. And his minimal social life revolved around family and church. He had done almost nothing to expand beyond his immediate circles.

As for his liquors, they were also provincial. Other than regular customers, few outside Smirnov's controlled, insular world recognized his concoctions as anything more than standard fare. He had garnered no awards or honors attesting to the high quality of his drinks, and the packaging and labeling of his bottles were no different than others on store shelves. These oversights contrasted with the tsar's reining vodka purveyors. Aleksander Shtriter, for example, held an array of titles and honors. His drinks had been recognized in international competition. Moreover, Shtriter was a philanthropist and civic leader.

UP IN HIS second-floor office, seated in his favorite leather chair, Smirnov contemplated his predicament. He possibly consulted his father, who now lived with him, as well as his Uncle Ivan. Perhaps he even spoke to Nataliya, who maintained a presence in her husband's commercial affairs. But their voices were drowned out by Smirnov's own internal counsel. The vodka maker trusted his own judgment most. As one of Smirnov's admiring managers noted at the time, "Pyotr Arsenievich is *the* brain of our business."[1]

Smirnov devised an ambitious campaign, as calculating, comprehensive, and tactical as any plan ever conjured. The plan was visionary, too. Smirnov was on a mission to make his the most well-known—and prestigious—name in vodka. By Russian standards, this goal of branding was a novel, almost ground-breaking quest because brand-making was, at this time, a primitive concept. Only a sliver of Russians—the little more than 1 percent considered aristocrats—noted the image or origin of goods. They had the means to pay for products differentiated by prestige or quality—and the education to read and understand promotional materials distributed by vendors.

For the rest of the population, these things meant nothing. Products were commodities purchased directly from local networks of sellers, who maintained a stable set of repeat customers. These relationships were far more important than impersonal brand names.

Notwithstanding the widespread illiteracy of customers, few businesses had reason to spend their limited resources on brand-building anyway. The legal system offered no formal protection for trademarks or copyrights until 1896—more than three decades after Smirnov opened his first vodka factory. A law, which required manufacturers to stamp their names on their goods, did exist to authenticate one product from another and help deter counterfeiters. Smirnov, for instance, had "Pyotr Smirnov in Moscow" etched into the glass on his bottles in the 1880s. But the stamps were used more to track sales and revenue for tax purposes than for promoting one brand over another.

Beyond the lack of legal protections, advertising was a largely foreign phenomenon. Years of censorship meant that newspapers and periodicals were almost entirely official entities, reporting government announcements and other state-related business. After emancipation, more ads began appearing in publications, particularly the newer, more liberal ones, promoting soaps, perfumes, and other products. Liquor makers, however, did not join this marketing wave, preferring instead to rely on their old, tried-and-true grassroots methods to reach consumers.

Smirnov's genius, then, stemmed from his ability to look beyond what *had been* to see what *could* be. His vision was grandiose, culminating with no less than complete dominance of his industry. His blueprint to getting there, which wrapped his company's future inside his personal brand, was a veritable labyrinth of opportunistic initiatives aimed at building up Smirnov's public reputation and increasing the profile of his products. He would be famous—not just for vodka. He would be known for his leadership, his charitable giving, and a bevy of upper-crust awards. He intended to cater to the entire social spectrum, servicing both the poor and the rich with an array of targeted, differentiated offerings.

Smirnov's ambitious proposal required a personal quantum leap. Shy and reserved by nature, appearing almost robotic at times, he would have to pry open his clamshell of a soul and thrust himself into the limelight as a leader and an activist. He would have to immerse himself in the philanthropic needs of the lowest classes as well as the high-brow demands of the nobles. He would have to travel to new places, too, hawking his wares to a discerning international clientele. Under this scheme, Smirnov's comfortable anonymity would evaporate, a casualty of the race for vodka supremacy.

And there was the vodka itself. Smirnov needed to create greater demand for it as well as convince people that his brand was superior to any other in the marketplace.

The first step in rebuilding his image, Smirnov concluded, was finding the right charity to support. Meticulous in his evaluation, he likely investigated the thirty-two organizations that fell under the supervision of the Moscow Merchants Society. These included orphanages, hospitals, schools, and shelters for the homeless. Since 1862, the society had decreed that one of the primary duties of its members should be the social welfare of the community. Merchants, especially the most successful ones, were still vilified for their self-serving attitudes and lavish lifestyles. Nineteenth-century Christian Russians took the Bible at its word: "It is easier for a camel to pass through the eye of a needle than for a rich man to enter the Kingdom of God."[2] The most savvy industrialists, in turn, supported charities to atone for the sin of wealth. And most did so through one of the groups overseen by the Merchants Society.

Smirnov, however, was not convinced that this route was the best. His agenda for social advancement trumped the convenience and familiarity of the organizations sponsored by the society. Besides, Smirnov was reluctant to participate in the Merchants Society's programs. The group often hosted rowdy, all-night affairs, and the newspapers reported on these wild parties, causing members after-the-fact embarrassment and indignation. This behavior fell far outside of Smirnov's comfort zone. He rarely drank or gambled and was still an outsider when it came to organized, social encounters.* He had never been one for mindless chitchat or gossip, nor did he want to participate in unstructured intellectual banter.

So Smirnov looked beyond the Society's sanctioned charities, focusing instead on institutions that operated outside the merchants' charter and the government. These tended to be older, more established, more prestigious charities whose patrons came largely from the nobility. And they were not always hospitable, particularly to newcomers. Smirnov had previously tried to donate money to a private, exclusive school that catered to the children of nobles. His gift, however, was rejected and deemed inappropriate by the school's officials because Smirnov was not an established member of the upper crust.[3]

The rejection must have humiliated Smirnov, but he quickly moved on, taking particular interest in the Moscow Committee on Beggars. Founded in 1838 by a nobleman who was also Moscow's most influential official, the committee took in vagrants, housing them, finding them jobs, training them, sending them

---

* Smirnov's name never appears in attendance records of these events or in the memoirs of other merchants at the time.

to mental institutions, if necessary, or returning them to their families. The group provided a laudable and much-needed service. Since emancipation, the problem of unemployment and homelessness had soared, primarily in large cities like Moscow and St. Petersburg. An estimated 320,000 Russians a year had found themselves in need of social services following emancipation, a 32 percent increase from just before the reform.[4]

Apart from its good deeds, the Committee on Beggars also offered unique benefits. Members of the committee automatically received the title of Titular Counsel. According to the all-important civil table of ranks in nineteenth-century Russia, this honor, also held by Pushkin at the time of his death, was rather low. It ranked ninth out of fourteen possible titles. Nonetheless, Russian society treasured these awards. They served to differentiate people from one another and placed them atop "artificial social stilts," explained one baron critical of his country's hierarchical customs.[5]

Within the same vein, committee members were also afforded the right to wear stately uniforms to special events. These full-dress, formal costumes publicly displayed the lofty status of whoever wore them. This prerogative was priceless. "Status meant both privileges and prestige, and the merchant scrambled after these by whatever means available."[6] Smirnov could hardly resist.

In 1870, less than a year after his imperial rejection, Smirnov became an agent of the Moscow Committee on Beggars. Almost immediately, he began to enjoy the fruits of his choice. After donating a sizable, inaugural sum to the organization, Smirnov received his first medal. It was a round gold coin with a picture of the tsar on one side and the words "for zeal" engraved on the other side. Smirnov could wear this medal around his neck on a special ribbon, known as St. Vladimir's ribbon, offering up more evidence of his largesse.

His charity established, the vodka maker turned his attention to his merchant status. Still one of 4,500 members of the second guild in Moscow, Smirnov realized there was far more to be gained by moving up a rung. Moscow's first-guild merchants held a lofty place in the Russian state. Indeed, the most powerful men of industry were veterans of the first guild, including the Bakhrushin and Ryabushinskiy textile dynasties, and the Perlovs, famous tea traders. Uncle Ivan was also part of this exclusive 630-member group.

From a financial standpoint, members of the first guild were entitled to operate an unlimited number of business entities, to import and exports goods at will, to structure their companies using the most economically beneficial methods, and to enter into contracts of any amount. On a more personal note, they could receive a variety of important titles, including that of "honorable citizen" and "counsel of commerce." They also had the right to wear illustrious uniforms, complete with a rapier, special collar, and cuffs. Another privilege gave them the right to ride in a fine carriage pulled by two horses. Those in the second guild and below could only harness one horse to their carts. Members' children received benefits, too. After serving for twelve years in the guild, the children of members were granted access to elite, aristocratic educational institutions. Second-guild merchants were far more restricted in their school choices.

Of course, it cost significantly more to be in the first guild— 565 rubles annually versus only 120 rubles (565 rubles was about $367 in 1871, or about $6,425 today; 120 rubles was about $78 then and roughly $1,365 today). By this time, though, the added expense was more than manageable for Smirnov—and worth it. He entered the first guild in 1871, according to his license, "as a wine trader in his own house in the Pyatnitskaya district."[7] Smirnov's profile was elevated instantly. He attended regular meetings with business leaders and high society. They were getting to know him and soon, Smirnov hoped, they would know his liquor, too.

. . . .

SMIRNOV UNDERSTOOD THAT there was still much to do to turn his bit of a brand into a household name. In a sea of distillers, how could he stand out? How could he convince peasants and royalty alike that bottles bearing his name were synonymous with smooth taste and eminent quality? It did not really matter whether his vodka truly was better than the rest of the competition, even though Smirnov believed it was. What mattered most was that drinkers, when hearing the name, instantly associated his bottles with the best Russia had to offer.

Smirnov's plan was to go directly to his would-be customers. The streets were already flooded with alcohol. Taverns already had their favored brewers; consumers already knew what they liked—changing their minds would not be easy. Although Smirnov knew the mind-set of the peasants and lower classes, he was no longer accepted as a brother. He would have to find surrogates to make his case.

Artist Nikolay Nikolayevich Zhukov recalled Smirnov's dilemma—and solution to it—in a short story he published titled "*Smirnovskaya Vodka*," or "Smirnov Vodka." Zhukov was an early twentieth-century graphic designer, book illustrator, writer, and painter for the Soviet military. He made his name mainly through portraits of Vladimir Lenin, which are now part of some of Russia's most prominent art collections and galleries. He also produced pictures of everyday military life during World War II and covered the Nuremberg trials, creating more than two hundred drawings during a one-month visit to the proceedings. Zhukov's colleagues recalled that he changed his seat daily at the trials to avoid the scrutiny of the defiant defendants.

One day, according to Zhukov's story (which could not be independently verified), he was doing a portrait of an old, bearded man. The man, tired of sitting motionless for so long, began

to stretch his body. He told the painter his hip hurt, probably
due to the strain of a fishing trip and recent rains. He asked
Zhukov, "Maybe you have something?" Zhukov fixed the man
a drink. "He wiped his beard haughtily, drank everything, and
ate a bit of something after it. Then he turned to me and said:
'Ah, Smirnov's vodka was really good? Have you ever tried it?
You must have been too young then. It was good, really very
good.'"

The story he then told Zhukov was of a canny, up-and-coming Pyotr Smirnov. The man's memories were vague in some
places and clearly mistaken in others, but his overall message was
vivid and insightful: Smirnov had been a marketing wizard. One
morning, the man said, Smirnov set out for Khitrov market, the
grimiest, smelliest, and saddest spot in all of Moscow. Crowds of
beggars, thieves, shabbily clad women selling spoiled food, and
shoeless ragamuffins haunted the square, located in the center
of the city. The people scurried about beneath a constant steam
that seemed to hover like a cloud. They slept on the ground or
in doss-houses; they ate tinned stew or fried sausages, prepared
by women who kept the food warm by covering the rims of their
huge cast-iron pots with their bodies. They drank in the two-
and three-floored pubs that surrounded Khitrov, washing away
their troubles with rancid vodka. At times, as many as 10,000
people passed through the place Russian journalist Vladimir
Gilyarovskiy described as "a moving rotten pit."[8]

Smirnov, dressed modestly, knew what he was looking for in
Khitrov. In the mix of vagabonds and panhandlers were newly
arrived men in search of a job. They came to Khitrov directly
from the train stations and planted themselves under a huge
awning where employers of all kinds came to find day laborers. Smirnov studied the eyes of the men he saw, unconcerned
with their stained or ragged clothing, scruffy beards, or straw
shoes. He could fix that. What he could not tolerate were sloppy
drunks. Smirnov needed sober men, respectable enough to be

taken seriously and proper enough to command attention. He rounded up fifteen of them.

He invited them back to his house where a long, narrow table had been already set with vodka and snacks. He sat them down and gave the men some time to warm themselves and have a bite to eat. He then asked each of them where they lived and where they were from. Smirnov learned that he had selected a broad assortment of residents and visitors who came from many different areas in and around Moscow. Smirnov then took out his wallet, tossing down three rubles in front of each man's plate.

"Beginning with this day, you will drink and eat as much as you want on my treat. All I ask is that you work well for me. Now I want you to go back to your neighborhoods, order meat soups, and demand Smirnov vodka everywhere you go. Of course, people will first look at you with great surprise and try to suggest another vodka. They will try to persuade you to take another drink. But you should complain loudly so that everybody pays attention to you. A waiter will run away to get his manager and report that a strange guest demands Smirnov vodka. The manager will come to you. You should tell him loudly: 'How is it possible that your respected establishment does not have such a vodka? It is absolutely the most remarkable vodka there is!'" Smirnov told his new hires to refuse all substitutions they might be offered and leave the pub in a huff. The men were then to go to the next bar and "begin this performance again. Then come back to my table."[9]

The entourage did as they were told. And they did it well. At least that's how the old man told it. "That very same night, Smirnov started to accept numerous calls: People demanded ten, fifteen, or twenty boxes of vodka. The vodka gushed out across Moscow."

Once most of the drinking establishments in Moscow had been hit, Smirnov summoned his emissaries again. "Well, my

dears, we have finished one thing. Let us promote another."
He then instructed the men to travel along the rail lines that
jutted from Moscow's central hub and disembark at every
stop. "Demand our vodka everywhere." The men were delighted to carry out Smirnov's latest orders. He had fed them
well, given them plenty of good vodka to drink, and paid them
handsomely.

Zhukov listened as his storyteller continued, remembering
that calls for Smirnov's vodka traveled like a virus, infecting
one town after another. In no time at all, orders were pouring
in and Smirnov's vodka "became popular all over Russia and
then—worldwide." The old man sat up, returned to his pose,
and sighed. "Paint now!" he commanded Zhukov.

And so the story goes. Smirnov, as master puppeteer, put
on the perfect show. He convinced people that his vodka was
special and he had done so simply—and cheaply—relying on
his innate sense of human nature. Smirnov knew he could not
sway drinkers through advertisements or shiny labels or fancy
titles. Neighbors had to hear praise for his vodka from a fellow
drinker, the man seated on the bench at the far end of the bar.

Almost overnight, Smirnov had transformed his good,
cheap vodka into something fashionable, almost trendy—and
extremely profitable. By the end of 1872, Smirnov employed
more than sixty workers and oversaw three managers. He
produced up to 100,000 pails of alcoholic drinks and grossed
600,000 rubles annually, or the equivalent of almost $7 million
in today's dollars.[10] He had expanded his menu of offerings
well beyond vodka, too, hoping to broaden his appeal to consumers differing tastes. He produced an array of Russian and
foreign wines, hard liquors, cognacs, and *nalivkas* (fruit and
berry-instilled vodka). He had also kept his prices low, at least
in the beginning. Smirnov did not want to alienate those consumers most responsible for his success. He charged just thirty

kopeks, or twenty-one cents, for a bottle of wine, significantly less than the average of sixty-eight kopeks a bottle.*

Smirnov was now wealthy and enjoying enormous success. This good fortune, though, was confined to business. Smirnov's personal life was another matter.

SINCE ALMOST THE beginning, 1872 had been a difficult and traumatic year for Smirnov at home. His seven-year-old daughter, Anna, died in January of "throat inflammation."[11] Just a few months later, in May, his mother Matryona died at the age of seventy. Then in November, Smirnov's one-and-a-half-year-old daughter, Olga, was buried after contracting scarlet fever. All three were laid to rest in the Pyatnitskoye cemetery.

Sorrow was the unwelcome visitor in Smirnov's vast home, inhabiting every room, every piece of furniture. Nataliya likely suffered more than Pyotr—at least outwardly. The death of her daughters left her heartbroken, but now, thankfully, she was pregnant again. This baby, she vowed as she stroked her growing tummy, would survive, joining its five brothers and sisters. She could not bury another child.

Smirnov mourned, too, but he would not allow himself to dwell. Ever the pragmatist, Smirnov accepted these misfortunes as the unhappy, normal consequences of life. Besides, Smirnov still faced serious, distracting business challenges. His liquor was flowing, to be sure, thanks to his ingenious marketing ploys. However, it was being consumed more by the under class than by the upper crust.

This class distinction presented Smirnov with a unique problem. In some ways, he, like many other merchants, might have detested the haughtiness of Russia's upper echelons. Many had

---

* The average cost of a bottle of wine was calculated from retail prices listed by participants in the Russian Exhibition of 1870.

done nothing to earn their positions, their wealth, or their pedigrees. They fed off the good fortunes of ancestors and the imperial protections they inherited. Yet Smirnov also yearned for their acceptance. Indeed, he wanted his children to live the way they lived. He wanted, eventually, to be one of them. It was not unlike the tug of a magnet, at once irresistible and then repellent, with just the slightest twist. It was this tug that Smirnov felt most.

Wooing the gentry would require a different approach from the one he had concocted for the lower classes. These people did not hang out in dark, neighborhood pubs. They attended lavish balls; they frequented the theater, the ballet, and the opera; they socialized in plush, exclusive clubs that served only haute cuisine and fine, mostly imported spirits. The Moscow English Club, founded in 1772, was the best-known of these stylish gathering spots. Tolstoy, a member for a time, wrote of it in *War and Peace*, noting that visits to the club were part of the regular routine for aristocratic ladies and gentlemen.

The Moscow English Club was indeed a place like no other. Grand carriages parked alongside one another in the large yard before the entrance. Members, only three hundred in total, and their guests ascended a white stone staircase surrounded by two rows of marble columns to reach the club's doors. Servants opened the double doors that led to the entry hall. From there, visitors could head to the portrait hall, which housed portraits of emperors and important members. Or they could go to the drawing room, reserved for card play. Or they could play in the billiards room. The library offered one of the most complete collections of Russian and foreign periodicals dating back to 1813. The rooms seemed to go forever, ending with the dining room, the most majestic room of all. It was expansive, stretching the entire length of the building. During dinners, prepared by a coterie of the most prominent chefs in Russia, a small orchestra might play, followed by performances on a stage that featured some of Moscow's best actors.

It was a world far away from anything Smirnov had ever known, yet he wanted his liquors to be as much a fixture of the Moscow English Club as they were at neighborhood taverns. The question was how to turn that desire into reality. Smirnov's answer, like the one he crafted for the peasantry, relied on the nature of Russia's aristocracy. Perception mattered as much if not more than reality—especially the perceptions of Western Europe's high society. Nothing would be more meaningful than its endorsement of Smirnov's products. It would make them chic. And Russians would be proud that one of their own had so impressed the foreign elite.

Smirnov went to work, making plans to travel to Vienna. An international exhibition would open there in mid-April. These competitions were visited by thousands of people from all over the world. More importantly, awards were handed out to vendors with the best products, ranging from shoes to steam engines. If Smirnov could collect such an acknowledgement, it would prove invaluable to his commercial aims.

This would be the vodka maker's first trip abroad. He was probably nervous about the journey—but also invigorated by its promise. He hoped Vienna would put some distance between him and the previous year's sorrows. The year 1872 had been both professionally exhilarating and personally wrenching. What Smirnov did not know was that it would be nothing compared to what came in 1873.

Chapter 6

To Vienna and Back

The dawn of 1873 began peacefully. Moscow had taken on the look of granite, as a warm cloud cover left the city feeling still and dull. The nation was experiencing a relative calm, as the biggest news of the day related only to the death of the tsar's aunt and an illness suffered by a young prince.

Smirnov was not so calm. He knew the next few months would be hectic—and vital to distinguishing himself and his goods in Vienna. The exhibition, which was just a few months away, had taken on extra significance. The Austrian Empire hoped to polish its image, which had been tarnished by a war with France, financial difficulties, and social unrest. The country intended to demonstrate its emerging economic and political prowess, as well as showcase its picturesque capital city. For their part, the Russians were keen on flaunting their blooming industrialization, proving that they were a flourishing, dynamic nation. Russia had participated in previous international fairs, but none had attracted so many entrepreneurs and inventors before from such a wide array of industries. Fully loaded travel packages and special trains from St. Petersburg had been organized to transport participants and visitors to the fair. At least 1,500 merchants, artisans, and engineers from Russia were expected in Vienna in 1873. Just 700 had displayed their wares at the International Exhibition of 1862 in London while 1,300 showed up in 1867 at the Paris World's Fair.

Growth in the vodka industry provided one of the sharpest illustrations of Russia's advancements—and more capitalistic mind-set. Just two spirits makers from Moscow presented in Paris six years ago. The Vienna exhibition was expecting products from more than thirty Russian distillers—plus dozens from other countries. Smirnov, unknown outside of his native country, concluded wisely that he would have to be exceptional to earn any notice.

Preparations for the fair began in earnest months before the scheduled April (May 1 in Austria, which followed the Gregorian calendar) opening. Smirnov's first order of business would be to file the necessary paperwork with government officials in charge of organizing Russians going to Vienna.* The special department would handle most of the administrative tasks for its exhibition participants, from transportation to lodging. Smirnov, however, was responsible for the selection and display of his own drinks. He had to choose which wines and liquors to send and, perhaps, figure out how to get them there. Uncle Ivan would have been able to lend a hand with some of the details, such as what to enter in the fair. He had taken part in another competition a few years earlier and had experience to share. But Ivan's event had been a Russian-only affair in 1870, so he knew little about navigating the international community. Smirnov would have to figure that out for himself.

---

* Evidence regarding Smirnov's preparations for, and the journey to, the fair is scarce. This account is a likely scenario based on available archives, documents, and family accounts.

International exhibition juries tended to consider above all else the pricing of products, manufacturing technologies, output volume, and treatment of factory workers. Smirnov was still relatively small time. He had no schools or medical facilities set up for his sixty or so workers. At least eight other vodka makers produced more alcohol than he did. And his use of modern machinery was no better than his rivals. The one edge Smirnov did possess was price. He sold high-quality alcohol at exceptionally low prices.

Smirnov decided to send a variety of his liquors to Vienna. He hoped that a parade of offerings, which included wines, *nalivkas*, and vodkas, would make him appear more prolific, more of a heavyweight to the judges in Vienna. He also probably decided to use carriages and carts instead of trains to transport his goods to the fair. It was a more cost effective means, but it was also easier for Smirnov to maintain control of his products at all times since one of his men would accompany the cargo.

In all likelihood, he directed his managers to prepare crates for packaging his bottles. They would need to be ready by early March since the journey west would take about a month, depending on the weather. Smirnov's horse-drawn carts would join a convoy of others heading for the exhibition. Celebrated artists such as Ilya Repin and Vasiliy Perov were sending paintings, the Tretyakovs entered furniture fabrics into the competition, the Morozovs sent muslin and velveteen, and other exhibitors dispatched everything from caviar to porcelain to steel cannons to toothache remedies.

There is scant evidence about Smirnov's personal itinerary or his stay in Vienna. But based on experiences of other Russian participants, his journey would have unfolded much like others. Smirnov boarded a train in Moscow, which took him and other exhibitors some four hundred miles to St. Petersburg. From there, it was on to Warsaw. (Passengers needed to change trains in Warsaw as the Russian rails were a different width than those in other parts of Europe.) Adding to the trip's duration, locomotives and conductors had to be switched every fifty miles. All told, the exhibitors would arrive in Vienna approximately four days after departing Moscow.

The vodka maker probably intended to leave at the beginning of April. This timetable would allow him to settle into Vienna and assess the exhibition. He was determined to arrive early enough to snag the most prominent location possible within Russia's allotted display space. He also wanted the chance to glad-hand the fair's officials and judges before they embarked on their reviews. They might not know his name now, but Smirnov was determined that they would before the fair ended.

Nataliya was due to deliver their baby during this time. But Smirnov, the traditional Russian patriarch, did not consider his presence a necessity—or even desirable. His assorted family members and a midwife were more than equipped to see Nataliya through the birth, and they would telegraph him with the news when the time came. The thought of delaying his trip likely would not have crossed his mind—or his wife's.

The trip to Vienna, though, must have produced a cobweb of emotions. He knew he was days away from having another child. Would it be another boy? He prayed it would be. And what about the fair? At one moment, he was exuberant about his upcoming foreign adventure—certain he could carry away the event's top honors. But then again, what if he failed? What if his peers at the exhibition saw him as no more than a former serf? What if his provincial roots kept him from garnering the professional accolades he so desperately wanted? As it turned out, Smirnov, clad in his finest dark European suit, was much more prepared for Vienna than it was for him.

THE AUSTRIANS HAD pinned much on the event's success. No expense had been spared erecting multiple buildings in Vienna's Prater Park, including a grand rotunda, and new hotels sprang up like mushrooms. Apartment owners, hoping to lease their spaces to a sell-out crowd, expected giant paydays. Dignitaries were invited, too, to witness the country's triumph. As a Russian journalist observed: "The exhibition was expected to satisfy the [Austrian's] boldest hopes and dreams. Organizers of the exhibition were ready to spend any amount because they were certain the whole world would gather under the exhibition roof."[1]

Yet as the opening day approached, the fair looked more like a glorified flea market than a premiere international spectacle. The majority of participants had yet to unpack their goods or arrange their displays. Many waited anxiously for the arrival of their precious packages. Throughout the halls, unopened boxes and crates blocked walkways, constant reminders of the lingering chaos. It would be weeks before all the exhibits were ready, delaying the full opening of several pavilions. The Americans, who had dispatched such items as Colt revolvers, soaps from Colgate, and Pratt & Whitney milling machines, had nothing set up in their section. Part of the problem was administrative. Just days before the scheduled opening, officials still had not assigned space to many participants, leaving foreign exhibitors frustrated, impatient, and unimpressed. "The cases are only half-filled. And if you ask an exhibitor for his specifications, he is sure to ask you to delay any mention of his goods until his better qualities arrive," wrote one correspondent for the *New York Times*.[2]

More to blame, though, was the lack of a cohesive, logical floor plan. Products were given space without regard to aesthetics or common sense. Each country was allowed to design its own area, giving the halls an inconsistent, jagged feel. Spain, for instance, placed an old edition of *Don Quixote* alongside a piano and mosaic floor tiles. Russia displayed silver necklaces next to malachite caskets. Jurors, charged with evaluating one country's technological progress and quality of goods against another, were befuddled. Critics pounced on the gaffe. "There was no single system. Each country used its own ideas of how to organize the exhibition. That is why it was impossible to compare countries in a sense of industrial development," wrote one Russian critic.[3]

Smirnov was at a loss, too, sorting through the melee in his designated division, the Department of Agricultural and Food Products. An estimated 282 exhibitors from Russia attended, showing everything from jams to cigars to champagnes. Given his penchant for order, Smirnov must have been underwhelmed. Presumably, his bottles arrived on time, thanks to his efficiency and good planning, and somehow amid the chaos he found a way to get them into a prime position. Scores of visitors and jurors alike would be hard-pressed to miss his wares. The vodka maker, like his mentor, Uncle Grigoriy, always understood the importance of location.

Smirnov must have felt a sense of elation. He had arrived in Vienna as a novice. He did not know the city nor the exhibition nor the language. He may even have had trouble finding his own name in the German index of participants, where Pyotr Smirnov was Peter Smirnoff. Still, he had thus far managed to outmaneuver more experienced entrants—and was awed by much of what he saw, according to a book commissioned by his great-great-grandson, Boris. "Vienna astonished him with its abundance of music, flowers and love of life. Wearing a European suit, the Moscow merchant walked around the exposition grounds, glancing at the wine booths. What and how were they selling?"[4]

Matters in Vienna were shaping up nicely for the former serf. Back home in Moscow, though, circumstances were growing grim. Nataliya had delivered a baby boy, born April 8, on Easter Sunday. His name was Nikolay. The Smirnovs would not lose this child, but the delivery had not gone well. According to church records, Nataliya had developed a nasty infection following Nikolay's birth that left her exhausted, feverish, and at times, delusional. The condition was all too common—and its outcome was just as well known. The doctors were powerless to stop the disease that raged through Nataliya's body.

The opening of the exhibition was just days away when Smirnov likely heard the news. His head must have been spinning. He was delighted to have another boy. But Nataliya was dying, perhaps already dead. Smirnov, thousands of miles away, could do nothing.

He faced an untenable dilemma: that of choosing between his family and deep-seated religious convictions, and his towering business aspirations. Both options were fraught with difficulties. Emperor Francis Joseph himself was scheduled to appear on opening day to tour the halls, so it was a unique opportunity to catch the eye of royalty. The emperor's endorsement would indeed be invaluable in promoting Smirnov's liquor to the nobility.

On the other hand, the vodka maker had obligations to fulfill. Nataliya had been a beloved wife, mother, business partner, and trusted confidante. She had sculpted the Smirnov family, which now included six children ranging in age from a newborn to eleven years, into a solid, cohesive unit. Her gentle, warm nature had been an essential counterweight to Smirnov's own strict and rigid approach to parenthood. Without her, the vodka maker would have difficulty finding his footing at home. Even worse, if Smirnov did not follow the raft of religious rituals required after a spouse's death, his reputation might suffer. His priest, fellow parishioners, business associates, and family members might not understand this sin—or forgive it.

Smirnov hesitated. He embodied the Russia of yesterday as well as the modern Russia. He often found himself challenged by these polar forces, making decisions based on the overwhelming ambition and traditions that guided so much of what he did. No one knows which path Smirnov chose to take in this instance. But six days after Nikolay's birth, Nataliya, at the age of thirty, was dead. By the time Smirnov received the news, she was probably already in the ground.

Smirnov's choice had been mercifully made for him. Ever the pragmatist, he pushed through his grief and fulfilled his responsibilities as a business owner. He had already missed the funeral and a commemorative dinner held three days after Nataliya's death. He could not make it home in time for another meal held nine days after death. Arseniy and an assortment of relatives and friends were probably managing the situation without him.

Smirnov, as a compromise, probably initially kept to his schedule. He would attend the inaugural event, wearing the requisite white tie and black tails. He would do all he could to attract attention to his products and corner as many officials as possible to make his case. But then, Smirnov would cut his visit to Vienna short, returning to Moscow as widower. He would be seen in nothing but black and be home in time for the most sacred of occasions, the fortieth-day commemoration of his wife's death. It would be then, according to the Russian Orthodox Church, when Nataliya's final resting place would be determined. The family would pray for her salvation.

The vodka maker again probably called upon his time as a serf to help him cope. He had spent years in his village perfecting the art of unflinching emotional control. No one would see his inner turmoil or debilitating grief. People around him would see only what Smirnov wished them to see—the next vodka purveyor to the tsar.

OPENING DAY WAS a grand affair. At noon, the emperor and empress rode up in a ceremonial carriage pulled by six horses. No less than seven orchestras played for the event, including one conducted by the famous Johann Strauss. A cannon boomed, sounding the fair's official launch. Smirnov lingered near his display as visitors, including the emperor, streamed into the halls. They snaked through the rotunda, machine hall, and other pavilions. But much to Smirnov's disappointment, the emperor never made it to his section of the fair. And the crowds overall were thinner than expected. The weather had turned cold and rainy, driving down attendance. Still, officials—and Pyotr Smirnov—remained optimistic.

Vienna, though, was not in a mood for optimism. Just one week into the fair, Vienna's stock exchange crashed. Its effects, which included massive bankruptcies, suicides, and unemployment, were widespread. It deflated the whole atmosphere of the exposition, as officials panicked and attendance plummeted. Exhibitors, builders, and organizers had borrowed heavily to pull off their architectural feats and create their dramatic displays. Now, it was becoming a real possibility that the proceeds from the fair would fall far short of what was needed to repay those debts. No one, not even the shah of Persia, who had come to town, was feeling flush.[5]

Oddly, the financial crisis may have been a blessing for Smirnov. It stunted the flow of the exhibition, putting it into slow motion as Austrians tried to regain their composure. It was the final straw for visitors who had come or planned to come to Vienna. Now, they largely stayed away, hoping for the foul weather to clear and the financial crisis to stabilize. They wanted to see a complete exhibition, with pavilions full of bountiful displays and jaw-dropping inventions. As the Austrians needed more time, so did Smirnov.

This interlude of sorts provided a perfect opportunity for Smirnov to get back to Russia without anyone noticing his absence. He boarded a train bound for home in the aftermath of the stock market collapse. He hoped to return to Vienna, perhaps for the judging of drinks or for the awards ceremony itself in August. In the meantime, Smirnov planned to use the trip to take measure of his current circumstances. Losing Nataliya presented a whole host of challenges beyond the obvious. Smirnov was prohibited by custom from remarrying for at least a year. But he knew his future required that he find another wife. At a time when his image was critical to his strategy, he could not afford to be viewed as somehow socially incomplete.

Landing back in Moscow when he did turned out to be a gift. Just days after Smirnov's arrival, his Uncle Ivan died unexpectedly on May 16 from a heart attack. Whether uncle and nephew actually saw one another before Ivan's death remains a mystery, but Smirnov was likely present for the burial.

Ivan's death was big news in Moscow. The papers placed his passing on the front pages. The focus was not so much Ivan's considerable business accomplishments, earned over a lifetime. The newspaper articles barely mentioned his leadership roles or successes related to his liquor franchise, noting only that rumors suggested "the deceased left an enormous fortune."[6] Instead, they emphasized his service as a churchwarden, his philanthropic endeavors, and his awards and titles. This charitable activity was what resonated in the Russian community, which Smirnov never forgot. This was why newspapers could report that "a huge number of people" came to pay their respects.

For Smirnov, his eyes bloodshot, his body weary, the funeral must have been exhausting, agonizing. Ivan's grave was a mere few feet from the fresh graves of Smirnov's wife, daughters, and mother. Almost as soon as Pyotr stepped away from Ivan's grave, it was time to bid a final farewell to his Nataliya. The fortieth-day commemoration for her was on May 23. As tradition demanded, he donated a sizable sum to the church, an act intended to pay off Nataliya's sins and ensure that she be forgiven and delivered to heaven. Smirnov and his children prayed heartily for her soul.

In a sense, Ivan's passing left more of a void for Smirnov than losing his wife had. It left him with no choice but to transition from a supporting role in his expansive family into a leading role. Without Ivan, Pyotr Smirnov, at age forty-two, was a natural patriarch. The extended family could now look to him for authoritative guidance and care as well as to his father, Arseniy. At age seventy-three, though in the twilight of his life, he retained some of the vibrancy and vigor acquired after decades toiling in the rural farm fields.

Pyotr, of course, had little time to adjust or wallow. His household was in disarray. He had to find appropriate caretakers for his newborn son and the other children. He had a large and growing business to run. And from the reports he was receiving, the situation in Vienna had gone from bad to worse. Foul weather continued to taunt the city, with a wild storm causing widespread damage to several pavilions. Then cholera hit. Some one hundred residents of Vienna died daily in the middle of that summer, keeping would-be visitors far, far away. Reporters described the dirt and stench, concluding that the plague and other misfortunes had greatly damaged the exhibition. As if that were not bad enough, cash-strapped exhibitors were failing to pay their rents. "There is scarcely a misfortune [the exhibition] has not experienced, and the elements have done their best to cause its ruin," wrote a *New York Times* correspondent.[7]

The vodka maker viewed the turmoil with, perhaps, only mild interest. Sales at the fair had been lackluster. Attendance was on track to be down by more than two million visitors from the last international exhibition. But since Smirnov had left Austria, visitors, or the lack of them, had not dampened his outlook. Indeed, none of the fiascos bedeviling Vienna mattered much to him now. His only remaining concern was the awards.

Smirnov made his way back to Vienna in time to do a last-minute marketing blitz. He wanted his prize and nothing more. But even that began to look problematic. Suggestions of jury corruption surfaced as did alleged payoffs and favoritism. Unhappy exhibitors charged that some judges were conflicted in their evaluations of products because they were also entrants in the categories they were judging. Organized rallies now demanded the appointment of new judges. A Russian newspaper reported that few people had faith in the integrity of the jury's decisions.[8]

In the end, a commission was appointed to investigate the charges, which included evidence that awards were granted to some people who had not even participated in the fair. But by that time, few cared. Miraculously, however, the exhibition ended on a high note. Attendance recovered somewhat, and revenue, though less than anticipated, was not as meager as feared. Besides, Vienna had been generous in its praise, handing out more accolades to entrants than any previous exhibition. A majority of participants had gotten medals, honorable diplomas, or testimonials—helping to appease angry exhibitors. Some 70 percent of the competitors from Russia received some sort of award or acknowledgement, including Pyotr Smirnov. He took home an honorable diploma, which was awarded surprisingly not for his vodka but for his red and white grape wines. His flavored vodkas also won acclaim.

To Smirnov, it didn't matter why or for what he had been awarded. It was enough of a breakthrough to come away with anything. Other Russian award recipients in the liquor categories were largely known, established manufacturers. Some, such as Rouget and beer makers Korneyev & Gorshanov, were already purveyors to the Imperial Court. So for Smirnov to win any acclaim was a step in the right direction.

The success in Vienna helped Smirnov focus away from his personal tragedies and achieve some much-needed perspective. As dour as his home life had turned, his business had momentum that it would not relinquish for more than two decades. In just three years, the number of employees working for Smirnov had increased fourfold—from just fifteen to about sixty. He had tripled the number of managers overseeing his operations, including the addition of his sister Glafira's husband, who had moved from Uglich to join the ballooning enterprise. His real estate holdings, which now included a factory, warehouses for both vodka and wine, and several shops, had swelled, too. Smirnov was even set to buy up Ivan's kiosks in the Gostiniy Dvor shopping mall, thereby solidifying his place as one of Russia's largest liquor retailers.

Vodka prices, though on the rise since the first days after the end of tax farming, were still relatively cheap, helping drive consumption up. The state's income from alcohol sales was also increasing, keeping nascent efforts to curtail excessive drinking at the fringe. But Smirnov was never one to compartmentalize his professional life from his personal life, particularly when matters lay unresolved. He saw the two as intertwined.

Smirnov needed a wife. So now he went looking for one.

Chapter 7

Mariya

Mariya Nikolayevna Medvedeva was just a school-girl when Smirnov met her. "When visiting one of the women's institutes, he noticed a girl, one of the older students, whose beauty made an impression on him," Smirnov's third son, Vladimir, later told his wife Tatiana.[1] Mariya was on the cusp of womanhood, yet despite her tender years, she had an inherent grace about her, a natural dignity that suggested there was more to this girl than lovely features. She had light eyes and rich, light brown curly hair that was usually piled in a bun at the back of her head. Her classic, straight nose was perched perfectly above full red lips, giving her face an easy, soft symmetry. She carried her tall, well-proportioned frame confidently upright, as if continuously balancing a book on the top of her head.

There was a sweetness, too, about Mariya, the daughter of a deceased, second-guild merchant. One man who knew her described her as "like a kind fairy." Perhaps it was a way of being that she had acquired while attending Aleksandro-

Mariinskoye college, a finishing school of sorts for girls. The school's stated goal was to "bring girls up and to teach them to do their duties zealously and with responsibility so that, in time, they could become kind wives and helpful mothers."[2] The seven-year curriculum, though, went beyond such female staples as religion, needlepoint, painting, music, and general homemaking. It also promoted the study of foreign languages, literature, history, and mathematics. When a girl graduated from Aleksandro-Mariinskoye, she was both educated and cultured.

Mariya's sophistication would have appealed to Smirnov. Unlike his first two wives who shared similar backgrounds to Smirnov's own, this time the vodka maker wanted a woman who could improve or even augment his prospects. That meant choosing someone who was not only educated but who also had at least some knowledge and understanding of the mainstays of Russia's upper crust. The daughters of true aristocrats, who were often schooled at home or attended exclusive institutions, almost universally married within their own class. They were off-limits to a man like Smirnov—despite his healthy bank account.

Many of the young ladies at Aleksandro-Mariinskoye would have seen Smirnov quite differently. In fact, they might have even been in awe of him. He was a leading benefactor of the school through an umbrella charity known as the "Patronage for Poor People." The organization, founded by an aristocratic woman, provided services and financial assistance to groups working with the needy. Among other things, it helped fund the educations of girls whose families faced hardships. Involvement in this particular group was considered an easy way for merchants to earn their charitable chits. Smirnov embraced the opportunity and, for his generosity, added to his collection of awards. He received a gold medal from the group in 1873 "as a result of zealous labors."[3]

Smirnov personally knew the school's founder and head-master, Varvara Chertova. She was familiar to Russia's royal family for her philanthropy and contributions to girls' education. Indeed, Chertova transformed Aleksandro-Mariinskoye from a school for orphans so poor that all students had to drink from just two glasses into a well-financed, first-class institution in Russia's three-tiered education system. The differences in the three tiers were mainly the social classes from which children were admitted and the makeup of curriculum. Students at first-tier schools, for instance, received 28.5 hours per week of sciences and foreign languages while third-tier students only received 16.5 hours. Girls in the bottom rung spent more time polishing up traditional homemaking skills rather than academics.

A girl like Mariya would have understood the advantages someone like Smirnov could bring to her future. Beyond financial security, he offered a ready-made platform from which she could pursue her own social agenda, unencumbered by the daily drudgeries of life. Knowledgeable about literature and the arts, she would have the means to attend the theater or the ballet, perhaps even as a patron. She might be able to travel, too, utilizing some of the languages she had learned at school. The prospects were clear for Mariya. They were also clear for Smirnov.

He had approached his hunt for a wife like an employer seeking to fill a job opening. This was an opportunity—and Smirnov wanted to make the most of it. He might even have seen Mariya as a stepping stone. Despite her youth, she could easily handle the conventional duties of a wife and possibly contribute something to his vodka operations, given her education and family's history in the merchantry. But what really convinced Smirnov was her ability to help him navigate the growing demands of Russian society that seemed to accompany his increasing wealth. She would not shy away from cultural or social obligations. Indeed, she might even seek them out.

To Smirnov, Mariya was young and lovely—and simply the best candidate to fill the post of wife.

. . . .

IT SEEMS THAT the couple's courtship was brief and unexceptional. Smirnov, not wishing to violate the customary one-year waiting period, held off the nuptials. But just one year and two weeks after the first anniversary of Nataliya's death, and after Mariya's graduation from school, Smirnov married for the third time, on April 28, 1874. Smirnov was forty-three years old, and Mariya was sixteen—just three years older than Smirnov's eldest daughter, Vera.

With the marriage complete, life moved along uninterrupted. Indeed, there was hardly any chance to notice a newcomer in the Smirnov household. Mariya took her time, however, trying to understand the comings and goings of the house by the Cast Iron Bridge. She quickly realized she was surrounded by a buzz of activity—in the living quarters, at the store, pub, and cellar downstairs, or at the factory right next door. The constant commotion was something undoubtedly foreign to Mariya, who had lived a relatively cloistered existence at Aleksandro-Mariinskoye. The Smirnov's corner of Pyatnitskaya Street and the Moscow River was anything but—especially during the springtime.

Beginning in May, just a few weeks after the wedding, each morning began with a cacophony of sounds. Policemen barked orders to peddlers and pedestrians. People shouted, fighting to get through the narrow walkways outside the vodka headquarters. Wagons and carts, lined up along the embankment and beyond the bridge, inched by, horses clomping and snorting. And the noise was all thanks to Smirnov.

He needed tons and tons of the freshest fruits and berries to create an assortment of popular flavored vodkas and other drinks; this produce was imported in bulk from the farms and orchards outside of Moscow. It came to the city via train, most likely into the Kursk station, just three miles from Smirnov's home. From there, the fruits, which included strawberries and

raspberries, were loaded on to carts heading for the vodka maker's factory and storage facilities. The colorful, aromatic caravan resembled floats in a parade.

The route from the station was circuitous and jam-packed with
people, cargo, and horses. To get from the station to Smirnov's
factory, located on the Ovchinnikovskaya embankment of the
Moscow River, required carts to pass over a new bridge that had
been built perpendicular to the river while the road it connected
to skewed in another direction. This meant that the horses had
to navigate their way through a jagged opening that was not
large enough to accommodate the scores of pedestrians, peddlers, and carriages that used it. The passageway, particularly
during Smirnov's processions of fruit, functioned like a clogged
drain, trapping those caught up in the mess.

Once across the bridge, the aromatic caravan encountered an
island known as "the bog." It got its nickname because the area
often flooded, making it muddy and difficult to pass. By the time
the carts made it to the embankment, they still had to contend
with the chaos of Pyatnitskaya itself, a neighborhood stuffed
with shops, residences, and traffic. As Smirnov's son Vladimir
later told his wife Tatiana: "Huge carts of cherries, strawberries,
and raspberries blocked the courtyard of the factory. Even the
streets leading to the Iron Bridge were made impassible because
of the fruit wagons. . . . The business of receiving the fruits,
weighing, sorting and paying for them, all of which took many
hours and days, added to the confusion surrounding the streets.
The air was resounding with the cries and insults from the cart-
ers and the people whom they were obstructing. Ladies closed
their ears or hid themselves behind umbrellas."[4]

Luckily for Smirnov, he had the personal clout to get away
with creating such pandemonium. In less than a decade, he had
become one of the top two producers of liquor in Moscow. His
1 million rubles accounted for one-third of all alcohol annual
revenue coming into the city, the equivalent of about $11.6 mil-

lion today. He now employed one hundred workers, or one-fourth of all vodka factory employees in the city.[5] He had also recently purchased another warehouse and building. Smirnov, with products ranging from vodkas to brandies to wines, was indisputably an industry heavyweight.

This clout also allowed him to work the system. Just before the season, policemen would visit Smirnov's home regularly. Here, they drank tea with one of the factory managers. Even the police chief would come by. After these encounters, Smirnov's wagons had an easier time getting through. "The policemen made sure all was in order, usually favoring the carts with berries and telling the regular carriages to drive around," Smirnov's son recalled.[6] In time, Smirnov's factory processed more than 36,000 pounds of berries and herbs annually.

MARIYA NOW INHABITED this life. Of course, she was not involved in the elaborate processing of fruit or the day-to-day manufacturing of vodka and other liquors. Her concern was establishing her authority within the Smirnov household. It would take time to win over the hired help who had been loyal to Nataliya, but she did not hesitate to assert herself, especially when it came to the question of education. Mariya knew there was not much she could do to remedy her husband's elementary handwriting and other blind spots, but she could help shape the destiny of his children.

Mariya wanted Smirnov's girls to marry into the most prominent merchant families—or better. The boys would learn languages, history, math, and music. Mariya shared Smirnov's desire to stand equal with members of the nobility, and she had the same calculated cunning as her husband to plot the best avenues for their social climb. In time, Mariya would bring all the trappings of high society into the Smirnov mansion—from governesses and horseback-riding lessons to occasional evenings in Moscow's theaters and art galleries.

Smirnov supported Mariya in this regard. It was, in fact, one of the reasons why he had chosen to marry her. Life had shifted in Moscow, especially for merchants. The liberalization of the 1860s had given the most enterprising group of entrepreneurs greater freedom to pursue their business agendas. And now, a decade later, these men, including Smirnov, who had once belonged to a regimented class of inward-looking traditionalists, shunned, mistrusted, and resented by much of Russian society, were coming into their own. They were gaining power and voice, both civically and culturally. Instead of bystanders, merchants were an integral part of almost every aspect of Russia's political, artistic, economic, and municipal scene—especially in Moscow. Observed one American historian: "A group [merchants] that had been closed, bolted in, and walled off had escaped the real and metaphorical padlocks. . . . In a burst of civic activity and organizational patronage, it helped preserve the past, mold a national identity, and provide leadership and vision for the future in learning, the arts, and science."[7]

Pavel Buryshkin, a wealthy Russian merchant who chronicled the lives of merchants in an authoritative book titled *The Merchants Moscow*, wrote about the flurry of activities that surrounded merchants beginning in the 1870s. "The merchant is everywhere. He is both the circle and the center of Moscow life."[8] Much like the Rockefellers, Morgans, Warburgs, or Carnegies in the United States, Russia had its Tretyakovs, Morozovs, Ryabushinskiys, and Shchukins, among others. These titans of industry had financial power, which afforded them access to whatever else they wanted. They held public office, founded charities, opened art galleries and theaters, sat on school boards, and supported numerous of public causes. Textile magnate Pavel Tretyakov, founder of the famous art gallery in Moscow, was a prolific collector and patron of young painters. Pyotr Shchukin collected antiques and rare books, which were later donated to the Lenin Library (now the Russian State

Library), while his brother Sergey opened a gallery for French impressionists. Aleksey Bakhrushin maintained a theater collection and founded the Theater Museum. Other merchants seeded schools and technical institutions, underwrote hospitals, or built orphanages.

The Merchants' Club, too, reflected the changes among its member class. Apart from its commercial role, it became a social and intellectual command center. The club hosted balls, masquerade parties, and concerts. It introduced literary evenings and held banquets with political overtones. It even began to sponsor more aristocratic pleasures such as horse breeding, hunting, and racing.

For his part, Smirnov shunned these organized group functions. He had no use for them in his myopic world. He had never aligned himself with the Merchants' Club and he saw no reason to change his mind now. With Mariya as his partner, though, Smirnov managed a bit better than in previous years. But he still participated only in what was essential to maintain an upstanding reputation and improve his social status. Perhaps it was his lack of education or his singular obsession with his vodka business. Perhaps it was just his personality, shyness, or social uneasiness. Whatever the reason, Smirnov avoided venturing through society whenever possible.

Despite this aversion to upper-crust gatherings, he appreciated the accoutrements of a more genteel lifestyle, as did Mariya. Their home displayed exquisite imported furnishings and the finest craftsmanship in all of Russia. They wore beautiful clothing and maintained luxurious carriages, and they had plenty of servants. The couple embraced the aristocratic life.

IN THE AFTERMATH of so much death and despair, Smirnov was content. Almost exactly nine months after their marriage, Mariya gave him his third son. Vladimir was born on February 7, 1875, just weeks after the first installments of Tolstoy's celebrated novel, *Anna Karenina*, appeared in the *Russkiy Vestnik* magazine. Vladimir favored his mother in looks with light hair and deep blue eyes. In the years to come, it would be apparent that Vladimir had also inherited his mother's appreciation for the aristocratic pleasures of life.

Smirnov's professional life was flourishing, too. His share of Russia's excessive drinking populace continued to increase—as did his collection of awards and honors. Smirnov sent his spirits to the Centennial Exhibition in Philadelphia in 1876. It was a momentous occasion for America, commemorating independence while showcasing the nation's emerging industrial prowess. Among the most notable exhibits was Thomas Edison's electric pen and duplicating press, Otis's steam elevator, and Alexander Graham Bell's telephone. In addition, thirty-seven foreign countries came to display their wares and innovations.

Russia sent a bounty of impressive agricultural machinery, tobacco products, confectionaries, and china. But what gained the most attention was its beverages. Some thirty-six Russians brought alcoholic drinks to Philadelphia, nineteen of whom focused on vodkas. "The first thing that strikes one is the variety of wines, brandies, and liqueurs Russia must make and drink. Here is *vodki* in every imaginable kind of bottle. When people travel for months in temperatures below zero such elegant bottles must be very comforting," wrote the *New York Times*.[9]

Though Smirnov had earned accolades in Vienna for his wines and vodka, in Philadelphia he emphasized only his vodka. Wine was quite well known in the United States already; it was an industry dominated by Western European producers. When it came to hard liquor, though, Americans preferred bourbon whiskey. Vodka was still mysterious, a drink yet to be discovered.

In the end, Smirnov received medals and high praise from the judges for his "high quality of manufacturing." It was praise enough to catch the eye of the tsar's ministers. Following his showing in Philadelphia, the Russian Ministry of Finance granted Smirnov the extraordinary right to place the prestigious state emblem on his products. This honor was rare, reserved primarily for people from the highest social orders whose products were of eminent quality.

This nod was the first real indication that Smirnov's strategic odyssey, hatched ten years earlier, was paying off. He had pursued his business aspirations with all the capitalist gusto he could muster, all the while adhering to the strict Russian order and its arcane rules. It had been a precarious balancing act, and now, with the state emblem on his products, consumers throughout the country would recognize in Smirnov an exceptional business, a laudable personal reputation, and a demonstrated dedication to community service. Other recipients of the privilege included Karl Fabergé, the famous jewelry designer, and Ludwig Nobel, an oil tycoon and the brother of Alfred Nobel, inventor of dynamite and founder of the Nobel Prize.

The Centennial Exhibition was a milestone, quickly followed by another, this time at the World's Fair in Paris. Smirnov's vodkas and wines snatched two gold medals there.[10] These awards from France carried particular sway with Russia's aristocracy, which bowed to all things French. They imported their governesses from France as well as their clothes, champagnes, and furnishings.

Smirnov's good fortune, like so much else throughout his life, was tempered by more personal tragedy. In 1877, within months of Smirnov's success in Paris, his father died at age seventy-seven. By Russian standards, Arseniy had lived a long, full life. Born into a peasant village in 1800 as a serf, he had overcome prejudice and stigmas to move himself and his family out from the depths of society. While Smirnov recognized his father's extraordinary contribution, few beyond him noted them. There were no front-page stories or crowds at his funeral.

Arseniy's death was a private affair. It left Smirnov, now forty-six, the undisputed patriarch of his clan. He was now the father who would steer his family through the next two tumultuous decades. Already Smirnov might have begun to feel rumblings of discontent.

THE TUMULT HAD begun during the days of the Vienna fair, a severe depression that left no nation unscathed. The stock market crash in Austria had spurred a chain reaction, collapsing one country's economy after another. In the United States, about 18,000 companies declared bankruptcy between 1873 and 1875 while banks failed and industry struggled. In Western Europe, unemployment soared and business profits plummeted, as the railroad buildup and other industrial projects slowed. Russia suffered similar fallout, with layoffs and bankruptcies mounting. It also endured poor harvests and a high-profile bank failure in Moscow in 1875. Russians were shocked that an enterprise backed by the government could go under. A run on banks resulted, as depositors rushed to pull out their funds from what they assumed were now unsafe institutions.

These hardships left many Russians feeling vulnerable, but they also emboldened a burgeoning group of young, radical intellectuals. They were populists, and their movement was known as *Narodnichestvo* (*Narod* is the Russian word for "people"). Many of them came from prominent families and attended universities throughout Russia's metropolitan centers. These activists were united in a core belief that the peasants' life was unjustifiably miserable. These poor souls, they argued, lived in dire poverty, lacked education, and served as tools of a rigid and hopeless state and class structure.

In the spring of 1874, hundreds of these radicals fanned out into the Russian countryside. They prepared fake passports, dressed up as peasants, and trained themselves to perform odd jobs, such as carpentry or farming. They planned to blend into village life, working alongside their less fortunate brethren. They believed that "going to the people" would gain them access to the hearts and minds of the masses, enlightening them on the unfairness of their condition. They believed it would be only a matter of time before an outright revolt, with peasants from every corner of Russia taking on the establishment and demanding a better way of life.

Instead, the activists were met with suspicion and mistrust. Many villagers were frightened by their revolutionary discourse, either unwilling or unable to understand such fanaticism. Some peasants even snitched on their new neighbors to the police, who then embarked on a quick and powerful crackdown. About 770 populists were arrested in thirty-seven provinces throughout Russia. Most were jailed or forced underground, failing to achieve any of their lofty goals. The movement, though, had its effects: Revolutionary, anti-tsarist thought was seeded.

Smirnov had little sympathy for such activism. He would have viewed the radicals as rude, disrespectful, almost criminal. How could they be so cavalier about order and authority? The tsar, as far as Smirnov was concerned, was God on earth, untouchable and all-knowing. To go against his wishes or policies was heretical. These people, Smirnov would likely have thought, were trying to undermine Tsar Aleksander II—and his reforms—the very actions that spawned Smirnov's enormous success. He was probably glad when the police arrested the protagonists and extinguished their campaign.

Other small demonstrations and uprisings followed the *Narodnichestvo*, but these were snuffed out and viewed by most Russians as sporadic nuisances rather than true threats to the stability of the nation. Of more concern, at least to Smirnov, was the growing unrest among factory workers. In the 1860s only a handful of labor strikes occurred each year, but in the 1870s, these incidents multiplied, peaking late in the decade when nearly sixty factory strikes were recorded by authorities with an unknown number of others occurring outside the government's official notice.[11]

The increase was due, at least in part, to the presence of more manufacturing facilities in the wake of industrialization. But also to blame was the growing discontent among workers about their shabby treatment and lack of basic rights. Paltry wages and irregular pay schedules were among the chief complaints. Typical salaries at Russian factories were two times lower than in England and nearly four times lower than in the United States.[12] Worse, perhaps, was the random way in which employers paid workers. Delays were routine, with no explanation. At one Moscow factory, for example, a notice was posted by a manager after the regular payday, October 22, had passed: THERE WILL BE NO PAY BEFORE THE 20TH OF NOVEMBER. ANYONE WHO DARES TO ASK ME FOR IT EARLIER WILL BE DISMISSED.[13]

Beyond poor wages, employees also complained about harsh working conditions. The average workday was thirteen hours, with some factories demanding as much as eighteen hours at one stretch. Another problem was excessive fines, assessed against workers for infractions ranging from tardiness to failure to attend church to smoking on the job to not taking off their hats when the owner entered a room.

The standard of living was yet another matter of concern. As peasants swarmed into cities for seasonal employment, they depended on their bosses to provide not only jobs but also shelter and food. Often beds were no more than rows of dirty planks, sleeping two or three men side by side. At one confectionary workshop, workers slept on the same tables where sweets were made. The food they served could also be substandard—and expensive—as employers sometimes deducted the cost of such staples from workers' paychecks.

Smirnov watched as his comrades, some of the leading business figures of the day, grappled with these issues. At one

of the Morozov's factories in 1876, some 540 workers participated in a strike largely against excessive fines. A textile factory
owned by the Tretyakov brothers saw 1,500 peasants rise up to
protest low wages in 1878. But it was the troubles faced by his
fellow vodka makers that would have most captured Smirnov's
attention.

Two strikes occurred in December. The first was at Keller
& Co. in St. Petersburg. It operated the largest vodka factory,
taking in 2.5 million rubles annually and producing roughly
574,000 pails of alcohol. By comparison, Smirnov took about 1
million rubles making fewer than 200,000 pails a year. During
the strike, 250 workers protested a one-and-a-half-month delay
in salaries as well as cruel treatment and work on holidays. According to an official report, one worker was beaten so badly
that he could no longer work and had to return to his village.
Another was found dead after being accidentally strangled by
unsafe machinery. "Every night after work, workers gather in
crowds, making noise, protesting oppressions," the report said.[14]
The other strike was at Shtriter's factory in St. Petersburg, with
claims of cruel treatment. One of the tsar's vodka purveyors and
a rival of Smirnov's at international competitions, Shtriter also
produced more alcohol than Smirnov.

Smirnov had yet to face an employee rebellion. He might
have privately congratulated himself in this regard. Smirnov
had figured out, long before it was fashionable in Russia or anywhere else, that satisfied workers meant more productive, more
efficient, more devoted workers. Consequently, Smirnov the
factory owner saw his role as much as a caretaker as he was a
manager. At least that's how his son Vladimir recalled it.[15]

Smirnov's village upbringing served him well in this regard.
He was a father figure to his workers, supplying the modest necessities of life in exchange for loyalty and obedience. It was a
fair and decent trade. Smirnov's factory was still small enough
for him to know personally, or at least be familiar with, most

of his employees. Managers were primarily family members or close friends; his 140 employees in 1878 were mostly known imports from his village or home region.

There were also solid business reasons behind Smirnov's management choices. In marketing himself and his brand, he recognized the benefit of having employees boast, rather than grumble, about their employment. It could only help build the impression of Smirnov as a benevolent and generous man if his lowliest employees were proud of their Smirnov affiliation.

Smirnov also paid many of his workers better than others in his industry. Machine operators and bottlers, for instance, could earn as much as twenty-five rubles annually with Smirnov while only eighteen rubles working at a competitor's factory.[16] Smirnov also employed no children or women, the converse being a relatively common practice among his rivals as well as at larger, more industrial operations. Some years later, Smirnov also paid for the educations of the children of his less fortunate workers.[17]

Perhaps the clearest demonstration of Smirnov's attitudes toward his workers surfaced during a brawl outside his home one evening. Pyotr and Mariya were entertaining guests that night, drinking tea and conversing in their spacious living room when two workers stormed in. One had a black eye; the other's cheek was bloodied. They ran directly to Smirnov, according to the recorded memoirs of his son Vladimir.

"Pyotr Arsenievich! Father! Forgive us for having dared to disturb you. Only it is an urgent affair. Allow us to speak with you Pyotr Arsenievich," one of the workers implored.

Smirnov jumped up, alarmed. "What's the matter? Speak."

"They are beating our boys, Pyotr Arsenievich. On the cross, [I swear] we won't manage without help. The [opposing team] has formed a strong wall while our strong men are working at the factory trying to fulfill an urgent order. There are three times as many of them as us."

"What?" replied Smirnov. "They are beating our boys? This is not to happen."

Fistfights were common among young workers from opposing factories. More a sport, they formed teams and dueled, following strict rules that no one could hit an opponent below the waist or while on the ground.

Smirnov immediately sent word to his factory foreman. "Let all who wish to go [to the fight], go quickly." Then he turned to his men. "Go on back. With new help you will beat the opposing team. If you beat them, I will treat you to a nice meal and you will be on paid vacation until 2 PM tomorrow."

"Hurray, Pyotr Arsenievich. Hurray! Don't doubt us. We will not falter." And the men were gone.

When they returned later in the evening, they were bloody and bruised, but they were also happy and proud, having trounced the opposition. The men were rewarded for their performance with vodka, food, and time off. Smirnov "was like a happy child." He boasted to his guests: "See how well the Smirnov boys showed their character." Smirnov then called in his factory foreman, berating him for not respecting his men's right to defend their good names—and the Smirnov name. "You wanted to make a laughing stock of our boys?" he scolded. "If the workers have organized a fistfight, then it is a question of honor for them. For this reason, you should let them leave work and that's the end of it."[18]*

Smirnov understood what the scuffle represented to his men. He shared their competitive spirits, and he knew he would gain more standing with them than against them because of a pressing liquor order. He demonstrated his unbending support for their cause and then rewarded them for their determination and toughness. He put their needs before the company's. "My

---

* The anecdote comes from a translation of Vladimir Smirnov's memories in the Bakhmeteff Archive at Columbia University, New York City.

father knew how to treat his subordinates. The white- and blue-collared workers respected and loved him. They carried out his orders not out of fear but for their own conscience," Vladimir later told his wife, Tatiana Smirnova-Maksheyeva, who recorded her husband's memories.

In time, Smirnov's harmonious relationship with his workforce would be a bright spot in an otherwise contentious, increasingly hot-headed environment. Already in Russia, the gap between the haves and have-nots had widened. Revolutionary ideas fomented among small pockets of opposition leaders and their followers. Temperance crusaders were finding their voice. And a series of attempts on the tsar's life, the latest of which came in April 1879, spooked the reform-minded, liberal leaning monarchy. It involved Aleksander Solovyov, a participant in the "going to the people" movement earlier in the decade. He tracked down the tsar during one of his walks near the Winter Palace in St. Petersburg. He fired his revolver five times, injuring a policeman but missing his royal target. Solovyov, easily captured, was hanged a month later.

With so much tumult, Smirnov may have wondered how long his good fortune might last. Little did he know that he was already under the scrutiny of temperance advocates and his industry rivals. Even Anton Chekhov, then a young, unknown journalist, had his sights on Smirnov. And soon, he would find out why.

Chapter 8

Vodka Wars

Tsar Aleksander II was a reformer. Thrust into his country's leadership role in the wake of the Crimean War, which exposed Russia's shortcomings to the world, Aleksander came away from the experience with new-found conviction. As daunting and risky as the task was, he would embark on a campaign to modernize his country and motivate his people.

His first major act was to free Russia's 22.5 million serfs, roughly two years before President Abraham Lincoln issued the Emancipation Proclamation in the United States. The tsar moved on from there, reforming the justice system, sanctioning localized governments, loosening censorship, establishing more progressive economic policies, and abolishing the wine farming tax. In short, Aleksander II presided over one of the most prolific periods in Russia's history. At times called "The Thaw," "The Russian Renaissance," and "The Icebreaker" by the country's media, his reign was marked by rapid industrialization and an unprecedented artistic awakening.[1] The masterpieces of Tolstoy, Dostoevskiy, Turgenev, Repin, and Tchaikovskiy all occurred under his watch, and now, the tsar was on the brink of ratifying Russia's first constitution. Talks were underway to form a kind of parliament, too, with representatives from every province.

While these fundamental shifts had been pivotal for the advancement of industry and for the fortunes of men like Smirnov, Aleksander II had made more than his share of enemies. Many intellectuals were frustrated by what they saw as the slow, uneven pace of the tsar's reforms—and they wanted to end the monarchy. Peasants and members of the petite bourgeoisie were angered as they saw no personal benefits from the country's modernization. They had not received the land promised after emancipation, which meant that their other freedoms were also limited. And nobles, who feared that their privileged positions were eroding, worried that the tsar was making too many concessions to his liberal advisors. The most radical objectors took their acrimony to the extreme: Aleksander had eluded death at the hands of would-be assassins seven times. The eighth attempt came on March 1, 1881.

That morning, the tsar met with his progressive minister of the interior, Count Loris-Melikov, and approved a draft announcement that moved Russia a step closer to a constitution; he then arranged for a follow-up meeting with his Council of Ministers on March 4. As the tsar prepared to leave the Winter Palace in St. Petersburg, the police chief drove up in a sleigh to escort him to his appointments. Aleksander II climbed into a closed carriage, accompanied by the chief of the royal guards and seven of his men.[2] Security had of course been tightened in anticipation of further attempts on the tsar's life.

Aleksander II attended to official business before having tea with his cousin at Mikhailovskiy Palace. He then climbed back into his carriage to head home. On his way, a young man approached the royal caravan, holding a small white package, which he hurled at the carriage. Seconds after the blast, the carriage was encased in white smoke. When it cleared, the tsar, unharmed, could see one of his guards was dead and a young boy lay on the street dying. He climbed out of the carriage, bent over the child, and crossed himself.

Despite pleas from aides to reenter the carriage, the tsar moved first toward his attacker and then in the direction of the crater left by the bomb. Suddenly, the force from another deafening explosion slammed Aleksander and his protectors to the ground. This time, some twenty people lay injured, including the tsar. His legs had been nearly pulverized and he was bleeding profusely. In a weak voice, Aleksander reportedly commanded: "Take me home quickly." He died little more than an hour later in his study at the Winter Palace, just a month shy of his sixty-third birthday.

The news of his murder spread like a contagion, sickening thousands of Russians. To Smirnov, a traditionalist and conservative to his core, it would have been devastating. For him, the tsar was holy, a father and protector. He represented knowledge and order and embodied authority and power. In a time-honored tradition, Smirnov, like many merchants, is thought to have kept a portrait of the tsar hanging in his office, a constant homage to his beloved monarch.

This tsar, Smirnov reasoned, had played a pivotal role in the vodka maker's own destiny. Had someone else been sitting on Russia's throne, Smirnov might never have achieved so much or advanced so far. Now, uncertainty engulfed the ex-serf and his nation.

It took just one week after the tsar's death for his eldest son, Tsar Aleksander III, to reject his father's nascent constitutional drive. His mandate, he determined, would be to restore discipline to his country. His father's legacy of reform had been dangerous and unhealthy, he concluded. After all, it had spawned repeated assassination attempts. Aleksander III issued a manifesto after ascending to the throne, attesting to his "belief in the strength and truth of autocratic power." He wanted to "put an end to the lousy liberals."[3]

The revolution that the assassins and their supporters hoped the emperor's death would spark did not materialize. On the contrary, Aleksander III moved quickly into crackdown mode, giving his special police force new authority to sniff out undesirables and revolutionaries. The perpetrators of his father's death were rounded up and executed in a public setting. And then, in an official statement, Tsar Aleksander III laid out a plan for the future. He vowed to close liberal schools, to transfer certain lawsuits from civil courts to military courts, and to stop the dissemination of some independent-minded newspapers and magazines.

Smirnov might have supported some of this backpedaling, figuring that Russia had grown too unpredictable and unstable. Order was always paramount in his mind. But just how far would this new tsar go? Would he revisit the vodka issue? What if the tsar determined that Russia's most popular spirit was better off back in the government's firm control? What if he decided to reintroduce a monopoly? Or wine farming? What if concerns over excessive drinking seeped into state policy?

Smirnov's worries were justified. The vodka industry was already undergoing considerable growing pains. Increased competition and the proliferation of greedy, rogue vodka makers had turned once tolerant rivals into ferocious enemies. In fact, the entire complexion of the business had changed.

In the previous decade, the number of legal alcohol manufacturers in Russia had grown by more than 40 percent—at least judging from the number of liquor-related participants in the All-Russia Industrial and Artistic Exhibition of 1882.[4] The swell came, at least in part, from the nation's continuing alcohol fever. The author Ivan Turgenev commented that liquor was "saturating Holy Russia."[5] But the growth was at least as much a consequence of the ease of the business itself. Producing spirits was relatively cheap and simple, especially when it came to flavored vodkas, which were not required to be 40-degree the way pure vodka was. Vodka makers would often water down their alcohol two to three times, increasing the volume of the products they were selling. This meant that retail prices for their drinks could run as high as 1,000 percent of production costs.[6]

The industry also operated without much regulation. Distillers paid an increasingly hefty excise tax and assorted other taxes while retailers paid licensing fees. There were also charges for mandated labels, which were glued onto bottles containing liquor. Beyond that, the spirits trade was free to do as it pleased. This arrangement made rich men out of skilled entrepreneurs like Smirnov and contributed to Russia's fiscal health. Vodka continued to be the largest single source of revenue for the treasury, averaging 30 percent or more throughout the nineteenth century.[7]

With so much easy money up for grabs, corruption seeped even deeper into the alcohol trade. Illegal distillers, underground vodka makers, and other unscrupulous profiteers flooded the marketplace. They did not pay taxes, purchase licenses, or buy the required labels for their products. They produced their own liquors that they then sold cheaply to taverns, directly to consumers, or to unsanctioned distributors. They undercut legal vodka makers like Smirnov on price. The government, recognizing it was missing out on a sizable chunk of revenue, struggled to tackle the conundrum caused by these vigilante producers, instituting a few insignificant rules. But it was like trying to capture tadpoles with a fish net. As one observer put it: "We know very well about how many cases of secret vodka-making take place, how many cases of cheating and swindling are discovered every day at distilleries. Illegal, secret spirits making is so unbelievably easy to do that we have no chance even to dream about stopping such violations."[8]

The problem was simply too immense. Data shows that the

number of bulk warehouses used to hide unlawful spirits rose an astonishing 31 percent, from 4,896 in 1878 to 6,395 just eight years later.[9] Other rampant offenses included the spicing of food sold in taverns. It was routinely doused in pepper and salt in an attempt to increase the thirst of revelers. At the same time, more liquor retailers illegally opened their doors, and their hours of operation went beyond the legal limits.

For Smirnov, this situation was more of a nuisance than a serious worry. He occupied a position of great strength in the spirits industry. By then, he was the biggest vodka manufacturer in Moscow, raking in almost 3.2 million rubles annually with 280 employees. He was outdone in size by only a handful of rivals based in St. Petersburg. Smirnov's brand was prominent and secure, synonymous with high quality and good taste. A reviewer from the All-Russia Industrial and Artistic Exhibition of 1882 praised Smirnov's drinks as "excellent." His factory, too, was singled out for being "respectable."[10] The vodka maker's market share was strong, both with aristocrats as well as with the masses. And he could charge a premium for his most superior goods. He knew he was losing out on some income due to the sale of illegal moonshine, but this alone was not enough to worry Smirnov or prompt him into action. Besides, illegal alcohol had always been a problem in Russia—even before the removal of state controls.

Smirnov would weather this minor aggravation. He might even use it as an opportunity to tout his products as the most genuine, most trusted in the land. But what he could not and would not tolerate was the surge of vodka counterfeiters. Vodka was the product of choice for nineteenth-century Russian imitators. And increasingly, it was Smirnov's brand that came under attack. It was a top target for counterfeiters, ironically, because Smirnov had been one of the few manufacturers to aggressively pursue the formation of a meaningful brand.

Copycat bottles displaying his labels in the marketplace infuriated him. To the casual consumer, these products were practically indistinguishable from the real Smirnov bottles. Looking closely, however, the name of the imitator could sometimes be found on a label or a notation stating that the bottle had been produced "at the request of P. Smirnov." This distinction did little to dissuade customers since so many fans of Smirnov's liquor were either unable to read or too unconcerned to take the time to authenticate the bottle.

More insulting to Smirnov than the fraud itself was the inferior product that counterfeiters pushed. Always with an eye toward earning the title of purveyor, Smirnov knew his reputation for quality was paramount. He would not be awarded this ultimate prize if customers complained about the caliber of his liquor. Smirnov pondered his options. He could not sue the perpetrators because no law existed forbidding counterfeiting or protecting copyrights and trademarks. He could not enlist the help of the police, some of whom were likely in cahoots with the offenders, because producing fakes was not a crime. He could not hunt down the no-name distillers either. There were just too many of them. Still, Smirnov was determined to defend his turf.

He devised a comprehensive, two-pronged campaign. First, he would do everything in his power to distinguish his products from the copies and confound his imitators. Beginning no later than 1881, Smirnov introduced caps on his bottles with corks stamped with both the state emblem and his factory's signature. He then sealed those corks with resin, a white waxlike substance. The second part of Smirnov's strategy was more novel. For the first time, he decided to advertise.

Smirnov, along with most other liquor merchants, had always taken a dim view of advertising. To them, it would have been a waste of money as well as an ineffective way to reach potential customers. The state had historically controlled most of the content in the media, from placed announcements to news stories. In addition, the readership of newspapers and periodicals was largely limited to the aristocracy.* Few publications targeted the other castes, which were too diffuse to reach or overwhelmed by illiterate citizens. As Smirnov put it, according to Vladimir's recorded memories, "Our firm is known everywhere. There is no need to talk about it with ads or with loud words."[11]

But by the 1880s much had changed, thanks in part to Aleksander II's reforms. A slew of new, more independent publications had emerged, which reached all levels of society. What's more, they were now stuffed with commercial advertisements for everything from perfumes to syphilis remedies. Smirnov was one of the first from the alcohol industry to join the fray, and he did so in a big way, thereby becoming a central figure in what would later be called the vodka wars.

SMIRNOV'S FIRST KNOWN advertisement ran on April 27, 1881—less than two months after the tsar's assassination. Displayed prominently on the front page of the progressive, widely read *Russian Courier*, the ad took up about a sixth of the page. Smirnov, as usual, was direct and unequivocal.

> From the main office of P. A. Smirnov's wine trade in Moscow at the Cast Iron Bridge:
> As a consequence of our factory labels imitations, our office recently had to replace caps on our table wine bottles #20, #31, and #21 with white tarring that features our vodka factory stamp. The imitators did not stop their tricks and also started to put the same kind of white tarring on their bottles with imitations of our labels, with bad wine inside.† In this way, they confuse our customers. Now, in order to evade this evil, we find it necessary to

---

* The conclusion about the change in commercial advertisements comes from an analysis of six leading newspapers in Moscow.

† In Russia, vodka was referred to as wine.

use corks on both our large and small bottles stamped
with our company stamp and have the State emblem
stamp on it as well. The cork will be covered by white
tarring which will also have our factory stamp. These are
the news items our office has the honor to announce.

It was one in a series of infomercial-like ads purchased by
Smirnov over the next several years in a variety of publications
and regions. Some of the ads announced store locations and
products for sale; others pounded on the makers of fraudulent
alcohol. Increasingly, too, Smirnov grew more sophisticated
in his announcements, buying up space in newspapers to brag
about his industry track record and the superiority of his beverages. His ads, which appeared in numerous issues of the *Moscow
Sheet* starting in 1881, dominated that newspaper. One ad from
1882 (January 7, 1883, Gregorian calendar) in the *Moscow Gazette*
used the copycat problem as an opportunity to tout Smirnov's
own successes.

In view of the necessity to stop this forgery of labels
under our firm's name, we are going to depict on our labels
two state coats of arms, received in 1877 and 1882 at the
All-Russian Artistic-Industrial Exhibition in Moscow, for
the excellent merit of our products. Moreover, the office
most humbly asks Gentlemen buyers to pay attention to
the corks on which is printed the stamp of our firm and a
representation of the State coat of arms.[12]*

Smirnov's boastful claims did not go unanswered or unimi-
tated. His leading rivals, also victims of counterfeiting to one
degree or another, joined the battle for public opinion. Each

---

* The ad and its translation were obtained from the Smirnoff Vodka Archive collection
at the Davis Center for Russian Studies in the Fung Library at Harvard University.

distiller lambasted the copycats and then tried to make his or her alcohol concoctions sound the most pure, the most delicious, or the most revered. Soon, from almost nothing, liquor industry advertisements were ubiquitous, with spots running almost daily in publications throughout Russia's major provinces.

Smirnov's competitor Shtriter, for instance, promoted his employment of a doctor at his factory, a man he told readers not only controlled his vodka's quality but could also attest to its superior purity. He then went on, boasting that his cinchona (an alkaloid similar to quinine) vodka, submitted to the medical administration in St. Petersburg, could be a healthy part of any diet.[13] Another of Smirnov's rivals, Koshelev, used the newspapers to brag about his technical prowess, noting that his alcohol was the finest because it was produced with the most cutting-edge machinery of the day.[14] Popova, who featured pictures of her awards and highlighted the premiere taste of her vodka, noted its "special mildness." Popova also carried out a nasty dispute with another distiller through her print advertisements. She claimed that her labels and brand name were being ripped off by another vodka maker of the same last name.[15]

Smirnov had his own public feuds with which to contend. In 1884 he charged a female factory owner named Zimina with producing table wine falsely promoted as having been made "on a special request of Pyotr Smirnov." Smirnov shot back that all his wines came from his own factory. "We have never made any requests to other companies," one advertisement read. He then went on to complain about the terrible quality of imitator's drinks—meant to be passed off as Smirnov's own incomparable blends. He also had to fend off a claim by another rival who advertised that "a Master of Chemistry had found turbidity in the table wine of a famous Moscow factory," a blatant attack on the clarity of Smirnov's popular #21 vodka.[16]

In truth, liquor in Russia was often as corrupted as the business behind it. No producer, including Smirnov, escaped criticism. In one report issued a few years later by the Distillers' Congress, an industry group organized to improve the image and operations of the alcohol business, Smirnov's raspberry nalivka #15 was found to contain traces of aniline, a poisonous derivative of benzene used for coloring.[17] Ivan Smirnov's ashberry liquor #1 had sulfuric acid. Other chemicals found in drinks produced by most distillers included fusel oil and sulfuric acid. Beyond the potentially harmful additives, the industry report also criticized excessive watering down of products, so much so that a wide range of flavored vodkas contained a third less alcohol than unflavored vodka.

The brouhaha caused by these accusations, the intensity of the vodka makers' mud-slinging, and the hotly competitive environment was something new for Russians. The more liberal policies of the late tsar yielded many of the benefits of a more market-driven economy, particularly in consumer-driven industries such as liquor where the barriers to entry were few. Competition cajoled the most savvy merchants into devising gimmicks and other tricks to win over customers. Chocolate maker Abrikosov was especially creative, announcing that beautiful blonds would sell his candies in one location while beautiful brunettes would man counters at another store. The by-products of this Russian capitalism were not always so playful or positive. Some of them, like the rampant corruption and the vodka wars, were downright ugly. Smirnov now represented both sides.

One man who took notice of the unusual melee was twenty-five-year-old Anton Chekhov, who one day would be among the most celebrated playwrights in Russian history. He had come to Moscow from his birthplace in Taganrog, a seaside town in Southern Russia. His first literary endeavors were mainly satirical stories published in various tabloids or humorous journals. Chekhov, educated as a doctor, enjoyed mocking uncomfortable social situations or critiquing the pettiness he often discovered in the mundane, routine details of living. The vodka wars, a phenomenon chronicled by Chekhov, was one such case.

Chekhov's piece on the wars appeared in May 1885 in a St. Petersburg humor magazine called *The Shards*. He was a regular contributor to the weekly publication, poking fun at everything from wicked in-laws to excessive eating during holidays to the amusing foibles that accompanied the art of courtship. In a column titled *The Shards of Moscow Life*, Chekhov took on vodka manufacturers. He was merciless in his assessment of Smirnov and his fellow liquor producers, bluntly referring to them as peddlers of "Satan's blood."

> We have no news about the Afghan borders [where a conflict was occurring] but we have war in Moscow already. . . . Englishmen are not waging war. Nor Russians. But Satan's blood makers—the tavern keepers and the vodka makers do it. Casus belli [a reason for war]—is a competition.
>
> Each enemy, trying to prove that his competitors' vodkas are no bloody good, sends torpedoes toward them and sinks them, and bores with politics. Any means are used to pour pepper into the sleeping competitor's nose, to snooker him, and to hurt his reputation. Vodka-maker Shustov denounced all existing vodkas and created, to his enemies' fear, English Bitter.
>
> Zimin eats Smirnov, Smirnov eats Zimin. And some Avdotya Zimina, in order to exterminate Pyotr Smirnov, created vodka #21—the stark fake of Smirnov's #21. The bottle and the label are absolutely Smirnov-like. To make the picture more complete, she wrote on the label "At the request of Pyotr Smirnov. (Pyotr Smirnov is some Moscow tavern-keeper whose acquaintance Zimina used for these purposes.)" A bit above this inscription she wrote in very

small type 'By order.' To demonstrate that she, Zimina, knows French, she put her name in the label corners: Eudoxie Zimina. People say that because of this inscription the vodka received a special, specific flavor.

Brothers Popov hired a Master of Chemistry who found turbidity in the table wine of a famous, Moscow factory, (interpret: Smirnov's) #21 and of another factory's #20, which tried to promote itself with advertisings.

Vodka manufacturer Koshelev lays himself out about his rectified spirit. In an eager rivalry, everybody issues huge announcements and exterior messages in the newspapers where they fling mud at their competitors. Even brothers Popov, who charge Smirnov with desiring to make himself more prominent, buy up entire pages. Smirnov occupied a position in the [Moscow] Sheet and nobody can pluck him out of there.

The war, obviously, will end with all the manufacturers exchanging blows with each other and starting lawsuits against one another. Fighting spiders eat each other in such a way that only their legs remain in the end.

If all this will result in a favorable way, then we can be thankful for our good fortune. Talents won't be ruined by drinking; the small press employees [here Chekhov refers to himself] won't be inspired [to write about the subject]; and a sobriety realm would have come.[18]

The sharp critique appeared under the name of Ulysses, one of sixty pseudonyms the author used throughout his career. The tactics vodka makers employed against one another as well as the public gushings over how delicious and healthy their liquors were disgusted Chekhov. His negative views were deep seated. The evils of alcohol were a constant theme in his writings, which included several specific references to Smirnov's most popular liquors. In *The Shards* a year earlier, Chekhov summed up his attitude: "Vodka is a colorless drink that paints your nose red and blackens your reputation." His byline that time translated as "Man Without a Spleen."[19]

If statistics are reliable, Russians were not the most prodigious drinkers in Europe. That distinction went to France, where the annual per capita consumption of alcohol was 15.7 liters compared to just 2.7 liters in Russia.[20] But alcohol was built into the French and other Western European cultures, a bit like beer in America. A glass or two of wine with a meal every day was the norm and part of an epicurean tradition. In Russia, however, the objective of drinking was different. "The real problem was not so much the absolute quantities consumed—per capita consumption was lower [in Russia] than most European countries—as the ways in which it was consumed. Instead of drinking small quantities regularly, peasants confined their drinking to a few festive occasions on which they drank to oblivion."[21]

Chekhov's charge that Smirnov had something to do with Russia's liquor excess—not to mention his calling vodka makers "fighting spiders"—would have enraged Smirnov. He never saw a real connection between his business endeavors and alcoholism, at least none he publicly acknowledged. Smirnov's self-image was of an ethical, utterly moral factory owner. He viewed himself as a humble, self-made man who had, through hard work and perseverance, achieved great success. To be compared to the most unscrupulous elements within his industry was an unjustifiable, unforgiveable insult. Like it or not, though, many intellectuals did not perceive a difference. To them, Smirnov had prospered at the expense of the weakest elements of society.

There is no record that Smirnov responded directly to Chekhov's attacks, but it may be more than a coincidence that his ads, following the Chekhov article, changed their tenor. For a time, no longer did Smirnov call attention to his opponents or counterfeiters, in general or by name. Instead, he concentrated more on his own business, his own distinguished record, and his own product line.

Perhaps Smirnov figured that enough attention had been paid to the industry's thorny controversies. The government had weighed in, taking steps to address some of the grievances aired by Smirnov and other prominent vodka makers. The state had raised the excise tax paid by distillers from seven kopeks in 1880 to eight kopeks in 1881 to nine kopeks in 1885. The idea, along with collecting more money for the treasury, was to discourage new entrants into the liquor industry by making the process too expensive and onerous.* The state also implemented a series of penalties aimed at alcohol abuses. Anyone seeking to sell alcohol without a license would be fined 300 rubles. Anyone producing illegal vodka would be fined up to 1,000 rubles and could face up to three months in jail. For hiding alcohol that should have been taxed, violators could face stiff fines, as much as sixteen months in prison, and a lifetime ban from the alcohol industry. A commission was even set up in the mid-1880s to try to tackle the rampant counterfeiting problem, which affected a variety of consumer products other than vodka including tea, yeast, and chocolate.

Smirnov was relatively unaffected by these efforts, which were at best cursory. More notable for him was the slow mind-shift taking place inside the Imperial Palace. After a steady stride toward more openness since the 1860s, the new tsar's agenda continued to scale back some of the freedoms his father had advanced. Moreover, the tsar was showing a renewed willingness to look at the alcohol issue again, including examining whether changes over the last two decades had contributed to what many argued was a liquor epidemic. Smirnov's fears were coming to the fore.

---

* In reality, the law encouraged more producers to enter the business illegally. They did not want to pay higher fees and therefore launched their operations outside the law.

. . . .

Among the first initiatives undertaken by the state to address the alcohol problem was a ban on pubs.[†] The government decreed in 1885 that alcohol could be sold only in taverns alongside food. The thinking followed the traditions elsewhere in Europe, where the combination of food and drink led to fewer instances of drunkenness. Russian officials also tried to address drinking in another manner, passing a law in 1886 that made it a serious crime to pay a portion of wages with vodka or other noncash substitutes. Violators of this common practice could face fines of up to 300 rubles.

These were small steps, having no discernable impact on consumption. Still, they foreshadowed the future direction of Imperial Russia. For the time being, Smirnov was comfortable and not directly threatened. He knew, though, he would need to monitor the reign of Aleksander III closely. He would, to the extent possible, need to take an interest in government affairs. Mostly, though, he would need to focus on turning his business into an even more formidable force, one with heft and staying power.

The vodka maker moved quickly. It had been thirteen years since he had begun supplying the palace with his goods, well beyond the requirement of eight years for obtaining the purveyor title. He had chased and obtained honor after honor, winning awards from Philadelphia to Paris for his alcoholic achievements. From a philanthropic point of view, Smirnov considered himself a model citizen, a prime candidate for purveyor. It was time to find out if the tsar thought so, too.

---

† Pubs were places where only drinks could be served.

Chapter 9

The Vodka King

O n May 23, 1885, Smirnov was all confidence when
he sat down to compose his letter to the tsar. Gone
was the fledgling entrepreneur, who fifteen years earlier
had begged for the chance to sell the tsar his liquors. Now
Smirnov was a fearless titan, a man recognized widely for
his varied accomplishments. He had been on an unrelenting
roll. He sat atop a 3.2 million-ruble empire ($34.8 million
in current dollars), according to a government directory
of Russian factories, which continued to multiply at an astonishing clip. Now, as he wrote to Aleksander III's court,
Smirnov came across like a pupil who had seen the answers
to a test.

> For many years, I have been trading foreign and
> Russian wines in Moscow. My wine is consumed in
> all corners of the Russian Empire and is even sold
> abroad. With tireless personal labor, I have grown
> my business to the widest of proportions. I pay to
> the state treasury, in the form of excise taxes and

customs duties, more than 2.5 million rubles per year. I was honored to receive the highest awards for the quality of my wine—two State Coats of Arms for the Philadelphia International exhibition of 1876 and for the Russian exhibition of 1882. It is my wish to attain the greatest of joys—to become the Purveyor of wines and vodkas to the Court of His Majesty. My moral qualities are known in Moscow and beyond. In Moscow, I'm honored to be a patron of the Court College and a wine purveyor for the Court Church. This is why making inquiries into my personality, starting with the Moscow Excise Department, will give Your Highness confidence [in me] . . . Your Highness is known all over Russia for his merciful attention to the Russian entrepreneurial spirit.

As for my wine and vodka, I have no doubt that they are of high quality and moderate prices and that they are known . . . Your Highness's attention to a Russian trader [Smirnov] will encourage me to further perfect my business. I trade in Moscow, at the Cast Iron Bridge, at my own house.[1]

Smirnov likely consulted a more literate member of his staff to help with grammar and ensure that his elementary prose and penmanship were proper. But the content of the letter, signed in the ex-serf's own hand under the title of First Guild Moscow Merchant, was all Smirnov, formal, respectful, and to the point.

Petitioning the tsar was an especially cumbersome and bureaucratic undertaking. An individual's entire business history for the previous decade needed to be supplied to the court. It was a task pursued by many but mastered by few. At least half the applications submitted were immediately rejected for being incomplete or unworthy of consideration. Fabergé, who had already gained notoriety for his glamorous jeweled Easter eggs, had to wait a full year to win the purveyor title in 1885 because he forgot to include some accounting information with his application. And paperwork was not the only hitch. A string of officials had to approve every applicant, including the tsar himself. This requirement often added months to the awarding of titles, which occurred only late in the year or during Easter.

Smirnov's wares were well known to the court by this time. They had been primarily provided to the palace in Moscow. The main royal residence in St. Petersburg was not as familiar with them and, therefore, in June 1886, it requested that Smirnov send his drinks to its court for further review. Although more than a year had gone by since the vodka maker first petitioned the Imperial Court, he was delighted to receive and comply with the request. It was the first tangible signal that the tsar and his advisors were taking Smirnov's application seriously.

In fact, Smirnov was so elated to have received notice from St. Petersburg that he wrote to Count Illarion Ivanovich Vorontsov-Dashkov, a personal friend of the tsar's who functioned much like a chief of staff. In his June 1886 letter, Smirnov touted his wines and vodkas again, noting that they were unparalleled. He also took the opportunity to bow to the throne and demonstrate his deep, unwavering devotion. It was an awkward show of respect, but the intent was clear.

I shall be bold and tell Your Majesty, true, Russian grand seigneur that you are, that for me, a Russian person, there is no higher reward in this world for my personal labor, which I have performed for almost a half-century, than the gracious words of our Great Tsar about the worthiness of my products. My products are famous far beyond the fatherland, where I have received many of the highest awards: a first State Coat of Arms in 1877 and a second State Coat of Arms in 1882 at the All-Russia Industrial-Artistic exhibition in Moscow. Moreover, I have also received the following awards: Diploma at the

Vienna Exposition in 1873; Grand Gold Medal at the Philadelphia Exposition in 1876; and Grand Gold Medal and Small Gold Medal at the World's Fair in Paris in 1878. But all these awards mean nothing to me in comparison to one word of praise from the Tsar.[2]

Before receiving word from the court, Smirnov might have wondered whether something unforeseen had occurred. Had his adversaries sabotaged his campaign? Had Chekhov's writings swayed the court? Or worse, had Smirnov himself blundered, appearing too eager and pompous rather than congenial and deferential? The uncertainty may be what prompted Smirnov to buttress his credentials once again.

He applied for and received the Order of St. Stanislav, third degree. This order was the lowest in the Russian hierarchy of orders but it was, nonetheless, a prestigious honor. More important, those who obtained it were granted hereditary honorable citizenship, a century's-old distinction also known as "eminent citizenship." Smirnov knew he would never be accepted as a member of the nobility; he lacked the blood lines. But this title was almost as grandiose. It was an acknowledgment directly from the palace that raised the recipient's stature to the highest levels of society. It also made it possible for Smirnov to pursue a more prestigious position in his longtime charity, the Committee on Beggars.

Smirnov had been an agent of the committee since 1870, donating as much as 200 rubles per year to assist in the placement of homeless or indigent workers into meaningful jobs. It was an admirable cause, but joining the elite, ten-member operating group had other advantages. Most notably, the tsar himself had to approve all nominations, including Smirnov's. The vodka maker reasoned that this nomination could help his case for the purveyor title if the tsar associated him with a serious, old-line charity. In his application, Smirnov pledged to contribute 500 rubles annually to the Committee on Beggars. He also provided a full accounting of his work history, religion, education, family background, and financial situation. Of his origin, Smirnov was as strategic as ever, noting only that he was the son of a Moscow merchant. He said nothing about his roots as a serf.[3]

The months went by as Smirnov waited for news from St. Petersburg. He knew that the government had been preoccupied. Russia, like the vodka industry, was in transition. The latest evidence of turmoil came in the form of Russia's first large-scale, organized industrial strike. The Morozov's cotton mill was the backdrop for an ugly scene. Wages of some 11,000 workers had been cut five times between 1882 and 1885 while excessive fines levied against them for a variety of offenses ate up as much as half of what they took home. The rank-and-file were fed up. Almost immediately, the 8,000-person strike turned violent, as participants ransacked managers' apartments, destroyed offices, and smashed the factory food store. Damage caused by the unrest was estimated at over 300,000 rubles. The tsar and the governor of the Vladimir province, fearful of a more widespread revolt, called in the military.

The strike was repressed and its instigators arrested, but the incident was a success for society's downtrodden. Morozov was forced to make concessions and, more importantly, the state recognized the collective power of its workforce. In little more than six months, reforms, however nominal, passed, including laws that limited fines against workers to no more than 5 percent of wages. It marked an initial decisive victory for Russia's labor movement.

Smirnov no doubt watched these events unfold as he awaited word from St. Petersburg. The distraction held his attention, but it could not shake him from his grander purpose. He was focused on a future in which he was not only purveyor to the tsar but also to royalty throughout Europe. With the title in hand, Smirnov could see no end to his opportunities. He had already hired a prominent architect and ordered plans be drawn up to enlarge and renovate his house in a way that would be more fitting for one of the tsar's suppliers. He intended to add an entire third floor with thirteen new rooms to his already expansive mansion, which included a formal ballroom. He would also upgrade the interior design, installing several indoor toilets, a convenience enjoyed by Russia's wealthy.* The most significant addition, at least to Smirnov, would be plastered on the outside of the house. He intended to inscribe "Purveyor of His Imperial Majesty's Court—Pyotr Arsenievich Smirnov" in bold letters. The large Cyrillic lettering would go on both street-facing sides of the house, making absolutely sure that no passersby could miss the designation.

Mariya was also ready to assume a more prominent place in society. She had slipped easily into the elite ranks of merchant wives, leaving most of the household drudgery and child-rearing to hired hands so she could concentrate on her own cultural and philanthropic activities. As her son Vladimir told his wife Tatiana, his mother "took little interest in the children and preferred to lead the life of a society woman."[4]

Not that anybody suffered, at least not outwardly. Smirnov's children enjoyed the best his money could buy. His daughters were likely home-schooled by private tutors early on and later attended gymnasiums, learning all that was necessary to assume their places among the most sophisticated echelons of society. Smirnov's sons attended one of the finest schools in Moscow, a private German institution affiliated with the Lutheran church that catered to boys from Moscow's eminent families. One of the school's renowned graduates was Boris Pasternak, author of *Doctor Zhivago* who received the Nobel Prize in Literature in 1958. Studies for younger boys were intense, with classes taught

---

* Smirnov's interior design plans come from floor plans obtained from the Moscow Committee on Heritage.

in both German and Russian. Students learned about language, music, math, and religion. Once initial studies were finished, the boys were split up into two levels: Either they attended gymnasiums that provided a traditional education, including literature and the arts, or they went to so-called "real schools," named for their more practical approach to learning. These institutions functioned more like trade schools, preparing students for careers in business and industry. This path was chosen for Smirnov's boys.

Smirnov fully expected his sons to be his successors. Having worked so hard to leave behind his peasant roots, Smirnov could not imagine his own flesh not doing whatever it would take to maintain their place among society's elite. His sons had had plenty of exposure to the good life, from novels to foreign languages to artists and composers, far more than Smirnov had ever had. What they needed now was an understanding of how to manage a growing business.

Smirnov might have been worried about the future of his boys. Pyotr, the oldest, was a comfort. He seemed to have inherited Smirnov's serious soul. He was dashing, just like his two next-youngest brothers. At seventeen years of age, he was shorter than his father, his full head of hair and bushy, handlebar mustache were similar in color compared to his father's complexion. Pyotr was also smart, and he studied hard. Even better, he was the one child who seemed genuinely interested in stepping into the role of heir apparent. The same could not be said for the next two brothers, Nikolay, age twelve, and Vladimir, age ten. They were decent students, getting average grades or better in most subjects, according to school records.[5] But both relied more on charisma than on brainpower. They were handsome boys with playful, almost frivolous demeanors. Management was not necessarily a natural or obvious choice for them.

The purveyor title, though, could make things easier for everyone. It was the ultimate symbol of success, an achievement that few others could match. The purveyor badge stood for impeccable quality, longevity in the marketplace, and unrivaled personal ethics. The holder was instantly elevated in status— both in business and in society.

THE DAYS WERE growing shorter and cooler as November came to an end. It had been almost eighteen months since Smirnov first petitioned the tsar. Finally, he got his answer. It did not come the customary way, by post. Smirnov had the honor of hearing the news in person—from the Moscow General-Governor. This informal notification from Moscow's chief on November 22 was followed by a formal letter, dated November 26, 1886, and signed by Minister Vorontsov-Dashkov.

> The Emperor deigned the Moscow First Guild merchant Pyotr Smirnov to be named purveyor of the Highest Court with the right to carry the State emblem on his signboards. This highest honor is reported to the Head of the Court department in Moscow.[6]

The very next day, Smirnov ordered that all his labels be changed to carry the new distinction. He also began running large, front-page ads, notifying his countrymen of the exciting news. "I have the honor to inform my customers that I was honored to become a purveyor of the Highest Court; this is why I have begun the process of changing my company labels for the table wine, vodka, liquors and for grape wine too. Customers will be informed when new labels are issued. Signed: Purveyor of His Imperial Majesty's Court, Pyotr Smirnov."[7]

There could no longer be any doubt—no one had intervened; Chekhov's rants had not soured the court; Smirnov himself had not erred. As of 1886, Pyotr Smirnov could claim the title: the king of vodka.

Chapter 10

From Pursuit to Preservation

Pyotr Smirnov was a man motivated by the end game. He thrived on the very act of striving, strategically assessing his current circumstance and then looking beyond it to pinpoint his next maneuver. The proverbial carrot was ever-present, essential to his continuous cycle of advancement. It was how he had reached the pinnacle of his industry, the unlikeliest of champions among a sea of staunch rivals.

Now with the purveyor title secured, Smirnov found himself in unfamiliar territory. His steady and indefatigable climb to the top of the mighty vodka world looked to have crested. For so long, this quest had shaped his every move, from philanthropic endeavors to exhibition appearances to the selection of a spouse. It fueled his drive and provided structure where none existed. Of course, there would be more medals to win, more honors to obtain, more money to be made. But Smirnov seemed to no longer crave them. He dominated the vodka trade, employing more than a third of all the industry's employees in the Moscow

Province, and producing more than two-and-a-half times more liquor than his nearest local competitor. His expansive operation, which included products made from some three hundred recipes, grossed 3.2 million rubles yearly, nearly two-thirds of all the commercially sold alcohol in the metropolis.[1]

With such a commanding presence, Smirnov needed new inspiration. At the age of fifty-six, he was entering the backstretch of his career. His rise had come during a unique period when Russian serfs, the powerless, faceless underbelly of the population, had gained their freedom. A shift toward rights for the masses had followed, as the tsar had undertaken steps to modernize and democratize his nation. Merchants, too, had enjoyed a rebirth of sorts, transitioning from the scourges of society into wealthy, influential, and philanthropic businessmen. By contrast, nobles and landowners, the dominant figures of the ages had had to accept somewhat lesser roles. The rigid hierarchy over which they had reigned was branded by an increasingly vocal chorus as outdated and backward. Class lines had blurred like smudged ink.

But a new tsar was at the helm, and Smirnov could see the pendulum swinging away from him. He had become a master at reading the machinations of his nation and its leaders, using them to guide his own conduct and plot his own course. Smirnov knew, before many others, that within a handful of years he would be facing a far more adversarial government and a far more critical populace.

Aleksander III was grappling with a huge budget deficit stemming from a series of poor harvests, excessive bureaucratic and military expenditures, and sluggish progress in the industrial sectors. The country was in financial trouble. "Weakness in the economy all over Russia has reached an enormous scale," concluded one newspaper.[2] In late 1886, the tsar sent for his new finance minister, Ivan Vyshnegradskiy, a descendant of clergy with a keen business mind, and demanded a solution be found. It did not take long for Vyshnegradskiy to propose one. Among other things, the minister suggested the introduction of a vodka and tobacco monopoly. The idea had been floated in previous years but this time, it quickly gained momentum, playing into the widespread, long-standing notion of the state as all-knowing.

From a certain perspective, even Smirnov had to see the proposition had merit and potent support. The aristocracy, the primary beneficiaries of the vodka trade before the excise tax was implemented in 1863, had grown strident about the need for change. Along with state officials, they grumbled that the liquor industry was more corrupt than ever. Distillers, vodka makers, and retailers, they charged, had grown adept at hiding their true production levels and sales figures, a situation that meant the government was not collecting a substantial amount of taxes it was due. Moreover, they argued that the quality of liquor was slipping, that it was either too watered down or spiked with harmful chemicals and additives. Monopoly proponents claimed that having the government take over responsibility for the liquor trade would not only prop up the treasury but also rid the industry of greedy cheats and scoundrels.

If these had been the only motivations for the monopoly push, Smirnov might have found himself supporting or even promoting the drive. After all, the state would be doing his dirty work, eliminating unscrupulous producers of fake Smirnov booze as well as the small-time illegal manufacturers. Government control and stiffer taxes would have reduced the number of vodka makers overall and consolidated liquor sales, most likely in Smirnov's favor. But unfortunately for Smirnov, there was much more heft to this debate.

The conservative, pro-autocracy press, which was airing the abuses of the excise tax program, was also calling for a return to firm imperial control. Articles characterized the state's previous efforts to combat alcoholism and reform the vodka trade as failures. More and more editorials appeared supporting the monopoly as an essential fix for a ballooning moral and health crisis. They took inspiration from similar, anti-alcohol efforts in other European countries, such as Switzerland, Germany, and France. They also looked to raw data, often considered unreliable or contradictory, to support their convictions. Russia, for instance, experienced five times the number of deaths related to alcohol from 1870 to 1887 than France did even though statistics showed per capita consumption of liquor in France was higher.[3] Nonetheless, high society, backed by growing numbers of clergy, medical experts, temperance advocates, and state officials, believed excessive drinking was a key contributor to Russia's ills.

Lev Tolstoy, perhaps Russia's most famous private citizen, held that viewpoint. Tolstoy wrote endlessly about the evils of drink and other immoral behaviors, proselytizing his positions of abstinence to anyone who would listen. Tolstoy contended that 90 percent of all crimes were committed by drunk perpetrators and that half of all women who had sex out of wedlock were intoxicated. He came to this conclusion, in part, after overhearing a cab driver discussing a crime. "It would be a shame to do that if one were not drunk," the driver reasoned.[4] The comment was an epiphany for Tolstoy, convincing him that people planning to engage in criminal conduct used liquor to steel themselves for the task. It let them be free to rob, rape, murder, or commit other heinous acts they could not carry out while sober. "They drink and they smoke, not from boredom, not to become merry, not because it is pleasant, but in order to stifle their conscience," Tolstoy concluded, recalling his own feelings and conduct during the Crimean War.

The novelist had a point. A study by a respected Russian academic looked at the connection between consumed spirits and unlawful activities over a period of ten years. He concluded that there was a 10 percent increase in crimes carried out by men who had been drinking and a 25 percent rise among women who had done the same.[5] The relationship between alcohol abuse and criminal acts or violence was especially notable in poorer communities or at factories. "They punch, slash, and beat each other for no particular reason. Life is cheap. If a fight starts, you can expect a murder, especially during holidays. The young people here are inclined to behave like hooligans. They often gather at the various mill towns and organize mass brawls. All this has become a daily phenomenon."[6]

To Tolstoy, the evidence was incontrovertible: Russians were drowning in liquor, destroying themselves one bottle at a time. In 1887 he publicly renounced drinking and launched the grassroots Union Against Drunkenness, one of the first national sobriety movements. A handful of others cropped up, too, but none had the punch of Tolstoy's. He was a public figure, beloved and admired by an impressive number of his countrymen. His activities were widely covered in newspapers and well known outside his small village of Yasnaya Polyana. Even among the many who opposed his views, Tolstoy's words carried weight and ignited passionate debate.

Thanks to Tolstoy and conservative rants, Smirnov was likely on edge. He could see that vodka was viewed both as the solution to and the cause of Russia's many ills. He realized it was only a matter of time before the monopoly would take hold, threatening his business empire and his lavish lifestyle. Smirnov needed to consider carefully how to proceed in this emerging, treacherous environment. His relationship with the Imperial Palace would shelter him some from the coming storms—as would his hard-earned, lofty reputation. But it would not be enough to ward off a financially needy government, a growing chorus of anti-alcohol proponents, or a citizenry who increasingly viewed his industry as dirty, corrupt, and immoral.

. . . .

BY NECESSITY, SMIRNOV was in transition. He was evolving from a man in pursuit of a future into a man bent on preserving his future. Never before had his private interests clashed so directly with the positions of the tsar. Given Smirnov's patriotic disposition and that in the eyes of the aristocracy and state, he was still an ex-serf, the vodka maker had limited options. He could not speak out against the vodka monopoly. Such a move would brand him as a rebel, or worse, an anti-tsarist. He would be seen as the worst kind of capitalist, a profiteer at the expense of the less fortunate. As a purveyor to the court, he could not survive such a hit to his reputation, nor could he risk leaving the impression that he cared more for his own livelihood and future than he did for Mother Russia. Smirnov would almost surely lose his royal support—and with that loss a large stream of reliable revenue from the Imperial Court.

He also could not highlight his own drinking habits to improve his stature. Smirnov was never known to drink to excess. His personal practices and the watchful eye he kept over his employees to discourage alcoholic binges would have pleased the government, which was interested in teaching people to drink with restraint and common sense. Flaunting a teetotaling image, however, could have been interpreted as a haughty act and might offend a slew of Smirnov's best customers, the rowdy imbibers, mostly peasants and blue-collar consumers, to whom he still catered.

Smirnov, being Smirnov, could not sit by idly either. He embarked on an inconspicuous, multipronged strategy that was neither openly political nor confrontational. It was purely personal, advantageous to Smirnov's agenda alone. He would stay undeniably loyal to the tsar while creating an image so impeccably moral and devoutly Christian that few could claim it was otherwise. In this way, Smirnov must have believed he would make out better than all other liquor manufacturers and retain his privileged position when the inevitable monopoly became reality.

It was a calculated bet—and the only one Smirnov must have determined he could reasonably make. In 1888 Smirnov applied for and received the title of Commercial Councillor.[7] It was a prestigious, eighty-eight-year-old honor that represented the highest distinction a merchant could receive. Granted primarily for outstanding charitable giving, its broader meaning was what Smirnov valued most now. Recipients were judged to be successful, prominent experts in their chosen industries. They were held to the highest professional standards and placed within an elite group of upstanding philanthropists.

Smirnov ramped up his charitable activity, too, giving funds to a variety of causes, including those associated with and supported by the Imperial Court or aristocracy. Having already received his first award, the Order of St. Stanislav, third degree, Smirnov decided to pursue the Order of St. Anna, third degree, an award named after Peter the Great's daughter, Anna. To obtain this award, Smirnov had upped his contributions to the Moscow Court Primary College, a trade school also backed by the tsar. Smirnov wrote that his donations were made "to support children by all possible means in their studies in crafts and trade . . . by organizing scholarships for the best male pupils and best female pupils. In this way, children will have a chance to continue their education and to prepare for useful labor."[8] Within a short time, Smirnov received the award, another outward sign that he was no ordinary, low-class merchant.

Smirnov sought to emphasize his faith, too. He had always been a Christian, attending church regularly, contributing to its financial needs, and passing on its teachings to his children. Like many merchants, he was also a collector of religious icons. One icon was particularly precious to Smirnov. His father had brought it with him when he came to Moscow. Its image, representing the head of Christ, was based on a story that when

Christ wiped his face with a towel, his features remained imprinted on the cloth. In Smirnov's antique wood painting, two angels held the corners of the sacred towel. The icon was placed in a luminous golden frame weighing more than five pounds, according to the recorded memories of his son Vladimir. At the beginning of every year, both Arseniy and Smirnov added a precious jewel to the frame, such as a pearl or sapphire. Smirnov hung the heirloom in a prominent place in his home.[9]

This piety, however, was not enough to win the admiration and open support of clergy and other religious leaders. For that, Smirnov would need to go far beyond routine gestures. So he donated money to restore a shrine to a Russian saint in one of the Kremlin cathedrals. He also took on the prestigious position of churchwarden in not one but two cathedrals located near the Kremlin.[10] The job, which involved managing the churches' business affairs as well as overseeing and paying for its structural upkeep, was a typical route for prominent merchants. Merchants served as churchwardens in more than half of Moscow's churches and cathedrals in the last quarter of the nineteenth century. For Smirnov in particular, this undertaking was clever and essential. "Personal participation of the entrepreneurial elite in church life became a demonstration of religiousness on the one hand and a means of strengthening the social image on the other," wrote one researcher.[11] The peasants' view was more cynical. "The heavier the sin on the merchant's conscience for abusing his countryman . . . the louder are the bells he cases and the bigger are the churches he builds." To them, it was a cure-all for sinful acts of capitalism, an antidote to self-interest.

Emphasizing his devotion to Christianity turned out to be timely. Religious persecution in Russia, namely anti-Semitism, was rampant and on the rise. The tsar had already forbidden Jews from residing in St. Petersburg, and in 1891 the general governor of Moscow ordered many Jews expelled from his city, noting that it was time to "secure Moscow from Jews."[12] Some

20,000 Jews were sent out into the suburbs and beyond, along with criminals and other unsavory characters. Smirnov probably knew some of these people personally. Many Jews worked in the spirits industry, as distillers, beer makers, or retailers. Keeping himself separate from their troubles might not have been Smirnov's aim; he may not even have supported these bigoted initiatives. But it was a political plus for Smirnov to be seen as a devotee to the favored national religion.

Smirnov then turned to his immediate family and to his eldest son, Pyotr Petrovich, in particular. Russia's raging vodka debate necessitated the expedient grooming of a competent, socially adept successor. Smirnov recalled all too well the difficulties he had encountered at his launching when he lacked both the proper pedigree and the appropriate social credentials. He was determined to protect his son from similar humiliation. The younger Smirnov, just twenty, was far better prepared than his father. He had not only inherited Smirnov's intellect and knack for business but also had had the advantage of a first-rate education. He knew the family business, having been engaged in his father's enterprise, working alongside him in the factory and back office. What the younger Pyotr lacked, though, was a public portfolio. Smirnov decided to sponsor his son for a spot on the Committee on Beggars. Pyotr Petrovich became an agent of the organization in June 1889. Smirnov then turned his attention to his employees.

SMIRNOV WANTED TO be certain, to the extent possible, that no one working in his factory or shops could embarrass him or bring shame upon his enterprise. That is one reason why Smirnov had always kept a hand in hiring, honing a simple yet revealing screening process. According to family lore and a book written by Smirnov's descendants, a typical exchange went as follows: Smirnov, working in his second-floor office, would come downstairs to meet an applicant for the position of, say, clerk. After a few pleasantries, he would offer his would-be employee a drink. "Would you like some?" he'd ask. The applicant would not hesitate. "No, no, Pyotr Arsenievich," he'd say. "God forbid. On my word, I don't drink, sir."*

The man, more than likely having heard about the vodka king's conservatism, was trying to make a good impression. Smirnov would consider the man's firm refusal before continuing on with the interview. He then asked the applicant a routine roster of questions, inquiring about his background, experience, and hopes for the future. Smirnov paid little attention to the predictable responses, preferring instead to gaze at the carafe on the table before him. "Sure you won't change your mind?" Smirnov would say, smiling warmly. "Too bad you're refusing. This is very good vodka."

Feeling confident about their exchange and certain he would be hired, the man relented. "Well, Pyotr Arsenievich, I see you could even convince a dead man. Go ahead and pour," he would say, returning the smile. The man would swallow some of Smirnov's fine vodka, all the while waiting for an official nod from his future boss. Instead, Smirnov would stand, his words unequivocal. "Why were you fooling with me?" he'd demand. "'I don't drink, I don't drink.' Why didn't you just say in the first place, 'Please, pour?' The way I see it, there's no doing business with you. You don't keep your word." With that, Smirnov would spin around and head back to his office. The applicant would be left alone, bewildered and shaken. It was quintessential Smirnov: Unwavering in his conviction, unforgiving in his critique.

WHILE SMIRNOV AND his many liquors and wines were at the forefront of Russia's robust alcohol business, they, like other

---

* Anecdote provided by Anton Valdin, a genealogist who worked with Smirnov's descendants. The anecdote also appears in *The Vodka King*, a book published in 1999 that was written by Smirnov's descendants.

alcohol producers and their wares, were increasingly under attack. It was not just the notion of a monopoly that threatened them. The real trouble stemmed from the state's pursuit of the monopoly. The Imperial Court was not about to tamper with a commodity so central to the Russian culture and economy without first convincing its people that a change was vital. M. G. Kotelnikov, an official who worked on the monopoly issue said the proposed reform "touched the interests of a considerable number of businessmen and people. It was determined that it was necessary to shape public opinion so it would favor the establishment of a wine [vodka] monopoly."[13]

The tsar's offensive, launched over a period of several years in the late 1880s and early '90s, was as direct, as compelling, and as comprehensive a marketing campaign as anything Smirnov himself might have hatched. It was like an elite military offensive, flawless in its execution, overpowering in its scope and message. The government wisely de-emphasized its primary reason for pursuing the monopoly: money. It instead portrayed itself as rescuer, the people's protector against unscrupulous liquor mavericks who encouraged excessive drinking, poisoned the products peddled, and hid profits that rightly belonged to Russia and its people.

Mikhail Fridman, a noted Russian economist close to the minister of finance and who later wrote a definitive work on the vodka monopoly published in 1914, summed up the government's stated intentions as full of altruism and a kind of fatherly love. The minister, Fridman wrote, had a strong belief that "all measures undertaken by the State to regulate drinking were of a palliative character; that free wine [vodka] trade undermined the economic and moral power of the country and its population and that it devastated and demoralized the people. Private wine traders negatively influenced people by inducing them to compete against one another to see who could drink the most. And they willingly sold wine on credit, allowing people to secure their purchases with personal belongings, future harvests or future wages."[14]

There was a great deal of truth to the charges, but they reflected only a small portion of the industry, the most deviant, immoral elements. Moreover, they completely ignored upstanding players, such as Smirnov, as well as the state's very real, very dire fiscal motivations. Still, the government managed to persuade the masses to see the situation its way. One of its most convincing arguments emerged after it commissioned for the first time scientific studies of alcohol, particularly vodka. The idea was to analyze the contents of the liquor and uncover an array of dishonest or harmful practices. That the quality of liquor was a perennial issue, including when it was under the government's control decades before, was irrelevant. The state needed to demonstrate that such wrongdoing was rampant.

A group of pure-vodka distillers known as the Distillers' Congress proved an unlikely source for the government in making its case. These producers did not like the use of additives in vodka as it cut into the demand manufacturers like Smirnov had for their unadulterated product. Watered-down or fruit-infused nalivkas did not require as much alcohol as did pure vodka. So, like the government, the Distillers' Congress saw potential in underwriting scientific studies that might uncover the unhealthy or unsavory practices during the production process.

A hygiene commission organized at Moscow University undertook a number of these studies. Its members, made up of academics and health professionals, were responsible for monitoring the quality of consumer products. One study looked at thirteen factories producing vodka. It found that the typical manufacturing process yielded fusel oil as a by-product. The fusel oil, deemed harmful to a person's health and specifically barred by the Russian military's code of laws, was making its way into the vodka consumers were drinking. It was most easily detectable in the cheapest liquors because of its strong smell. But it was present in all the alcohol tested. Other additives discovered to varying degrees in flavored vodkas included ethane diacid, sulfuric acid, and aniline dye, which was linked to stomach, mouth, and kidney maladies. The Distillers' Congress did not hide its disgust. "Then this slush is poured into bottles with beautiful labels. . . . Then it is baptized with names such as raspberry nalivka and sent first to the Moscow market and then, by railroads, to all ends of Russia," wrote one of its members.[15]

Another review tested only nalivkas, which were particularly popular with the aristocracy. Fusel oil was again found along with fuchsin, a dye that could contain arsenic, cochineal, a rather benign crimson dye additive, and aniline. Indeed, aniline was used as a coloring agent in Smirnov's raspberry nalivka #15. "All nalivkas, without exception, were more or less impure," reported Fyodor F. Erisman, a leading scientist specializing in hygiene and sanitary conditions, who authored the state-sponsored report on vodka.[16]

In the same review, the commission looked at the quantity of spirit used in vodka recipes. It found that most of these drinks were made with about 25 percent alcohol, much less than the 40 percent strength found in straight, unflavored vodka. Smirnov's cherry *nastoyka*, for instance, had 24 percent alcohol.[17] Nalivkas and nastoykas, which were mixed with water, fruit, or herbs, were not expected to have as high an alcohol content—and might have arguably been less harmful than more potent beverages. Nonetheless, researchers cast their findings in a negative light. "Cheap nalivkas have extremely poor alcohol quality. If you let the flavor evaporate and then rub the liquid in the palm of your hand, you'll feel fusel oil, which is an undoubtedly harmful substance. The distilling industry must do its best to get rid of it by all possible means."[18]

Despite the specific derogatory references to Smirnov's beverages, intended to demonstrate that even the most prestigious vodka producers were guilty of using hazardous chemicals in their goods, Smirnov also got some favorable news from the hygiene commission. It conducted a separate analysis in 1892 of the products offered by the three most prominent, most expensive vodka makers, including Smirnov and one of his chief rivals, Popov. The intent of the review, again, was to show that premium goods also contained unhealthy ingredients. Smirnov's drinks, though not free of additives, were found to be the purest and of the highest quality. Even his cheapest, most popular vodka, #21, was deemed better than similar products from his closest competitors.

Smirnov came out better than most in the group's assessment, perhaps good enough for him to claim that he was making the purest vodka in Russia. In the current climate, though, this distinction was dubious. The government's drive toward monopolization was on—and it was unstoppable. The only consolation for Smirnov may have been his ability to distance himself from the most corrupt businesses in the liquor industry. The government, to buttress its agenda, intended to highlight this group of bad actors. The findings from the Erisman report and Distillers' Congress went a long way toward proving their unsavory practices. Beyond that, the ministry shined a light on the enormous profit margins of the alcohol trade. It noted that a pail of wine sold for more than six rubles, but it cost only about half that to make the pail, including all taxes. "The rest of the money goes into a wine trader's pocket."[19]

Before the Ministry of Finance could claim that money for its own account, it decided it would be well served to acknowledge the dangers associated with Russia's cultural alcoholism. The state echoed Tolstoy to an extent, encapsulating drunkenness as the enemy of all that was moral and right, a hurdle to productivity, economic stability, and civility. Unlike the famed author, though, the Imperial Palace did not preach sobriety, aiming instead to educate people about moderation. "Russians drank wrongly," the state maintained.[20]

Among other things, officials wanted to promote drinking

in the home under a family's watch instead of in pubs filled with rowdy imbibers. They also intended to distract heavy drinkers by offering more sober entertainment alternatives, such as tearooms, theatrical performances, and public readings. The government even planned eventually to launch its own temperance organizations.

It was all rather convincing; the government's proposal for the vodka monopoly would have proceeded without a hitch had it not been for a series of unrelated blunders that diverted the attention of the tsar and his advisors, particularly the minister of finance Vyshnegradskiy. From the outset, Vyshnegradskiy, a self-made millionaire, was preoccupied with erasing the state's budget deficit and strengthening its overall economic health. His blueprint involved raising taxes, reorganizing the railroad system, increasing exports, and launching the vodka and tobacco monopolies. He hoped to prop up Russia's international profile, attracting new foreign investors and capital.

Vyshnegradskiy's plan worked—to a point. He managed to erase much of the deficit through higher taxes on sugar, tobacco, alcohol, and kerosene. He also increased tariffs on imports, adopting the strictest customs taxes in all of Europe. At the same time, Vyshnegradskiy aggressively exported the nation's abundant grain crops, doubling the amount shipped outside of Russia. Farmers raced to sell not only their surpluses but their domestic stockpiles as well, hoping to meet state-imposed deadlines and cash in on high-export bonuses to raise money to pay for all the new taxes. State revenues climbed and the value of the ruble strengthened.

Russians, namely peasants, did not share in the state's largesse. Rather, they suffered greatly under the heavy weight of mounting tax obligations and a decline in world grain prices. Their living conditions plummeted. A devastatingly paltry harvest in 1892 complicated matters further. Vyshnegradskiy had not accounted for this—or the famine that settled in throughout

Russia's central provinces. Gone was the cocky, myopic Vysh-negradskiy, who had once said of his aggressive economic plan: "We'll not eat, but we'll export."[21]

In the end, Vyshnegradskiy was forced to halt grain exports and provide more than 160 million rubles to aid Russia's starving citizens. Hundreds of relief efforts were launched throughout the country as volunteers, including Chekhov and Tolstoy, rushed to help their countrymen. "I cannot describe in simple words the utter destitution and suffering of these people," wrote Tolstoy to his wife, Sonya. Then, the writer and his two older daughters organized canteens throughout the hardest hit regions.[22]

Vyshnegradskiy's reputation sank, as newspapers skewered him for pursuing policies built on little more than quicksand. Shortly thereafter, perhaps due to the crisis itself, sheer exhaustion, or the harsh words hurled his way, Vyshnegradskiy had a stroke; his health never recovered fully. On August 30, 1892, Vyshnegradskiy tendered his resignation, leaving much of his agenda, including the wine monopoly, incomplete.

Smirnov presumably welcomed the reprieve, but he knew it would be brief. Momentum for the vodka monopoly was on the tsar's side. What's more, Vyshnegradskiy's replacement was not a man to get sidetracked. Count Sergey Witte was a nobleman by birth who would ultimately become one of the country's most powerful, most progressive, and most controversial statesmen. He made his intentions clear from the start. He wanted to craft a new Russia—a nation that was modern, industrialized, and economically formidable. The vodka monopoly, he predicted, would help him do it.

Chapter 11

Monopoly Capitalism

Sergey Witte was an imposing figure in just about every way. He was a head taller than the average Russian male, and sported a solid, square physique. His wide shoulders looked as if they had been chiseled out of a slab of giant marble. His massive head and expansive forehead seemed out of proportion with the rest of his body while his nose, appearing long and almost fractured, caused at least one person to observe that it made him look "like a crocodile."[1] According to one of his closest friends, it was impossible not to notice Witte. "He was a man of strong mind and hard will, with notable originality in his physical appearance, way of thinking, and way of doing. Everything in him demonstrated passion, inspiration, spontaneity, and inhuman energy. He was a warrior in his nature, a bold warrior."[2]

Smirnov probably already knew of this man and his outstanding qualities. Witte arrived at the Imperial Palace preceded by an armload of achievements. He was a shrewd businessman, having turned the Southwest Railway into one of the most profitable railroads in Russia. He also was a courageous man of deep convictions. One story, possibly apocryphal, tells that Witte first caught the tsar's attention while he was working as an administrator for the busy Southwest Railway, which covered the Ukraine and Belarus regions. Despite urging from the tsar's officials, Witte declined to increase the speed of the imperial train when it passed through, which was known for its excessive, sometimes dangerously fast pace. Witte's bold refusal in 1888 infuriated the imperial party until the tsar's train, returning to St. Petersburg from the summer residence in Yalta, derailed later that year. The royal family luckily survived, and it was at that moment that Aleksander III recalled and appreciated Witte's stubbornness and his prophetic warning that "it was better to sacrifice speed than the life of the Emperor."[3]

Within a year, Witte was rewarded when he was appointed to the prominent post of the tsar's Director of Railway Affairs. He immediately proved his worth, relying on his work experience and a degree in mathematics to streamline operations and improve the department's financial health. He also made a name for himself by overseeing the massive construction of the all-important Trans-Siberian Railway, which began in 1891, and by introducing an effective freight tariff to pump more money into the treasury and protect domestic industries. By the time Witte became Russia's minister of finance in August 1892, he had earned an admirable reputation and had the complete confidence and support of Aleksander III.

When it came to the vodka monopoly in particular, Witte also could count on the tsar's personal commitment. In his memoirs Witte contends that controlling liquor sales was one of Aleksander III's primary objectives. "He was very grieved that the Russian people squandered so much money on liquor and saw a liquor monopoly as a means of reducing drunkenness. . . . He was ready to take the bold step of replacing the excise tax system with one under which the government, as the exclusive

purchaser of liquor from distilleries, could regulate liquor production and then be the sole seller of liquor to the public."[4]

Although Witte was more fiscally than morally motivated,
he embraced the mandate. Almost immediately following the
tsar's official approval of the monopoly on June 6, 1894, Witte
moved into offense. He continued the state policy of playing
down the government's budgetary needs and emphasized once
again the more popular notion that the monopoly would "put
an end to the grievous influence of the retailers of spirits on the
moral and economic condition of the people."[5]

Smirnov, not the intended target of the minister's insults,
nonetheless had to have recognized that his support from the
monarchy was on the wane. His spirits industry was being singled out—by the tsar and his top lieutenants, all of whom wholeheartedly backed the monopoly, as did the church. Clergy were
more and more taking up the cause of sobriety, organizing and
leading temperance groups throughout Russia. The anti-alcohol
message was a cornerstone of the church's fledgling movement
aimed at improving the deteriorating lives of workers and peasants. Strikes, some supported by a young and determined new
leader, Vladimir Lenin, reappeared with the industrial boom of
the 1890s. These incidences increased steadily, and like a mutat-
ing virus became more and more immune to the state's efforts
at suppression.

It seemed that the one thing on Smirnov's side now was time.
The vodka monopoly could not escape the quagmire of politics
and government bureaucracy. Implementing such drastic reform
would not be accomplished overnight. The state had to set up
mechanisms for collecting new taxes and fees; it had to hire
locals free from any association with the private spirits industry
to monitor liquor supplies and their quality; it had to educate
officials and citizens about the details of the new measure; and
finally, it had to assume responsibility for a gigantic, unwieldy
industry. This monopolization would include the building of

more than 350 distillation warehouses and the opening of up to 18,000 state wine shops by 1899 alone.[6] Witte recognized the enormity of the task and determined that he should seed the reform first in places where both alcohol consumption and vodka revenue collected by the state were historically low. In this way, the government would exercise more control over the reform rollout and not be overwhelmed by it. He could also see whether the monopoly would indeed capture more money for the monarchy and reduce drunkenness at the same time. Four eastern provinces—Samara, Orenburg, Perm, and Ufa—were selected as testing grounds.

This methodical rollout became Smirnov's advantage.

FROM 1893 TO 1895 Smirnov turned outward. Russia was changing quickly throughout the decade, and Smirnov realized his personal and commercial longevity depended on his doing so as well. No longer could he be singularly focused on his own image—whether he appeared pious enough, charitable enough, or honored enough. A variety of troubles loomed on the horizon, above and beyond the pending monopoly. Smirnov had to grapple with a shifting business environment as well, which under Witte was moving swiftly toward more expansive industrialization and more Westernized business practices. A variety of capitalistic institutions, from commercial banks to stock exchanges to ventures with private shareholders, were multiplying across the country. Industries from oil to iron to transportation were undergoing enormous growth.

Closer to home, there was the man himself, who at the age of sixty-two in 1893 was beginning to show signs of his advancing years. The debonair vodka king, though still quite distinguished, was losing his sharp features, particularly around his bluish gray eyes. In place of the taut gaze was a more haggard look. Puffy bags drooped from Smirnov's eyes, stretching it seemed for the floor where they could rest. But they could not rest—not yet. Smirnov had three grown sons with varying interests and abilities to consider and for whom he must make plans—not to mention five daughters and two younger sons. He also had to think about Mariya, a woman swirling within high society who at thirty-five was still beautiful, energetic, and full of want for aristocratic pleasures.

Turning to his family, Smirnov might have found himself wondering where he had gone wrong. He had given his children everything, including a deep and often tender love evidenced in letters he wrote to them.[7] They had first-class academic, religious, and cultural educations, as well as rich social lives. They had traveled abroad to destinations throughout Europe, often as a family.[8] They had never known hardship, certainly not the kind that had defined Smirnov in his youth. In a world so limited for so many, the opportunities for Smirnov's children seemed boundless. Taken together, the Smirnovs should have been the idyllic family.

But as Smirnov's children grew into adulthood, their differences and potential shortcomings began to fracture the family. Perhaps it was the stereotypical consequence of wealth's corrupting influence, or the natural result of having fathered children by different mothers, or simply the nature of life in nineteenth-century Russia. Whatever the reason, Smirnov's plan for a smooth transition to the next generation was in jeopardy.

Smirnov could and did depend on his eldest son. In most ways, Pyotr Petrovich was the model heir. At age twenty-five, he was serious, hard-working, driven, and full of promise. Smirnov did not hesitate to put his eldest boy in charge of his operations in St. Petersburg, dispatching his son to the capital city for two years to oversee a large cellar and vodka warehouse. While in St. Petersburg, Pyotr demonstrated not only his managerial prowess but also his own entrepreneurial zeal, opening and operating a popular teashop on top of his other duties.[9]

Smirnov was more than pleased with his son—except for one thing. While in St. Petersburg, Pyotr had an illicit affair with a married woman. Few details are known about the romance between Pyotr and Eugeniya Ilyinichna, an elegant woman believed to have been married to a doctor when the two met. According to family lore, Pyotr fell desperately in love with Eugeniya, and despite the threat of scandal they carried on a passionate relationship. Eugeniya ultimately chose to leave her husband for Pyotr, risking the deep-seated stigma and disgrace attached to divorce in pre-revolutionary Russia. The couple married in 1893, according to church records, the same year Eugeniya gave birth to a daughter, Tatiana.

There is little doubt that the sordid affair angered Smirnov. It went against his rigid religious convictions and strict moral compass. He may have ordered his son to end the relationship or face serious repercussions. The conflict between Pyotr and his father was mentioned briefly in a letter to Aleksandra, Smirnov's youngest daughter, by a suitor who was having trouble gaining Smirnov's blessing for his own attempts at courtship. The suitor asked to meet Pyotr to get some advice on how to deal with what he regarded as Smirnov's fanatical and unflinching disapproval. "Tell your older brother [Pyotr] to set a date when I could come and speak to him about some things . . . I would like to know, because your brother suffered from him [because of his affair], to what extent your father's despotism may spread and what I should beware of."[10]

Smirnov could be tyrannical in business and at home, though with age his stronghold had begun to loosen. Pyotr was unquestionably Smirnov's best shot at an enduring legacy, and he probably knew it. In a highly uncharacteristic act, the father, whose threats went unheeded, essentially condoned the son's affair. He appointed Pyotr to handle a vital restructuring of his business in 1893. In a letter addressed to "my dear son, Pyotr Petrovich," Smirnov granted his son the right to represent the elder's interests. Confidence in the young man was unwavering. "I trust you in all the acts which will be done by you according to the laws. I will not argue nor will I contradict you," wrote Smirnov.[11]

He wanted Pyotr to spearhead the establishment of a joint-stock company, a tool used widely in other developing nations and an increasingly popular one employed by Russian businesses. The structure allowed for ownership stakes to be distributed among a select group of directors. Until this time, Smirnov's vodka business was managed like most other family-run operations in his country: as a vast, one-man show. But Smirnov and other progressive business leaders could see they needed to move beyond this antiquated, autocratic model. When the vodka maker applied for his joint-stock company in 1893, there were just 522 of them with a capitalization of about 600 million rubles. By the end of the century, the number had swelled to 1,996, according to the Ministry of Finance, with overall capital estimated at nearly 2 billion rubles.[12]

Along with issuing stock, which required approval from the tsar, Smirnov took the unusual step of asking the ruler to allow him to pass all his personal awards and honors to his company, including his cherished title of Purveyor to the Imperial Court.* This request, believed to be the first of its kind for a vodka enterprise in Russia, proved yet again Smirnov's foresight and ability to craft innovative measures before others. Smirnov was arming his business for the post-Pyotr Arsenievich era, concerned that his decades of hard labor, which had made him one of the wealthiest and most prominent businessmen in Russia, would evaporate with his passing. Smirnov's assets at the time included nine houses in

---

* Prior to Smirnov's request, the title of vodka purveyor to the tsar could be held only by an individual.

Moscow, a *dacha* (country home), and a vodka factory. In addition, he leased twenty-one warehouses for his liquors.

Witte personally signed off on Smirnov's restructuring in 1894, which valued his company at 3 million rubles, roughly $39 million in today's dollars. Newspapers carried the announcements informing the public that Smirnov had selected his son Pyotr, and Nikolay Venediktovich Smirnov, a cousin, to serve alongside himself on the company's new board of directors. Mariya, Smirnov's wife, took on the post of alternate director. The omission of Smirnov's two other eldest sons from the slate of directors was telling. They were still quite young, of course. Nikolay was just twenty then and Vladimir eighteen, but Smirnov had other reasons to keep them removed from his commercial affairs.

Nikolay had often been cause for concern. He began life when his mother, Nataliya, died. Physically, he appeared fit and robust. His face was long like his father's, and his dark handlebar mustache and goatee were full. He was handsome, though he lacked the confident air about him that both Pyotr and Vladimir had in abundance. In school, according to records, Nikolay received average marks. Whether these factors contributed to what family members later described as his unstable, neurotic temperament, remains a mystery, but it appeared that Nikolay did not possess a sense of responsibility and was therefore ill prepared for the demands of business—at least in his father's mind.

His brothers stated in legal documents some years later that Nikolay had battled alcoholism for years. He tried, to a large extent successfully, to keep his outsized appetite for liquor in check for the sake of his disapproving father, but he had a propensity for dangerous and deviant conduct. Later, Nikolay's freewheeling spending of his father's fortune would cause problems. He once purchased a diamond necklace made by Fabergé for a favored lover, an extravagance that cost 16,000 rubles ($200,000 today).[13] He also purchased a silver chamber pot for 200 rubles, or more than $2,500 today. A regular around Moscow's raging nightclub circuit, Nikolay often shepherded different women on his arm. He was not interested in gainful employment of any kind, preferring instead to spend his time more playfully.

Not surprisingly, Smirnov found his son's destructive and erratic behavior disgraceful, viewing Nikolay like a raft with a small leak in it. Smirnov, who did love his son, could not afford to allow Nikolay to take his company down with him. His son's drinking binges could be lethal, playing right into the hands of temperance advocates and monopoly proponents. If Nikolay Smirnov could not control his thirst, how could helpless peasants be expected to? Smirnov, always the pragmatist, made the practical choice. He kept Nikolay away from his business, focusing instead on finding him a mate able to help control him.

Vladimir, handsome, charismatic, and talented, presented a different conundrum for Smirnov. "Vladimir looked like his mother—blond, with blue eyes, well proportioned, well put together, and tall. He was naturally charming and always elegant."[14] He was in some ways the ideal heir. He had a smoothness about him that stemmed from supreme confidence. He was smart, conversant in at least three languages beyond his native tongue. He was quick-witted and artistically and musically gifted. He also had a powerful advocate in his mother, Mariya, who was devoted to securing her eldest son's place in the family hierarchy.

Vladimir, too, had his vices. Like Nikolay, he had a passion for unsuitable women, a love of gambling, particularly horse racing, and a spending problem. He often sought out the company of actresses or singers. Unbeknown to his father, Vladimir loved to pass time at a fashionable restaurant in Moscow that played host to the best gypsy singers in town. It was a party hub, attracting many fellow playboys. According to the memoirs of Vladimir's third wife, Tatiana Smirnova-Maksheyeva, this penchant for the carefree, somewhat debauched lifestyle, cost Vladimir a great love and drove a wedge between son and father.

He was 18 years old when, secretly from his father, he became a regular customer at the famous Moscow restaurant called Yar, where a gypsy choir sang. Vladimir made friends with the choir members, learned how to play the guitar, and often stood behind the choir, singing along with pleasure. Among the gypsy women soloists was a young girl named Katya. He fell in love with Katya and signed promissory notes for a large sum to a Moscow money-lender to purchase lots of brooches, bracelets, earrings and rings, decorated with diamonds. He gave all this to Katya and, as was required, paid the choir 50,000 rubles for her. His involvement with Katya and his prank with the promissory notes soon became known to Pyotr Arsenievich. He became upset, calling the money-lender, paid him for the promissory notes, and forbade him to ever show himself again and threatened to sue him if he ever lends money again to any of Smirnov's sons.

After this, Pyotr ordered Vladimir be locked up in his room and not allowed to leave or to go anywhere. Before this, they had a confrontation. Vladimir pleaded with his father, saying that he had "fallen in love with Katya forever and could not live without her."[15]

It is impossible now to verify Tatiana Smirnova-Maksheyeva's remembrances of her husband's youth in Moscow, but plenty of evidence confirms that Vladimir adored women, loved the good life, and squandered money. It is also certain that Smirnov saw his third son differently than he saw Nikolay. He was more optimistic about Vladimir's future prospects and took steps to set him on a more respectable path, suggesting that he seek work experience and adventure away from his homeland.

I [Smirnov] have decided to send you on a business trip for a year to China to deal with some affairs of our firm. If your love endures the separation, I will allow you to marry your gypsy woman. For now, you will sit in your room, locked up. [Smirnov told his son.]

Vladimir was in complete despair but had to obey his father's wishes. Sitting in solitary confinement, he burnt the letter "K" above his elbow, using a very hot pin. This "K" remained on his arm for the rest of his life.

Soon, Pyotr Arsenievich sent his son to China, under the guardianship of his own brother to whom he [Smirnov] gave a sum of money for the trip. Pyotr allowed his son to say good-bye to Katya. She came to the train station when the train was about to leave. They were both crying. That was their last meeting.[16]

Vladimir's granddaughter, Kira Smirnova, who lives in Moscow, believes her grandfather went to China.* She has an incense burner she says Vladimir purchased during his time there, a keepsake that has been handed down to her. The trip also would have been in keeping with Smirnov's image as a strong patriarch, decisive and authoritative when it came to his children's upbringing and social standing. He did not tolerate indecent behavior, particularly when it could undermine his company or his own finely sculpted image. What's more, the trip abroad might have been part of an effort to expand Smirnov's global presence prior to Russia's enactment of the vodka monopoly. Indeed, Smirnov opened up in markets where liquor was traded more freely—from Japan to China to France. In the 1890s his liquors were on the menus in fine hotels across Europe and in other locales where wealthy Russians might be

---

* Kira Smirnova related this story during interviews in Moscow in July 2005 and in October 2007.

found. He also became purveyor to the royal courts in Sweden, Norway, and later, Spain.

Vladimir likely spent his year in China, building relationships with local traders and learning more about the Chinese liquor industry. But according to his third wife, the journey did not mellow Vladimir—at least not right away. Almost immediately after leaving port, he reverted into his old habits.

> On the steamship to China, Vladimir was bored and got involved in a card game, losing a large sum as a result. He had to ask his uncle for help. The uncle became upset and categorically refused to pay for his nephew's losses. What was to be done? Without giving it a second thought, Vladimir took up the guitar he had taken with him on the trip and started singing gypsy romances, walking around the deck and at the dinner table during meals. He was a great success. People stuck cash into the round opening of his guitar. Each performance was followed by loud applause. He paid back the money he had lost in the card game in full but did not play cards again, suspecting that he had been the victim of card sharks.[17]

The gambling was one thing; Vladimir's weakness for women was another. After arriving in the country, he began romancing a married woman. The doomed affair ended abruptly when Smirnov called his son back to Russia. It had been exactly twelve months since Vladimir had gone away. Upon returning, he pleased his father by involving himself more in the company's affairs and business operations. Still, though, he thought of the woman who had so thoroughly captivated him. He went to Yar in search of Katya. Instead of finding her, Vladimir learned that she had married and suffered a mental breakdown after giving birth to a stillborn child. Her body was later found in a ravine.

"It was never known whether she had committed suicide or fell prey to a murderer."[18]

THE MONOPOLY STILL loomed for Smirnov. It was like an immense gray cloud in the distance, blackening as it made its approach. It was advancing, slowly though, bogged down in a thicket of logistics. The big question for Smirnov was how much damage it would cause.

In the meantime, the vodka maker prepared himself. More exposure to his name and products on the world stage was imperative, if only to remind the monarchy of its pride in Smirnov's brand. Witte, in particular, was sensitive to Russia's economic reputation, desirous that the world see his country as a leader among modern industrialized nations, ready to embrace new technologies and more capitalistic institutions. That was likely one reason behind Smirnov's decision to send a sizable collection of his rum, vodkas, liqueurs, and cordials in 1893 to the World's Columbian Exposition: the famous Chicago World's Fair. It was a highly visible platform internationally and an ideal location for affirming Smirnov's goods as Russia's best. In a company profile submitted for the fair, Smirnov stated that he employed 1,200 men, produced 2,000,000 pails of 40-degree vodka each year, and had annual revenue of 15 million rubles ($180.3 million today).[19]

Russia sent plenty of other representatives to the exposition, including a delegation from the monarch himself and more than 1,000 exhibitors. Products ranged from furs to samovars to silks. The fair also boasted a variety of firsts, including an entire building devoted to electrical exhibits crafted by the likes of Thomas Edison and Nikola Tesla. The fair debuted the Ferris wheel, Juicy Fruit gum, and Aunt Jemima pancake mix. For Smirnov, who likely did not attend the event personally, the agenda at the fair was simple and self-serving. He got what he wanted, receiving top honors for his liquors.

This strong showing in Chicago was significant. Russia, under Witte's direction, was pursuing a broad economic agenda, hoping to improve the domestic economy and buttress the nation's international stature. Protectionist policies, inspired and developed by renowned chemist Dmitriy Mendeleyev, best known for creating the periodic table of elements, helped fuel heavy industry growth at home. Sectors ranging from iron to steel to railroads thrived as a result of dramatic influxes of cash collected from steep import tariffs. By 1895 Russia had become the largest producer of oil in the world. Foreign investment was up almost fourfold in the decade. Moscow was booming, too, as villagers flooded the city in search of work in factories and on construction projects.

The 1890s were a healthy period overall for most Russian businesses. New technologies and modern infrastructure kept the marketplace buzzing. Smirnov, too, advanced his manufacturing capabilities, adding electricity to his factory operations. Though not claiming to be first, Smirnov advertised that he was *among* the first to install electrical lighting in his factory, demonstrating to the Imperial Palace his willingness to embrace progress no matter the cost.[20] Smirnov wanted to be seen as part of his country's economic future, somebody who could thrive in and adapt to a changing environment. The Chicago fair and cutting-edge facilities helped make the point.

Smirnov also expanded his philanthropy, cementing his reputation as an upstanding, charitable merchant and strengthening his ties with the monarchy. Among other acts, he paid for the renovation of twenty-eight sterling silver arks containing bones of Russian saints. The project, which included the building of a reliquary made of metal and thick glass in the church where Smirnov served as church warden, was important enough that it had to be approved personally by Aleksander III. The newspapers wrote about Smirnov's gift and the sanctification of the reliquary, noting that the priest called Smirnov "a God-loving donator."[21]

The attention to Smirnov's largesse benefitted his cause, but it was the Imperial Court's personal support of the vodka maker that mattered most. Unfortunately, just days after the reliquary's sanctification, Aleksander III died of pneumonia. Prayers had been said for the tsar's failing health at one of Smirnov's bulk wine warehouses as well as at other operations throughout Russia, but it was not enough. Nikolay II, the last Russian tsar, prepared to assume the throne.

His ascension was a wild card for Smirnov—and Witte. The new tsar was relatively unknown and untested. The *New York Times* described him as a "slender young man, something under the middle height, with narrow, sloping shoulders and an awkward carriage of the neck and head. He has yellowish hair and a beard which is trimmed so as to produce an almost grotesque resemblance to his cousin, the Duke of York. . . . The Tsar Nikolay has small furtive gray eyes, unpleasantly close together." An interview with a royal tutor in the same article suggested Nikolay II was less interested in autocratic rule than his father, Aleksander III, had been. The tutor commented that the new tsar was "an amiable, light-hearted youngster of extremely limited brain power. . . . He detests the military life and is bored by politics. The notion of authority and personal power rather repels than attracts him."[22] Of course, other commentators of the time hailed the new leader, praising Nikolay's strength of character and looking on his future rule with great optimism. They predicted that he would serve as a formidable champion of a strong monarchy.

It is unclear how Smirnov viewed the leadership shift and what it might mean for Russia. He had been through these royal machinations before, but he had never before been in such a precarious situation. With the monopoly just months away from its trial run, Tsar Nikolay II's loyalties and intentions would be pivotal in determining how quickly the private vodka trade might come under attack.

Witte, who had been a close confidante of Aleksander III, still looked on Nikolay II as a youngster, someone too immature to lead Russia. Witte, nevertheless, was hopeful his new boss would be a strong partner, even if he adopted a different blueprint for the government than his father had. "When Emperor Nikolay II ascended the throne, he had, if one may put it this way, an aura of resplendent good will. He truly desired happiness and a peaceful life for Russia, for all his subjects, whatever nationality they might belong to. There is no question that he has a thoroughly good, kind heart," Witte wrote in his memoirs.[23] This meant that the new monarch would likely be sympathetic to any effort to rid Russians of their liquor dependency. This again was Witte's focus when he stated in 1894: "The reform must be directed, first of all towards increasing popular sobriety, and only then can it concern itself with the interests of the treasury."[24]

Looking at its details, much of the reform was focused on combating drunkenness. It banned consumption in retail shops, requiring customers to leave as soon as they had completed their purchases. Liquor could be sold only in sealed bottles. Pictures of the emperor and of saints were to be posted on the walls of state wine shops. Organized sobriety was also a feature of the monopoly. In 1895, Witte established the Guardianship of Public Sobriety. Its mission was to oversee the quality and quantity of liquor sales and advocate moderation in drinking.

The problem with the state's more altruistic emphasis was that it was overshadowed by its monstrous financial appetite. When the monopoly was launched in four provinces in 1895, the government took over the wholesale and retail trade of pure vodka, making it the only legal buyer of vodka from state or private distilleries. Anyone wishing to trade other spirits in territories covered by the monopoly, such as flavored vodkas, liqueurs, grape wines, or beer, would be permitted to do so, but they had to remit to the government 15 percent of the revenue earned. This tax resulted in a surge in state revenue. In one province alone, Ufa, income from alcohol sales grew from 2 million rubles in 1894 to 3.6 million rubles in 1895.[25] "As a fiscal system, the government spirits monopoly was truly a stroke of financial genius," wrote one observer.[26]

Critics pounced on the hypocrisy of the double-edged policy, blasting the state for trying to curb alcoholism as it peddled alcohol. Lenin dubbed the reform "monopoly capitalism."[27] Tolstoy's opposition to it was more cutting. Witte had tried to entice the writer into backing his, Witte's, sobriety organization, believing that Tolstoy's endorsement would lend it credibility. Tolstoy, though, refused even to meet with Witte, instead asking his brother-in-law, Aleksander Kuzminskiy, to convey his displeasure to the minister. In a letter to Kuzminskiy, Tolstoy outlined his position. "In my opinion, if the government really was making every effort for the good of the people, then the first step should be the complete prohibition of the poison which destroys both the physical and the spiritual well-being of millions of people. . . . Thus, the temperance societies established by a government that is not ashamed that it itself sells the poison ruining the people through its own officials seem to me to be either hypocritical, silly, or misguided—or perhaps all three."[28]

Witte knew the monopoly would attract plenty of detractors, but he also knew the vast majority of Russians welcomed it. Smirnov, too, knew it and he had prepared well. When the monopoly took hold in 1895, Smirnov could see that its impact on his own operations would be negligible. The four trial provinces represented a miniscule piece of his business. The vodka maker had also sought out new avenues to reach customers. His vodka, particularly the popular #21 and other unflavored vodkas, continued to be the favorite, especially in Russia's heavily populated central provinces. It was the drink of choice for Russia's military as well after Smirnov landed a contract to provide #21 to soldiers. The drink was consumed "everywhere, in all the regiments, in the officers' canteens, in soldiers' tearooms, and also in the Russian Navy, in both the Baltic and Black Sea."[29]

Smirnov also beefed up production of other liquors. Throughout the 1890s, he expanded his product menu, focusing in particular on unregulated beverages. He introduced a variety of new flavored vodkas (nastoykas), including ashberry flavor, an instant consumer favorite. He also increased his production of grape wines. This diversification, along with his new global reach, minimized the effects of the monopoly after its introduction. His business did not suffer greatly in those first years, when the monopoly covered only a handful of provinces.

The government, though, was enthused by what it saw. Witte personally toured the four provinces where the monopoly made its debut and reported back to the tsar that drunkenness was down while revenue to the state was up. The preaching of the moderation had taken hold, Witte concluded, and he told Nikolay II that "a peace came to families, harmony came to spouses. . . . Wives no longer have to look for their husbands in drinking places and then bring them home in a horrible condition. . . . There was a notable shift to a better life."[30]

Such enthusiasm made the government impatient. The state initially planned to test the reform in the four provinces for three years, but the tsar, at Witte's urging, quickly scrapped the old timetable. Instead, the government accelerated the monopoly's rollout, introducing the reform in nine provinces in 1896, six in 1897, and another four in 1898, which included St. Petersburg. In the face of such an unrelenting assault, Smirnov might have given up, but that was not his nature. The government's aggressive anti-vodka campaign emboldened him, setting in motion one of the greatest and most satisfying triumphs of his life.

Chapter 12

The Tsar and 3,000 Flashing Bottles

Nizhniy Novgorod, a commercial center located 250 miles east of Moscow, sits at the juncture of major trade routes and two grand Russian rivers, the Volga and the Oka. At the turn of the century, it took more than eleven hours to get there by train from Moscow, longer by ship. Despite the lengthy journey, most who made the trek annually, like Smirnov, did so without reservation. It was that important.

Since 1817, the city had come alive from July to September with the arrival of thousands of merchants and traders representing almost every industrial sector in the Empire. They invaded this commercial hub, hawking commodities ranging from wool to metals to rice to leather. Smirnov, who had been the largest buyer of grape wine at the Nizhniy Novgorod Fair for years, contributed to the 416 million rubles worth of transactions consummated there annually.*

---

* The equivalent of about $5 billion today.

"The prices established at the fair constituted the benchmark values for the entire commercial year. So important was the fair that when it was open, financial and commercial establishments often shifted their operations entirely to its territory. It was also there that the Moscow merchants carried out their largest annual transactions, thus confirming the centrality of the fair."[1]

Nothing before, though, could compare to the late spring and summer of 1896 in Nizhniy Novgorod. That year the city of almost 82,000 people hosted the All-Russia Industrial and Artistic Exhibition, one of the most spectacular technical achievements in the history of the country. The tsar, Witte, and Russia's top business leaders pledged to use the exhibition, the first of its kind in fourteen years, to demonstrate to the world that the nation's economic power was vast and its industrial development expansive. It was to be the marketing event of the century, a show of fortitude so undeniable that it would inspire even the most skeptical observers to concede Russia's status as an industrial superpower. "Russia grows, its productive forces grow, and with them grows the wealth of the country, its powers, and the recognition of its strength," proclaimed Witte at the opening of the exhibition on May 28.[2]

No expense had been spared to create just the right atmosphere. The government pledged 3 million rubles to pay for a new transportation system, new buildings, a modern sanitation system, pavilions for entertainment, and a variety of other attractions. Private industry contributed another 7 million rubles, constructing eye-popping exhibits and cutting-edge facilities. When all was done, the site boasted 172 separate buildings. Electric streetlights replaced kerosene lamps. A theater big enough for almost nine hundred people had been erected, complete with steam heating, electric lights, and a sophisticated ventilation system. The first funicular railway in the country had been installed there, too, which guided two trams shuttling visitors to and from the exhibition grounds. A magnificent new park provided respite from the daily commotion, complete with fifty-one fountains and artificial ponds containing swans. "The exhibition is the most important business for the entire state, a result of activity of more than 100 million people who have been working for fifteen years, counting from the Moscow exhibition of 1882," wrote famed writer Maxim Gorkiy, a native of Nizhniy Novgorod who covered the event for a local newspaper.[3]

Beyond the infrastructure, the displays were also designed to impress. Among the most technical advances unveiled at Nizhniy Novgorod was the first Russian automobile, which topped out at a speed of 13.5 miles per hour. The first hyperboloid steel tower, created by architect Vladimir Shukhov, was constructed and shown there. A tractor with a steam engine made its debut, too. Technical presentations by an array of esteemed scientists, including Mendeleyev, botanist K. A. Timiryazev, and scientist/inventor A. S. Popov were also featured. The parade of serious achievement was enough to entice a slew of foreign dignitaries, ambassadors, some 180 Americans, and nearly one million Russians.

They came to witness and evaluate Russia's industrial prowess, to be sure, but it was the most fanciful exhibits, including one by Smirnov, that truly delighted. Henry Brokar, the tsar's perfume purveyor, made columns out of transparent soap. Electric lights inside the soap lit up the structure, giving it a luminous, magical quality. He also put up a tent made out of roses carved from soap. Another exhibitor showed a belfry constructed completely out of stearin candles. There were railroad booths made out of chocolate, a grotto made of 108 different gemstones and rocks, and a two-headed eagle made out of dried fish.

Smirnov would not be outshown by these other participants, particularly not when the tsar, the empress, and Witte were among the fair's visitors. Smirnov occupied a superior position at the exhibition—at least among the sixty-six vodka makers and distillers. His display was right at the entrance to the vodka department, signaling to everyone his supremacy in his industry. His showcase was unparalleled, a true reflection of Smirnov himself: a potent combination of master showman, ingenious marketer, and Imperial loyalist.

As visitors approached the vodka section, they were awestruck. A colossal arch built entirely out of bottles and little wine barrels greeted them. The bottles, 3,000 of them, were the colors of the Russian national flag—white, blue, and red. Light bulbs inside those bottles flashed on and off, creating a fluorescent, glowing, and utterly patriotic spectacle. The symbolism was not lost on journalists who covered the exhibition. They wrote about Smirnov's "fiery effect."[4] Nor was it lost on the exhibition's officials. Smirnov, his exhibit, and his company received a huge write-up in the exhibition catalog. The vodka king was praised for his fine products and continuing success, particularly in the face of the liquor monopoly, which the catalog authors euphemistically described as "new conditions in the market."[5]

As laudatory articles at the exhibition proved, Smirnov's business was still on a tear. His revenue now topped 17 million rubles annually, with 9 million rubles going straight into the state treasury. His pure vodka production was up to 120,000 bottles a day, or 45 million annually. This required some 3 million kilograms of charcoal per year, which was used to rectify the vodka. Smirnov contracted with seven different glassmakers, each one supplying an estimated seven million bottles a year. The 60 million labels and tags needed annually came from four printing factories. Corks alone cost 120,000 rubles each year. Smirnov's nastoykas required purchases of huge lots of raspberries, currants, strawberries, bilberries, cherries, cranberries, and ashberries. Sales of foreign and domestic grape wines also increased to 100 million bottles per year.[6]

There was simply no denying Smirnov's preeminence. It was on full display at the Nizhniy Novgorod exhibition—in his assigned location, in his flashing arch, in the stories carried in newspaper, and in the fair's printed catalog. He also collected top honors again, earning the right to display another state emblem, his fourth, on his products. None of the adulation bestowed upon him during the event, though, moved Smirnov the way his brush with royalty did.

ON MAY 18, the tsar's coronation, intended to be a magnificent celebration of his reign, turned into tragedy. Smirnov's vodka had gushed like a river at the largely symbolic event. Indeed, one-fifth of all the alcohol purchased for the occasion by the Imperial Court for its own pleasure came from Smirnov's cellars and warehouses, including four different kinds of flavored vodkas.[7] On top of the tsar's elite party, more than 500,000 revelers showed up the day before the coronation for a traditional gathering held for commoners. They drank and ate throughout the night in a large outdoor field outside Moscow, all the while waiting for the moment when packaged gifts from the tsar would be distributed to the crowd. Rumors swirled among the assembled that herds of horses and cows would be given away, that fountains of beer and wine would flow, and that trained elephants would perform.

None of these rumors were true, but the anticipation, along with the drink, made people anxious and impatient. Then someone shouted: "They give it," referring to the presents from the tsar to this subjects. The crowd went wild, pushing, shoving, and charging. Mayhem ensued, as throngs frantically chased packages thrown into the air. In the end, an estimated 2,000 people were killed in the crush, many of them women and children. The tsar's gifts, a souvenir enamel cup, a spice cake, a sausage, and some bread, offered little consolation.

Nikolay II was reportedly grief-stricken, putting even more pressure on officials to ensure his experience at Nizhniy Novgorod would be refreshing and positive. The plan was for the tsar to arrive on July 17, spend three days touring the exhibition, meet with prominent attendees and participants, and attend a sumptuous dinner given in his honor. Smirnov, who had been commuting from Moscow to Nizhniy Novgorod since the exhibition's opening, returned to the fair with childish anticipation. He brought Mariya and his children, including his youngest daughter, nineteen-year-old Aleksandra, and five sons. In Smirnov's mind, greeting the monarch was not only an honor and a thrill, but also a duty that ought to be shared.

The weather turned foul on the day of the tsar's arrival. Until then, the summer in Nizhniy Novgorod had been quite pleasant. The days had been warm enough—but not too warm. A few small showers and breezes had kept the air clear and clean. Only once, in June, had it been hot. The air was so stifling then in the Machinery and Industrial Departments of the exhibition that glass bottles split, wax displays melted, and engines overheated. Officials reacted quickly, painting white over windows on the sunny side of the buildings and bringing in more fans.

Now, though, as the tsar approach Nizhniy Novgorod in July, officials were frantic over the thunderstorm that trailed him. The skies darkened, giving way to sheets of rain mixed with hail the size of walnuts. The downpour knocked out windows and blew over several displays at the exhibition. Despite the inconvenience, the emperor's welcome from the awaiting crowds was unabashedly enthusiastic. They cried out "Hooray!" as the royal party, comprised of Nikolay II, his wife, Empress Aleksandra Fyodorovna, and the Grand Duke Aleksey Aleksandrovich made its way from one hall to another.

Order and decorum, unlike at the coronation, ruled the majesties' tour. Everywhere the tsar and his companions went was paved in red carpet. An honorary guard made up of the young sons of prominent merchants shadowed them. Seventeen of the boys came from Moscow's leading families, such as Morozov, Mamontov, and Ryabushinskiy, while ten came from business dynasties in Nizhniy Novgorod. They were dressed in expensive white kaftans with poleaxes on their shoulders, some made out of sterling silver. They stood in a line, motionless, as if anticipating a military style drill.

This honorary guard was an unusual, calculated move by merchants to appeal to the tsar. They wanted to demonstrate simultaneously their importance to the country's economic growth and their allegiance to Russia's traditions and heritage. An editorial in the *Volgar*, a regional newspaper, suggested that the merchant class had proven its power and loyalty to the crown more fervently than the age-old aristocracy, which was leaning increasingly toward Western ideals. "The *kupechestvo* [merchantry] has preserved the genuine Russian spirit more than any other [social estate]. Nowhere else does the national feeling appear with such strength, conviction, and breadth. Of all groups in Russia, it alone is strong also in an economic sense. There is nothing it cannot do."[8]

The royal entourage was impressed with what it saw, even though they did not share the views expressed in the *Volgar*. The tsar greeted his guardians and then made his way through a sampling of the displays. The royal couple returned several times to walk through the exhibition, always guided by Minister Witte dressed in a summer coat and hat. Finally, on July 19, the tsar stood before Smirnov's flashing arch. The nature of the exchange between the tsar and Smirnov is unknown, but given standard protocol and the vodka maker's devotion to the Imperial Court, it is more than probable that Smirnov bowed deeply, perhaps even expressing his thanks and hope that the tsar and tsarina had enjoyed his exhibit. Other members in the imperial party certainly did. The Great Prince Vladimir Aleksandrovich and his wife, who later came to the exhibition, were so amused by Smirnov's showcase that their appreciation made the Moscow news.[9]

The tsar's tour was possibly not the only encounter with royalty that Smirnov had at the exhibition. The banquet for the emperor took place that same night in a building that usually housed shops and kiosks on its first floor and apartments for city officials on the second. For this occasion, the place had been transformed into something out of a fairy tale. An entirely new staircase had been constructed, with decorations representing the heroes of Russian folk tales carved into it. Columns at the bottom of the stairs were draped in velvet and gold lace. Flowers, including snow-white lilies, roses, and azaleas, were everywhere, lit up by electrical lanterns to render the petals and leaves transparent. Garlands of lights surrounded the state emblem and a makeshift throne was set up under a thick cherry-velvet canopy. The Smirnovs joined a guest list packed with 1,700 international luminaries. "The fair has never seen such glitter," commented one observer. "Along with the tsar's family, there were almost all the ministers, ambassadors from foreign countries, the vice king of China, the diplomatic corps, the court, three general governors, and lots of various grand people."[10]

To join such company on that night made clear Smirnov's eminence. Any lingering doubts the former serf or anyone else might have had simply faded away. That evening, he was a known man, a wealthy man, with his wife and children, gazing through the curling wisps of cigarette smoke, at Tsar Nikolay II. Smirnov was where he had always wanted to be: in the warm embrace of his motherland, a member of the inner circle.

Chapter 13

Twilight

In the twilight of his life, Smirnov continued to oversee his business operations and go about his daily routines. But more and more he turned his attention to other pressing concerns: his family, his inevitable death, and his ensuing legacy. His commercial and financial affairs needed more ordering, and his philanthropy, already sizable, demanded one more major initiative—or so Smirnov thought. His sons and daughters, who had thus far produced a dozen grandchildren, still had complicated issues to resolve. Smirnov may not have seen it coming, but as 1897 came into view, he entered one of the most unsettling periods of his life.

Rumblings of the turmoil began even before Nizhniy Novgorod. Aleksandra, Smirnov's youngest daughter and Mariya's only girl, reluctantly accompanied her parents to the exhibition, more out of duty than genuine desire. Smirnov and Mariya, in a show of steely determination, had given her no choice in the matter.

By the time she was nineteen years old, Aleksandra had

grown into a glamorous young lady. She had wide, gray-blue eyes and a thick mop of wonderfully curly hair, which she styled according to the latest European trends. Her lips and body were full and voluptuous, giving her an innocent sensuality. She was charming, too, displaying a natural vibrancy. Aleksandra was indeed her mother's daughter, independent and thrillingly passionate.

It would have been hard for Aleksandra to imagine that any yearning in her young life could not be fulfilled. Like her siblings, she had experienced nothing but privilege. Her schooling revolved around all the fundamentals of good breeding, including music, art, foreign language, and literature. She traveled a lot, too, according to passport records, both for pleasure and out of necessity. For example, when she was diagnosed with an eye disorder as a young girl, Aleksandra went abroad in 1890 with her mother to find a cure.[1] Aleksandra's affliction probably inspired her father to become a primary benefactor of an eye clinic in Moscow.

She seemed the model daughter, and it was assumed she would follow the lead of her sisters, who had selected worthy men and then slid comfortably into the traditional ranks of high society. Vera, Nataliya, Mariya, and Glafira all married sons of prominent merchants. Nataliya married Konstantin Bakhrushin, a member of the well-known family who later founded the Bakhrushin Theater Museum in Moscow. Mariya's first husband was Pyotr Rastorguyev, a member of a prominent merchant dynasty. Her second husband, Mikhail Komissarov, was also well respected and adept at business. And Glafira married Aleksander Abrikosov, heir to a candy empire.

Then came Aleksandra. In the spring of 1896, just a few months before the exhibition began, Aleksandra met a man more than twenty years her senior. Devilishly handsome and suave, he appealed to her instantly. His name was Martemyan Nikanorovich Borisovskiy. His family of merchants had been well respected and wealthy. The Borisovskiys owned a sugar refinery and a small textile factory, but a bad business deal and falling sugar prices had reversed their good fortune, plunging the family into bankruptcy. They were devastated, forced to sell their estate and close their factory. Borisovskiy's father despaired while his son turned to more frivolous pursuits.

Martemyan was a drinker, a gambler, a debtor, and a cad. He was also married. According to a contemporary merchant who knew him, Martemyan "didn't possess elementary or basic notions of honesty."[2] He was a regular on Moscow's party circuit, known to drink prodigiously at breakfast, and to seduce unsuspecting women at will, using deceit and a smarmy charm to get his way. It was rumored that Martemyan took a girl up to the belfry of a church located at the Kremlin where, in an act of utter blasphemy, he made advances on her. After this, according to his contemporary, Borisovskiy was caught and forced to marry the girl.[3]

None of this debauched behavior, however, could derail the budding romance between Martemyan and Aleksandra. According to several personal letters Martemyan sent to Aleksandra between 1896 and 1897, the relationship unfolded routinely. He began to call on Aleksandra at Smirnov's home. The visits were formal, chaperoned most often by Mariya. Relations between the Smirnovs and Aleksandra's suitor were cordial and friendly. Once the Smirnovs realized the couple had more than friendship on their minds, they made inquiries around town about Martemyan. They quickly learned of his wretched reputation. Still, it appears that Martemyan was struck by the support the Smirnovs continued to demonstrate. In one letter he wrote, *"I [Martemyan] still can't understand why, after all this unpleasant feedback about me, your father talked to me so willingly. Your mama also seems to have a liking for me. It means that they do not believe the wicked people who want to blacken my reputation. It means that everything may be arranged on mutual agreement."*[4] In another,

Martemyan refers to Mariya as their "guardian angel," an ally in their quest for true love.

Within a few weeks, the couple openly expressed their feelings to one another—and to their families. Aleksandra, unable to contain her ardor, disclosed her devotion to Martemyan to her parents, believing they would yield to her desires. Borisov-skiy made plans to divorce his wife and pledged to renounce his playboy lifestyle: *"Before I met you I lived like a pig because, as you know, I expected nothing from life and did anything I wanted to do. . . . I led an immoral life"* (April 8, 3 AM). In a letter eleven days later, Martemyan declared, *"Though I have had many affairs when I was young I've never really loved anybody. And I love you, not for your appearance but for your wonderful soul, which shines through your wonderful eyes. I even feel fear. I've never looked at a woman the way I look at you. And you are not just a woman but a goddess embod-ied in a woman"* (April 19, 1 AM).

The Smirnovs were not swayed by Martemyan's poetic pro-nouncements nor were they convinced that Aleksandra was anything more than an innocent girl behaving rashly under the influence of an unscrupulous, manipulative man. They viewed Martemyan as a poor match for her, a scoundrel who would bring nothing but scandal to them and unhappiness to Alek-sandra. Even though they forbid her to see him, the Smirnovs knew how headstrong their daughter was. From letters, it looks as if Mariya paid off Martemyan's wife, getting her to contest a divorce that had been thought to be an already closed matter. Martemyan wrote to Aleksandra about his outrage. *"Somebody, probably somebody from your family, gave money to my ex-wife to start a lawsuit against me. She hired a lawyer, some Jew man, and now he plays mean tricks on me. . . . He insists on delays in my divorce, on receiving lots of papers concerning my finished divorce. He appealed the decision. He wants all the witnesses to be interrogated again in his presence. It's disgusting!"* (Case 497, #100, June 3, 5 PM).

At the same time, Mariya, likely in collaboration with her

husband, pursued an alternative, riskier strategy. She approached Martemyan. Still a beauty herself and about the same age as her daughter's suitor, she tried to seduce Martemyan, hoping to elicit direct, incontrovertible evidence from him about his base, unchanged character. He wrote to Aleksandra about the incident. *"M. N. [Mariya Nikolayevna] . . . wanted not to make a son-in-law out of me but a lover. She was cruelly disappointed in her aspirations and will probably start looking for a partner for a fun pastime outside the house. Then you'll have more freedom"* (#87, May 22, 11 PM).

The niceties practiced during the first days of the courtship had vanished. Martemyan only had his all-adoring mother and father to spur him on in his quest for a Smirnov. They embraced their son's relationship with Aleksandra, according to several letters his mother wrote to Aleksandra, seeing the girl as a more-than-suitable match for Martemyan. She would bring money, respectability, and renewed stature to her son and his family. Moreover, she believed Martemyan genuinely loved Aleksandra and would make her a good husband. She wrote, *"Believe me, my Mortya* [a nickname for Martemyan] *is a very good, very kind boy. He will always love you. And I love you beforehand. And his father also loves you. . . . It is such a pity that your parents oppose your love so much. I don't understand them. You will live with Mortya, not them"* (Case 497).

Martemyan's anger grew as each day brought more frustrations. In his letters, he expressed his raw hatred for the Smirnovs as well as his fears that they would try to force Aleksandra into abandoning him for another more suitable partner. *"Your parents will definitely exert every effort to make you interested in a fiancé who would be more favorable to them"* (Case 496, #21, April 19, 1 AM). Then later:

> They [the Smirnovs] will terrorize you because of me! They will torment you! They are animals, monsters! . . . Your father, though he gave you both education and good

breeding, he still remains that terrible type of despot merchant—an emigrant from the people. . . . He accepts his opinion only while he's indifferent to other people's opinions. . . . Alas, I am very sorry to have to write all these things about your father but he seems to be a person like this. He really is. A person, who earns money not for life but for money's sake, and is alien to any kinds of feelings where money plays a second or third role. And you wrongly call him religious. . . . No my darling, these are not religious people. These are fiends! (Case 496, #55, April 25, 10 AM).

Martemyan's rants directly aimed at Mariya were just as visceral—and more pointed. "*Let her go to hell,*" he wrote (Case 497, #172, June 20).

Pyotr Petrovich, Aleksandra's half brother, was the one Smirnov for whom Martemyan had kind words. Aleksandra confided her troubles to her older brother, begging him to help her find a way to circumvent her parents' opposition. She believed the younger Pyotr would be sympathetic to her predicament given his own struggles with their father over a married lover. From Martemyan's letters, it is certain that Pyotr met with him and promised to assist the couple in their quest. "*What a pleasant person! How he took our problem so close to his heart.*"[5] It's not clear what, if anything, the younger Smirnov managed to accomplish on his sister's behalf. He may not have had much opportunity to help. When it became evident that Aleksandra would not easily relinquish her love affair, Smirnov and Mariya decided to get their daughter out of Moscow and away from Martemyan. Their strategy, at least in part, was aided by coincidental good timing. A series of trips was already on the calendar that spring—from the Nizhniy Novgorod exhibition to a visit to Smirnov's boyhood village in the Yaroslavl province. The vodka maker had ached to return to his roots and build a cathedral, an act that was thought to justify wealth and alleviate the sin of capitalism. For this deed, Smirnov chose Potapovo, a village within two miles of his birthplace and roughly 165 miles from Moscow. As a child, Smirnov had attended church there, but the building was now too small to hold all of its worshipers comfortably. It was also old, having been erected in 1757, and it needed major repair and renovation. The new structure commissioned by Smirnov was to be enormous by comparison. It would be built of stone, contain three altars, five domes, and a modern heating system. Decorative touches, such as iron-curved rods and brick columns, would create a grandness more akin to cathedrals found in the bigger cities than in the rural countryside.* Smirnov spared no expense for this undertaking, donating an estimated 250,000 rubles [more than $3.3 million in today's dollars] from his own pocket.[6] And it seemed that Smirnov was proudest of this one project. Local townspeople hailed their native son, treating him as a hero come home.

For the sanctification of the church, Smirnov insisted on Aleksandra's attendance. As it was natural for Smirnov to want his family around him on such a momentous occasion, he could make this demand without seeming overbearing or punitive. Martemyan, though, saw the voyage as an assault on their relationship. His letters reveal the rage he felt when Aleksandra told him she would be going away for many weeks.

In truth, the Smirnovs wanted to keep the couple apart for longer. They had moved their daughter for the summer to their dacha just outside Moscow, hoping Aleksandra would forget about her romance. But she did not. Despite being watched closely by the home's caretakers, Aleksandra and Martemyan managed to see each other repeatedly, infuriating Smirnov. He and Mariya remained steadfast in their opposition to Martemyan and his daughter. By

---

* Description is based on a personal interview on Nov. 12, 2005, with Varvara Niko-layevna Petukhova, a resident who saw the cathedral. It no longer exists.

necessity, though, they dropped their active campaign against the courtship. Perhaps they realized it was a fight they could not win. Or, perhaps, there was simply too much else for which they had to fight.

IN THE SAME year that Smirnov's church in Potapovo was completed, the state council voted to accelerate the rollout of the vodka monopoly. Minister Witte successfully argued to the state in May 1897 that it was having its intended effects: reducing alcohol consumption, eliminating corruption, improving morality, and lastly, aiding the treasury. It was an easy argument for Witte to make because no one opposed him. In just a few years, the government's take from alcohol sales had climbed more than sevenfold, leaving it with a net profit of 20 million rubles. Smirnov had anticipated as much. But now he was confronted with a definitive timetable. His factory, warehouses, and the heart of his operation would be under the government's full control by 1901. All his elaborate maneuvering and clever strategizing, which had kept the business thriving, would be rendered useless.

Worse still were the results of technical tests undertaken by the Central Chemical Laboratory within the Ministry of Finance in the mid to late 1890s. Trying to determine what vodka recipe the state should adopt when it took over all manufacturing of the spirit, the organization focused on the vodkas produced by twelve private distillers, including Smirnov.[7] Scientists took dry residue from the liquors and tested them for a variety of potentially harmful ingredients. Smirnov's vodka, considered among the tastiest of the bunch, was found to have the largest amount of ethyl acetate, a substance that irritates eyes, nose, and throat. "According to the results of the analysis into the production process, it would be difficult to find that P. A. Smirnov's table wine [vodka] was the best, though it is still extremely popular. . . . This finding demonstrates that the product's reputation doesn't always depend on the quality. Obviously a very considerable role here belongs to the way a factory distributes its products and on the talent to make a product's appearance more attractive. Very often, the product's reputation depends on its harmonious name, bottle's shape, colorful label, or just a more expensive price of the product."[8]

The revelation was insulting. Smirnov had always strived to offer the highest quality products at the most reasonable prices, and he had a long list of awards and honors to prove it. He repeatedly demonstrated that he cared about the purity of the ingredients used in his recipes. He had even responded to the criticisms lobbed his way from earlier studies, which had found too much fusel oil in his liquor. He had changed his manufacturing method to address the concern, greatly increasing the amount of birch charcoal he used to filter his spirit. The charcoal absorbed fusel oil and gave the vodka a smoother, more pleasant taste. Smirnov used between ten and thirteen pounds of charcoal per pail, an amount that was significantly greater than what was used by other vodka makers.[9] The switch had done its job, ridding Smirnov's vodka of almost all traces of fusel oil. More and more, other vodka makers adopted more modern methods for rectifying their spirits, which produced more purified liquor, while Smirnov deliberately stuck to the old system.

That Smirnov's vodka was not proven to be the best or most pure in Russia by the government's scientists would have been an enormous blow to Smirnov. Rumors were not flying about his products being harmful or subpar. Indeed, the chemical report was solely for the state's use and not publicly disseminated. And Smirnov would not lose his large customer base, at least not immediately. Even the Imperial Court was still a big buyer, placing an order for almost 9,000 bottles of Smirnov's vodka in 1897.[10] Vodka was a regular fixture at the tsar's table, particularly during the lunchtime meal when it was said that Nikolay II himself drank two full wineglasses of it. But the coming monopoly coupled with the government's finding forced Smirnov to see that his vodka, responsible for the largest chunk of his profits, would not likely survive beyond 1901. If the state had chosen to adopt his recipe, he could have argued that it was his vodka alone that sat on the tables of Russian citizens long after his death. But now it would not be so.

SMIRNOV HAD SOME hard choices to make. Russia was changing. The labor movement, still not unified or all-mighty, was nonetheless gaining momentum. Intellectuals had begun joining the ranks of workers, aiding and organizing them in their quest for better treatment. Strikes at factories throughout the country were becoming as common as borscht—as were the government's harsh crackdowns. The Imperial Palace was increasingly intolerant of the dissent, enacting a series of decrees to combat the unrest. First, it issued an order that outlawed the printing or publication of any materials relating to the labor movement, factory conditions, salaries, or negative attitudes toward employers. Then local authorities were instructed on how to suppress agitators. Police were to keep close watch over factories and their workers, paying particular attention to intellectuals who sat among the rank and file disseminating antigovernment propaganda. Meetings of workers were strictly prohibited, and anyone found to be inciting protests, peaceful or otherwise, was to be arrested. Lenin, among many other radicals, became a high-profile example. In 1897 he was arrested and sent into exile in Siberia.

Smirnov himself had escaped the taint of the labor problem. His workers never went on strike and, like many in his industry, he had upgraded the benefits his employees received, offering medical care, housing, and modern conveniences such as electricity.[11] Still, he could see that the business climate overall was growing more unstable. This realization, combined with the advancing government initiatives against his own industry and enterprise, convinced Smirnov that it was time to galvanize his three eldest sons. He would need them, unified, in the battle for long-term survival.

Smirnov did not delay. He pushed ahead to see that Pyotr would have the necessary social status to step into his own well-polished shoes. Proper standing within the greater community, Smirnov had learned long ago, could be a great asset to commerce, and the younger Smirnov had already racked up an impressive string of qualifications. He had joined the boards of several of his father's charities, including the Moscow Council of Children Orphanages, the Moscow Committee on Beggars, and the parish at John the Baptist church. He still lacked an order, though, an incontrovertible symbol of a much-revered, lofty reputation. Smirnov joined his son in petitioning the Moscow Merchants Administration in 1897 for an order.[12] As was the custom, the committee requested numerous reference letters stating that Pyotr was worthy of such a distinction. The letters came in, but they were not what father and son had envisioned. In typical Russian fashion, several of them questioned the younger Smirnov's readiness, stating that he seemed to rely on his father's position instead of earning honors himself. The letter from the Moscow Exchange Committee, which oversaw the Moscow Stock Exchange, was particularly pointed. "I notify the State Chamber that the hereditary honorable citizen P. P. Smirnov, being only twenty-seven years old, was not and could not be recommended to any order or sign of excellence by the Exchange Committee because his activity in the trade world not only is not outstanding but is unknown. Further, before this year, he had no independent significance and has been one of P. A. Smirnov's directors for only one year."[13]

The negative comments may have been an outgrowth of Smirnov's choice years earlier to concentrate on aristocratic institutions for his accolades rather than those dominated by merchants. He had indeed participated in only those merchant activities that were essential to his business interests—and nothing more. Consequently, the Moscow Exchange Committee, ruled by eminent merchants, might have relished the chance to reject Smirnov and his son.

Still, Smirnov forged ahead. He filed a petition with Witte's office in 1897, asking that his company be allowed to expand its board of directors from three members to four. The change was necessary, he explained, due to the increasingly complicated business environment in Russia and abroad. Vladimir was selected to become the company's fourth director while older brother Nikolay, still undoubtedly a question in Smirnov's mind, joined as a member of the revision committee.[14] Mariya remained a shareholder, and Smirnov himself retained solid control of his company, keeping all but seventeen of the six hundred shares issued. This structure gave board members a voice in business affairs but kept any real decisions from being enacted without Smirnov's personal agreement.

That both Vladimir and Nikolay were brought into the inner circle of the company suggests that Smirnov's views toward his sons' suitability had softened. It was not so much that the two had reformed. But they had started to take on the appearance of respectability. Both agreed to marriages supported by their father that were possibly based on practical concerns rather than love. Nikolay's wife, a little-known woman by the name of Darya Nikolayevna, offered him stability. His wayward conduct also seemed to be more under control. According to his brothers, his drinking, gambling, and prodigious spending decreased during this time.[15] Vladimir married Mariya Gavrilovna Shushpanova. From all accounts it was an unhappy coupling, one that Vladimir entered to satisfy the elder Smirnov's hunger for the appearance of harmony.

All of Smirnov's children seemed to crave their father's approval. They were willing to do almost anything for him regardless of the personal sacrifice. Even rebellious Aleksandra seemed to be easing away from the stranglehold Martemyan had on her. The two were still engaged, but it looked as though Aleksandra's commitment to the union was waning. In a succinct letter sent to Aleksandra in late 1897, Martemyan lashed into her for speaking to another man in public. *"This made me really angry. I demand your complete obedience and ask that you live your life according to my directions. Otherwise, I don't know what will come next!"*[16]

Meanwhile, Smirnov's health was now failing, as evidenced by a request he made to the Moscow Court Administration in April 1898, which oversaw the Kremlin churches where Smirnov had served as church warden. He had held the position since 1892, enjoying the associated respect and reverence. Now, Smirnov was concerned that he lacked the energy necessary to fulfill his responsibilities. "As a consequence of my unhealthy condition, I have no ability to carry out the position of church warden of the Moscow Court Cathedrals: Blagoveshchenskiy and Verkhospasskiy," wrote Smirnov, asking that the archpriest find a replacement.[17]

Death may have been in sight. Smirnov could wait no longer to craft his last will and testament. According to a report in the Russian edition of *Forbes* in 2005, Smirnov was one of the richest men in Russia by the end of the nineteenth century.[18] His name appeared on a list dominated by such textile titans as the Tretyakovs, Prokhorovs, and Konovalovs and also included more than a dozen multimillionaires whose origins, like the vodka king's, harkened back to peasantry or serfdom. Smirnov's assets, estimated from official sources at roughly 10 million rubles (the equivalent of $133 million today), were numerous, including property, artifacts, and commercial interests. Smirnov may have been even wealthier, underestimating his worth for political and economic reasons. Nonetheless, distributing such bounty was a delicate matter—and not something Smirnov could entrust to anyone else.

His legacy was a crucial objective for a man who had spent a lifetime molding an image about which he was so obviously proud. Perhaps that is why Smirnov made the decision, unusual for merchants of his stature, to retain all his assets within the family and leave nothing to charitable causes. It was a decision many aristocrats criticized: "When Smirnov died, note was duly taken of the fact he left none of his money to charity."[19] Smirnov must have had his reasons. He may have figured that the vodka monopoly and temperance movement left his sons with little opportunity for future growth. They might then need all he had acquired to prosper in the coming Russia.

Smirnov invited Andrey Andreyevich Pol, a known notary he had used before, to his home by the Cast Iron Bridge. His will, which relied on the bonds of blood and a protective measure or two, was ready to receive his signature. The bulk of his assets would be disbursed evenly between his wife and five sons, including thirteen-year-old Sergey and nine-year-old Aleksey. They would split the real estate as well as the stock in Smirnov's company. Mariya retained the right to live in the Moscow residence and had full use of the dachas. She was also given sole ownership of all the contents of Smirnov's homes, including "icons, pictures, gold, silver, bronze and metal objects, furniture, horses, carriages, harnesses and other equipment relating to the horses and carriages." His five daughters were allotted 30,000 rubles each, and 40,000 rubles was set aside to cover Smirnov's burial expenses. A gift of one month's salary was provided for most employees.[20]

There was one catch to Smirnov's equitable distribution. His sons could not receive their shares in the company until reaching the age of thirty-five. "While exercising the rights granted to them by the charter of the company, none of my sons has the right to either alienate or mortgage their acquired shares of stock until they achieve the indicated age." The intent was to prevent infighting among the sons as well as the possibility that one of them might try to sell his interest in the business to an outsider, and it was sound reasoning. If only events had unfolded more predictably, it just might have worked.

Chapter 14

Two Dead Bodies

As winter approached in 1898, the house by the Cast Iron Bridge was devoid of its usual commotion. Muffled chatter among family members and servants periodically broke the quiet, but otherwise, a somber stillness settled in. Smirnov refused to see doctors any longer. He was dying.

In recent months Smirnov's face seemed to have literally deflated, thinning and lengthening like taffy does when it is pulled. It was thicker at the forehead and chin, but the cheeks were sunken and pale. Photos show that his eyes, which once blazed, now glowed like small embers. They were encased by bags so heavy and pronounced that Smirnov's gaze was perpetually weary. Even his hair, a once abundant fixture, had lost its luster and heft. The man's body and soul were vanishing, it seemed, one cell at a time.

Reports differ on exactly what ailed Smirnov. Undoubtedly, he was suffering from a debilitating heart condition. The official cause of death was recorded as congestive heart failure, but the memoirs of Vladimir's third wife reveal that he may have been in a far more precarious state toward the end of his life. "Pyotr Arsenievich had a stroke. He was virtually paralyzed, spoke unclearly, and could not use his legs," wrote Tatiana Smirnova-Maksheyeva.[1] Whatever his precise physical condition, dying for Smirnov had taken on a quality he had not known since his days as a serf. It was inefficiency. Dying was an infuriatingly plodding exercise—nothing like the workmanlike crispness Smirnov had embraced throughout adulthood. The dullness of it, and the dread, for much of 1898, consumed the Smirnovs.

On an unusually warm day in late November, the stillness in Smirnov's home crackled. The wait had ended—Smirnov lay motionless, dead in his bed. Almost immediately, the commemoration of his unusual and unexpected life story began. Saluting the vodka maker's sixty-seven-year voyage was a national affair, involving representatives from all walks of life. There were his ties to the Imperial Palace, his relations with the clergy, and his notoriety among merchants and community leaders. For the masses, though, the remembrances came in another form. For them, Smirnov had stood out as an icon, an authentic example that rising up from the lowliest echelons of society was a possibility. Even in tsarist Russia, with its autocratic rules and entrenched social hierarchy, capitalism and capitalists could flourish, even those with peasant roots.

Crowds assembled to bid their farewells on what turned out to be a bitterly cold and snowy day in early December. They came and went, as Smirnov's passing was noted, his afterlife prayed for. Mariya, dressed in all black, played her wifely role well. She, too, was known in Moscow circles and, still a relatively young woman, attracted her share of attention. What would Mariya Smirnova do now? Would she remarry? How would she spend all that money?

The questions were frivolous and obvious, although little else that transpired afterward was. Smirnov had been meticulous in the preparations of his will. He had selected three executors:

his son-in-law Konstantin Petrovich Bakhrushin, a wealthy and notoriously fat man; Nikolay Venediktovich Smirnov, a trusted cousin from the Yaroslavl province; and Grigoriy Yakovlevich Arsentyev, a merchant's son whom he had known for many years.[2] But within weeks of Smirnov's death, Bakhrushin inexplicably withdrew from his charge as executor.[3] He cited no specific reasons for the unusual move in court documents, but the fact that he did so suggests that trouble may have been already brewing within the Smirnov family—trouble that Bakhrushin, who was married to Smirnov's daughter Nataliya, preferred to stay far from.

One clue to Bakhrushin's bizarre behavior emerged within weeks of his withdrawal. Smirnov had divided his real estate holdings into six equal parts, giving a sixth to each of his five sons and to his wife. Smirnov stipulated, however, that his boys could not take ownership of the properties until after Mariya's death. Nonetheless, the two remaining executors petitioned the court on behalf of Smirnov's sons asking that they be allowed to inherit their portions of the real estate immediately. This bequest included shares in the Cast Iron Bridge mansion and the family's dachas.[4] The executors did not explain why the Smirnov sons were in such a hurry, but one possibility is that both Vladimir and Nikolay may have needed more capital to fund their carefree lifestyles, and Pyotr sought more financial independence and personal control over the vodka business. Sergey and Aleksey were too young to have opinions of their own or much input. The request was rejected by the court, which saw no reason to alter Smirnov's wishes so soon after his death.

As it turned out, the Smirnov sons need not have bothered with their request. In what was one of the most unexpected turn of events, Mariya contracted meningitis and fell into a feverish stupor, unable to carry out even the simplest tasks. Prior to her illness, she had valiantly stepped into her husband's former role as the elder statesperson in the family. It was Mariya who had provided stability and maturity, a strong hand corralling the unwieldy Smirnov brood into something resembling functional. It was Mariya who had demanded respect for the vodka maker's memory, who controlled the direction of Smirnov's legacy.

Now she was powerless. Less than four months after Smirnov's death, Mariya died on March 7, 1899. As with her husband, newspapers carried prominent announcements about her passing. The typeface was large and surrounded by thick framing. Most of the news was perfunctory, noting the date and time of the funeral. She would be buried March 9 next to her husband, memorialized in the same church he had been. Smirnov's shops, warehouses, and factory would be closed out of respect. The *Moscow Sheet*, a paper read mostly by the lower classes, addressed Mariya's death more creatively. She was a curiosity of sorts for its readers, a wealthy, high-profile widow who was a prime target for gossip seekers. The *Sheet* took full advantage, publishing a fictional, largely inaccurate conversation between two women:

-Maybe you've heard? Mariya Nikolayevna gave her soul to God.

-She was a true beauty. She was going to keep on living. Pyotr Arsenievich left her two million rubles in his will.

-What happened to her?

-People say she had heart pain. And she hasn't left a will. Her kids will have everything.

-What a pity. How many kids did she leave?

-People say she had three.

-What do you say, darling? She had more, about five, hadn't she?

-The other two had another mother. They are not counted here.

-I guess they will give money to the poor people to pray for her soul.

Mariya Nikolayevna Smirnova's death caused a lot of talk in the merchant's society. Nobody thought she was going to die so fast. Let the peace stay with her ashes. [5]

That peace soon disappeared: Smirnov was dead; Mariya was dead; the twentieth century was dawning—and nothing would ever be the same.

PART II

Chapter 15

A New Century, a New Reality

Russia came into the twentieth century resembling a tree in early autumn. All of its leaves were still intact and bountiful, some even quite beautiful. But they had begun to lose their vibrancy. A gradual weakening was taking place, brought on by the country's increasingly contentious political, economic, and social realities. Though few said so openly, there was a growing sense among certain sectors that it was only a matter of time before the nation, like the decaying leaves, fell to the ground exhausted. Tsarist Russia could only hang on for so long.

The emerging difficulties could be traced to a series of contradictory yet telling circumstances. Economically, Russia had made great strides throughout the 1890s. Production in industries such as coal, steel, iron, and oil had tripled. Railroad mileage had doubled, placing Russia second only to the United States. Foreign capital, led by money from France, Belgium, and Germany, had poured into as many as half of Russia's corporations. By 1900 few could credibly challenge the notion that Russia had taken its place among the leading developing nations of the world. The historian Gregory Freeze wrote that Russia's rate of industrial growth through the 1890s would not recur until the 1930s and that industrial production, which increased an average of 8 percent per year, was higher than even that of the United States.[1]

The story was a powerful one, even though it had come at the expense of the majority of Russians. About 80 percent of the citizenry were tied in some way to agriculture, which contributed about half of the nation's income. The largesse from Witte's capitalistic drive toward modernization had not filtered down to them. Instead, most peasants grappled with high taxes and the inability to buy land offered to them after emancipation. In general, their standard of living, far from improving, was deteriorating, and they were not alone in their frustration. Members of the emerging working class, which flocked to the big cities in search of jobs, were voicing grievances of their own. Many endured brutal working conditions, long hours, paltry wages, and substandard living situations. These two seemingly disparate groups found common ground with other such disaffected circles as conservative intellectuals, who feared that Russia's tilt to the West would contaminate its beloved heritage, and an increasingly active socialist movement germinating on university campuses across the country.

The budding resentments, which were fomenting in almost every stratum of society, intensified even more as a worldwide financial downturn settled in. Unemployment spiked, factory production sank, wages dropped, and businesses went bankrupt. All this distress came at a time when the state's budget and spending had mushroomed out of control. "The country was seething with discontent and unrest," wrote David Floyd.[2]

Inside the Smirnov's insulated household, the sentiment was much different. The deaths of Pyotr and Mariya, sad as they were, also had a liberating effect on a number of the Smirnov siblings. No longer did they need to keep their conduct in check.

No longer did they need Smirnov's approval for their choice of lovers or extravagant spending habits. No longer did they feel compelled to pretend to be something they either were not or resented. They were young, beautiful, wealthy—and now free. This emancipation, though, came at a price. Much like their homeland, the Smirnovs had begun to fracture. The common bonds of blood were thinning, strained as personal differences surfaced and financial interests began to collide. In this sense, the Smirnovs were not so different from their motherland. Both faced a polarizing uncertainty—one that would ultimately send them down a calamitous, destructive path.

LESS THAN TWO months after Mariya's death, the seven remaining shareholders in Smirnov's vodka empire assembled at the house by the Cast Iron Bridge for their annual board meeting.[3] They climbed to the second floor of the elegant mansion and settled into their seats. The room was exquisite; the ceiling resembled an artistic sculpture, full of elaborate floral motifs cast throughout the periphery of its surface. The windows were elongated with lovely rounded tops that captured the natural light as it filtered in. A heating oven enveloped by an opulent frame filled up an entire corner, though on this spring day it remained unlit and cool.

Most often, the board meeting was a routine affair, a yearly gathering held every April. Shareholders would conduct a detailed review of the state of the business and then make preparations for the coming year. But the April 28, 1899, assembly was anything but typical. The usual course of business needed to be suspended so a new order could be crafted. By this time Smirnov had been dead for five months, and his absence left a gaping, unpredictable hole in the proceedings. Thirty-one-year old Pyotr Petrovich now occupied his father's old chair, the obvious and unanimous choice to do so. His brothers, Nikolay, now twenty-six, and Vladimir, twenty-four, took up two other places at the table while a guardian representing the interests of the two youngest brothers occupied another spot. The remaining seats were reserved for cousins Nikolay Venediktovich Smirnov and Dmitriy Venediktovich Smirnov, both of whom had been with the company for twenty-five years, and for Vasiliy Kouvaldin, a long-time employee who was close to the business and Smirnov's family. The three eldest Smirnov sons and their cousin Nikolay Venediktovich held the majority votes on the board, giving them ultimate control. The other attendees were nonvoting shareholders.

The exact agenda of the meeting is unknown. What *is* known, according to a financial report issued by the Ministry of Finance for 1899, is the substance of the most critical actions of the day. These details provide ample evidence as to the long-term intentions and aspirations of Smirnov's sons. At this time, the vodka firm was still thriving. The previous year had delivered the largest-ever profit for the enterprise, more than 1 million rubles.[4] The bounty was due in part to Smirnov's keen foresight and business acumen, which had not only cushioned the company but had enabled it to prosper during treacherous market conditions. It was also the result of an unforeseen outgrowth of the state's vodka and temperance initiatives. According to published accounts, the closer the date came to implementing the monopoly in certain communities and cities, the more money consumers spent stocking up on their favorite, soon-to-be-vanishing brands of vodka. Sales of Smirnov's liquors, as well as Popov's, soared in 1898 when the monopoly came to larger population centers like St. Petersburg.[5] The purchases fell into two categories: The vodka was either being preserved for personal use during future occasions or used as a means for turning an illegal profit later.

Smirnov's sons were smart enough to see that this spike in profits would be a temporary phenomenon. Consequently, they did not hesitate to take full personal advantage of the good times. They had lavish lifestyles to support. Pyotr had purchased one of the most elaborate homes in all of Moscow. It was a second home, a showplace designed by the renowned architect Fyodor Shekhtel, and Pyotr used it most often for entertaining members of the Russian establishment. His primary residence was most likely his father's home by the Cast Iron Bridge. Vladimir's indulgences were also many, including underwriting theater performances, buying expensive gifts for women, and hosting his favored actors and actresses at grand after-performance parties. In the late 1890s, he had also purchased a 740-acre estate some fifty-four miles west of Moscow. It was a spectacular country hideaway complete with its own electric power source, boat dock, stables, and horse-racing track.[6] As for Nikolay, he had resumed his drinking habit in the wake of Smirnov's death, spending money without restraint. Often seen buying precious jewels from Moscow's most exclusive retailers, he was also known in shady circles for lending significant amounts of money to people he barely knew in exchange for an informal, most often worthless IOU.

The Smirnov brothers, for the first time in the history of the company, proposed that board members be given yearly bonuses. Select employees would also be eligible for the additional payouts, though presumably at a rate much less than the directors. They voted to put aside a pot totaling 64,000 rubles (the equivalent of about $33,000 in 1899 and more than $851,000 in today's dollars) to split as the bonus for 1898.[7] All three of the eldest Smirnov sons would receive checks despite Nikolay's recent appointment to the revision committee. The two youngest sons, since they were only shareholders, would not receive a cut. Pyotr headed off any objection his younger brothers or their guardian might have had by also proposing a dividend hike. Instead of garnering the previous year's 1,000 rubles per share, stockholders would now get 1,425 rubles. A total of 855,000 rubles ($441,341 then and more than $11 million now) would be paid out to the handful of shareholders. This dividend came on top of the 300,000 rubles in cash each son had already collected as part of the inheritance from Smirnov's estate.*

The escalation of these payouts continued unabated as the monopoly spread. The following year, bonuses jumped to almost 80,000 rubles. And in 1901, the year the monopoly was to be implemented in Moscow, the Smirnovs enjoyed an unprecedented windfall. Muscovites bought up barrels of Smirnov's vodka, helping push profits to a record 1.8 million rubles.[8] Consequently, the brothers voted to split 226,000 rubles (about $117,000 then or more than $2.9 million today) in bonuses, triple the amount from the previous year.[9]

Aside from these financial machinations, the Smirnovs also took up the company's management structure and spearheaded a shakeup of the board's oversight committee. This maneuver was especially telling because, in addition to verifying financial reports, the committee also had a policing role. The panel had the authority to investigate any questionable or suspicious actions by management or the board. Smirnov's sons named their own wives to replace a cousin and a loyal accountant who had worked for Smirnov for many years. Having the Smirnov women in charge of an oversight function, even though by then Vladimir's and Nikolay's wives were their partners in name only, was an easy, efficient way to consolidate information and influence within the bounds of the family.

Smirnov himself would have been pleased to see all three of his eldest sons seated at the helm of his empire. It had been one of his greatest wishes. But it is highly unlikely that he would have condoned the blatant self-dealing—or the beginning signs of divisiveness that would soon transform brothers into warring factions.

---

* The five sons and Mariya were each left 260,000 rubles in cash. After Mariya's death, her share was, as far as anyone knows, divided equally among the sons.

. . . .

THE BROTHERS DID not begin in battle. Indeed, following Mariya's death, the dynamic among the brothers appeared to be harmonious and loving. Both Pyotr and Vladimir applied to the court to take over guardianship of their youngest brothers. Pyotr, who had a solid track record of charitable giving and religious activities, was appointed guardian over Sergey. Vladimir's application, however, was rejected. The court determined that his penchant for gambling and overall poor reputation would not be in ten-year-old Aleksey's best interests. "His sinful behavior was the reason why the court refused to allow him to be my younger brother Aleksey's guardian," explained Sergey later, adding that his brother was "known all over Moscow for his passion for the [horse] races and for [betting on horses]."[10] Konstantin Bakhrushin, Smirnov's portly son-in-law and chosen executor, was appointed Aleksey's guardian instead.

The rejection should not have come as a great surprise. Although Vladimir could appear the responsible, upstanding citizen when necessary, his natural disposition was much more whimsical. He liked nothing better than a good time—whether playing cards, betting on horses, partying at one of Moscow's nightclubs, or attending his own, frequently raucous fetes. "Vladimir enjoyed lively, cheerful company. Artists from the opera, operetta, theater, and farce often came to his home," recalled Vladimir's third wife, Tatiana Smirnova-Maksheyeva.[11] She wrote that among the frequent guests to Vladimir's home was Varya Panina, one of Russia's best-known gypsy singers. She had gotten her break singing at Yar, the wildly popular night spot in Moscow where years ago Vladimir had met his first love, Katya. Panina, known for her low, seductive voice and perpetually lit cigarettes, was a favorite of Chekhov, Tolstoy, as well as the tsar.

This was the company Vladimir liked best. Despite being married to Mariya Gavrilovna, he strutted around town like a committed bachelor. Jovial, light-hearted, and handsome, Vladimir was often seen out with members of Moscow's theater community, cavorting with various women at Yar. This playfulness might have gone on for years had it not been for Aleksandra Nikitina.

Nikitina was classically beautiful. Everything about her, from her soft eyes to her elegant nose to her diminutive stature, was lovely and feminine. Her sister, Mariya Nikitina, was well regarded for her work in operettas and for performing with a well-known acting troop. Aleksandra Nikitina performed in the troop as well, which was how Vladimir, a fan, most likely met her.

The two fell in love. They carried on their affair openly, caring little about Vladimir's marital status or the scandal the relationship could spark. Soon, they were living together, with Vladimir continuing to support his wife in a luxurious manner. It had likely been a loveless marriage from the beginning, constructed out of practicality. Nikolay, who also carried on with other women while married, commented: "My brother Vladimir also spends money for a woman he lives with, Miss Nikitina—much more than I do. He bought her two houses at considerable expense. He doesn't feel embarrassed about giving gifts to her or other women."[12] Nor was he embarrassed when the two had a child together a year later. It was Vladimir's only child, a son named Vladimir, born to unwed parents. The two eventually married after Vladimir divorced his first wife.

This questionable conduct was not unique to Vladimir. Within a four-year period, four of Smirnov's children had babies out of wedlock, including Vladimir. Aleksandra, the youngest daughter, had a son named Vadim. He was the result of an affair with a well-known merchant named Vasiliy Bostanzhoglo. Aleksandra was still involved with her former lover, Borisovskiy, but Bostanzhoglo, who was married to the sister of famed director and acting pioneer Konstantin Stanislavskiy, was a thrilling diversion. He eventually broke off his relationship with Aleksandra, and when it was over, she was left with little choice but to marry Borisovskiy. Sergey, on the other hand, at just seventeen years of age had his first child. He moved in with the mother of his first son, Oleg, who was joined by brother Viktor later.*

It was as if all the years of Smirnov's strict fathering, the constant preaching of society's expectations and the imperative to meet them, had been abandoned. This second generation followed guideposts of their own making. Their passions, rather than their pasts, ruled their minds, enabling them to inhabit worlds Smirnov would not have dared enter. It was not just their vast inheritances that enabled their carefree behavior, it was also their environment. The Smirnovs had stature, money, and their father's legacy to gloss over whatever they did.

More and more, though, it seemed as if the siblings were monitoring one another like spies. They were taking note of each other's foibles, storing these observations away as defenses against a future assault. Perhaps they already sensed that their alliances were ephemeral, convenient only as long as the status quo could be maintained, which of course it could not. The events of 1901 and beyond left little doubt of that.

---

* This information comes from extensive research conducted by Sergey's son Oleg in the 1970s.

Chapter 16

Monopoly Madness

Evidence of the shifting landscape was inescapable. Scores of neighborhood taverns and liquor shops, once identified by folksy, personal monikers and cozy barrooms, were shuttered. In their place were sterile, state-owned-and-operated outlets. Yellow and green placards hung above the doorways, announcing the class of the establishment where state-produced, 40-degree vodka was now sold. Inside, the scene was sobering. Nothing except a religious icon, pictures of the tsar or saints, a clock, and announcements related to the rules and regulations of the monopoly could appear on the walls. A partition cut the hallowed room in half. The bottom of the partition was all wood while the top was made of wire mesh. On one side, workers collected money through a small window while other workers handed off bottles of purchased vodka through another opening.

Swarms of thirsty, sometimes raucous, customers packed these shops starting at seven o'clock in the morning. Often, so many people showed up that they spilled out onto the streets; while they waited, they would play cards or dominoes. Sometimes, they just lingered, swallowing newly purchased vodka despite strict laws forbidding drinking on the premises or in public. Observed one contemporary outside a shop one morning: "There is a line of about a hundred people who have lost themselves with drinking and are ragged. They are waiting for the door to open, when it will be possible to go inside under the yellow-green sign. They are waiting, shivering in the cold."[1] It was 1901—and the vodka monopoly had come to Moscow.

The changes were jarring. According to one source, whereas 2,664 locations sold alcohol in the Moscow province before the monopoly, fewer than 870 now did. The number of state vodka shops, which totaled 513 a year earlier, was just 260. And the number of inns in towns surrounding Moscow, those that operated like taverns or cafes, had plummeted from more than 900 in 1900 to just 60.[2] It was a difficult adjustment in general but particularly trying in Moscow, which had served as the home base for many of Russia's most beloved vodka brands. "Those who have been far away from Moscow . . . and have had no chance before to see the monopoly in Moscow were surprised. They could not recognize their favorite restaurants and they were shocked by the appearance of new wine [vodka] shops and by the abundance of monopoly signs. . . . A merchant can't find Smirnov's vodka, to which he has gotten used to over many years. He's offered only the . . . state vodka, which may be good but is unknown to him."[3]

The mood was equally unsatisfying—and downright somber— at Smirnov's vodka factory during the last day of its operations. According to a newspaper photograph, men wearing long white aprons and dark caps darted in between a maze of large wooden barrels that sat motionless in the middle of a dirt courtyard. These barrels most likely had been removed from Smirnov's storage area inside, no longer required for housing his vodkas. Men were hauling away large wooden crates, which might have been used for boxing up glass bottles. In the background, a tall ladder stretched to the top floor of Smirnov's building. It was closing day: no one in the photograph was smiling.[4]

The Smirnovs, of course, had no intention of fading away. Apart from the state prohibition against producing pure vodka, they were allowed to sell a variety of other, less popular alcoholic beverages. In an announcement that ran on the front page of the *Moscow Sheet* just days after the monopoly's official start, the Smirnovs made it clear that they were still very much in business.

> The Administration of the association of P. A. Smirnov has the honor to inform our dear customers that as a consequence of the implemented state monopoly on [vodka], our exports to nonmonopoly provinces and abroad will continue without interruption while production of [flavored] vodkas, nalivkas, and liqueurs has increased considerably. We especially recommend our Russian and foreign grape wines and Russian and foreign cognacs, which are stored in our cellars for many years.[5]

Smirnovs' sons fought to stay afloat. In addition to commercial advertisements, they introduced a variety of cost-cutting measures to combat slumping sales and dropped their father's lifelong demand that all Smirnov liqueurs be flavored only with fresh fruit. Instead, they began using essences, a much less expensive alternative. "Thanks to this, we were able to deal with the losses that occurred due to the introduction of the state monopoly over liquor," recalled Vladimir.[6]

Other adjustments were flashier and riskier. Vladimir recounted to Smirnova-Maksheyeva the story of an especially creative spectacle the sons concocted for one of the fairs at Nizhniy Novgorod. He and his brothers wanted to stand out, to demonstrate that they were still owners of a flourishing enterprise. They erected a stage in the main pavilion, which was grand and luxurious. They then hired bears who walked around a large stage, danced, bowed, and brought people drinks. "This unprecedented spectacle and free refreshments attracted a huge number of people. The crowd was dense. It was hard to move through it. Everyone wanted to toast with the bear."[7]

All the bears, except two held tightly by a leash, according to Vladimir, had been either people in bear costumes or wind-up animals. The live bears had been "fed so much vodka that they could not stand. First, they lowered themselves onto all four paws, then sat down and then finally fell asleep. Bears are big lovers of vodka. You did not need to ask them to drink it. They drank willingly, holding the bottle in their front paws."[8] The Smirnovs later ran advertisements featuring bears holding Smirnov bottles.

The scheme may have grabbed people's attention, but it did little to prop up sales. Significant layoffs at the factory followed; contracts with bottlers, label suppliers, and cork-makers were either cancelled altogether or significantly scaled back. These measures helped some, but in the first year after the monopoly came to Moscow, the Smirnovs' losses were devastating. Profits sank by a factor of four, from 1.8 million to 441,000 rubles.[9] While the monopoly was by far the primary reason for the collapse in business, it was not the only reason. The Smirnovs, along with the state, were also battling the growing threat of bootleggers.

These bootleggers were like parasites multiplying faster than authorities could hunt them down, expert at disappearing into their secret hideaways, the crevices buried deep within a neighborhood's routine comings and goings. Sometimes they purchased the state's vodka and resold it. Other times, they distilled their own vodka concoctions, selling them to eager consumers at prices that undercut the government. Beyond the alcohol, the most enterprising bootleggers also provided a social environment, similar to the speakeasies that would later sprout up all over America during prohibition. These places enabled Russians to drink together outside their homes. Satirical magazines chronicled the unsavory trend as if it were commonplace. One cartoon featured a crowd of innkeepers running frantically trying to capture a stick inscribed with nothing but the word "secret."[10]

No one seemed to care that the punishment for making moonshine or selling it was time in prison. Demand was simply too great and the police, for the most part, tended to look the other way. "Following the imposition of the monopoly, without exaggeration, one can say that for each ten peasant households there is one bootleg establishment."[11]

The abuses proliferated, even inside state-sponsored anti-alcohol locations. Teahouses, for instance, established as part of the sobriety movement, were meant to be a gathering place for Russians, offering entertainment and socially acceptable alternatives to drinking liquor. Newspapers reported, however, that some of these venues were known to pour vodka—not tea—straight from their kettles.

Perhaps most disturbing was the exponential rise in public drunkenness. Since consumers could no longer drink in taverns or inns, they took to the streets. They were aided by cunning entrepreneurs who tried to capitalize on the trend by supplying everything from drinking glasses to corkscrews—for a fee. In her book *Under the Influence*, the historian Kate Transchel writes, "Drinking did not abate but merely moved from the tavern into the streets."[12] A *New York Times* columnist observed: "Official and unofficial reports from all parts of European Russia agree in stating that the most noticeable result of the establishment of the Government monopoly is the great and alarming increase of street drunkenness and disorder. A peasant now buys a bottle of vodka, carries it away, and drinks himself into a state of helpless or quarrelsome intoxication."[13]

The tsar had some consolation while trying to tame the

nation's alcohol addiction. His treasury ballooned. In the year
following adoption of the monopoly in all provinces, the state
took in more than 488 million rubles compared to 23 million
during the first year of the monopoly. At its height in 1913, the
year before complete prohibition was instituted, more than 953
million rubles were collected as a direct result of the liquor monopoly.[14] A comparison of liquor revenues in 1909 illustrates just
how beneficial the monopoly was for the government. Had the
excise system remained in place, liquor sales for that year would
have generated 371 million rubles.[15] Under the monopoly, the
government's proceeds were greater than 720 million rubles.[16]

In 1901 the tsarist regime downplayed the financial aspects
of the reform. Its implications paled in comparison to other
issues confronting the administration. Violence and deep-
seated resentment were on the rise, made worse by the tsar's increasingly hard-line policies. The state had begun to arrest and
punish students who participated in protests or distributed antigovernment propaganda. One measure enabled the monarchy
to force these young rebels into the Russian Army. The tsar's
minister of education, Nikolay Bogolepov, ordered 183 students
at the St. Vladimir University in Kiev into the military. He also
fired a number of professors who openly opposed the autocracy.
Within short order, Bogolepov was fatally shot in the neck by a
student expelled from a university in Moscow for his revolutionary activities. Soon after, the minister of domestic affairs, Dmitriy Sipyagin, a hard-liner who backed several harsh measures
aimed at noncompliant workers, peasants, and students, was also
assassinated. Two years later, Sipyagin's successor, Vyacheslav
Pleve, was blown up by a terrorist's bomb.

Labor disputes had also turned more combative. In May
1901, a strike at the Obukhov steel plant in St. Petersburg was
sparked by the firing of twenty-six metal workers. They had not
shown up for their jobs on May Day, a workers' holiday. Several thousand employees gathered outside the factory less than

a week later demanding that the fired employees be reinstated. They also presented a litany of other demands, including wage increases and a shorter workday. The steel factory had approximately twenty socialist circles operating within it, evidence of the increasingly political nature of strikes, which prompted police to come to the demonstration prepared to fight. Laborers who battled back with stones were overpowered, but the confrontation set the stage for more bloody strikes.

Nikolay II also faced a growing chorus of high-profile critics. Tolstoy, who sympathized with the protesters and much of the underclass, was one of the most outspoken. His uncensored barrage of critiques and a large, loyal following contributed to his excommunication from the Russian Orthodox Church in 1901. His crime: heresy. In his writings, particularly in his last novel, *Resurrection*, he denounced the church, Russia's government, and the country's antiquated social customs. He supported the student uprisings, lambasted the monarchy's increasing censorship, and championed the needs of the poor. Finally, he directed his appeals to the tsar himself in a passionate letter dated January 16, 1902. He pleaded for reforms that would aid impoverished peasants and suggested that the ways of the monarchy no longer met the people's needs. The fervent entreaty, along with other anti-tsarist chants, only seemed to embolden Nikolay II—he dug in his heels.

THE SMIRNOVS DUG in, too. Whether it was the turmoil engulfing Russia or the overriding uneasiness seeping into the heart of the vodka clan itself, the siblings took up battle stations. The war began in earnest in 1901, the same year Moscow's vodka trade came under the government's control. At first, it appeared to be no more than a few simple legal maneuvers aimed at divvying up assets equitably among family members. Smirnov's sons and their still-unmarried sister, Aleksandra, jointly owned their father's various properties, but they decided it would be better for the youngest sons to own property individually instead of as part of a group. "We don't wish to continue common ownership and we agree to voluntarily divide this property," a legal document signed by the siblings read.

Smirnov's real estate holdings were valued at 1.89 million rubles (about $24.6 million today). Aleksey, the youngest son, would receive seven retail outlets at the Gostiniy Dvor shopping district as well as some land. Sergey would acquire a residence in Moscow, a commercial building near the family mansion, and some retail shops at the Nizhniy Novgorod fair. All the other properties, including the house by the Cast Iron Bridge, the factory, the dachas, and land in Moscow would be owned collectively by Pyotr, Nikolay, Vladimir, and Aleksandra. The siblings who signed the document pledged not to contest its substance. "We are completely satisfied with the given real estate division. We find it to be profitable for the minors [Sergey and Aleksey] . . . We promise not to raise questions about further divisions of the real estate and not to lay claims against one another."[17]

It looked like an amicable, sensible transaction. The Smirnovs, given the nation's precarious state, may have believed that they would be unable to convert so many properties into cash should the need arise. Or they might have worried that disagreements or misunderstandings among them would prevent or delay a necessary sell off. But given what happened next, it appears that the elder Smirnovs may have wanted to preserve the most precious assets for themselves. The real estate division in 1901 turned out to be the first of several divisive actions that ultimately transformed blood brothers into fierce, feuding rivals.

Sergey was the first Smirnov to break from the pack. His youthful face held surprisingly mature features for a sixteen-year-old, and he had a confidence about him that he inherited from his father. His dark hair, thick brows, and dark peach-fuzz

mustache gave Sergey the look of someone who was fearless—
and he was. Having been orphaned at the age of thirteen years,
Sergey had grown up fast.

He had been under Pyotr's guardianship since Mariya's
death. The two, with a seventeen-year age gap between them,
were not as close to one another as the three older brothers,
but they appeared to have a decent relationship. When Sergey
began romancing a singer he met at the Yar nightclub, Pyotr
sent him money to woo her. He also helped him buy horses from
Vladimir and paid to spruce up the house Sergey had been al-
located in the real estate agreement. Still, relations between the
two began to deteriorate shortly after the monopoly came to
Moscow. When Sergey turned seventeen in April 1902, he successfully petitioned to have Pyotr replaced as his guardian. The
two had been increasingly at odds over what the older brother
termed Sergey's "wastefulness."

Soon after, Pyotr teamed up with Vladimir and petitioned
the court to appoint a new guardian over Sergey, at least until
he turned twenty-one. In legal filings, they claimed that Sergey
was squandering his inheritance. Nikolay was not a part of this
effort, presumably, because of his own extravaganzas. Sergey
fired back in filings with the court that his brothers were spread-
ing lies about him in an attempt to discredit him and gain greater
control over the family business. "My brothers say they have the
best intentions toward me. . . . I find it necessary to explain that
only self interest motivates my brothers." He pointed to the salaries the brothers paid themselves as well as the bonuses to make
his case. "My older brothers, having the majority of voices [in
the company], chose themselves to be directors of the company.
They gave themselves each a 60,000 rubles salary yearly and
70,000 rubles bonus, even when the company started to suffer
because of the introduction of the monopoly. Objections by my
younger brother's guardians couldn't change anything."[18]

In a letter to Moscow's general-governor dated July 6, 1902,

Sergey outlined the ugly charges against him as well as his strident rebuttal.

My brothers Pyotr and Vladimir spread rumors about me—that I have a passion for gambling, that I play the stock market, that I bet on horse races. They say this has led me to a situation of debts. . . . All these accusations, from the beginning to the end, are the fruits of pure imagination. I've never been to the stock exchange and I've never participated in such speculations. I also haven't gambled in a long time and I haven't visited the horse races for a long time. About a year ago I did visit the races several times and sometimes gambled, investing negligible sums of money. My brother, my guardian, knew it. All this was done just to have fun and it was done under the influence of my brother, Vladimir, who is known all over Moscow for his passion for the races and gambling. . . . My brothers Pyotr and Vladimir find it immoral and wasteful that I have lived with one woman for some time and that I spend a lot of money to support her. This is the only thing among their accusations that has some merit. But it is necessary to take into consideration some facts that accompanied my getting closer to this woman. My brother, Pyotr Petrovich, before accusing me, should have remembered that this affair started while he was my guardian and he knew about it and assisted me with it by giving me three times more money than I had received before when we started living together. My other accuser, Vladimir, openly left his wife to live with another woman. His sinful behavior was the reason why the court refused to allow him to be my young brother Aleksey's guardian. As for me, I'm physically older than my true age. I was scared about the possibility of getting a bad [venereal] disease. So I found a solution. Nobody can charge me with having close relations with other women. I don't drink vodka. I don't smoke. I did have to spend money on this woman but the expenses . . . are greatly exaggerated by my brothers.[19]

Sergey's letter covered other alleged extravagances as well as his charge that Pyotr's and Vladimir's actions were motivated by greed. Their goal, he argued, was nothing more than obtaining as much control as possible of their father's enterprise. As it turned out, Sergey's arguments carried the day. The court declined the request for new guardianship, but his success was fleeting. The elder Smirnovs, helpless to stop the hemorrhaging of their father's business, decided to restructure it. This time, Nikolay was given a role. He explained the troika's thinking in a letter to company management. "As a consequence of the state vodka monopoly, trade operations of the Association [of P. A. Smirnov] have decreased considerably. . . . I ask the administration to call an urgent meeting of shareholders to address the question of the Association ceasing."[20] The brothers argued that the company's capital, 3 million rubles, far exceeded the income generated by liquor sales and that it no longer made sense to continue conducting its affairs under the same business framework.

An emergency shareholder meeting was called for eleven o'clock on the morning of November 20, 1902.[21] According to affidavits, Pyotr, as chairman, proposed that the company be dissolved. Then, Bakhrushin, Aleksey's guardian, spoke up. He was furious that he had neither been given better notice of the meeting nor a financial report outlining the reasons behind the proposed reorganization. Sergey echoed Bakhrushin's complaints and asked that they be given more time to study the issue.

The majority of the shareholders did not want more time. Nine shareholders wrote their votes on secret ballots, which were placed in a closed envelope. The ballots were counted: seven shareholders favored the dissolution while two, Bakhrushin and Sergey, voted against it. Incensed, both stormed out of the meeting in protest. The remaining shareholders formed a committee to head up the process of winding down Smirnov's forty-two-year-old empire. It took just two days for a petition on the company's dissolution to be drafted and sent to the minister of finance for approval.

Bakhrushin, a favored son-in-law, could not sit by idly while the company his wife's father had spent a lifetime building simply vanished. He, too, in collaboration with Sergey, sent a letter to the finance minister. He argued that the eldest Smirnov sons were essentially looting the vodka business and hurting the two youngest Smirnov boys. As evidence, Bakhrushin pointed to the annual salaries and bonuses the brothers awarded to themselves.

The greatest injustice, according to Bakhrushin and Sergey, was the intention of Pyotr, Nikolay, and Vladimir to purchase *all* the assets of their father's company at a steep discount. These assets included the remaining real estate, inventory, and supplies, valued at more than 3.2 million rubles. The brothers proposed to pay 2.2 million rubles. Sergey and Aleksey were conspicuously excluded from the buyout plan.

The objections were filed in a letter dated December 7, 1902, but they were too late. By the time they arrived in St. Petersburg, Witte's office had already rubber-stamped the dissolution papers. By November 30 Smirnov's three eldest sons owned the remnants of his liquor firm; by December 3 a new trading house, a private one without outside shareholders, had been founded. Its name: A Trading House: Pyotr, Nikolay, and Vladimir Smirnov, trading under the company P. A. Smirnov in Moscow. The threesome represented the company's sole members, with equal say about its future. They intended to carry on, as much as possible, in the same traditions as their father, but one thing would never be the same: the Association of Pyotr Arsenievich Smirnov, just four years after his death, was gone forever.

Chapter 17

From Bad to Bizarre

Nikolay Petrovich was never the same after his father died. He had always been a nervous personality, unsure of his place in the family, anxious in its business matters, and uncomfortable in obligatory societal affairs. Smirnov had likely fretted about his second-born son, but he steadfastly provided a pivotal service to him, offering up solid moral and emotional guideposts to make sure that Nikolay not lose his way. With the patriarch gone, no one was left to shield him from his self-destructive impulses; no one was strong enough to keep his demons in check.

While Nikolay closely aligned himself with Pyotr and Vladimir when it came to decisions affecting the vodka business or family matters, his attentions were far from the company's boardroom. He was again drinking heavily, and his drunken binges could last weeks or several months at a time. A constant fixture at Moscow's toniest nightclubs and gambling halls, known throughout town for recklessly showering money over virtually anyone who had the gumption to ask for it, Nikolay did not seem to care how much he spent or what he bought—or for whom. Nikolay was a multimillionaire and he seemed to feel that he was more than entitled to his indulgences.

His marriage to Darya Nikolayevna, except in law, had been over for years. Still, perhaps out of guilt for his absenteeism and behavior toward her, Nikolay bought her a barrage of expensive gifts. These presents included a primary residence near the Red Square as well as a second home near his family's dacha. The total cost: 425,000 rubles (roughly $5.6 million today).[1] Nikolay explained later in legal documents his rationale for the largess: "I believe it is absolutely appropriate. By making this gift . . . I meant to improve the strength of our marriage and to provide a future for our possible descendants. In the case of a divorce from my wife, by offering her such a big gift, I would consider myself to have met my [financial] obligations toward her" (ibid., 24).

Nikolay often hatched schemes to appease his wife or evoke sympathy from her. Once, according to a police affidavit, he simulated a suicide. In his drunken, paranoid state, he took a gun and locked himself in his room in their home, fired a shot into the ceiling, then took some red ink and painted his temple to make it look bloodied (ibid., 37 [affidavit of Oct. 24, 1903]). Even though it was all a ridiculous act, he likely hoped Darya would see how troubled he was. Then, he reasoned, she would forgive him for his transgressions. She did not—especially after he began openly courting another woman, who was also married, in 1902. Darya instead became enraged and demanded 24,000 rubles annually for the rest of her life, in addition to sole title to the properties her husband had purchased for her (ibid.).

Nataliya Trukhanova was Nikolay's new love interest. She was a twenty-one-year-old singer at Omon's Theater, a popular performing venue located in a park known as Aquarium. Vladimir knew Trukhanova from his own escapades around town and characterized her as a common prostitute. He told police that

Trukhanova, who sang under the pseudonym of Tarnovskaya, behaved no differently than the other gypsy singers (ibid., 17 [evidence by V. Smirnov re: guardianship of N. P. Smirnov]). Police reports verify Vladimir's assessment of her through an associate of Trukhanova's named Ivan Morozov. He was a pimp for the women working at Omon's Theater and he "accompanied this coquette [Trukhanova] everywhere" (ibid., 16).

Nikolay fell hard for Trukhanova, and she used his weakness for her to great advantage. In one year he spent 65,000 rubles at one of Moscow's most exclusive jewelry stores. Among other gifts, he purchased a gold matchbox made with sapphires and diamonds, a pair of earrings with two emeralds and twenty-four diamonds, and a silver serving spoon for fish that cost twenty-five rubles (ibid., 32–34). Nikolay had always been extravagant, but now under Trukhanova's influence, all manner of rational thinking seemed to have left him. Explained Vladimir: "Five years ago, after our father's death, my brother Nikolay Petrovich received an overall amount of about 3 million rubles. . . . [This was equivalent to about $1.5 million in 1898.] Then, as a member of the Society, he received dividends of about 400,000 rubles before the monopoly was established. He has spent all that money" (ibid., 17 [evidence by V. Smirnov re: guardianship of N. P. Smirnov]).

Initially, Pyotr and Vladimir tolerated their brother's erratic and irresponsible conduct. But when Trukhanova entered his life, their patience evaporated. They went to court together to have him declared incompetent to manage his own financial affairs. It was a difficult and embarrassing undertaking that involved filing a petition with the Moscow general-governor, packed with evidence of their brother's pattern of wild, scandalous behavior. Police reports were filed, too, sparked by the multitudes of people who swindled Nikolay out of money or property. The court collected numerous affidavits attesting to Nikolay's antics and questionable state of mind.

At first Nikolay agreed to the guardianship his brothers sought for him, petitioning the court for assistance on his own behalf. But he quickly changed his mind, perhaps at Trukhanova's urging, once he realized how hampered his lifestyle would be without control of his own affairs. "I hadn't understood all the consequences of a guardianship," Nikolay explained in a document requesting the court to rescind his previous petition. He argued that Vladimir was no better than he when it came to morality or excessive spending. "My brother Vladimir . . . also spends money on a woman he lives with, Miss Nikitina. He spends much more than I do. He bought her two houses at considerable expense. He doesn't feel embarrassed about giving gifts to her or to other women that are of no less value than my gifts for Trukhanova" (ibid., 23–24).

For Nikolay, the battle was uphill. He was not fit to rule his own destiny, and his brothers, with the help of cousins, debtors, the police, and an uncooperative Trukhanova, were intent on proving it. In a letter to Moscow's general-governor, Vladimir and Pyotr wrote of their brother, "He is always drunk. . . . His last period of hard drinking lasted for four months. He has gotten involved with courtesans and he spends huge amounts of money on them. Since he no longer has any money, he gives out promissory notes that have no relation to his true financial position" (ibid., 8 [letter from Vladimir and Pyotr Smirnov to Moscow's general-governor, June 1903]).

The accusations mounted. Pyotr assigned blame for the problem largely on alcoholism and Trukhanova. He expressed his concern that if Nikolay were not reined in, he would lose everything, including the 500,000-ruble inheritance he was entitled to when he turned thirty-five. Pyotr noted that Nikolay, then thirty, had already put up as collateral against his debts his share in the house by the Cast Iron Bridge as well as some racehorses he owned. Then Pyotr and Dmitriy Venediktovich Smirnov, one of Smirnov's closest cousins, scrolled down a list of extravagances made on behalf of Trukhanova, including 7,000 rubles at a fashionable dress shop, 30,000 rubles with an exclusive jeweler, and lavish furnishings for her flat (ibid., 18). Nikolay had even ordered an ornate chamber pot for her, which Dmitriy Venediktovich guessed was made of gold and cost upward of 8,000 rubles; the pot was, in fact, made of silver and cost just 200 rubles (ibid. 20, 22). Still, Smirnov's cousin argued, these were not the acts of a rational person. "Under the influence of Trukhanova, Nikolay Petrovich drank so much that he became insane," Dmitriy Venediktovich testified (ibid., 20).

The proof for the insanity claim made by Nikolay's relations came from a statement made to police by Trukhanova herself. She recounted a bizarre episode in which she was called to Nikolay's house by his butler, Grigoriy. He told her that Nikolay planned to commit suicide by hanging himself. She rushed to his home to find that he had not hanged himself but had slashed his own penis instead. "He told me that he had cut off his penis. I sent for a doctor . . . who came and sewed up the wound. According to how the wound looked, I concluded that he, Smirnov, did it while he was drunk," she recalled (ibid., 35 [Trukhanova's affidavit of Oct. 21, 1903]).

Trukhanova tried to minimize the implications of Nikolay's deceptions and self-inflicted injury. She explained that the message about committing suicide was a simple ploy to get her attention and that the cut was nothing serious or life-threatening. She also downplayed the cost of the gifts she received, arguing that they were not as expensive as Nikolay's brothers wanted everyone to believe. Trukhanova also made the case that Nikolay was more than competent to manage his own affairs, despite his ongoing battles with alcohol. "He has recovered and is a perfectly healthy person," she told police (ibid., 37).

Trukhanova's credibility, however, was thin. Too many witnesses provided testimony that ran counter to her claims, including one from a jeweler who worked at Fabergé's shop in Moscow.

According to a statement made to police, Nikolay came into the store to buy some jewelry for Trukhanova. He asked to take twenty-seven diamonds with him "to test them" and make sure they were what his girlfriend wanted. Their cost: 16,000 rubles (about $200,000 today). Trukhanova apparently wanted to make a necklace out of the diamonds. Since Nikolay was a regular customer, the management of the shop agreed to his request. But nearly a month later, the diamonds had neither been returned nor paid for. Moscow's chief of police reported that Trukhanova and her pimp had attempted to take the diamonds to St. Petersburg when police apprehended them (ibid., 47).

The court could not ignore the mountain of evidence and declared Nikolay incompetent. As a consequence, Smirnov's two cousins, Nikolay Venediktovich and Dmitriy Venediktovich, became his guardians. They controlled Nikolay's checkbook, properties, and other financial interests. He would receive a relatively modest allowance of 15,000 rubles annually ($7,711 then, about $187,434 today) to cover his living expenses (ibid., 68). In addition, at the end of 1903, Pyotr sent his brother to an alcohol treatment clinic. It was the right thing for Nikolay at the time, though sadly it would not be enough to put an end to his struggles.

NIKOLAY WAS NOT the only Smirnov brother embroiled in a bizarre legal entanglement in 1903. That same year Vladimir sued his wife, Mariya Gavrilovna Smirnova, claiming that she had ignored his greeting when the two met by happenstance during a summer stroll in Moscow. Worse, she had refused to shake his hand after it was offered. Not long after the incident, Vladimir went to court to seek revenge. He demanded that a house he purchased for Mariya be returned to him. He asserted that he had been humiliated by Mariya because the slight had occurred in front of friends. Moreover, he claimed that the law required a recipient of a gift always to show the gift-giver the proper amount of respect. When an act of "obvious disrespect" had been committed, like Mariya's, the gift had to be returned.[2]

The determination to initiate such a petty claim against Mariya reveals much about Smirnov's third-eldest son. Despite his father's humble roots, Vladimir considered himself a member of the aristocracy, entitled to its privileges and lofty place in the social hierarchy. Vladimir did not deem his own shortcomings as a husband, including a history of infidelity, abandonment, and the fathering of a son by another woman, as justification for his wife's insult. To him, Mariya behaved imprudently, and she needed to be punished for it.

Interestingly, Mariya did not mention her husband's infractions to the court. She seemed to have already accepted that her marriage was doomed. Her interest was solely on preserving her financial position. She filed a counterclaim against Vladimir, arguing that he failed to pay her the 18,000 rubles annually that the two had presumably agreed to as a condition of their separation (ibid.). She asked the court to enforce their agreement. Vladimir replied by urging the court to force his wife to move back in with him, a hallow gesture at reconciliation given that he was still living with Aleksandra and their toddler son. More likely, Vladimir made the request to create the public appearance that he was a decent husband, willing to let bygones be bygones. He hoped to convince the court that, if reunited, an alimony payment was unwarranted.

The newspapers delighted in the bickering Smirnovs. Gossip-mongers dove into the sordid details of their relationship while other reports focused on the ridiculous nature of the legal arguments. They reported every titillating hiccup.

Moreover, the news accounts noted, Mariya had good reason to reject Vladimir's proposal that they live together again. "Mariya Gavrilovna Smirnova refused to move back in with her husband. She explained that the motivation for her refusal was her husband's indecent behavior and offensive attitude toward her as a wife and as a woman. As a consequence, Mrs. Smirnova has asked to invite witnesses to testify and the court has agreed" (ibid.).

The account made Vladimir look foolish. It was far more damaging and embarrassing to him than the unrequited handshake. The court sided with Mariya and stuck Vladimir with her legal bills, adding more insult to his injury. Still, Vladimir refused to walk away. "The Court found that the rude treatment did not give Vladimir Petrovich Smirnov the right to ask that his presents be returned," his lawyer wrote in his appeal. "Also, the Court found that the significance of the case was diminished by the fact that the spouses had been leading separate lives for quite a long time. . . . There is no doubt that, according to the social circle to which the Smirnovs belong, refusal to shake a hand is a serious offense and can be considered an act of obvious disrespect" (ibid., 2).

Ultimately, Vladimir must have realized his folly. He dropped the case, and the two resolved their differences privately. The incident provides valuable insight into the psyche of the Smirnovs at that time, particularly that of Vladimir. It was a vivid indication of how much trivial matters may have occupied his mind rather than the travails of his own family. Close to home, he had an alcoholic brother who had faked a suicide, cut his own penis, and was frittering away every cent he had. His father's business, once a thriving national treasure, was in disarray. His two younger brothers, having been on the losing end of the company struggle, were now estranged from the core of the family. And his sister, Aleksandra, had married Borisovskiy, a sharp critic and adversary of the three eldest Smirnov brothers.

Russia, too, was slipping further and further into disarray. Strikes were more prevalent, due to political unrest and the growing influence of Vladimir Lenin. While in exile, he wrote his seminal piece titled *What is to be Done*, a pamphlet that out-

lined the framework for a revolutionary organization. At about
the same time that Vladimir was dueling with his wife, Lenin
founded the Bolshevik Party. From afar, he helped organize one
of the largest industrial strikes of the time. It began in Baku,
Azerbaijan, and spread to Ukraine and other southern regions,
ultimately encompassing more than 200,000 workers. They
issued leaflets, demanding not only salary increases and shorter
workdays but also an end to the autocracy.

Of course, the Romanovs still occupied the Imperial Palace
and the tsar was going nowhere. He did, however, conclude that
it was time to end the tenure of Russia's minister of finance,
Sergey Witte. Witte had been increasingly under attack within
the tsar's inner circle and among the conservative nobles for
causing the country's economic woes. They believed the nation's industrial growth was too tied to Witte's aggressive notions of state-sponsored capitalism, which among other things
depended too much on foreign investment and not enough on
reforms within the enormous agrarian economy. He also championed a series of unpopular, seemingly liberal policies that few
if any members of the Imperial Court backed, such as support
for the Jews and the granting of more civil and economic rights
to the peasantry. Witte simply had made too many enemies
during his time, and with the economy sagging, his critics went
on the attack.

On August 3, 1903, the tsar called Witte to his office. After
some customary discussions, he removed him from his ministry post and installed him as the largely powerless head of
the Committee of Ministers, which functioned as an advisory
group to the tsar. The departure of Witte, known to some as
the "father of Russian capitalism," left a void within the tsar's
cabinet. The Western influence he brought to business policies,
along with the conviction he poured into industrialization, were
waning, leaving a lasting impact on his motherland. "Not all
elements of the Witte system came to an end with their author's

fall. . . . But gone was the industrial tycoon's zeal and experience, gone the passionate plea to make rapid industrialization the order of the day. Witte's successors were again products of the bureaucracy."[3]

It is difficult to know how focused the Smirnovs and others within their sphere were on Witte's fall or on the other troubling developments of the day. A wide swath of the aristocrats, statesmen, and prominent merchants had no clear grasp of what these happenings signaled about their own futures. But they would soon pay for that naïveté.

Chapter 18

A War, Uprisings, and Then There Was One

War can be like a mirror. Within its triumphs and failings, leaders see a truthful reflection, an unadulterated and penetrating view of what got them there in the first place—and a sense of what must be done to move beyond the stark realities. In the aftermath of the Crimean War (1854–56), Tsar Aleksander II saw an image he did not like. He could no longer deny his nation's economic, technological, and societal shortcomings, which were exposed by a spectacular loss of human life and the embarrassing snafus of the conflict. The emancipation of serfs followed, along with numerous other reforms, all aimed at reinvigorating and modernizing Russia.

In the early twentieth century, Tsar Nikolay II would face a similar predicament. He did not want to see or acknowledge the depth of discontent surging through his countrymen, but as the country edged closer to war with Japan over Korean and Chinese territories, he would be left with no choice. Combat began in earnest on

February 8, 1904, when Japan launched a surprise attack on Russia's Far Eastern fleet harbored in the Port Arthur naval base. Despite the initial drubbing, the monarchy was confident about its position, certain it would handily defeat Japan and hopeful that it could then use the victory to subdue the burgeoning anti-autocracy movement. As the conflict wore on over the next eighteen months, it became increasingly clear this would not be the hoped-for outcome. Russia was routed on land and at sea, with enormous casualties for both sides. The now-legendary mutiny aboard the battleship *Potemkin*, which began as a protest over the quality of food in the mess hall, became a prophetic symbol of the resentment raging throughout the military ranks and among civilians—before, during, and after the war.

Russia's loss was devastating. The economy stalled as resources were diverted in order to fund the fighting. People suffered, too, with many losing their jobs, unable to scrape together enough money to cover basic needs. Even the tsar himself was a victim of the war. Public opinion about his government soured further, feeding into the heated rhetoric of revolutionaries. "That war, and especially its glaringly unsuccessful conduct and the resulting national humiliation, served to raise the level of political unrest in almost every layer of society and within every political grouping, pushing Russian political dialogue several degrees to the left," wrote one historian.[1]

The war underscored all that ailed Russia, from poverty to unemployment to a lack of workers' rights to estrangement of the classes. It also highlighted the nation's dependence on vodka sales to fill its coffers. Former Finance Minister Witte, who had somewhat resuscitated his career by negotiating an end to the conflict with Japan, spoke out on behalf of many who agitated that increased liquor consumption—and the rising cost of vodka—had helped bankroll the failed war and other unpopular government initiatives. The comments may have been self-serving since Witte had actively advocated for the monopoly as a way to curtail excessive drinking, but they were backed up by striking evidence. During Witte's tenure, per capita consumption between 1893 and 1903 remained relatively static. But in 1904, after the start of the war, it began a steady climb, a progression that critics claimed proved that the state wanted its subjects to drink more. Witte did not temper his views, arguing that the new finance minister, Vladimir Kokovtsov, "directed his attention to the monopoly chiefly from the point of view of profits, to extract maximum returns from the reform. . . . The decrease in drinking was not and will not be a task of the officials, but an increase in the profits from the sale of alcoholic beverages will remain their goal."[2] Cartoons later appeared in publications featuring the tsar getting rich off his drunken subjects.[3]

The hypocrisy was not lost on sympathizers of the revolutionary movement or other disgruntled citizens, some of whom decided to make a political statement out of the monopoly's two-sided agenda. In tandem with other antigovernment strikes and protests, small groups of peasants and laborers organized liquor boycotts in urban neighborhoods and villages. They abstained from drinking vodka or patronizing state liquor shops to cut into the government's revenue stream. The boycotts sometimes turned ugly as riots broke out, destroying state liquor outlets.[4] Other protests were more contained yet also effective. In one St. Petersburg district, for instance, women who were the wives or relatives of disaffected men banded together and forced the closure of all state-run liquor shops and inns.[5]

The tsar may not have wanted to hear the cries of his people or the calls for reform, but they would not be muffled. They reached a crescendo on January 9, 1905, a date that coincidentally would have been Smirnov's seventy-fourth birthday. It was a frigid day; the Neva River was frozen solid and snow blanketed the streets. A metal workers strike in St. Petersburg had occurred some days earlier. The walkout was typical, with demands for higher wages and a reasonable work schedule. But the charismatic leader of the large Russian Factory and Plant Workers Union, Father Georgiy Gapon, wanted to make more of it. He sensed an opportunity to galvanize thousands of his followers and publicly present the tsar with a petition of grievances and demands. They would ask for civil liberties, democratic freedoms, and improved working conditions. They would also call for an end to the autocracy. "Russia is too great and its needs too varied and profuse to be governed by bureaucrats alone," the five-page petition stated. "Popular representation is essential. The people must help themselves and govern themselves."[6]

In the morning, at least an estimated 140,000 working class men, women, and children gathered in locales throughout the city with the intention of uniting at the Winter Palace, Nikolay II's primary residence. They carried religious icons and portraits of the tsar and his wife to demonstrate their devotion and peaceful intentions. The people sang hymns and patriotic songs. As the demonstrators approached the palace gates, armed guards ordered them to halt. Without weapons of their own, they continued on. Maxim Gorkiy, the great socialist and political activist and author, described the crowds he observed in an essay as a "dark, liquid mass."[7]

The leaders of the procession, including Gapon, were only twenty yards from the gates when it is believed that one of the tsar's uncles, Grand Duke Vladimir, panicked and gave the order to fire into the throngs. Pandemonium gripped the terror-stricken crowds. In just a few short minutes, bodies littered the square. Some lay lifeless atop the snow, now stained crimson. Hundreds of others groaned in agony. Elsewhere, near the Neva River, other protesters were shot down in a flurry of gunfire. Few, if any, of the protesters had known that the tsar was away, having left the city a few days earlier.

It would forever be known as Bloody Sunday, an uprising so potent and heart-wrenching that the future of the Romanov dynasty, which had ruled Russia since 1613, was left in serious doubt.

No corner of the empire could escape the chaos and violence that unraveled faster than a tightly bound ball of string. In 1905 alone, an estimated 14,000 strikes hit the motherland, many massive in scope. In Moscow, a walkout of some 60,000 laborers, or 40 percent of the entire workforce, swept in, pounding local commerce. A railroad strike spread throughout the country, eventually encompassing more than 40,000 miles of tracks. Protests at universities throughout Russia were commonplace, with some students forming voluntary armed brigades. Peasants in rural areas revolted, too, seizing estates, crops, and livestock from landowners. Terrorism raged. Grand Duke Sergey Aleksandrovich, the general-governor of Moscow and another uncle to the tsar, was assassinated by a homemade bomb a little more than one month after Bloody Sunday. He was a staunch conservative and a known supporter of the Imperial Court's most repressive edicts. By the end of 1905, some 1,500 government officials had been slain.[8]

The Smirnovs had been one of the grand duke's vodka purveyors as well as the tsar's. The family had been linked to the monarchy for decades, loyal subjects and ardent followers. This association, along with their extraordinary wealth and aristocratic lifestyle, made them prime targets for insurgents who increasingly unleashed their fury on those they considered surrogates for the tsar or enemies of the people. In memoirs recorded by his wife, Vladimir explained the unsettling development. "Under the influence of demoralizing, revolutionary propaganda, the people began to despise the ruling classes, capitalists, landowners, and government officials. Having been thoroughly exposed to this propaganda, the people began to speak out against the 'exploiters,' attack landowners, and burn their estates. Some of the far-left intelligentsia were involved in terrorist activities, robbed banks, made assassination attempts against individuals who occupied administrative positions. The majority of victims were ministers and governors."[9]

Plenty of the victims, though, were like Vladimir himself. His own terrifying accounts of harassment in the wake of the 1905 revolt were indicative of the often spontaneous brutality that infiltrated Russia's cities and towns. One incident occurred at the beginning of what Vladimir thought would be an uneventful trip from Moscow to one of his provincial estates. He had traveled it countless times before, riding in his car, a rare luxury at the time, with his French chauffeur at the wheel.

> Suddenly, a crowd of peasants, armed with staffs and pitchforks, blocked his way. Someone came forward, yelling "Stop! Get out of the car here. We'll show you how to ride around in an automobile while people are starving." After this came a flood of heavy obscenities. The chauffeur stopped the car because otherwise he would have driven over the demonstrators. Vladimir did not falter and immediately ordered him "Allez en avant, ecrasez-les, mais n'arretez pas." (Forward, crush them, but do not stop.) The chauffeur let the car gather speed. The crowd immediately dissolved. No one was hurt but they threw dirt and rocks at the car as it sped away.[10]

The event was frightening, but the second attack was far more pointed as it demonstrated the particular threat faced by the Smirnovs because of their family's liquor heritage. It also illustrated the moblike, random nature of much of the rebellious outbursts. A woman had been hit by a tram in Moscow and killed. She was found clutching a bottle of Smirnov liquor. Bystanders assumed her tragic fate transpired because she was drunk. Whether this was true did not matter, as Vladimir, who had been riding in his carriage near the site of the accident, soon learned:

> Someone in the crowd that had gathered recognized him and started to yell. "This is the vodka man, Smirnov, exploiter and destroyer of the people." They caught onto one of his horses and the crowd surrounded the carriage. They pulled Vladimir out onto the pavement. He would have gotten a good beating but, luckily, policemen who knew and respected the Smirnov family showed up at the scene. They immediately "arrested" Smirnov, holding him arm-in-arm on both sides and calmed the crowd with the promise that they would take him to prison immediately. Then, they took him to the carriage, sat down with him, and safely delivered him home.[11]

No reliable tally exists about the frequency of such attacks at the time. Most were probably minor scuffles, noted by few, but these tense encounters were symbolic of an undercurrent, a swelling of resentment among the population and echoed in the media that the wealthiest members of society had somehow acquired their fortunes through the exploitation of workers and consumers. A study of the business elite from 1840 to 1905 found that "it was extremely unusual to find any suggestion in the leading organs of the Russian press that the fortunes of Russia's successful businessmen might have been attributable to business abilities, entrepreneurial initiative, hard work, intelligence, or other such characteristics. In fact, the very idea that Russian merchants and industrialists might be considered good businessmen, capable of showing initiative and working hard, met with frequent and emphatic denials in the press."[12]

In this electric climate, the Smirnovs, along with much of the establishment, were like salmon swimming upstream. Despite their stature, or because of it, they were lumped together with the emperor as perpetrators of the people's woes. Lenin's pronouncements against capitalism and capitalists, as well as those by a number of other revolutionaries, did not help their cause. Nor did the support many merchants openly demonstrated for the principles being promoted by liberals and revolutionaries. For these elite Russians, the situation in their homeland was turning ominous and they wanted out. In 1905 the government reported a surge in the number of applications for foreign passports and a tenfold increase in the passports being issued daily.[13] The majority of the requests came from Russia's most prosperous citizens, a telling trend but not a full-blown exodus. Most people, like the Smirnovs, insisted that the tumult would ease and resolve itself.

In the two years that featured war with Japan, Bloody Sunday, and countless other episodes of instability, the Smirnovs did nothing visible to rein in their ostentatious propensities or to minimize their public profiles. If anything, they drew more attention to their largesse. It was as if they wanted to prove to all the naysayers that little fundamental had shifted inside Russia. They still topped the nation's pecking order, the rulers of civil society. Vladimir's flamboyant infatuation with horse breeding and racing was one of the most vivid examples of this sentiment. He owned and operated estates that featured high-profile stud farms, a hobby associated with Russia's nobility and most eminent merchants in the early twentieth century. In addition to breeding, Vladimir raced his own horses. One of his trotters, named *Pylyuga*, a derivative of the Russian word for dust, was among the country's most renowned thoroughbreds. This horse won the prestigious Emperor's Prize in 1909.[14] The subject of numerous articles in the media as well as a march composed in his honor, the horse won multiple races, netting more than 138,000 rubles ($1.7 million in today's dollars).[15] Another one of his well-known horses was *Gulyaka Molodoi*. The name, meaning "young playboy," was a testament to his owner's lifestyle. Vladimir basked in the glory of his animals, never shying from the attention it brought to him. It was hardly the kind of undertaking pursued by a doomsayer or someone worried about the future.

Nikolay enjoyed stud farming as well, though he concentrated more on raising carriage and work horses, at least to the extent that his condition would allow.[16] Despite the firm presence of guardians and a stay at an elite alcohol treatment center, Nikolay's destructive behavior continued without interruption. He kept up his drinking binges, which were now intermittently accompanied by hallucinations. Complicating matters further was his continued association with "dark personalities." In a report filed with the Moscow Orphanages Court, his guardians claimed that these unsavory characters went beyond just cheating Nikolay out of his money. Now, they were tutoring him on how to break the law. The guardians alleged that Nikolay had been taught how to bypass his financial restrictions by issuing fraudulent promissory notes. In one case, Nikolay wrote to his wife from the treatment center asking that she get 30,000 rubles for him from someone to whom he had issued a promissory note.[17] The problem was that Nikolay backdated his guarantee to a time before his guardians were put into place. And this act was not the first backdating ploy; Nikolay repeatedly took money from lenders under suspicious circumstances only to find himself unable to repay the loans when they came due.

Pyotr and Vladimir realized Nikolay's troubles and extravagances were not going to disappear any time soon. Moreover, if their brother was not competent enough to manage his personal finances, relationships, or alcohol dependency, then he was certainly not competent enough to serve as a member of the trading house. It was time to cut Nikolay loose. An agreement, blessed by the court, was reached between the brothers and Nikolay's guardians by the end of 1904. It was signed on January 28, 1905, a little less than three weeks after Bloody Sunday. In short, Nikolay Petrovich Smirnov, "who has been limited in his legal capacity for over-extravagance," would receive 500,000 rubles (more than $6 million today) over a five-year period, plus interest.* In exchange, Nikolay gave up any and all claims to his father's company and its assets.[18]

Nikolay was not the only Smirnov to opt for—or be forced into—a hefty payout. Vladimir also cashed out, although the reasons behind his departure are less clear-cut than his brother's. It is undisputed that Vladimir was never devoted to operating or managing his father's empire since his interests lay more in theater, horses, hobnobbing, and in other less structured, less business-oriented activities.

The brothers had perpetually struggled with the liquor business ever since the monopoly took hold. The financial data for 1905 is not known, but it was clear that things were not going well for anyone selling vodka in Russia other than the tsar. One of Smirnov's chief competitors, Bekman & Co., a large St. Petersburg-based outfit, described its "huge losses" resulting from the monopoly. Despite reporting decent sales from other products ranging from flavored vodkas to champagne, Bekman, like Smirnov, could not replicate anything close to its earnings prior to the state's takeover.

The prospect, then, of a windfall large enough to underwrite anything Vladimir might choose to do for the rest of his life, without the headaches of business hassles, would have been an immense temptation. Looking at all the evidence, Pyotr and Vladimir seemed to have enjoyed a warm relationship, they trusted and understood one another. Vladimir might have rea-

* The 500,000 rubles payment is an assumption based on the amount Vladimir officially received for his interest in the family business, though it could have been more. In addition, the agreement was changed in April 1905 to cover eight years.

soned that his father's company had a better shot at survival under Pyotr's firm, singular control. He agreed to sell his third of the family business to his older brother at the end of 1904 for 500,000 rubles to be paid in installments over eight years, plus some additional payments.[19] In addition, and perhaps more importantly, Vladimir gave up his right to everything—from the factory equipment and buildings to the company trademarks, according to the agreement.

When the ink dried, only one Smirnov remained atop the once omnipotent vodka empire; it was a circumstance that would have saddened their father. His valiant efforts to preserve the company for his five sons had failed. Worse, perhaps, the woman with whom his first son had once carried on an illicit affair was now a shareholder in her own right. Pyotr had made the appointment official as soon as his brothers vacated their posts: "I, Pyotr Petrovich Smirnov, remain the sole and entire owner of the said Trading House and the entire business with all its active and passive capital. I will continue to manage its business under the same trademark and to invite new partners in replacement of those who have left. My wife, Eugeniya Ilyinichna Smirnova, will become a partner with conditions described in this agreement and a separate agreement to be prepared. However, the right to administer and manage the complete business without exception of acts and documentation belongs to me."[20]

The second tangle over control of Smirnov's firm was over. Like the dizzying strife swallowing up Russia, this tussle had been emotional and contentious. In the end, though, Moscow had a new vodka king. His name, not surprisingly, was still Pyotr Smirnov. And Russia, thanks to the October 1905 "October Manifesto," which was a comprehensive guarantee of civil rights, had the beginnings of a democracy. The tsar, under extreme pressure, agreed to grant his subjects such liberties as the freedom of speech, conscience, association, and assembly. In addition, he established the State Duma, the people's representative with authority to approve—or reject—laws backed by the monarch.

Whether either newfangled institution, the state's or Smirnov's, would flourish was an open question. Both were committed to trying, unsure of which steps to take next. On the night after signing the manifesto, Nikolay II wrote in his diary: "After such a day, the head is grown heavy and thoughts are confused. May the Lord help us save and pacify Russia."[21] Pyotr might have written the same.

Portrait of Pyotr Arsenievich Smirnov issued in commemoration of his death in 1898. The inscription under the photo reads P. A. Smirnov, Councillor of Commerce, November 29, 1898. *Source:* The Moscow Sheet.

Mariya Nikolayevna Smirnova, Pyotr Smirnov's third wife. She died about four months after her husband. *Source: M. Zolotarev*.

The house by the
Cast Iron Bridge
was the Smirnov
residence from the
1860s up until the
revolution. The
family lived on the
upper floor, while a
factory, office, and
shop operated below.
Source: M. Zolotarev.

View of Pyatnitskaya
Street. Smirnov's
home is on the left.
The belfry pictured
is part of St. John the
Baptist Church, where
Smirnov's funeral
service was held in
1898. *Source:
M. Zolotarev.*

Pyotr Petrovich
Smirnov, the vodka
king's eldest son.
He ran the liquor
business after his
father died. *Source:
M. Zolotarev.*

Коннозаводчикъ
Николай Петровичъ Смирновъ.

Nikolay Petrovich Smirnov (above), Smirnov's second-eldest son. He is identified as a horse breeder in the photo, which appeared in a book on the subject in the early twentieth century. *Source: M. Zolotarev.*

Vladimir Petrovich Smirnov (below), Smirnov's third-eldest son. He is identified as a horse breeder in the photo, which appeared in a book on the subject. After spending time in a Bolshevik prison, Vladimir fled Russia post-revolution and revived his father's business in Europe. *Source: M. Zolotarev.*

Коннозаводчикъ
Владимиръ Петровичъ Смирновъ.

Smirnov's showcase exhibit at the All-Russia Industrial and Art Exhibition of 1896 in Nizhniy Novgorod. Russian royalty praised Smirnov's display, which featured flashing liquor bottles in Russia's national colors. *Source: The fair's catalog of participants.*

Aleksandra Petrovna Smirnova, Smirnov's youngest daughter. A beauty in her time, Aleksandra's correspondence with her lover was a valuable resource in re-creating the Smirnovs' lives. *Source: The widow of Vadim Borisovskiy, Aleksandra's son/M. Zolotarev.*

Sergey Petrovich Smirnov, Smirnov's fourth-eldest son. He broke from the family after Smirnov's death. A feud with his brothers over the vodka business and the distribution of his father's assets was the catalyst. *Source: M. Zolotarev.*

Aleksey Petrovich Smirnov, Smirnov's youngest son, and his wife, Tatiana. Just nine years old when his father died, Aleksey had little to do with the vodka business. *Source: M. Zolotarev.*

Closing day at Smirnov's vodka factory after the state's vodka monopoly went into effect in Moscow in 1901. This photo ran in the local newspaper. *Source: The Moscow Sheet.*

Зданія призовой рысистой конюшни В. П. Смирнова въ Москвѣ, по Скаковой ули

Vladimir Smirnov's grand horse stables in Moscow. He was an avid horse breeder and actively participated in horse racing. *Source: M. Zolotarev.*

Aleksandra Smirnova, Vladimir's second wife, with their only child, Vladimir. *Source: M. Zolotarev.*

Smirnov family photo, date unknown. Vladimir is standing second from the left, his wife, Aleksandra, is standing on a swing. Pyotr Petrovich is standing third from the right. *Source: M. Zolotarev.*

Eugeniya Smirnova, Pyotr Petrovich's wife. She remarried and fled Russia after the revolution, resettling in Nice, France. *Source: M. Zolotarev.*

Tsar Nikolay II, Russia's last tsar, is greeted on a military ship with a small glass of vodka during a routine visit. *Source: M. Zolotarev.*

Wounded soldiers being cared for at Smirnov's dacha during World War I. Several Smirnov properties were turned into makeshift hospitals during the war. *Source: M. Zolotarev.*

Vladimir Smirnov and his third wife, Tatiana Maksheyeva, in boyar costumes. Tatiana sent the photo to her brother in Estonia on December 29, 1926. A note on the back of the photo describes the difficulty of life in France. *Source: Vadim Maksheyev.*

Valentina Piontkovskaya, a famous operetta star who was Vladimir Smirnov's lover and companion before and after the revolution. With Vladimir, she fled Russia in 1919. *Source: Bakhrushin Museum.*

Rudolph Kunett, a Russian émigré who purchased a license from Vladimir Smirnov in 1933 to market Smirnoff vodka in the United States. He is pictured here in front of St. Basil's Cathedral in Red Square on a visit in 1978. *Source: Diageo.*

Rudolph Kunett, seated, sold his interest in the Smirnoff franchise in 1939 to John Martin, then president of Heublein, a company based in Hartford, Connecticut. *Source: Diageo.*

Chapter 19

Life and Death and Love and Death

It did not take Pyotr long to come up with a plan. Like so much else at the time, it was laden with risk. He must have determined that he had few alternatives—and he sensed a unique opportunity. Public sentiment regarding the vodka monopoly was in a downward spiral following the events of 1905. Religious leaders, women's groups, peasants, intelligentsia, and others were all adopting anti-alcohol mantras. They, like so many Russians, were increasingly appalled by the hordes of cash being channeled from vodka sales into the state's kitty. These critics, who referred to the monopoly as the state's "drunk budget," did not need to look far to make their case.[1] By 1909, 760 million rubles (720 million rubles from vodka sales and 40 million rubles from other nonmonopoly alcohol sales) came into the treasury annually, two-and-a-half times more than the amount collected the year before the monopoly's enactment.[2] In addition, a sharp spike in alcoholism horrified much of the populace. "It was not a rare phenomenon to see drunkards totally passed out on the street. Commentators of all political orientations cited alcohol abuse more than any other factor as a sign of moral degeneracy and social decay."[3]

The situation regarding alcohol abuse had deteriorated so greatly that the State Duma took up the topic in 1907. Sixty-five members urged the tsar to reduce his dependence on revenue generated from liquor. They argued that Russia could no longer rely on an immoral and destructive habit to fund its government. Resentment, they said, was building almost daily inside Russia. Abroad, the state's central role in peddling alcohol was attracting more than its share of unwelcome attention. "The most important thing for Russia at the present moment is not the Duma or freedom or a responsible Cabinet," wrote the *New York Times* in 1908, "but the question of vodka . . . [t]he whole empire is becoming more drunken, and the government is directly interested in the increased consumption of liquor because in Russia vodka is a state monopoly. The more the people drink the more revenue the government gets."[4]

These assessments underscored the increasingly hard-line stance adopted by leftist members of the Duma when it came to the matter of vodka. Although it did not yet advocate repeal of the monopoly or an outright liquor ban, the Duma considered a number of measures aimed at sobering up its citizens, including shortening the hours spirits shops could operate and selling liquor only in small containers. The political body also established the Commission on the Struggle Against Drunkenness, an organization dedicated to finding solutions to the deterioration of society. Among other things, the commission proposed limiting the sale of alcohol to one bottle per customer and banning liquor concessions at train stations and piers. The Ministry of Finance rebuffed these measures, arguing that they would encourage more illegal, more hazardous vodka making.[5]

Still, Pyotr was emboldened. Going against his own father's history of political neutrality, he readied for an imperial battle.

Of course, he, too, ardently opposed the vodka monopoly, believing it had created more problems than it had solved. He and a cadre of other vodka insiders argued that the quality of liquor had plummeted while consumption had soared, and the result became an unhealthy and dangerous mess for the government and its people. Their solution to this crisis was self-serving and predictable, though not entirely without merit: Give control of the vodka trade back to the private sector.

The real question was how to make that happen. Pyotr turned to a decidedly Western strategy for the answer: lobbying. He and other industry leaders brought together members of Russia's alcohol trade to form an organization dedicated to promoting its interests. The Central Bureau of Wine and Beer Industry and Trade was, in every sense, an experiment in modern-day influence peddling. The bureau would pursue its agenda through two means. It would lobby key decision-makers in the Duma and Imperial Court, and it would seek to persuade the public by disseminating a periodical devoted to topics important to liquor businesses. The bureau's first assignment was to issue a report on the state of the vodka monopoly. Pyotr pledged 500 rubles of his own money to fund the research and the publication of a special brochure.[6]

One of the most intriguing and bizarre arguments advanced by the bureau was the idea that beer, grape wines, cognacs, and flavored vodkas were "healthier" than 40-degree, pure vodka. "You can't evaluate the following drinks to be equally harmful: three-degree beer, 14-degree grape wine, or 25-degree flavored vodka in comparison to 40-degree vodka or 90-degree spirit."[7] The bureau went further, claiming increasing production of these other beverages and lifting restrictions imposed by the state on the amounts of them that could be sold would help sober up Russians.

This argument was not a popular one inside the palace gates. That Pyotr, the tsar's own purveyor, would make it, though, let alone sponsor a group openly critical of a key policy of the monarchy, illustrates both the worsening state of Smirnov's business and of the times itself. Following the events of 1905, there was, albeit briefly, a period of more openness, a greater willingness by top officials to hear competing viewpoints. For example, a law passed in March 1906 granted people the right to form unions and associations. Some 123 such organizations in Moscow and St. Petersburg alone were officially recognized in the two years following Bloody Sunday. A variety of professions organized unions, including medical workers, pharmacists, and barbers. Businesses, too, from the railroads to candy makers, galvanized their collective strength.

That's not to say that the tsar tolerated outspoken radicals or those he deemed to be his most virulent adversaries. His administration suppressed the activities of the monarchy's ardent foes, prosecuting and imprisoning tens of thousands of revolutionaries, including such luminaries as Leon Trotskiy. By April 1906 the government had executed 14,000 members of the opposition, and another 950 people had been sentenced to death by military courts. The Duma, too, had to rein in its conduct. It was repeatedly formed, dissolved, and re-formed based on how Nikolay II and his top lieutenants evaluated the political leanings and intentions of its representatives.

Of course, Pyotr Petrovich was not a wild rebel but rather a shrewd businessman. Like his father, he believed in doing whatever was necessary to further his business interests as long as he remained within the boundaries dictated by Russia's longstanding hierarchy and traditions. He viewed the monarchy as his ally, an essential guide to navigating Russia, and like his father he believed that perception was a vital ingredient in persuading the nobility and the tsar to see things his way. He painstakingly cultivated an image of supreme integrity, a benevolent business leader who gave as much of himself to good works and religious endeavors as he did to his business pursuits. An elder at several churches, he gave generously to other charities, such as a hospital for the blind, a shelter for weak and sickly children, and the Moscow Archeological Institute.[8] Beyond that, Pyotr earned a number of coveted titles and honors, including the same Order of Vladimir that his father had also received.[9] As a model merchant with a pedigree that Nikolay II could understand and appreciate, he had a shield of sorts from whatever backlash might result from his association with the Central Bureau.

Beyond building up his own credentials, Pyotr also distanced himself from an unexpected threat: his brother Sergey. Ever since the three eldest brothers had clashed with him, their relations had strained. Sergey was now a bona fide Smirnov outcast, and he had begun to act every bit the part. He derided his family's devotion to what he viewed as the trappings of Old Russia, and he began to pursue reform. In late 1906 or early 1907, Sergey invested nearly $1 million in a daily, liberal-leaning newspaper *Stolichnoye Utro*, ("Morning in the Capital").[10] The newspaper, with a circulation of roughly 30,000 in Moscow, used its pages to criticize the tsar, report on revolutionary activities, and advocate for more civil rights. Stories depicting the woes of laborers and the harsh conditions faced by peasants were routine, as were stories about student activism and the socialist movement at home and abroad. The newspaper, whose top editorial post was held by a Jew, touted the idea that Russia's future rested on a break with its past.

It was a risky venture for Sergey. It was common knowledge that the emperor's henchmen kept a close watch on the media, never hesitating to shut down or vandalize publications if the anti-tsarist rants went too far. The individuals who contributed to such editorializing faced retaliation as well. *Morning in the Capital* was not among the most radical newspapers at the time, nor was it a champion of the complete abolition of the monarchy. Instead, it promoted the idea of a constitutional monarchy. Still, Sergey, who cared about the future of his country, made himself a target. He may have felt free, even compelled, to express his liberal opinions, as he knew he was dying. Around the time of the 1905 uprisings, he had contracted tuberculosis, a common disease in the early 1900s that killed more than 360,000 Russians annually.

It is not clear whether the other Smirnovs knew about Sergey's illness. Still, none of them, particularly Pyotr, would have been pleased with the message Sergey's newspaper trumpeted or that officials in St. Petersburg might link that message back to his family. Their displeasure became apparent after Sergey's death on November 16, 1907, at the tender age of twenty-two. His death left Yelizaveta Nikolayevna, his common-law wife, and his two young sons, Oleg and Viktor. He was buried in the same cemetery as his father, mother, and grandparents, though *next* to the family plot, not within it. No one knows why his siblings chose to banish Sergey in this way, even though there were plenty of reasons from which to choose. The most likely possibilities included their earlier dispute over Smirnov's vodka empire, the siblings' disapproval of Sergey's low-class spouse, and his sponsorship of *Morning in the Capital*. Even one of the death announcements placed by his brothers depicted the family's schism, mentioning Sergey's children and siblings, but not Yelizaveta.[11]

Yelizaveta might have looked for moral support from Sergey's younger brother, Aleksey. After all, guardians for the two boys had taken the same position against the eldest brothers during the feud for control of the family business, and Aleksey had a true gentleness and innocence about him. Unfortunately for Yelizaveta, though, Smirnov's youngest son was not equipped to defend the interests of his brother's children. As Vladimir later recalled, Aleksey was "feeble-minded."[12] His life existed largely outside the main sphere of the Smirnov clan, and he had a guardian to help him manage his affairs. A few years after Sergey's death, he married Tatiana Mukhanova, a woman from the lower classes who demonstrated none of the cultural or intellectual polish expected from someone in the Smirnov's social strata. This coupling possibly limited Aleksey's influence and aggravated the already chilly relationship he had with his family—much as a new marriage in Nikolay's life had.

Nikolay's new wife, Mariya Ivanovna, was the daughter of a retired file clerk. She suffered from an unknown and costly medical condition. Less than three months after Sergey's death, and probably at the behest of his new spouse, Nikolay filed a petition to have his own guardianship removed. He offered multiple arguments for his request, claiming that he had been sober for three years and that he no longer squandered money. Mariya Ivanovna testified that he was now a model family man. Moreover, Nikolay asserted that his guardians had not represented him well financially, selling his interest in the family's business as well as his real estate for prices well below their value. Nikolay claimed his home, for instance, had cost him 100,000 rubles but was sold at auction for 35,000 rubles.[13]

Nikolay's guardian, his father's cousin Nikolay Venediktovich Smirnov, protested, but various others backed up the younger Smirnov's assertions. His doctor, his valet, and a lawyer all swore that Nikolay had indeed stayed sober. His doctor, who saw him three times a week, testified that his patient led a quiet life, absent of alcohol or extravagances.[14] These assertions did not stop Nikolay's new father-in-law, Ivan Volkov, from stating otherwise. He sought to take over his son-in-law's guardianship, arguing that Nikolay was as reckless and irresponsible as ever. He told the court that Nikolay's drinking binges had not ceased. As evidence, he pointed to a five-day period during which he said Nikolay was so incapacitated from nonstop tippling that he, Ivan, had had to take away all his immediate access to money and jewelry to prevent him from frittering it all away.

The back-and-forth biting went on for months, with all sides spewing venom at one another. Volkov offered more evidence of

Nikolay's wastefulness, demonstrating that he had pawned his wife's diamond earrings and rings, and had lost the furniture in his flat due to an unpaid debt. Nikolay, in turn, claimed that his wife had married him only for money and that he had spent more than 25,000 rubles to pay for her medical treatments. Other doctors testified that while Nikolay tried to stay sober, he sometimes slipped back into his old habits. In the end, the court declined to change the status of Nikolay's guardianship, reasoning that his situation was still too unstable to go unmonitored.

Neither Pyotr nor Vladimir appeared to have taken any active role in the year-long dispute over Nikolay's guardianship. They may have been war-weary from their previous battles with both Nikolay and Sergey, preferring instead to leave the wrangling to his guardian and the court. They also may have been too preoccupied with other matters. While Pyotr was running the vodka business and playing a leading role with the Central Bureau, Vladimir was cultivating an entirely new chapter in his life. This one took him to St. Petersburg.

CONTRASTING MOSCOW WITH St. Petersburg in the early 1900s was a bit like describing the difference between cotton and silk. One was an invaluable essential, a durable and workmanlike staple. The other was more precious, a sumptuous, fragile, and somewhat elusive luxury. Vladimir had always seemed drawn to the latter.

Free of any obligation to the vodka business, he had begun to spend more time in St. Petersburg in the years after the 1905 revolution. Previously a frequent visitor to the city, Vladimir had taken in the theater, eaten in the finest restaurants, and mingled with the aristocracy, which had historically congregated more in St. Petersburg than in Moscow. But now, Vladimir sought something new. Following the sale of his shares in the family enterprise, the personal attacks he endured after

Bloody Sunday, and the anti-alcohol sentiment raging throughout the empire, he yearned for a fresh start. He had more than
enough money and could pursue his love of the arts, particularly
theater, with renewed vigor. In St. Petersburg, Vladimir could
reinvent himself.

His attachment to the tsar's hometown stemmed in part
from a stud farm he purchased there, where, in addition to his
stallions, mares, and colts, he kept the offspring of his prized
thoroughbred Pylyuga, the trotters Valentinochka and Piontkovskaya, named after the popular operetta star Valentina Piontkovskaya.[15] Vladimir had met the singer, most likely at one
of her performances or at one of the many theater parties they
both attended. She mesmerized him. Valentina's dark eyes were
expressive and memorable because they shone in the same way
diamonds do, changing their sparkle and brightness with the
slightest shift in her gaze. Her thick, dark mop of hair was often
pinned back by a jeweled clasp or hidden under an elaborate,
feathered hat. Valentina carried herself like a queen, dressing in
the most splendid gowns and furs, set off by expensive necklaces
perfectly draped across her neckline. She was, in a word, daz-
zling. Grigoriy Yaron, the son of a well-known director, actor,
and writer of operettas, was also an admirer. He wrote that Valentina was "amazingly graceful so that you started to want to
paint her every movement, her every pose."[16]

Her charisma came through as much on the stage as it did
off. Theater critics referred to Valentina as a superstar, an actress who possessed a trifecta of artistic gifts. She could sing,
dance, and act. Polish by birth, she studied her craft in Italy and
performed in cities throughout the Russian Empire. She landed
the lead role in the St. Petersburg production of Franz Lehar's
The Merry Widow, one of the most beloved operettas of the day.
She also adored men, especially rich men.

That was where Vladimir had his advantage, for she offered
him exactly what he craved. As a starlet, she was invited to the

most exclusive parties, and her social circle included an array of top Russian artists and actors. She reveled in the same ultraluxurious living as Vladimir did. He was also ideal for her, a dashing escort with seemingly infinite resources. As was the custom, he could be her lover and patron, underwriting her productions and funding the purchase of all the glamorous accessories necessary to maintain her highly cultivated public profile. "Diamonds and precious stones in general were something very peculiar to operetta actresses before the revolution [of 1917]. The quantity, quality and size of the diamonds were parameters used to judge the significance of a prima donna," wrote one contemporary. "It became clear that along with high salaries, actresses needed to find other sources of income. These sources of income were found in the faces of admirers who sometimes spent enormous amounts of money for their objects of adoration."[17]

In no time at all, Vladimir and Valentina began living together in Vladimir's spacious apartment in the center of the city. Vladimir showered his new muse with diamonds and an imported wardrobe; he hosted opulent gatherings or tributes for her, sparing no expense on the menu or entertainment. Details of the menu from one event reveal that Vladimir's parties featured an array of delicacies, which could include quail, Chinese pheasant, Siberian hazel grouse, red partridge, and French fatted fowl. He also planned the specific pieces he wanted the orchestra to play during the evening. One night featured a program of Mendelssohn, Brahms, and excerpts from Gounod's *Faust* and Bizet's *Carmen*.[18]

Those expenditures, however, paled in comparison to the money Vladimir paid out to underwrite Valentina's flourishing career. He purchased operettas for her to star in from a variety of composers. He paid for the other actors as well as supporting personnel, props, and costumes. He even rented out grand theaters such as the *Passazh* (arcade) for her productions.[19] The opulent Passazh was a complex on three levels, complete with shops, a restaurant, and a giant theater hall that seated more than five hundred people. While his desire to please Valentina motivated him, he also had personal aspirations that amounted to more than simply playing the role of financier. He wanted to gain recognition as a theatrical producer—and in some cases as even more than that. In one instance, Vladimir purchased the rights to a new foreign-language operetta and tried to hire the well-known Mark Yaron, Grigoriy Yaron's father, to translate the production into Russian. Vladimir then made another peculiar request. According to Grigoriy, Vladimir asked that his name be included on the poster advertising the operetta as one of its authors. Mark Yaron, outraged at the bold demand, fired back in a way that infuriated Vladimir. "I only told Smirnov that I was used to seeing his surname not on posters for plays but on vodka bottles," recalled Grigoriy.[20]

Vladimir was deeply wounded, much in the same manner he had been when his first wife refused his hand when it was offered. He was trying to move beyond his past, at least the part that associated him with liquor more than theater. To Vladimir, Yaron's comment, whether intentional or not, belittled his foray into the arts and insinuated that he would never be able to move past his vodka heritage. Vladimir sued Mark Yaron for what he claimed was an unforgivable insult. The outcome of the case is unknown, although its very existence demonstrates just how driven Vladimir was to develop his life in St. Petersburg, free from the taint of alcohol.

The potency of the brand his father built made Vladimir's goal of a new life unusually difficult. Vladimir's ties to his former life in Moscow were as solid as cement. Aleksandra, his second wife, and his young son, Vladimir, still lived there. Vladimir's cold and public snubbing of Aleksandra left her shattered even more than his first wife had been. Worse for Aleksandra was that her husband demanded and received custody of their son. Young Vladimir went to live with his father and Valentina in St. Petersburg during these years, leaving Aleksandra distraught and desperate—a condition that would later make itself known in a surprising and frightening way.

Vladimir also faced an increasingly hostile populace as the debate over what to do about the alcohol problem raged throughout Russia. The people's ire had been awakened by the events of 1905, and it had not dissipated in the least. As the debate widened and grew more heated, a series of high-profile initiatives in 1909 reflected popular attitudes, which condemned not just the uncontrollable drunkards but also the manufacturers and sellers of spirits. This rhetoric vilified old-time vodka makers like Smirnov, much in the same way as Chekhov's column had two decades earlier.

Mikhail Chelyshev was a merchant who had been elected to the Duma on an anti-vodka, anti-monopoly platform. Referred to informally as "a sobriety apostle," he crusaded against what he believed to be a chief cause of revolutionary fervor: "The system of national alcoholization." He fought against all aspects of the alcohol trade believing alcohol to be a core weakness that prevented his nation from achieving greatness. Wisely, he utilized Lev Tolstoy to sharpen his point.[21]

Chelyshev paid a visit to the eighty-one-year-old Tolstoy in October 1909. The distinguished writer, though frail, remained a passionate temperance advocate and was a supporter of Chelyshev. The two discussed how best to educate citizens about the harmful nature of liquor. One solution was to put a menacing label on all bottles of state-produced vodka. Chelyshev asked Tolstoy to design the label, which he did, proposing a simple yet powerful script. Alongside a sketch of a skull and crossbones, Tolstoy suggested just one word: "Poison."[22] He explained, "Wine [vodka] is a poison that is harmful for the soul and for the body. That is why it is a sin to drink wine [vodka] and to treat others with wine [vodka]. Also, it is a bigger sin to produce this poison and to sell it."[23]

It was a novel and brilliant concept. Had Russia adopted it, the country would have been decades ahead of the rest of the world in warning its people about the health dangers of alcohol. But that was not to be. Though the Duma voted in favor of the warning label, the Imperial Council discussed and then tabled the measure, dooming its passage. Among the chief critics was the tsar's minister of finance, who feared that warning labels would cripple the government's finances.

Still, the state got the message. It took concrete steps to demonstrate that it was not only taking the alcohol problem seriously but that it was also looking for solutions. At the urging of the conservative yet reform-minded prime minister Pyotr Stolypin, the state backed the First All-Russian Congress Against Drunkenness. It was to be a series of public meetings that would air the viewpoints of numerous factions, including doctors, academics, and women's groups. The Social Democratic Party also waded into the debate, urging its members to participate in the public meetings in order to "tie the private question of alcoholism with the general aims and tasks of the workers' movement."[24] The congress met in December 1909 and then again in January of the following year, fueling the aspirations of temperance advocates, which were moving from promoting a curb on drinking to an outright ban.

This trend complicated Vladimir's personal makeover. The more enlightened and incensed Russians became about their alcohol dependency, the more vilified the state and its vodka makers became. Vladimir persisted anyway, immersing himself in the beauty of St. Petersburg and in the love of Valentina. The two traveled together often during this time, both domestically and abroad. They headed to locales for weeks or even months at a time so Valentina could appear in productions and solidify her growing fame.*

As for Vladimir's brother, Pyotr Petrovich, the monopoly debates dovetailed with his agenda. It was beginning to look

---

* Based on the memoirs of P. Isheyev, a close friend of the couple.

as if it would be only a matter of time before the vodka monopoly vanished, a victim of anti-tsarist, anti-state propaganda.
With careful planning, maybe Pyotr would be able to regain
his father's former dominance. Pyotr was on the brink of landing the prestigious title of purveyor to the king of Spain. At
home, advertisements touting Smirnov's cognacs, grape wines,
and flavored liqueurs seemed to be having their intended effect
as Smirnov captured a greater share of the market. The trick for
Pyotr was to keep the public rhetoric focused on the state and
its vodka monopoly. He could not allow it to mushroom into
a referendum against the entire liquor industry, or worse, into
talk of prohibition.

The king of vodka's oldest son might have had the skills and
cunning to pull off such a feat, if only death had not gotten in
the way.

Chapter 20

Sudden Chaos

Pyotr Petrovich Smirnov died unexpectedly on April 25, 1910 "after a short but severe illness."[1] He was just forty-two years old. His passing was not a national event like that following his father's death, but it was noteworthy and, in some very tangible ways, much more consequential. The younger Pyotr's death was like a falling domino, the first in a series of occurrences that tore into the heart of the Smirnov family and crippled the vodka firm. No one had been prepared for the void he left. It had all happened too fast.

Pyotr had been a community and business leader, a man well known, well respected, and well liked. He had possessed and practiced his father's winning combination: a quick mind and an uncanny ability to appear conventional while quietly blazing new trails. Thousands of people turned out for his funeral and burial. Colorful wreaths piled high on his casket, as mourners expressed condolences to his widow, Eugeniya, and their five children. Tributes appeared in leading publications. Most emphasized his charitable work and business savvy, praising Smirnov's son for his inventiveness and foresight. Compatriots from his industry were particularly saddened by Pyotr's death, sensing that they had lost one of their most determined and effective advocates.

A publication representing the liquor and food trades summed it up best.

> At the funeral were thousands of people. Those crowds of people, who came to bury Pyotr Petrovich, knew whom they had lost. They knew that the heart that had stopped beating was that of a responsible, gentle, and kind man, always going to the aid of those laboring and burdened. Shelters, almshouses, and various schools knew that the most fervent guardian and protector had gone away. Merchants and industrialists, gathered in so great a number, knew that already there was no brighter and more energetic defender of their interests and needs. If the unfortunate and laboring felt a frightening loss, an even bigger loss was felt by industry and trade, having lost their bright representative. Home industry is struggling through heavy years, especially those branches to which Pyotr Smirnov stood closest—that is the food and drink business.
>
> Pyotr Petrovich was not only a man of words. He was mainly a man of business. He not only spoke but he also acted. Words for him did not walk a separate path from business. In particular, the deceased was unsatisfied with the state wine [vodka] monopoly. He understood that the monopolistic trade of wine [vodka] brings frightening damage both to the population and to closely adjoined branches of industry. He hotly fought for the destruction of the state wine [vodka] trade. Any project in this direction met with his special attention. . . . Recalling his

joyous memory, it is impossible not to say: Sleep peacefully! That work which you did in the span of your whole
life will be carried on. . . . There will come a time when
this work will yield its results."[2]

That time never came. Pyotr's death left the spirits industry
without one of its most outspoken defenders. No one stepped
in to galvanize the sector the way he had. Indeed, the passion
for its anti-monopoly crusade seemed to have withered, overrun
by an increasingly vibrant and vigilant temperance movement.
The anti-alcohol campaign had matured and strengthened. Its
rants about the evils of liquor had grown more confident, more
scientific, and more reasoned. Its endgame had broadened, too,
escalating beyond demands for a repeal of the monopoly or a
reduction in consumption into talk of complete prohibition.

This onslaught stemmed in good part from the deteriorating
condition of society and a general acceptance among Russians
that alcoholism was a leading contributor. This situation was a
chief topic of the day, its discussion no longer a sign of rebellion.
The public's grave concern was reflected regularly in articles
critical of the state's liquor policies and the tsar himself. According to *Novoye Vremya*, a large-circulation newspaper published
twice a day in St. Petersburg: "Everybody speaks about alcoholism now. The state could easily end alcoholism thanks to the
monopoly, as the alcohol income makes up one-quarter of our
budget."[3] Another article was more dramatic in its assessment,
charging that "Russia is dying because of alcohol."[4] The press
devoted buckets of ink to this topic. At one point, more than
thirty different journals were dedicated solely to the coverage
of temperance.[5]

Another factor boosting the anti-alcohol movement turned
out to be the death of Lev Tolstoy in 1910, less than seven months
after Pyotr Petrovich died. Tolstoy's vehement opposition to the
state's alcohol policies was well documented. He had railed for

decades against the ills of liquor, one of the few to emphasize that it was not a problem plaguing only the poorest segments of society. "The ugliness and, above all, the meaninglessness of our life stems primarily from the constant state of drunkenness in which the majority of our people of all classes, callings, and positions are now to be found," Tolstoy wrote toward the end of his life.[6] The Commission on the Question of Drunkenness called a special meeting to commemorate Tolstoy's passing and to celebrate his temperance principles. His death sparked numerous demonstrations among student activists and others throughout Russia. They marched against everything from poor working conditions to the death penalty. One protest drew 10,000 people to the streets of St. Petersburg, disrupting the flow of trams and pedestrian walkways.

Without Pyotr's leadership, the Smirnovs struggled to fend off the tidal wave headed their way. His untimely passing left the company defenseless in a sense. His will, hastily composed just three days before his death, bequeathed all his property and the rights to the remnants of his father's business solely to his wife, Eugeniya Ilyinichna Smirnova. She would have use of the family's real estate throughout her lifetime and was unilaterally responsible for the guardianship of their children, each of whom was to receive 50,000 rubles (more than $580,000 today) when they reached the age of twenty-five. Thus, Eugeniya became the chief executive and solitary owner of Smirnov's liquor firm.

Eugeniya had never shown any real interest in her husband's business, nor did she have any experience that would have prepared her for her new responsibilities. In fact, when Pyotr Petrovich appointed his wife in 1905 as his partner in the company, he did so as a formality to retain his status as a trading house. He had never intended for Eugeniya to work there, much less serve as its top executive. Like most women in high society, Eugeniya was the product of a private boarding school, a girl born and bred to assume her rightful place among the elite.

She loved traveling abroad and was a regular fixture at some of the grandest hotels in Europe. Her grandson described her as "a woman who didn't have a head for business, hadn't been involved in business matters. She was as free as a bird. That's how she had spent her life."[7] Her daughters were being groomed in much the same way. "Their prime concern was spending money, traveling," Eugeniya's grandson later recalled.[8]

Eugeniya, a widow at just forty-one, was not prepared to spearhead the company's next steps, particularly in the midst of such a turbulent environment. Although many Smirnov loyalists were still employed by the vodka factory, within a few short months Eugeniya tapped her eldest son, Arseniy, to be her surrogate regarding family business matters when she was otherwise engaged or unavailable. It was an odd, reckless choice for her to make, primarily because her son was sixteen years old. A special amendment to the bylaws of the company had to be drafted just to allow Arseniy to assume his new role.[9] What's more, he was not mature enough to grasp the depth of the struggle facing the vodka industry nor astute enough to manage critical relations with key business contacts. These weaknesses, and the irreparable damage that resulted from them, became apparent almost immediately.

Arseniy learned the hard way how pivotal his father's dedication and personal stature had been in preserving the financial health of the Smirnov's vodka business and its broader interests. In 1909, the last full year Pyotr Petrovich ran the business, it employed five hundred people and grossed 7 million rubles.[10] That was down considerably from its high of 19.7 million rubles in 1897 but still quite respectable in light of the monopoly and the contentious political landscape. Pyotr had done it in part by stepping up production of flavored vodkas, grape wines, and cognacs, and exporting greater proportions of vodka. In addition, he solidified his place as an industry ambassador of sorts, helping to launch and then pilot the Central Bureau. Competitors and allies alike held Pyotr in high regard and treated him with great deference.

The company had claimed for years that it had a right to display four state coats of arms on Smirnov's labels and in advertisements. But members of the Central Bureau questioned whether this kind of marketing was appropriate, particularly because it was Pyotr Petrovich's father who had earned the coveted awards and accolades. They argued that these rights could not be passed to a son who had eight years earlier dissolved the original business and formed another. His rivals had precedent on their side. Indeed, it was Pyotr Arsenievich Smirnov himself who had successfully argued that the inheritor of the Popov Trading House could not use a state coat of arms earned by the founder.

Still, the Central Bureau chose not to go to battle over its gripe. Instead, it approached Pyotr Petrovich directly. After some quiet discussions, the two sides reached an amicable agreement. Pyotr promised to remove one of the coats of arms from his labels and advertisements, conceding that it had been a mistake to use it. In the future, he would use only three. That would have been the end of the matter except that Pyotr died before making good on his bargain. The Central Bureau then followed up with Arseniy, but Pyotr's son repeatedly refused to honor his father's pact. He and other Smirnov managers claimed that the paperwork related to the use of the coats of arms was unavailable. They stalled for time, convinced that they had inherited the right to use the honors. They probably hoped the situation would simply go away, a costly miscalculation, exacerbated by Arseniy's haughty refusal to pay a bill for advertisements his father purchased to run in the Central Bureau's bulletin prior to his death.

Tensions boiled over between the two parties. Former allegiances to Pyotr were exhausted. Now, the Central Bureau concluded, it had no other choice but to take legal action. It filed a petition with the Ministry of Industry and Trade, which opened an investigation into the Smirnov's use of not one but all four state coats of arms. The Central Bureau contended: "The newly reformed firm Trading House P. Smirnov by law can buy only the movable and immovable property of liquidating enterprises. By no means can it buy distinguishing features, such as a coat of arms granted to the P. A. Smirnov Association. Consequently, the Trading House P. Smirnov has been enjoying up to this time a right not belonging to it, the right to carry on its labels and other such items the coats of arms, medals, and awards."[11] The Smirnovs fired back that they inherited the hard-earned designations: "We consider ourselves within our rights to use on signs and products four representations of the state coat of arms."[12]

The legal fracas was nasty. The Smirnovs had plenty of sympathizers, some of whom expressed their opinions publicly in periodicals. Industry insiders, especially the Central Bureau, broadcast their views the loudest. They seemed intent on wounding the Smirnovs, bitter over the shabby treatment they received from their former ally's son. Worse, the controversy bled over into the company's most cherished asset, its right to the title of purveyor to the Imperial Court. This distinction was still a coveted and invaluable marketing tool, despite the tsar's sagging public image. Indeed, when one of Smirnov's chief competitors, N. L. Shustov & Sons, received the purveyor title in 1912, it was rumored that Shustov was so anxious to show off his newly elevated status that he trashed all his old labels and replaced them with ones highlighting his award in just one night.[13]

Given the gravity of the situation facing the family, it appears that Eugeniya and a more business-minded representative working on her behalf intervened. Arseniy was no longer the point person on this issue, a wise last-minute shift. Eugeniya saved face by getting a temporary license to keep the purveyor title and one state coat of arms. The Ministry stripped the other three from the Smirnovs in late 1911, a devastating blow to the company.* The loss in stature, occurring in tandem with the raging anti-alcohol movement and disarray within Smirnov's management ranks, contributed to an alarming drop in profits. Gross revenue fell by more than 5 million rubles in 1912, and about 150 employees at the warehouse and factory lost their jobs.[14]

The Smirnovs suffered from even more negative press when the Shustovs sued the company for trademark infringement. Perhaps smelling blood in the water, the Shustovs claimed that the Smirnovs were copying the name of one of its popular specialty drinks, a cherry-flavored vodka known as *Spotykatch*, a derivative of the Russian word meaning "to stumble."[15] In point of fact, many vodka makers produced flavored vodkas under the *Spotykatch* moniker; the court threw out the case, concluding that the word could not be trademarked as it was too commonly used to refer to cherry-flavored drinks.

Still, the bad news just kept coming. Relations between Eugeniya and her son Arseniy grew contentious. He had begun to show troubling signs of behavior similar to Nikolay. Arseniy spent money like it was vodka, free-flowing and infinitely available. He overpaid for two homes, which cost him a total of nearly 1 million rubles.[16] He then issued promissory notes in the amount of 150,000 rubles, which returned to him less than 15,000 rubles.[17] No one knows why Arseniy's behavior turned so destructive: it might have been the pressure from the business, the loss of his father, or his absentee mother who, like many aristocrats, left her children in the care of trusted nannies and guardians while she traveled throughout Europe. Regardless, he had to be stopped.

Eugeniya implored Arseniy to curtail his extravagant spend-

---

* Documents explaining the aftermath of these decisions could not be located. It is likely the Smirnovs appealed the decisions. Company ads from 1914 to 1917 feature all four coats of arms and reference to the purveyor title.

ing. He sued her, in turn, alleging that she had short-changed
him on his inheritance. "Relations between my mother and me
are pretty strained," Arseniy wrote in his complaint. He questioned the financial allowances he had been given, noting that
this would be "an issue of a lawsuit."[18] A court found Arseniy's
charges against his mother baseless, but the rift between the
two remained. A court-appointed guardian was put in place to
monitor his finances, and Arseniy was removed from his position in the Smirnov company. Eugeniya still had no intention
of taking the helm of the company. By that time, she had met
Umberto de la Valle Ricci, an Italian diplomat and the man she
would later marry. It is likely that Eugeniya decided to spend
time with him, either in Japan where he would serve as ambassador, or in Europe. She gave her power of attorney to a trusted
confidante to run the vodka business in her absence.

Eugeniya seems never to have sought assistance from Vladimir during this period of crises. Their lives were completely
separate . . . and he was dealing with problems of his own.

Tensions in St. Petersburg were running high. The air in
the city was heavy, weighed down by an unspecified uneasiness in the atmosphere. For the most elite members of society,
like Vladimir, the mood was especially gloomy and foreboding. A book about St. Petersburg during this time described the
city's "doom, a [feeling of] closeness to the end of the existing
social structure."[19] People responded to their fears in different
ways—some did nothing, trusting tradition and the monarchy
to take care of them; some got passports and fled to seemingly
more stable lands; some dug in, intensifying their ardent support of the status quo; others joined the ranks of the disenfranchised, fighting for reforms and more humanistic policies. And
some, like Vladimir, took more drastic measures. They armed
themselves.

On June 26, 1910, Vladimir applied to the local police department on behalf of himself and a servant for the right to purchase and carry a revolver. He wrote in his application that his vast wealth and treasure trove of valuables made him a target of the city's criminals and the needy.[20] He still lived in a huge and luxurious apartment on Nadezhdinskaya Street, one of St. Petersburg's most fashionable neighborhoods. His lifestyle was opulent and showy, and he continued to host lavish parties at chic restaurants. This life was what Vladimir wanted—and he sought a gun to protect it. He recalled all too well the frightening attacks he endured following the uprising in 1905. Little did he know that the greatest threat, at least at that moment, lay within his own inner circle.

His estranged wife, Aleksandra, was stewing back in Moscow, pining away for her eleven-year-old boy who had been ripped from her to live with his father in St. Petersburg. She was frantic with grief over the loss of little Volodya. Aleksandra now plotted her next move. She went to court, in part to secure her divorce from Vladimir and in part to gain official permission to see her son. The judge acquiesced to her request, but he allowed her visiting privileges only twice a week for just two-and-a-half hours each time.[21] For Aleksandra, though, this access was more than enough.

In March 1912 she boarded the train to St. Petersburg. Vladimir and Valentina were "living abroad at the moment," according to a St. Petersburg newspaper, likely traveling on theater business. They had hired a tutor and a governess to look after Volodya full time. The tutor shared a room with the boy while the governess, who also inhabited the apartment, taught him music and foreign languages. When Aleksandra showed up on Vladimir's doorstep early one morning, it was not a day that she was legally authorized to see her son. According to newspaper accounts, which referred to Vladimir as a Moscow manufacturer even though he had not been in the liquor business for seven years, she explained that she was unable to visit on her designated day. So she had come at a more convenient time. This was a lie.

> The doorman let Mrs. Smirnova enter on the grand staircase and went away to distribute the mail. The servants who opened the door to Mrs. Smirnova also quickly returned to their usual duties—morning cleaning. The governess and the tutor were not prepared for the sudden meeting with [Volodya's] mother. So it is unknown where and under what circumstances a meeting between the mother and her son took place. It was a matter of two to three minutes. When the servants went to close the street door, Mrs. Smirnova and her son Vladimir were already out of the apartment. . . . A search brought no results.
>
> People say that the boy, who loved his mother madly, said to her many times before "Mommy, don't cry. I'll always be yours." The servants, the doorman, the governess and the tutor can't tell the police what happened. They say everything happened too fast."[22]

Another article ran under the headline "New Adventures of a Millionaire's Son." It reiterated the facts of the kidnapping, adding that Volodya had run into his mother's arms and that the whereabouts of the boy and Aleksandra were unknown. It was not Aleksandra's first attempt at nabbing her son. She had tried to escape with him earlier in March from a railroad station, according to the newspaper, but that plan had been foiled.

Aleksandra now had her boy back. The two soon surfaced together in Moscow. Although it is not clear what transpired next, in the end Vladimir declined to press charges against Aleksandra, allowing Volodya to remain with her. He may have determined that his son was better off with a more attentive, physically present parent. He had no intention of curtailing his travels or pursuits in the theater world. His life with Valentina demanded flexibility and spontaneity. And too, he could not deny Aleksandra's deep love for their child—and Volodya's love for her. What's more, as the situation in Russia, particularly in St. Petersburg, grew precarious he may have reasoned that Volodya would be safer in Moscow.

THE TSAR'S CENTURIES-OLD stronghold on Russia was weakening. Many factors contributed to this historic loss of confidence. First, the tsar's regime continued with its harsh punitive pursuits. Prosecutions, arrests, and exiles had accelerated as the Imperial Court sought to silence its critics. Executions, often in the form of public hangings, were commonplace; cruel, moblike displays of what could happen to those who spoke out against the tsar's authority. Censorship reigned, too, muzzling revolutionaries and their allies. The State Duma, once a promising symbol of democratic reform, had been virtually neutered. Its members heralded almost universally from the upper classes, and its legislative initiatives rarely amounted to more than political discourse since the tsar had retaken the power to reject any law it passed.

Contributing further to the instability was the emergence of Grigoriy Rasputin, the charismatic holy man from Siberia who penetrated the royal family's inner circle. Convincing the family that he was the only one who could heal the tsar's hemophiliac son, Rasputin came to be known by Nikolay II as "our friend," while his wife, Empress Aleksandra, viewed him among her most trusted confidants. She sought Rasputin's advice on matters as far flung as ministerial appointments and on managing relations with foreign nations. Rasputin's influence was highly controversial. Many observers claimed he was a womanizer, a sexual deviant, a fraud, even a spy. He was also later accused of having an affair with the tsarina. Citizens, particularly in aristocratic circles, were repulsed by his unorthodox opinions and lifestyle, and they secretly feared that his presence was poisoning the Romanovs and dooming their reign.

Overall, the public's tolerance of this situation and the monarchy was akin to a balloon on the brink of bursting. The government's two-faced stance on liquor did not help either. Despite the state's wishful thinking, consumption had skyrocketed under its vodka monopoly. The tsar's sobriety initiatives as well as private efforts to curtail drinking proved to be miserable failures. Inside the Duma, which was proposing a series of measures to combat drunkenness, verbal attacks focused on Witte's replacement as minister of finance, Vladimir Kokovtsov. Accused of manipulating the vodka monopoly for the benefit of the treasury, Kokovtsov opposed any proposal aimed at fighting alcoholism if it did not also account for the state's fiscal needs. This unbending posture made the new minister of finance a lightning rod. The newspapers were full of harsh criticisms and featured cartoons playing up the government's hypocrisy.

Finally, in January 1914, Nikolay II had had enough. He decided to see for himself how his people were faring when it came to the liquor problem. He was horrified by what he witnessed, noting that he observed "tragic scenes of the degeneration of the people, the poverty of families, and the decline of households as a result of drunkenness."[23] He immediately dismissed Kokovtsov and demanded that his successor embark on a series of reforms aimed at weaning the state off its own vodka dependency. "We cannot make our fiscal prosperity dependent upon the destruction of the spiritual and economic powers of many of my subjects, and therefore it is necessary to direct our financial policy towards seeking government revenues from the unexhausted sources of the country's wealth and from the creative toil of the people, to seek constantly, while preserving wise economy, to increase the productive powers of the country and to take care of the satisfaction of the people's needs. Such must be the ends of the desired changes. I am firmly convinced that they must succeed and that they are absolutely necessary for the good of my people, especially since both the Duma and Imperial Council have turned their attention to these needs of the people by revising our alcohol laws."[24]

The march toward prohibition in Russia was on.

OVER THE NEXT six months, the state restricted the amount of outlets selling liquor, closed distilleries, gave greater control over alcohol bans to local officials, and replaced its monopoly-driven revenue with other sources. More than eight hundred petitions requesting the adoption of local prohibitions were approved by July 1914, and 1,100 retail shops had been shuttered. The tsar then ordered that the vodka monopoly, which had provided jobs to an estimated 200,000 men, including 23,000 barkeepers, be rescinded. A gradual, carefully orchestrated drive toward a dry Russia was on course, bringing with it, it seemed, the fate of Pyotr Arsenievich Smirnov's once almighty vodka empire.

But then, Russia had not counted on the Great War.

Chapter 21

Revolution

For a time, it seemed that World War I might save Russia from itself. The country had been plagued by an almost daily parade of strikes and other disturbances. Confidence in the government was at an all-time low. Trust in the tsar and his leadership was nearly exhausted. But with the declaration of war, Russians had a new, more alluring target for their rage: Germany.

People throughout the country rallied around their emperor and motherland, replacing their deep-seated resentments with heartfelt patriotism and pride. From nearly every window and rooftop, the tsarist flag flew. Peasants and aristocrats alike listened with renewed admiration as their leader, dressed in uniform, addressed them from the Winter Palace, promising a thrilling triumph. The Duma, which had been a nest of political bickering, snapped into place as a cohesive body, fervently backing the tsar and his wartime pronouncements. There was nothing the nation would not do to demonstrate its collective devotion. Symbolically, St. Petersburg was renamed Petrograd to rid the city of its German-sounding moniker. Mobs raised and burned the German Embassy in the capital city; soldiers enthusiastically and confidently marched off to a battle certain they would win. "A torrent of love for Holy Mother Russia poured forth. The war had come at the right moment; it afforded an outlet for the frustrations and hatreds that for so long had been turning Russian against Russian. Once more, if only temporarily, things were back in proper order."[1]

So united was the nation around Nikolay II that he threw out his methodical plan for sobriety and replaced it with an all-out prohibition. In tandem with ordering the mobilization of troops, the tsar essentially banned the sale of vodka, wine, and beer. Other nations grappled with alcoholism to varying degrees, but Russia went the farthest. Temperance was to be a pivotal ingredient to Russia's war strategy. Memories from the conflict with Japan nearly a decade earlier were still hauntingly fresh as Japanese generals credited drunken Russian soldiers with handing them at least one of their major victories. Other wartime failures were also blamed on the bottle. It was openly quipped that Germany was counting on meeting inebriated Russian troops. For example, a satirical cartoon featured a German soldier, armed with sobriety, as he faced his Russian enemy.[2]

Neither the tsar nor his people could withstand a repeat defeat, so Russians enthusiastically cheered the edict of prohibition. The ban was to remain in place only until the mobilization was complete, but it turned out to be so effective, as soldiers readied for battle in half the time expected, that the tsar extended his order to cover the war's duration. The results were immediate—and stunning. At home, public drunkenness and overall consumption plummeted. Money that had been spent on vodka was now deposited in the bank, resulting in a sixfold increase in individual savings.[3] Crime eased, too. Reports from various regions heralded the newfound sober serenity. "Hooliganism has almost disappeared, and the police lockups, always filled on bazaar days with drunken men, are now empty," read one. Another stated that "the suspension of the vodka traffic has diminished crime in this city by 50 percent."[4] In Petrograd, cases going before the Justice of the Peace dropped by 80 percent while the number of male beggars plunged by 75 percent.[5] Part of the newfound civility could have been attributable to the deployment of so many men to the war front, but nonetheless, the results of the prohibition were tangible.

The military, too, had undergone a magnificent transformation. A war correspondent for the *London Times* remarked in a column in March 1915: "One cannot write of the Russian mobilization or of the rejuvenation of the Russian Empire without touching on the prohibition of vodka; the first manifest evidence of the increased efficiency was, of course, in the manner and promptness with which the army assembled; but, from that day, the benefits have been increasingly visible, not only in the army but in every phase of Russian life. . . . In nearly six months association with the armies in many different theaters of operations I have not seen a single drunken or tipsy officer or soldier. This, then, was the first of what New Russia intended to do in this war. At one stroke she freed herself of the curse that has paralyzed her peasant life for generations. This in itself is nothing short of a revolution."[6]

The Smirnovs, despite being further hobbled by this prohibition, did what everyone else did and joined the war effort. Russia endured overwhelming casualties throughout the four-year conflict, significantly more than could be handled by the existing medical infrastructure. The Smirnovs, like others in their class, opened their spacious private homes to care for wounded soldiers drifting back from the front. The family's elegant dacha in Sokolniki outside Moscow, the scene of Aleksandra's earlier forbidden trysts, was used to treat dozens of soldiers. Sergey's sons opened their residence with twenty beds less than two weeks after combat broke out. Smirnov's youngest son,

Aleksey, accommodated sixty wounded veterans at a time in his house. Two hospitals named after Pyotr Petrovich, Smirnov's oldest son, opened up in the mansion on Pyatnitskaya Street and in another family-owned property.*

These were immensely charitable gestures, particularly given the family's increasingly precarious financial status. The combination of war and the new dry laws had dealt the business a devastating blow. Factory production dwindled to a trickle, and the rank-and-file dropped by more than two hundred men. According to an official report, which did not include revenue figures, no longer did the Smirnovs produce much in the way of grape wines, cognacs, or other liqueurs, nor did they manufacture vodka for export.[7] Business was off so much that Eugeniya began leasing some of the inactive properties. Two buildings, including a stone, two-story warehouse, became movie theaters. The state also used some of Smirnov's real estate to store military supplies.[8]

There was one bright spot to the liquor ban. It had come with a slew of odd exceptions that were amended and altered throughout the war. Flavored vodkas, for instance, continued to be produced by manufacturers like Smirnov because they were less potent than other drinks and because forbidding them completely would have devastated the Russian fruit industry. These spirits also represented something uniquely Russian, a traditional symbol the state determined was worth preserving. The same exception was made for beer and grape wines—and for first-class eating establishments. Restaurants and clubs that catered to the wealthy were allowed to sell any kind of liquor its customers wanted.

These loopholes, though polarizing, kept the Smirnov business afloat, if only barely. Eugeniya, who spent most of her time

---

* The Smirnov's wartime contributions come from research conducted by Anton Valdin.

traveling with her Italian diplomat, signed over the day-to-day responsibilities to the company's remaining senior management. No members of Smirnov's immediate family seem to have been involved with the business. Vladimir and Valentina were mounting a new production in Warsaw at the outbreak of the war, followed by some work in the Ukraine region. Pyotr Petrovich's son, Arseniy, was still under guardianship, as was Pyotr's brother, Nikolay. Without the personal Smirnov touch, it looked as though the once-mighty vodka empire might be on a path to oblivion, right alongside the imperial traditions of the Russian Empire.

THE WAR REPRESENTED the tsar's last chance to reassert himself as the indisputable ruler of a powerful, fearless nation. His test began with genuine promise. In 1914 Russia's military was awesome, totaling 1.4 million and eventually enlisting almost 15 million men. It was taken for granted that this immense army would crush its enemies, but the reality soon became clear. The masses of men heralded largely from the lower classes. Though exceedingly brave, they were raw recruits from rural villages, men drafted for a job they had no training to do. In addition, a lack of professional, seasoned leadership, and a dearth of vital supplies greatly undermined the war strategy. "It is hard to imagine how ill-equipped for modern warfare the tsar's huge army was. Thousands had no shoes, one man in three had no rifle, artillery was in pitifully short supply, munitions even shorter. In such matters as wireless, airplanes, transportation, the Russian Army proved helpless."[9] There were some successes, of course, but the overall losses were nothing short of horrific. Hundreds of thousands of men perished, and vast areas of the motherland fell under German control. Troops were demoralized, hungry, and exhausted. The liquor ban took a toll, too, as the war wore on, with soldiers substituting their cravings with colognes, furniture polishes, and alcohol-based varnishes.[10] Increasingly, the tsar and his bureaucratic machine took the blame for this misery. The love fest that had been sparked by the war was vanishing.

Against the urgings of his most senior advisors, Nikolay II decided to follow in the noble footsteps of his ancestor, Peter the Great. He, personally, would assume control of his army, intent on bringing dignity back to his soldiers, respect to the monarchy, and an end to the constant suffering. It was a controversial move supported wholeheartedly by the tsarina and her most trusted adviser, Rasputin. With Nikolay II at the front, the duo assumed a greater hand in the daily affairs of the state, causing widespread mistrust and angst: Empress Aleksandra was German-born, a child of the enemy, while Rasputin's increasingly powerful influence was deemed by some as an unpredictable and frightening threat to the future of the empire.

The aristocracy was especially unnerved by Rasputin, fearing his presence could spark a mass overthrow of Romanov rule. Soon, a small cadre of nobles came together to plan the murder of Rasputin in December 1916 by luring him to the palace of Prince Felix Yusupov. First, as the legend goes, Rasputin gulped wine laced with enough poison to kill as many as ten men. Unaffected, his stunned murderers then shot him multiple times, causing him to fall but not die. They then wrapped Rasputin's body in a cloth and dumped it into the icy Neva River. When his body was retrieved on New Year's Day, the empress was hysterical with grief. Much of the rest of Russia, however, was relieved. The murderers were banished to their country estates but not charged with the killing. The tsar returned from the war to console his wife and assess the grave circumstances in the capital. A Swedish diplomat dispatched to Petrograd commented that the mood in Russia's capital city was "snappish and fretful. . . . One hears the thunder and sees the lightning . . . but the storm has not yet broken."[11]

Nikolay II returned to a Russia he did not comprehend. The

war had corroded the Russian psyche, and Petrograd stank of despair. Few had been untouched by the disastrous battles, losing sons, husbands, or fathers. The wounded languished in hospital beds, forever crippled by the bloodbath they had witnessed. For the population at large, debilitating hunger had crept into their daily lives as food and fuel grew scarcer and costlier, doubling and sometimes tripling week by week. Long lines snaked outside food shops as women and young children waited for their meager rations, constant reminders of the hardships the war had brought.

Winter temperatures plunged to forty degrees below zero. Food trains, hampered by a lack of fuel and frozen tracks, could not access Petrograd, choking off the city from essential supplies. Families tugged apart wooden fences and pilfered whatever they could to keep their stoves warm. Schools closed, newspapers stopped printing, trams stalled. Liquor, again, found its way into the hands of many in spite of the official prohibition. Illegal production of *samogon*, or homemade vodka, multiplied in both urban and rural locales. Established makers of alcohol, including the Smirnovs, skirted laws by selling spirits out of their factories directly to customers. These transgressions were most often condoned, though the Smirnovs were fined 3,000 rubles at least once for engaging in this practice.[12]

The tsar's advisors warned that he would face dark consequences if he did not do something drastic. The Okhrana, the secret police force of the Russian Empire, predicted the "possibility in the near future of riots by the lower classes of the empire enraged by the burdens of daily existence." The leader of the Duma sent a telegraph to the tsar: "The situation is serious. There is anarchy in the capital." Nikolay II remained unconvinced and worse, paralyzed.

Perhaps it was that so few in his circles were affected by the country's many calamities. Russia's rich still led glittering lives throughout the war. They packed into expensive restaurants and patronized the theater and ballet, insulating themselves from the suffering of others. Horse-racing went on without disruption, as did the seasonal parties and celebrations. Vladimir and Valentina, part of this bejeweled set, returned to Petrograd; once home Valentina continued to act as if she were the living embodiment of her role in Offenbach's *Beautiful Helen*. "The war had not changed the life of Russia's nobility and aristocracy, although many socialites wore mourning armbands for their fallen."[13] This ostentatious show became just another contribution to the population's discontent, an example of the imbalance ingrained within Russian society.

It was not until February 23, 1917, International Woman's Day, that the tsar began to grasp the depth of the fury raging through his people. In spite of calls for no strikes, women from some textile factories in Petrograd staged a walkout and asked for support from the metalworkers at the huge Putilov factory. An estimated 128,000 malcontents joined forces, parading down snowy streets with signs that read, DOWN WITH THE AUTOCRACY. They shouted "Give us bread," as they made their way through the heart of the city. The following day, the number of protesters swelled to more than 200,000, and a day later, the walkout exploded into a general strike, with participants filling the streets and chanting slogans opposing the tsar and the war. Crowds of supporters from all walks of life cheered on the mushrooming processionals.

The police erected barricades to contain the masses; guards nervously staked out positions while leaders from the Bolsheviks, Mensheviks, and Social Revolutionary Party sought to unify what they now understood to be the stirrings of a full-scale insurrection. With every passing day, the tension in Petrograd intensified. Clashes between workers and the tsar's still-loyal officers erupted sporadically. Now, gunfire pelted the crowds, clubs crashed down, delivering heavy blows to people's bodies and heads, looters ransacked food shops. The violence did not last long, though. The tsar's defenders, many sympathetic to the people's cause, abandoned their posts and threw down their weapons. The remaining troops were then simply overwhelmed, as armored cars bearing red revolutionary banners rolled into the streets. They stormed the police stations, providing arms to the masses. The Okhrana's headquarters was looted and then burned. Defenders of the great Fortress of Peter and Paul surrendered. Finally, the Imperial Guard at the Romanov's summer residence mutinied, and with this, Russia's last tsar had no choice. Nikolay II abdicated.

A Russian newspaper reported that people bid their emperor farewell "like they were blowing fuzz from a sleeve."[14] Most had no remorse, no regret. They were just glad to be done with him.

A HUGE RED banner floated over the Winter Palace, the residence of tsars since Peter the Great. Revolutionary fever spread to every corner of the country. For a time, a provisional government advocated freedom of speech and religion, equal rights, and a free press. It sought to revitalize the military, which was still in the throes of battle. Factories buzzed again with activity as a brief period of relief took hold. Officially, prohibition became a permanent fixture of the new Russia. Political exiles, including Vladimir Lenin, Josef Stalin, and Leon Trotskiy, returned to their homeland. Previously these men had had little power and meager support. But in the wake of the uprising, they had opportunity. Explained one Siberian peasant: "We feel that we have escaped from a dark cave into the bright daylight. And here we stand not knowing where to go or what to do."[15]

Lenin arrived by train from Zurich at Finland Station in Petrograd in April 1917. There, a crowd of thousands welcomed him with effusive cheers, waving flags branded with the Bolsheviks slogan: PEACE, BREAD, AND LAND! It was as if a parched nation had finally discovered the source of pure water. From atop an armored car, Lenin addressed his followers. He denounced the war, then embraced a revolution that had "opened a new epoch." Afterward, at a meeting of leading activists, he outlined his plans for the future. It involved dismantling the provisional government, ridding the country of capitalists, and rallying workers, peasants, and soldiers. They were to take control of the revolution and begin the new order in Russia.

The message reverberated throughout society. The Bolsheviks soon emerged as a leading voice among the opposition parties, wooing a sea of malcontents. They feuded openly with the fledgling leadership, which still faced sporadic disturbances and constant problems fulfilling people's daily needs. Food costs were outrageous, rations too skimpy to satisfy. Shortages of raw materials and transportation snafus snarled industry, and unemployment soared. The war worsened, too, with mounting casualties. The Germans were closing in on Russia, en route to Petrograd. The post-Romanov honeymoon was over.

To revolutionaries, it was time to finish the job begun in February. The summer of 1917 brought spontaneous, violent rioting in the streets of Petrograd. Soldiers joined by 30,000 metalworkers and other troops sympathetic to the Bolsheviks launched a demonstration against the government. In all, some 500,000 participated in the movement. Soon, as shops and factories closed, employees spilled into the streets to join the march. Angry mobs unleashed their fury, looting stores, smashing windows, charging liquor reserves. They swallowed what they could, thumbing their noses at the dry laws, and then headed for Tauride Palace, home of the provisional government. There, they met resistance from pro-government forces, who fired on the masses. The revolutionaries returned an avalanche of fire, and blood from both sides of the fray filled the cracks of the city's center. For forty-eight hours, everything in Petrograd seemed to turn a shade of red—from the bloodied ground to the signs and flags. The upper hand seesawed between the rebellious mobs and regiments called in by the state.

Finally, the edge shifted in favor of the government after it charged Lenin, Trotskiy, and other Bolshevik leaders with spying on behalf of the Germans. Officials released a document that, they said, proved that Lenin had organized the demonstrations to distract the state while its enemy mounted an offensive at the front. Despite emphatic denials from the accused, Bolshevik enthusiasts were horrified, turning their rage on the traitorous Bolshevik leaders. The offices and printing plant for *Pravda*, the Bolshevik's newspaper, were destroyed and the revolutionaries' headquarters stormed. Trotskiy and other top party members were arrested and thrown into prison while Lenin, with the aid of Stalin, slipped into Finland. The rebels' movement had not only failed, it had been disgraced.

It was a serious setback for Lenin but not a fatal one. The government still had no idea how to solve Russia's mountain of woes, and now Petrograd felt the threat of advancing German soldiers. As fall neared, people forgot the treasonous charges hurled at Lenin and other top Bolsheviks. They concluded that the state's leadership was too weak, too unstable, to hang on. No one was offering the answers they sought except the Bolsheviks. Lenin steadfastly preached for an end to the war and for sweeping social reforms, and increasingly, people turned en masse to these passionate, energized men. Lenin returned in disguise to Petrograd and settled into a Bolshevik hideout. On October 24, 1917, Trotskiy assumed the role of conductor, orchestrating a comprehensive strike. The Bolsheviks systematically seized control of Petrograd's infrastructure—from the post office to the train stations to telephone and telegraph offices. Red Guards infiltrated the Winter Palace, home of the provisional government where its anxious ministers were holed up. Late into the night, the government surrendered, with little bloodshed as the state's guards offered almost no resistance.

Announcements plastered throughout Russia notified people of the old regime's disintegration and the tenuous creation of a new one. Nobody understood exactly what it meant, but in the days and weeks and months to come, it became clearer that this fledgling reign would extract a great price from those who sought to undermine it, challenge it, or who were, by definition, in conflict with its tenets.

According to the recollections of Vladimir Smirnov, his family, like the majority of wealthy capitalists, fell into that latter category. After the revolution, which he described to his wife as "a dark cloud," the Smirnovs were "denounced as enemies of the people."[16] Vladimir fled south with Valentina to a resort town near Pyatigorsk. Full of spas, hot mineral springs, and other leisurely pleasures, it was a beautiful region to which many affluent Russians had retreated. Since the end of the eighteenth century, the town had been a refuge of sorts, where the rich and famous came to restore their weary bodies and nurse their bruised souls. Tolstoy, Pushkin, and Chekhov had all escaped at one time or another to this green, mountainous paradise. The home and resting place of one of Russia's most famous poets, Mikhail Lermontov, the quaint town was approximately 1,440 miles from tumultuous Petrograd and, most importantly, not yet under the control of the Bolsheviks. Vladimir and Valentina rented a nice home and settled in, figuring they would be safe there. They were wrong.

Chapter 22

Escape

The Smirnovs tasted firsthand the bitterness the new Russia served up. The Bolsheviks declared that all private property belonged to the people, including factories, private homes, churches, vacant lands, and even stud farms like Vladimir's. In addition, the state decreed that Russia's dusty social infrastructure would be no more. Overnight, the Smirnovs and others like them were stripped of their privileged standing. Titles ranging from prince to noble to merchant to peasant were hurled into obscurity. From then on, everyone was simply a citizen of the Russian Republic.

This new social order, or lack of it, elicited great fear and confusion from the upper classes. For almost everyone else, it represented liberation, albeit a complicated one. Lenin, sticking to his message, pushed hard to galvanize the pent-up frustrations of the masses. For too long, they had been downtrodden and oppressed, and now it was their turn to rise, he argued. He encouraged them to see wealth as an unforgivable sin, capitalism as a self-serving evil.

The collective good was what mattered most, and true virtue was the result of honest labor and shared prosperity. With the Bolsheviks running things, workers and peasants would finally have land and an equal say in matters ranging from economics to justice. The Marxist talk was intoxicating and dangerous.

In the ensuing months, virtual anarchy took hold of the country. The chaos stemmed from a variety of causes, including the hugely unpopular war with Germany and a continuing shortage of almost every basic need. Hunger gnawed at the majority of citizens. A lack of fuel and electricity stalled large swaths of the country's transportation network. Disease spread, too, as a dearth of medical supplies, personnel, and services overwhelmed an already crippled health care system. Severe unemployment gripped several pockets of Russia, as factories and once-prosperous retailers and restaurants stood idle. Angst was all that was plentiful. "Moscow and the other Bolshevik cities at this time were more drab than usual. Shops were closed, the streetcars rare or non-existent . . . public buildings were unheated and poorly illuminated, people died in offices and on the streets."[1]

The misery was indiscriminate. According to statements made by Eugeniya's grandson, Boris Aleksandrovich Smirnov, members of the once prominent vodka dynasty lived in a state of constant anxiety. "It was a very sad and sorry time," he recalled decades later in legal proceedings. "Everything had shut down and you couldn't buy anything. All the stores were boarded up. The well-to-do people would exchange antiques, antique furniture, just to get hold of a bag of flour." His mother, Tatiana Petrovna Smirnova, was pregnant with Boris in Moscow during the revolution. About a week after Lenin's takeover, she went into labor. She could not find a carriage or tram or car to help her. "In order to give birth, she had to walk across Moscow on foot to . . . go to the hospital. There was no transport. There was nothing left."[2]

Lenin knew his grip on the country was fragile and that he needed to maintain order, consolidate power, and instill obedience. To that end, he created the Cheka in December 1917, formally known as the All-Russian Extraordinary Commission for Struggle against Counter-Revolution and Sabotage. It was the government's secret police force, entrusted with snuffing out opposition groups by any means necessary. Its often-bloodthirsty mercenaries executed, tortured, or imprisoned anyone suspected of lacking complete faith in the new power. The Cheka took on the task of ridding Russia of its Romanovs, shooting to death the tsar, his captive wife and children, and some servants in a cellar in July 1918. To ensure that no evidence of this massacre survived, they took the bodies of their victims to an abandoned mine. After showering them with sulfuric acid, they dropped what remained down a mineshaft before burying the mutilated remains nearby.*

Although high-ranking officials from the Imperial Palace were among the first to suffer under the new order, ordinary citizens often fared no better. The Cheka, along with members of the Red Army, raided private homes, rummaging through drawers, desks, and closets, confiscating valuables and whatever else they found to their liking, including liquor reserves. Indeed, the looting of wine cellars, known as wine pogroms, was a particularly daunting problem for Lenin and his anti-alcohol comrades. Angry mobs would crash into warehouses that stored alcohol reserves, sparking drunken orgies that could last for days. Cellars in the Winter Palace were raided along with some 570 other storage facilities in Petrograd alone, despite the enduring prohibition. "Soldiers and civilians alike rocked Petrograd with a series of riots sparked by struggles over control of liquor supplies."[3] This unrestrained lunacy lasted for weeks

---

* Remains of all but two victims were discovered in 1991. The last two, including Nikolay II's only son, Aleksey, were found in 2007.

until the Bolsheviks issued an order proclaiming that anyone participating in the wine pogroms would be killed on the spot. "People were shot as if they were wild wolves," remarked Maxim Gorkiy in one of a series of articles he published about events between 1917 and 1918.[4]

It was not just those who were caught in acts of wrongdoing who suffered. The Bolsheviks seized suspected infidels on a whim, sometimes rousing them from their beds. No investigations, evidence, or formal trials were needed or expected. Eugeniya's grandson, Boris, believed his father had vanished in this fashion. He never knew much about him, except that his name was Aleksander. Shortly after his birth, recounted Boris, his father "disappeared, he was arrested. Nobody knows what became of him . . . it was presumed he was shot. A lot of people got shot around that time."[5] The same destiny awaited Vasiliy Bostanzhoglo, the wealthy merchant and former lover of Smirnov's youngest daughter, Aleksandra. He was also the father of her son, Vadim, Smirnov's grandson. He was reportedly shot in his factory during a routine raid by the Cheka, which was hunting for valuables believed to be hidden there.[6]

Daily life became a series of unexpected, often unexplained confrontations, especially for the formerly privileged. "The war on private wealth was a bloody purgatory on the way to a heaven on earth."[7] A great many homes owned by Smirnovs, like so many others, were subdivided. People from all walks of life moved in, taking up residence alongside aristocrats. In the home of Smirnov's youngest son, Aleksey, for instance, as many as fifteen people from one family could live alongside him and his family, shattering the comfortable life he and other members of the upper crust once cultivated.

The nationalization initiative, which saw thousands of private enterprises either abandoned by distraught owners or taken over by force by government bureaucrats, came on the heels of this chaos. The Smirnov vodka business was no exception. It was unceremoniously torn from the family—no Smirnov would ever play a role in its future management or operation. The 1918 order read: "All the stores of grape wine, cognac, flavored vodka and related to them, rum, liquor, fruit drinks etc. . . . are announced to be property of the Moscow Soviet of Peasant and Working Deputies. . . . All the warehouses where these products are kept, all the equipment related to the industry, i.e., glass, boxes, covering material, dressing and fuel; also cash money in the wine shops and warehouses belong to the company and to [private persons] . . . now belong to the Moscow Soviet of Peasant and Working Deputies."[8]

Instead of vodka, which was still outlawed, the factory began producing and selling vinegar made from sour, overaged wine, and berry drinks. Just fifteen workers, who petitioned to nationalize this department for fear of becoming an orphaned enterprise, were left to run this business. The former liquor empire also began producing an herbal, alcohol-based liquid sold as a remedy for digestive problems, though it was also drinkable. Grape wines, because of their weak alcohol content, continued to be produced at one of Smirnov's facilities. Comrade Mikhailov, a longtime Smirnov loyalist, oversaw the operation with the help of roughly three dozen employees. The Smirnov name, along with its Imperial distinctions, remained a fixture on all these products until the early 1920s. It was then that Lenin banned use of pre-revolutionary brands and awards, such as the state coats of arms and the status of having been purveyor to the tsar.

Smirnov's warehouses, still stuffed with bottles of flavored vodkas and other liqueurs, presented an unusual problem. Laws prohibited moving the inventory without special permission from local authorities. It also could not be sold. It is unknown exactly what happened to these remnants. Most likely, they were destroyed, confiscated by corrupt officials, or sealed off from the public. Whatever transpired, the closure seemed to have ended forever Smirnov's reign as Russia's vodka king.

It was a story repeated again and again. During this time at least 37,000 private enterprises were nationalized by the Bolsheviks, which became known as the Communist Party of the Soviet Union. The drive left Russians from all classes without homes, without jobs, and, sometimes, without their lives. Sergey Chetverikov, a leading Russian scientist, recalled an eerie vision he had one day while brushing snow from a railroad track in early 1918. His work was part of the Bolshevik's forced labor initiative. In the distance, he made out the figure of Arseniy Ivanovich Morozov, a leading member of one of Moscow's most prominent industrial families. He seemed to be wandering through the snow aimlessly, having just been evicted from his own spacious mansion and factory. Chetverikov saw that Morozov was clutching a family icon, the one thing he had managed to salvage before his banishment. "The fate of the leading lights of merchant Moscow at the hands of the Bolsheviks was truly wretched," wrote James L. West in his book, *Merchant Moscow*. "As arrests of prominent capitalists mounted in 1918 and nationalization decrees cascaded down from the Bolshevik regime, the once-proud captains of Russian industry were torn from the charmed lives they had known and thrust toward almost unimaginable extremes of human experience as prisoners, fugitives, refugees, and émigrés."[9]

For her part, Eugeniya was helpless to stop the government's heavy-handed takeover. Businesses that did not adjust or acquiesce to the new realities often ceased to exist. Besides, Eugeniya seems to have gambled that the Bolshevik's tenure in office would be short-lived. Like many in her class, she viewed Lenin and his cohorts as a temporary fix, a stepping stone to some other regime that would eventually return Russia to glory. She did not foresee her own poverty or that of her family. How else could she have justified leaving her children and her homeland behind shortly after the revolution? Eugeniya left Russia to join her new husband, Italian Marquis de la Valle Ricci, who was then stationed in Japan. "She took a little money but, of course, it was more or less worthless money," recalled her grandson, Boris. "They had a great deal of money in the Credit Lyonnais Bank in Moscow. When they went to a branch of the Credit Lyonnais bank in Japan, and then subsequently in France, they were told that all had been lost because of the revolution."[10]

The wrenching realities were disheartening. For some, they were also electrifying. In the months that passed, the disenfranchised, the displaced, and the disillusioned mobilized themselves into what became the White Army. They formed in locales throughout the empire, including the region near Pyatigorsk, the resort area to which Vladimir and Valentina had fled. These were the Russians who did not necessarily favor a return to the past, but they wanted something more democratic and humane than what the Bolsheviks were delivering. And they were willing to fight for it.

Lenin made good on his promise to end the war with Germany, but the treaty he signed had been costly, requiring Russia to sacrifice huge chunks of its territory, including the entire nation of Poland. He also empowered and equalized his people, or so they thought. These moves did little to quiet the rumblings of the opposition. Lenin and Trotskiy, who were amassing a new Red Army with thousands of trained officers culled from the tsar's own military, understood this discontent. Civil war, it was clear, was upon them.

PYATIGORSK ("FIVE MOUNTAINS") was a refuge. The quaint, chic city in the southern part of Russia was located in a lush green valley surrounded by a protective chain of mountains. The mineral waters flowing through this region in the Caucuses had restored the health and psyche of Russians for more than a century. Now, it offered its newest inhabitants a similar restoration, but this time it was the healing of souls tormented by the violent outbursts that raged in the Russia's cities. Vladimir and Valentina enjoyed the tranquil countryside in the dacha they now shared. Their new neighbors, some of whom included the ex-minister of finance Vladimir Kokovtsov and prima ballerina Mathilde Kshesinskaya, did as well. Still, they all must have known that the serenity they had discovered would be fleeting.

The Bolsheviks seized power in Pyatigorsk and its environs in the spring of 1918. They did not immediately impose their harsh reprisals, so life went along relatively peacefully. Valentina entertained former nobles as well as the newly appointed local leadership, providing her and Vladimir with some much-needed income. More importantly, it ingratiated Valentina with officials who not only enjoyed her performances but also appreciated her enormous charms. Valentina, Vladimir's third wife wrote, "was beyond suspicion since she gave concerts for the Red Army [meaning Bolsheviks]."[11]

Still, news of unrest and chaos elsewhere reached the residents living in and around Pyatigorsk. Each reported incident of brutality pierced the calm, protective shell that shrouded the community. Vladimir and Valentina, who resided in Yessentuki, a town nine miles west of Pyatigorsk, had lost everything they had not taken with them. Their home, furnishings, clothes, and keepsakes all disappeared, disbursed into the hands of ravenous strangers. Vladimir's prized thoroughbred, Pylyuga, described by a well-known Russian writer as "an adorable gray-steel he-horse," was bludgeoned to death by a raucous, club-swinging crowd. It was part of a senseless slaughter of animals throughout the country, explained away as acts of revenge against their greedy, capitalist owners.

This recklessness caught up to Pyatigorsk in September 1918 when the government implemented an order aimed at suppressing the rising insurgency throughout the country. It was direct and unequivocal, calling for anyone to be shot "during an attempt of counterrevolution or assassination directed at leaders of the proletariat." Moreover, hostages were to be rounded up for everything from belonging to the ruling elite to praying against the Bolsheviks. The party's newspaper, *Izvestiya*, ("The News") reported that anyone in the Red Army who did not follow the order would be punished. "The national commissariat of Domestic Affairs must be informed immediately about any cases of indecisiveness concerning this issue. . . . There must be no hesitations at all, no indecisiveness at all in the mass terror implementation."[12]

Vladimir would have represented a particularly enticing target— not just because of his former wealth. It was the *source* of his wealth that was most damning. Lenin and his party blamed liquor for the ruination of the Russian people. Vladimir, therefore, would have been deemed the worst kind of capitalist. He was a vodka maker, which by definition made him part of a class of exploiters.

Arrests and arbitrary searches began shortly thereafter. A number of notable people were jailed, including former generals, the tsar's ex-minister of communications, and a prince. Vladimir and Valentina held their breaths, as members of the Red Army appeared at their doorstep. According to recorded remembrances of Vladimir by his third wife, they had hidden what they had left of value in a garden—mostly some silver and jewelry. The only item they could not hide well was a treasured religious icon known as a Mandylion, a large and heavy heirloom Vladimir had managed to save that had belonged to his father. It was held in a large wooden frame decorated with gold, diamonds, and other gems.

The Bolsheviks tore into the contents of the dacha, turning over drawers in cabinets, desks, and dressers. They searched every corner of the house, eventually finding the Mandylion. In a panic, Vladimir pleaded with the men to leave his cherished icon alone.

"The commissar in charge of the search laughed and said, "We don't need this garbage," after which he ordered his subordinates to take off the golden riza [cloth covering] and he threw the icon on the floor with such force that the wood broke in half. "There, have your heirloom," he said. "As for the gold and precious stones, we'll find a use for them."[13]

It was the unleashing of what people in the region dreaded. Vladimir and Valentina were forced to move several times since they could no longer safely remain at the much-watched dacha. It was assumed that Vladimir was now in the sights of local authorities, a man to be hunted and caught. The police returned repeatedly to search the premises shared by the couple. One evening, during a search, Vladimir hid from the officers, climbing up a large tree. When asked where he was, Valentina replied that she had kicked him out after they had quarreled. After four days of hiding out in the tree, with Valentina secretly bringing him food, Vladimir could take it no more. He refused to behave like a coward and began to move about town again, going to restaurants and other public places. It did not take long for the authorities to confront Vladimir. This time, though, their actions were decisive. Smirnova-Maksheyeva recorded her husband's memories: "They gave him a document that read 'Vladimir Smirnov, stud-farmer, capitalist who used to sell vodka, enemy of the people. . . .' After his arrest, they put him in prison. Soon there was a trial during which he was sentenced to the highest punishment—execution by shooting."[14]

The verdict was devastating. Conditions in the prisons throughout Russia were known to be wretched, filthy holes crammed with diseased or malnourished bodies. An inspection of a prison run by the Cheka in Moscow in October 1918 found "overcrowded cells, no water, grossly inadequate rations and heating, and sewage dumped in the courtyard. Nearly half of the 1,500 inmates were chronically sick, 10 percent of them with typhus. Corpses were found in the cells."[15]

Valentina tried her best to save Vladimir—or at least soften the blow. She had ties to officials who admired her acting and delighted in her charms. These relationships were extraordinarily valuable—and they were also well-known. Other women with loved ones at the mercy of the Bolsheviks in Pyatigorsk sought out Valentina's powers of persuasion. One woman whose husband was behind bars sought out the actress on the advice of some of her confidants, imploring her to gather some news about his situation. "She [Valentina] had connections and friends in the Cheka," the woman recalled. "These relations were pretty old, made during her past performances on stage."[16] Valentina asked her contacts about this woman's husband, a high-ranking member of the social elite. What she learned, though, was inconclusive. Valentina reported back to the woman that twenty-eight hostages from her husband's prison had been executed. She was unable to find out whether this woman's husband had been one of them.

On Vladimir's behalf, Valentina begged local officials to spare his life. She sought out the wives of the commissars, giving them her remaining furs and jewels. She may even have offered sexual favors in return for her beloved's safety. But all this pleading ended up buying her, or so it seemed, was a chance to tell her lover goodbye. Smirnova-Maksheyeva's recorded remembrances reveal what happened next.

"Vladimir and other prisoners were loaded onto a tall truck bound for Pyatigorsk. The guards were instructed to shoot them on the way, at the foot of Mount Mashuk. Vladimir, thinking of his imminent death, turned to an old passion for comfort. He began to sing, loudly, encouraging his fellow condemned and the guards to join him. The two groups soon were singing in unison, with the guards forgetting their orders. They were several miles past Mount Mashuk when they realized they had passed their destination. Darkness was looming and the soldiers had to be fed. The officer in charge determined it was too late to turn back. *'Let's take them all to Pyatigorsk, hand them over to the prison, and then they can do what they want with them there,'* the officer said."

This incident turned out to be the first of several times that Vladimir cheated death.

PYATIGORSK WAS HOME to a trio of prisons, and it is impossible to verify which one held Vladimir. He did not make the distinction when reminiscing years later about his captivity, and the archives from the facilities have long since been lost or destroyed. All three, though, offered heavy doses of torment and humiliation. At least two practiced merciless murder. One of the prisons, known as "the hole," was especially horrific in its dark, dehumanizing treatment of its enemies. It is likely that Vladimir passed at least some of his time here since it tended to be a holding location for the recently incarcerated as well as for those awaiting execution. The hole, like many of the Bolsheviks' prisons created out of structures that previously served as restaurants, hotels, or theaters, was located in the cellar of a home. The entrance to the hole was through an opening dug into the yard of the property. Once inside, the height of the room from floor to ceiling was about ten-and-a-half feet. The glass from the few grated windows peering out from the ground had been knocked out, leaving an unrelenting musty and moist cold. There were no beds. Just a few desks, which were guarded by inmates panicked at the thought of having to sleep on the dirty, bug-infested cement floor. Sometimes as many as seventy men were packed into one of the cellars at a time.[17]

The commandant of this prison had a malevolent reputation. He reveled in his power, cruelly and spontaneously whipping or beating his prisoners. One of his favorite pastimes was watching the tsar's former generals and colonels clean toilets using only their bare hands and wearing filthy clothing. He executed several prisoners without a moment's hesitation. According to an investigation years later into crimes committed by the Bolsheviks, the commandant of the hole "confessed that he got inspired by shooting people, that it was a meaning of his life."[18] Vladimir learned this fact firsthand.

He spent his days in a cell crammed with some thirty prisoners. The stench was overwhelming, the food was rotten. Occasionally, guards would call out the name of an inmate for questioning who often would never return. One day, they called Vladimir's name. He was led outside to the yard surrounding the prison and told to stand against a wall. Soldiers a few feet away faced him, their rifles aimed at his body. Vladimir waited, listening for the expected pop of the guns. It never came. The soldiers lowered their rifles and laughed. The mock execution was repeated five times, always ending in the same horrible manner. According to Smirnova-Maksheyeva, Vladimir grew so weary of the torment that he wished for death.

This kind of heartless theater was a known method of psychological torture and may well have been the unforeseen consequence of Valentina's pleas on behalf of Vladimir. It is quite possible that she succeeded in convincing the commandants to spare Vladimir's life. In return, however, they may have kept him behind bars and used him for their own sadistic entertainment. This and other methods of torture, known as the Red Terror, were commonplace during this era of tumult and often resembled the same techniques employed by the tsar's former secret police. Indeed, many of the Bolshevik's most effective tormenters had spent time in jail during the tsar's crackdown. Gorkiy protested the Bolshevik's brutality, calling it "barbarism." He even addressed some of his outrage directly to Lenin, a man whom he had previously admired.[19]

Still, the bloodletting went on as if it would never end. Winter descended upon the region, though not the kind of strangling chill that smothered Moscow, Petrograd, and other more northern cities. Nonetheless, the cooling air would have felt frigid inside the moist and dark cells, as if it were freezing in place the daily horrors endured there. It would have continued, too, had it not been for the well-armed White Army. Its ranks swelled to as many as fifty thousand recruits at its height, though still it paled in comparison to the manpower of the Red Army. Its leaders were culled largely from the tsar's former military while the rank-and-file depended on rebels and the Cossacks, who saw the Bolsheviks as a menacing threat to their independent way of life.

In January 1919 a division of Cossacks overpowered the forces guarding the Pyatigorsk region, freeing all the prisoners and residents. The young general who led the charge, Andrey Shkuro, recalled the relatively bloodless battle for control. "Realizing that they were surrounded, the Bolsheviks escaped from Yessentuki [the place Vladimir and Valentina had first come], which we easily captured after an attack of part of our troop. On January 5, I sent the First Volzhskiy regiment to Pyatigorsk. January 6, the regiment invaded the town. . . . The loot was very considerable: Several thousands of captives, guns, cannons. . . . I was met enthusiastically by the local population, which had suffered under the Bolshevik regime."[20]

Vladimir and other freed men received passes that enabled them to leave the region—and Russia if they chose—immediately. He scooped up Valentina, and the two joined a long procession of refugees traveling south to Yekaterinodar, a city in southern Russia named to honor Catherine the Great. Renamed Krasnodar in 1920 (from the Russian word for red), it was a stronghold of the White Army and a center for refugees fleeing the civil war. According to a 1919 census, Yekaterinodar experienced a surge in its population, growing by thirty-four thousand residents. This rapid growth caused a variety of logistical problems, from a shortage of food and fuel to overcrowded dwellings to an outbreak of typhus. The problems intensified to the point where the town, a few months after Vladimir and Valentina arrived, closed off its city to nonresidents.

Vladimir's decision to go to Yekaterinodar and then eventually leave his motherland was clear-cut. He had no hope of reviving his father's business in Russia even if he had wanted to. By this time, the Bolsheviks had nationalized the vast majority of the liquor industry as prohibition reigned. He also likely had no idea what had happened to his remaining siblings, whether Nikolay had survived the revolution, whether Aleksey still resided in Moscow. He could not even imagine what might have befallen his former wife, Aleksandra, and his son, who he must have assumed were still in Moscow. He may have feared a worse fate for them than his own. As Vladimir explained, the risks of remaining, given his background and known name, were far outweighed by the possibility of finding passage to a safe, albeit unknown, haven.

It is most likely that Vladimir and Valentina wasted no time once they arrived in Yekaterinodar, stopping only long enough to make plans to reach the border. Trains were the fastest way to get to Novorossiysk, a port city on the Black Sea, but they were often stuffed with refugees. Luggage blanketed the platforms in the stations, making it difficult to move about. Once on the train, passengers stood for long stretches, unable to find comfort in a seat or on the floor. Once in Novorossiysk, the wait for a ship heading west commenced. It could be an Allied warship or a Russian cargo vessel, anything that was seaworthy. Space was at a premium, as thousands of desperate refugees clawed for a ticket out of Russia. Consequently, no baggage was allowed once aboard. Passengers could take with them only what they could carry compactly—mainly a few personal items, money, and enough food for the journey to Constantinople.

In the three years following the revolution, an estimated

two million Russians emigrated.[21] Such luminaries as composer Sergey Rachmaninov, prima ballerina Anna Pavlova, writer Vladimir Nabokov, and Nobel Prize–winner Ivan Bunin were among them. Vladimir and Valentina were there, too. They probably had enough valuables and important connections left to secure passage. The ship's typical route stopped in towns along the Crimea, including Yalta, before docking in Constantinople. This city was the first place to which thousands of Russians fled before migrating farther west, and the city to which Vladimir and Valentina escaped. They had only a fraction of their worth left when they disembarked. Unsure of how they would scratch out a living, where they would go, who they could trust, they had arrived—and survived—and that opened up possibilities for a future that neither could have anticipated.

Chapter 23

Smirnov with an "F"

The faces of the new arrivals to Constantinople, as many as 140,000 in one month during the evacuation of the White Army in November 1920, were at once relieved and bewildered. They were relieved that the life-threatening horrors they had faced were now far beyond the Black Sea, and bewildered upon realizing that they had nothing, knew no one, and had not a clue as to what they were going to do next. These refugees had to adapt to the local language and new customs. As one American relief worker in Constantinople observed: "It is pitiful. There are Russians who were colonels and generals in the army who are selling papers on the street, scarcely getting anything, trying to do what they can in order to get something to eat, but they can only get a little. They don't know the language; they have nothing to do; and with no business in Constantinople, there is no hope for them."[1]

This was the place Vladimir and Valentina now called home. Unlike many Russians who relied on Constantinople as little more than a way station on the road to cities farther west, Vladimir and Valentina decided to stay put. They had managed to bring some money and valuables with them from Russia, but it was not nearly enough, certainly not for a couple used to a privileged life. They needed time to generate some income and replenish their resources—and they knew just how to do it. The two enjoyed one pivotal advantage that most other new arrivals did not. They had recognizable names and well-established reputations.

Almost simultaneously, Vladimir and Valentina sought to revive the businesses and careers they knew best. For Vladimir, it was unquestionably vodka making. Even though he had tried to distance himself from the brand and industry that had made his father wealthy and famous, he realized it was his only real vocation. All his other pursuits, including horse breeding and racing, had been aristocratic pleasures, indulgences he could now not afford. It did not seem to matter that Vladimir had sold his interest in his father's vodka enterprise to his older brother, Pyotr. He was gone now, and no one probably knew what had become of his two other surviving brothers, Nikolay and Aleksey. The Smirnov brand was his heritage—and his only hope for survival.

Awhile after docking, he ventured into the heart of Constantinople in search of a suitable space for a vodka factory. He found one. It was to be a small operation, presumably producing mainly the pure and flavored vodkas for which his family had been best known. Vladimir still remembered many of the recipes his father had concocted. On January 10, 1920, the Russian consulate in Constantinople granted Vladimir a license to open his new firm. The certificate was full of references to a Russia that had been cast into history, calling Vladimir the son of a first guild merchant and the manager of a vodka distillery that once supplied the Imperial Court.[2] In Turkey, such references still had meaning within the bulging immigrant community.

Valentina was also working hard to reestablish herself. Constantinople had a thriving theater community, thanks in part to dozens of Russian actors who had settled in the city after the revolution. With Vladimir as manager, Valentina founded a cabaret theater called Parisiana. Its French-sounding name was meant to entice Russia's French-loving ex-aristocracy, which had always held France as the epitome of good taste and refinement. At first, Valentina found a loyal, appreciative audience, attracting "the cream of the [Russian army]," according to Pyotr Isheyev, formerly a high-ranking military officer who had come to live in Smirnov's vodka factory after escaping the revolution. However, that venture did not last long. Indeed, both Vladimir and Valentina struggled to keep these enterprises afloat, but the Russian customers to whom they catered were primarily a newly impoverished, inward-looking group, either unable or unwilling to spend their remaining rubles on drinks or entertainment. As for the Turks, they were merely uninterested in what Vladimir or Valentina had to offer. "The factory business did not go well. Turkish people didn't drink vodka," wrote Isheyev, a distinguished-looking man with a softness in his eyes. "And Parisiana, which had flourished in the beginning, for some reason became unpopular."[3]

Isheyev and other witnesses wrote about the unending difficulties faced by Russian refugees in Constantinople. Apart from shortages of everything from housing to food, Russians found themselves largely unwanted. Turkey was in the midst of a protracted struggle for national independence, led by Mustafa Kemal Atatürk, the founder of the Turkish Republic. The country had no ability or incentive to absorb another country's needy castaways, and the government was concerned that Turkish rebels might try to recruit ex-Russian soldiers for its own agenda. The local culture was also alien to Russians, culminating in a political, economic, and social environment that was often hostile.

Vladimir and Valentina accepted this unfortunate reality, but they were tired of running. They made a last-ditch effort to get something sustainable going in Constantinople. Valentina reprised her starring role in Offenbach's *Beautiful Helen* at a summer theater called Buff. The production had always been a favorite of her audiences, and it did well in Constantinople, too. Beautiful costumes, original staging, and inspired music and dancing helped lure a constant stream of enthusiastic attendees, according to the memoirs of several Russian exiles.

That success, though, came at a price: It piqued the interest of the Turks—at least the government's tax collectors. Nearly two years after Vladimir and Valentina arrived in Turkey, the tax agents showed up one morning and presented them with an enormous tax bill. It requested payment of an amount far beyond the pair's financial means.[4] Not satisfying the bill would mean certain jail time. Once again, regretfully, Vladimir and Valentina packed their bags and crossed the border into Bulgaria, a common stop for Russian immigrants after Constantinople. The couple landed in the capital city of Sofia where they met up with Isheyev, who had fled there a few months earlier with a small group of actors.

BULGARIA WAS A far more hospitable location for Russian émigrés. The languages were much closer to one another—as were the cultures. Both Russians and Bulgarians were of Slavic origin, creating a common bond between the two nations and its people. The Bulgarian government, too, was welcoming. It used public funds to provide Russians with a variety of social services. The government also offered certificates enabling Russians to take jobs with the state and to travel without needing Bulgarian citizenship.

Vladimir took advantage of the friendlier atmosphere. With Isheyev's help and a handful of investors, he established another outpost for Smirnov vodka. Isheyev would manage the factory while Vladimir would own the business. "The factory business went well," recalled Isheyev. "First, there were parts of the White Army there who liked vodka. And the Bulgarians started to appreciate it in time."[5] In short order, it appeared as if Vladimir may have sold or licensed the rights to his brand name, along with the rights to his family's liquor recipes. "A buyer appeared who proposed a good price for the factory," wrote Isheyev. It was no giant windfall but Vladimir was only too happy to pocket any profit, however small.

Valentina was doing well, too, continuing to entertain the hoards of expatriates from Russia, now resettled in Sofia. Valentina's reputation as a leading lady still loomed large. She managed to entice paying customers to her concerts, including a well-to-do Polish diplomat by the name of Ladislas Baronowski. Valentina and Baronowski had a great deal in common, starting with their Polish roots. It is not clear exactly when and how their relationship bloomed. Indeed, it appeared that at first all three, Vladimir, Valentina, and Baronowski, formed strong bonds of friendship. Soon, though, Valentina and Baronowski were no longer just friends. Valentina, according to Smirnova-Maksheyeva's memories, could not resist the allure of a man with money and position, making their budding romance not necessarily only a matter of love. More likely, Valentina's desperate desire to regain a sense of security and access to the finer things in life, neither of which Vladimir could now provide, brought the couple together.

The breakup shattered Vladimir. Valentina had been the one woman to whom he had been devoted. With Valentina, he had been part of a golden couple within the inner circles of Russian theater, and this had been the passion of his life. As was Valentina, who had traded much of her own remaining fortune, from furs to jewels, to help ensure that Vladimir did not perish at the hands of the Bolsheviks. He, in turn, had supported her, making sure there was nothing for which she could want. Theirs had been a true love, a genuine match that had superseded all the trivialities that made up their public lives.

The depth of their feelings was underscored by their remaining connection long after their split. Following the sale of Vladimir's vodka business in Sofia, the threesome moved again. This time they settled in Lvov, Poland. Baronowski had great influence there and was able to help Vladimir get established in 1923. It was in Lvov, now part of Ukraine, that Vladimir decided to formalize his efforts to preserve the Smirnov brand. His idea was to plant seeds in as many locales as possible, willing the spirits firm to endure and flourish. His company's main objective would be to license the Smirnov name and recipes to as many takers in as many communities as possible.

Vladimir reached into the heart of Russia and found his brother Nikolay in Moscow. He wrote to him, asking for his power of attorney to create a shell company that would be responsible for peddling the remains of their father's business, primarily its brand, reputation, honors, and secret recipes. It would most likely manufacture nothing itself. Vladimir and Nikolay would be part owners of that enterprise, along with Baronowski, Valentina, and a Russian lawyer they knew in Moscow. Nikolay, it appears, wasted no time in fulfilling his brother's request. There would have been no point in resisting. Nikolay could not revive the family business, despite the ending of prohibition in Russia and reinstatement of the vodka monopoly later in 1925. Too many obstacles stood in his way, and Nikolay did not possess the skills or ambition to navigate the new state system, particularly during a time of such economic turmoil. He also could not rely on his youngest brother, Aleksey, for help, for he had died of heart trouble a year earlier. Perhaps most daunting was that the old Smirnov company was now part of a large state-owned enterprise by the name of Vintorgpravleniye, later known simply as Vintorg. An umbrella organization that united many previously private businesses, including the Smirnovs, it produced the same drinks Smirnov had manufactured. It even used the same labels—absent the Smirnov name and the former company's array of honors.

Nikolay put his faith in Vladimir. In his own shaky hand, he signed over all his rights to Vladimir. The last two remaining Smirnov brothers, both of whom had sold their interests in the family business years earlier, were bound together once again by their shared vodka heritage. The letter, dated June 18, 1923, attested to the different fates that had befallen the men. It was signed: "Citizen Nikolay Petrovich Smirnov."[6]

The new firm was born in Lvov. Its name, Société Pierre Smirnoff Fils, registered in French, may have been the first time the brand was officially spelled the Western European way with two *f*s. The owners were also the firm's board of directors. In its first transaction, the company hooked up with a small local alcohol manufacturer who planned to produce about five hundred bottles of Smirnov liquor per day.[7] Vladimir then sold other licenses to groups in Prague and Paris. It is not known how much income these deals generated for Vladimir or his co-owners, or how much liquor was produced and sold under the brand.

Despite this success, Vladimir was deeply unhappy during his stay in Lvov. Valentina probably moved back to Bulgaria with Baronowski, leaving Vladimir alone. He had some friends from the old days and a handful of new acquaintances, but life was now so different for him—no matter how hard he tried to re-create what he once had had. He realized, like many Russians, that any hope of returning to the motherland was dimming. Thousands had chosen to return, but they knew, too, that Russia could never revert to its former self. Petrograd had been renamed Leningrad in 1924 following the death of Lenin. The former Bolshevik leader had left a will explicitly stating that Stalin should be removed from his position as general secretary of the Communist Party. The directive ignored, Stalin's iron fist grew stronger. On a personal level, Vladimir learned that his own son, now twenty-three years old, and Aleksandra, Vladimir's ex-wife, still lived in Moscow in the eight-room, one-bathroom flat that he had purchased for them years ago. But now, so did members of seven other families.[8]

Vladimir began to look ahead in earnest, strategizing his best chance at building a real, lasting future for himself. His thoughts took him to the one place he had long adored, a second home of sorts to much of Russia's former aristocracy. Many of the people he knew during his happiest years were there already, setting up little, self-contained Russian colonies, complete with Russian churches, schools, restaurants, music, and theaters. Vladimir applied to the Polish government for a passport, packed his bags, and hopped a train. He was going to France.

FRANCE, AND PARIS in particular, was like little Russia in the 1920s. Its chic style, sophisticated art and literary scenes, and its willingness ultimately to accept more than 150,000 Russians made it an enticing destination. Paris offered the added benefit of being architecturally reminiscent of St. Petersburg. A vast array of Russia's most prominent, promising, and ordinary citizens relocated to the French capital. Composers Igor Stravinskiy and Sergey Prokofiev, bass opera singer Fyodor Shalyapin, and painters Aleksander Benois and Marc Chagall all emigrated to Paris. Members of the late tsar's family, including his brother-in-law, Duke Aleksander Mikhailovich, and Grand Duke Dmitriy Pavlovich Romanov, who took part in the killing of Rasputin, now resided in France. Distinguished merchants and wealthy capitalists gravitated there as well, such as members of the Ryabushinskiy textile dynasty, industrialist Sergey Tretyakov, and textile magnate Sergey Shchukin, a prolific collector of French impressionist art. Shchukin's more than 250 magnificent works, which included masterpieces by Matisse, Monet, Picasso, and Gauguin, were expropriated by the Russian state after he fled to Paris.*

These leading lights were joined by scores of more typical,

---

* During Stalin's reign these paintings were hidden because Stalin saw them as decadent. Only after his death, in the 1950s, did they begin to be viewed publicly.

lesser known émigrés. They wanted nothing of the Paris spot-light. They faded away into the city's natural commotion, taking on odd jobs such as driving taxis, sewing dresses, or working in factories. They were just trying to survive and like them, Vladi-mir had come to France full of hope and in search of a home. Though he was probably better off than many of his downtrodden brethren, he was more like them than the extremely well-to-do.

Vladimir, now fifty, had aged greatly by the time he arrived in Paris. Still remarkably handsome, his looks had taken on the weight of his experience, leaving him under a constant fog of loss and fatigue. According to photos, he had done away with his trademark handlebar mustache, which left his clean-shaven, more fully rounded visage looking a bit fallow. His thick mop of wavy, sand-colored hair had thinned, graying at the temples. His light eyes, once overflowing with aristocratic entitlement and conceit, had mellowed, too. They seemed now to hold only longing and regret.

It is not clear why Vladimir's stay in Paris was short-lived. He spoke the language fluently and knew the local culture well, but he had an already established venture there. Smirnov vodka was being produced at a nearby factory, and it was selling, though it is unclear how well. Vladimir may have felt he needed to cultivate more opportunities elsewhere. Or maybe he just preferred to be away from the big city. After a while, he left a friend from Russia in Paris in charge of that small operation and headed south to Nice.

Nice was second only to Paris in its number of Russian émigrés. Like the country's capital, it also had spawned a little Russia, a bubble-like community full of restaurants, grocery stores, a library, and even a cemetery. Matisse was known to paint Russian émigrés during his regular visits to the beach city. There was a magnificent Russian Orthodox cathedral in Nice, full of parishioners. Part of this infrastructure existed as a result of decades of visits from wealthy nobles who, prior to the revolu-tion, spent entire seasons in the resort.

Now, of course, Nice's Russian population was two-faced. A small minority of the inhabitants managed to escape with a healthy share of their resources. They maintained luxurious lives, residing in opulent villas. They hobnobbed with the rich who arrived from New York, London, Paris, and Amsterdam, went to expensive cabarets, watched Isadora Duncan dance; they had the means to eat in the finest restaurants.

For the vast majority of émigrés, though, the air smelled more of fish, alcohol, and drying laundry. Their lives were simple yet onerous, overburdened by unemployment, poverty, and despair, overwrought by what had been and what could never be again. Wrote one observer: "You can distinguish a Russian person . . . without words. They have shabby clothes, down-to-the-heel boots, a washed-out hat, and, the main feature, they have unveiled sadness in their eyes, gestures, and gait."[9]

Shortly after arriving in Nice, Vladimir met Tatiana Maksheyeva, the woman who would become his third wife. He was likely in search of companionship more than anything, someone to fill the void left by Valentina and the loss of contact with his son and siblings. An attractive woman, though not as charismatic as Valentina had been, Tatiana grew up in St. Petersburg and received a first-rate education at the Yekaterininskiy Institute, a private girls boarding school. Her parents had been, like the Smirnovs, members of the wealthiest social class.

Tatiana, one of eight children, left Russia before the outbreak of World War I. Her first husband was ill and was advised for health reasons to move to the Mediterranean Coast, so the couple relocated first to Turkey before moving to Nice. The string of events—from war to revolution to civil war—kept Tatiana from ever returning to Russia. She yearned for Russia but determined there was nothing waiting for her in her homeland other than misery. For years, she didn't even know the whereabouts of her family, much less its fate.

Alone in Nice after her husband's death, Tatiana probably

ached for a Russian soul mate, someone to keep her connected to her roots. She was fifteen years younger than Vladimir and nothing like the other women who had dominated his life. Tatiana appeared to be a far more independent, less demanding spouse. Instead of coveting diamonds and furs, she was a lover of literature. She was a prolific writer, penning romantic novels and poetry throughout her life. She also made her own way rather than relying on a husband for income. With what little money she saved, Tatiana purchased a small antique shop in Nice with a dingy, two-room apartment on its second floor where the newlyweds would live. She also made and sold Russian dolls and hats, according to her niece, Alfonsina Frantsevna Mekhedinskaya. In her memoirs, Tatiana wrote succinctly, "In 1925, we met, fell in love, and got married."[10]

The two managed to scrape by. Vladimir collected a meager income from the concessions of Smirnoff vodka he managed to sell. Tatiana brought in a bit of money from her antique business. It was enough to send money in letters to relatives back home, recalls Alfonsina, who says her family might not have survived without the generosity of Tatiana and Vladimir. The couple kept to themselves, socializing mainly with friends and acquaintances from the old days. One of them was, surprisingly, Valentina. She had moved to Nice shortly after Vladimir and was performing there. Baronowski, still occupied with his diplomatic duties, was often away. In time, Tatiana, Vladimir, and Valentina developed a warm, comforting friendship. Tatiana recalled her interactions with Vladimir's ex-lover:

> In spite of her relationship with Baronowski and the fact that he supported her, [Valentina] was still in love with Vladimir. Once she came over unexpectedly and asked my permission to visit us, telling me that she was compelled solely by her friendship with Vladimir and that they shared a connection due to what they lived through

together during the revolution. Since I am not jealous by nature, I received her warmly, invited her to visit us. When Baronowski would visit Nice, they would visit us together. I never had to regret meeting Valentina. She was always proper, cheerful, and genuine in her dealings with me. She sometimes complained about Baronowski— most often that he sent her too little money too rarely. She would cry and my husband and I would comfort her. In another minute, she would start laughing on account of some trifle. Vladimir treated her as a brother would treat a sister. He never recalled the past except for the fact that thanks to her, he was able to leave the USSR and save himself from death.[11]

The affections were not so warm for another woman out of Vladimir's past. Eugeniya had also resettled in Nice. She had grown bitter and desperate, unable to adjust to a life without privilege. She had once been well known to workers in Nice's hospitality trade. She could walk into the lobby of her favorite hotel with her trunk and chambermaid in tow, and the manager of the hotel would greet her almost as royalty. Settled into her usual suite overlooking the Mediterranean, she could call for room service, and make plans to visit her regular crew of socialites.

Now, though, Eugeniya probably never visited her former haunt. She could no longer afford even a dinner there. She relied on charity and on money supplied to her by her daughter, Tatiana, who worked an array of odd jobs, but the money never amounted to much. "She [Tatiana] never tolerated the idea of working in a factory or any kind of nine-to-five job because she loved her freedom," said her son, Boris. "She was brought up with great freedom and in luxury, the grand life, very pampered. She never really wanted to buckle under and work."[12] For her part, Eugeniya never tried to earn her own way. When she had a chance to improve her situation when her third husband, the Italian diplomat died, she used the bit of money he left in typical fashion—she went on a vacation to Italy.

Eugeniya was even more disturbed when she learned that Vladimir claimed a right to the Smirnov brand name. It galled her that he or Nikolay would profit from a business that their older brother had bequeathed to her and she argued that she was its legal owner. Now Eugeniya tried to prove her position by making several attempts to contact former Smirnov employees in Moscow, hoping they might have access to the legal documents that would make it clear who owned the trademarks and copyrights. Those efforts were fruitless: Eugeniya stewed. According to her grandson, Boris, neither Eugeniya nor Vladimir spoke to one another directly about the matter. They staked out opposing positions about the vodka business and carried on a silent kind of bout. "I don't think [they ever communicated] because knowing my grandmother, enraged as she was, I would be very surprised that it would have even crossed her mind to get in touch with him. I can't guarantee this but, to my knowledge, that's simply not possible. . . . For both my mother and grandmother, he was a pariah. He had betrayed the family."[13]

Boris says that his mother, Tatiana, on Eugeniya's behalf, once tried to file a complaint against Vladimir with the local chamber of commerce. Her lack of evidence, though, thwarted those efforts. "There was very little she could do, in actual fact, because she had no money whatsoever and, of course, too few connections with the people who could help her to go to Moscow. Of course, this was tough for her."[14]

Bit by bit, Eugeniya slid into poverty, isolating herself from the people and world she had once dominated. She lived in a modest retirement home, supported by her daughter and grandchildren who had also emigrated. Eugeniya received assistance from some Russian charities set up by wealthy exiles to help less fortunate refugees. It was a humbling and humiliating experience for the former aristocrat.

Vladimir was down, too. His vodka business was sputtering—France was not taken by the taste of the colorless spirit, preferring its own wines and cognacs, nor did it seem that the rest of Europe had a thirst for vodka either. By 1930 Vladimir was thought to be receiving little to no income from the various licenses he had sold. With few options, he turned to singing, the only other skill he had. Not since his father had shipped him off to China had Vladimir sung for his supper. Music had been a joyful hobby for him, but now it was work. Making matters worse, Vladimir had to wear a costume harkening back to the days before Peter the Great while he performed. He sent a card to his old friend, Isheyev, who by then had immigrated to the United States. Vladimir made light of his situation, showing off to his friend a photo of himself in a boyar costume. "You see," Vladimir wrote, "I'm singing!"

Vladimir was running out of options. His bank account depleted, he had few prospects for replenishing it. More worrisome, he began to feel seriously ill. Soon diagnosed with a debilitating and unspecified illness, Vladimir would need multiple operations and significant medical care. The fight before him now was more than financial. It would require all his remaining energy and a good deal of luck. He was dying. If good fortune did not step in, the legacy his father had spent a lifetime crafting, the legacy Vladimir had clung to in the wake of the revolution, would die with him.

Chapter 24

The End Is a Beginning

In 1933 Vladimir was in an almost constant state of agony. His physical condition was deteriorating. Two complicated surgeries had done little to slow the progress of his illness or alleviate his pain. Medications aimed at easing his discomfort were largely ineffective and, worse, accompanied by debilitating side effects. "He would spend long periods of time in hospitals," recalled Smirnova-Maksheyeva.[1] "When the doctors allowed it, I would take him home, but he was always on a strict regimen." Confronted by what he believed to be the inevitable, Vladimir made the tough call. He ceased taking his medicines and stopped visiting his doctors. He would stay out of hospital beds and rely only on herbal remedies to find relief. After all he had been through, Vladimir did not want to spend whatever remaining days he might have in a drug-induced blur. Mostly, though, he did not want to leave his wife and friends in abject poverty. He still felt responsible for their livelihoods and was determined to somehow come up with more funds. In a letter to a Russian émigré, Vladimir explained his calculation: "I was ill the way I wish nobody to be ill. I faced two serious surgeries. So now, after four years of hovering between life and death, I've finally recovered. Now I only drink herbs and have left all doctors and medicines. And I feel fine."[2]

The decision may well have shortened Vladimir's prognosis, but it also left him more clearheaded and with enough fight in his battered fifty-eight-year-old body to take a last stab at a Smirnoff renaissance. The family's spirits had been one of the few pre-Bolshevik liquor products exported into international markets: surely there was untapped demand for it somewhere.

Vladimir cast his net. He placed numerous advertisements in *Posledniye Novosti* (The Last News), a Russian language newspaper widely read by the émigré community throughout France. One small, unadorned ad, which sought out businessmen to open up Smirnoff outlets in Switzerland, the Netherlands, Italy, Persia, Belgium, and England, gave no hint of the flourish or fanfare that once accompanied the flashy announcements from the tsar's favored purveyor. It was as bland and unpretentious as the gray blocks of cement Stalin erected during the Soviet era—with two exceptions. First, the ad made reference to the old company's honors, including its four coats of arms and special relationship with the Imperial Court. Second, Vladimir, the self-proclaimed head of the revamped company, demanded that anyone wishing to manufacture Smirnoff vodka mimic the precise distillation practices and marketing strategies that had transformed his father's little operation into a powerhouse. He may have been desperate, but he was not willing to sacrifice the hard-earned reputation and secrets behind the Smirnoff name. "Contractors have to pay particular attention to the products' high quality, to distill the products through our charcoal machines; and to keep the established bottle shapes and label designs," the ad stated.[3]

A second advertisement was more typical of Smirnoff during its heyday in the late nineteenth century, highlighting the company's accolades and dominant position with the use of a large typeset and darkened capital lettering.

DEMAND EVERYWHERE—in good **RES-TAURANTS** and in good **SHOPS** our **RUSSIAN MOSCOW** world-known, granted with **FOUR RUS-SIAN STATE EMBLEMS** and **HIGHER AWARDS, VODKAS AND NALIVKAS,**
the **QUALITY** is **BEYOND** any **COMPETI-TION**—the **TSAR'S VODKA #40—TABLE WINE #21, ZUBROVKA #19** . . .
The Administration of the Trade House Pyotr Smirnov's Sons offers the company to be licensed or bought in Germany, England, Sweden and Persia. For further information you should address solely to the Head of the Administration V. P. Smirnov, 52 rue Lamartine, Nice, France. The company has no representatives.

The bait was set, but unfortunately, no one bit. For Vladimir, hope of a revival was quickly fading. It is likely he knew that the remaining Smirnovs in Russia were living ghosts. Like so many of the formerly wealthy and influential who stayed behind, they tried to remain invisible, fearful that their identities would ignite renewed hatred and punishment. Vladimir's own son Vladimir had no affiliation with his father's former profession and had seemingly blended into the new landscape. He served in the Red Army for two years and then attended the now prestigious Plekhanov Institute of the National Economy, specializing in metallurgy. The house by the Cast Iron Bridge, the home in which Vladimir père had grown up, was now the headquarters of the Erisman Research Institute of Hygiene, a scientific research facility focused on advancing studies of worker productivity. Ironically, the institute was named for the same chemist who spearheaded the toxicity tests of vodkas, including Pyotr Smirnov's, in the 1890s.

The Smirnovs and their vodka heritage were on their way to obscurity. Then, in a bizarre twist of fate, an enterprising Russian-born American, living thousands of miles across the Atlantic Ocean, intervened.

RUDOLPH P. KUNETT was just twenty-seven years old when he arrived in New York City. He was penniless—and a world away from his agricultural roots and the comfortable life he had once known. He was born Rudolph Kunettchenskiy in Trostyanetz, Russia, now part of Ukraine. His father owned a large plantation and distillery that was believed (in 1912) to be the largest rectifier and blender of liquor in the world. Much of the grain harvested by the Kunettchenskiy family supplied the Smirnovs.

Kunett was an academic sort, believing his best opportunities would grow from a solid education. He studied philosophy at Odessa University and received his doctorate from the University of Berlin. At the outbreak of the revolution, he was in Denmark, working on behalf of the Red Cross. This assignment saved him from having to confront a wrenching choice for many anti-Red Russians—ride out the storm unleashed by the Bolsheviks or to embark on the hazardous journey over the border. Kunett just chose not to return.

He entered the United States like thousands of other Russians in search of a fruitful, new beginning. For Kunett, his arrival in 1920 coincided with the inauguration of America's own experiment with prohibition. The dry laws were in full force, giving rise to a subculture of bootleggers, speakeasies, and bad alcohol—a scenario similar to what Russia had experienced during its anti-alcohol era—and this precluded Kunett

from contemplating a career in the liquor industry, but he readily found other opportunities. He worked as a salesman for the
Standard Oil Company and later landed a job in New York with
Helena Rubinstein Inc., where in due course he rose to be the
general manager of the company's cosmetic enterprises.[5]

Kunett may not have known the Smirnovs well, but he was
certainly familiar enough with members of the family and his
own father's strong connection to them. Moreover, he was well
acquainted with their vodka, having been a frequent consumer
of it. "In Russia, Poland, Bulgaria, and Serbia, everyone drinks
vodka," explained Kunett in a published interview decades later.
"Until I was twenty-one and left Odessa for a German university, I didn't know there was any other liquor."[6]

Somehow Kunett heard about Vladimir's offer or his ads
placed in France in 1933, the same year prohibition in the United
States officially ended. The combination of the two seemingly
disconnected events piqued Kunett's interest and gave him what
he thought was an ingenious idea. If he could bring Smirnoff's
beverages to the United States, he might be able to introduce
the spirits to consumers, create demand for it, and make a fortune. Kunett was possibly one of the few people in America who
knew something about producing vodka. At the time, of course,
most Americans preferred bourbon or beer. Few had ever tasted
vodka, straight or mixed.

Kunett made arrangements to go to France, where Vladimir
was delighted to meet his former compatriot. The familiarity
elicited a rare and deep-seated level of comfort and trust. With
few other options, Vladimir was more than pleased to make a
quick deal. After some negotiation, they struck a bargain: For
54,000 francs, Kunett was sold "the exclusive right and license
to manufacture and sell within the territory of the United States
of America, within the territory of its possessions . . . all the
alcoholic beverages and all other products of the firm, together
with the exclusive right to use the firm's name, the trademarks

and labels as used and owned by the firm, and the exclusive right to reproduce and use the various models of bottles hitherto in use by the firm or its licensees in France."[7] Kunett also agreed to manufacture all his Smirnoff products using the exact formulas and processes introduced to him by Vladimir. The labels would mention Pierre Smirnoff Sons and use the subtitle "Firm of Pierre Smirnoff formerly by appointment to the Imperial Court of Russia." The deal was finalized on August 21, 1933. Vladimir, who continued to try to sell in other countries, signed the documents on behalf of himself and Nikolay, while the three other owners, including Valentina, signed for themselves.

Just after the repeal of prohibition, in March 1934 Kunett opened the first vodka factory in the United States. Located in a long, two-story building near the center of Bethel, Connecticut, a sleepy southern New England town just sixty miles from New York City, the factory's location was perfect for the fledgling operation. It was adjacent to the railroad tracks where boxes of vodka could be easily loaded onto trains for delivery. Kunett touted his new product immediately, exercising the same marketing zeal that had made him a force in the cosmetics industry. The company prepared a history of the business for the American media, highlighting its grand tradition. "The name Smirnoff was known from end to end of the Russian empire, and its product, which was referred to as Smirnovka, became a household standby alike in peasant cottage and Imperial castle," wrote the *Danbury News-Times* in 1934, citing the company's numerous awards, state emblems, and relationship with the last three tsars.[8]

Kunett was unabashed in his own advertisements as well. They prominently featured all four coats of arms, the purveyor to the Imperial Court distinction, and an enticing slogan: "Creating a new vogue in cocktails ... VODKA by Smirnoff." Each bottle, it was advertised, cost $1.75 and came with a booklet of recipes for mixed drinks. Kunett also emphasized what a good deal his made-in-America vodka was compared to the imported stuff, which cost as much as $4 a bottle due to tariffs.[9]

Smirnoff's newest evangelist kept Vladimir apprised of every development, writing to him about the business and about his associates in New York and Bethel. He made sure that Vladimir would have an active role in the factory's future, inviting him to be the chairman of the board and to visit the United States to meet everyone involved in the venture. Kunett, as president of the Smirnoff firm in the United States, wrote to Vladimir in 1934: "I'd love to connect you with my colleagues. That way, you will have relationships not only with me personally but with the company as well, and hence with my colleagues. . . . I'd love if you could establish relations with them so in case of my death, the connection won't be lost."[10]

Clearly, Kunett valued Vladimir's flesh-and-blood footprint on his fledgling enterprise, surmising that it legitimized promoting the product as a Russian original instead of an imitation. He showcased the Smirnoff family connection at every chance, putting out statements from Vladimir testifying to the authenticity of the vodka as well as its superior taste. Vladimir, in a statement, said he was confident that their venture would win over skeptical American consumers. "With [your] flair for cocktails and other mixed drinks, you will find vodka the ideal base. Because of its clarity and freedom from artificial flavor, it blends harmoniously with the Vermouths, Grenadines, bitters, fruit juices, and other ingredients. And it is worth knowing that Vodka by Smirnoff leaves you feeling fit after a convivial evening. It is so matchlessly pure."[11]

For Vladimir, it had been some time since he had been treated with such respect and deference. His other licensing partners had been dismissive of him, forgetting to report sales, sending insufficient money, or mismanaging operations without explanation. Vladimir complained that his surrogate in Paris, for instance, had been particularly unprofessional, cheating him out of money and botching the running of the vodka franchise. Kunett, though, was different. His ties to the Smirnoffs during their most powerful years stayed with him. He had come of age when all the trappings of old Russia mattered, from social titles to financial stature. The Smirnoffs had been important citizens; their products universally popular. It was natural for Kunett to exude reverence.

Vladimir must have felt like his old self again. He wrote to Kunett expressing his appreciation. In the letter, Vladimir's emotions overflowed as he thanked Kunett for his kindness and accepted the invitation to serve as chairman of Kunett's board.[12] Vladimir now pledged to come to America. He wanted to inspect the factory and further instruct Kunett regarding his father's vodka-making innovations. He also wanted to sample for himself the spirits Kunett was making, believing that "the drinks' taste is the most important thing in our business."[13] The trip, though, seems not to have materialized. Vladimir's health took a sharp turn for the worse and he never recovered. In the early morning hours on August 25, 1934, the fifty-nine-year-old, third son of the vodka king died in his apartment above the antique shop. It was almost exactly one year after he had made his pact with Kunett, transporting the Smirnoff name and drinks to America.

His passing, unlike those of his father and brothers, went almost unnoticed. It is unlikely that members of his family in Russia even heard about it. There was no mention of it in the news there, which was then dominated by Stalin's propaganda. Only Russians in France received word through a brief announcement that ran in the newspaper for émigrés. The end for Vladimir came like a whisper—without ceremony, without fanfare, without prestige. His simple grave in a Russian Orthodox cemetery in Nice was a communal one, its gravestone generic in its remembrances. It was a testament to how far Vladimir's life had veered away from the once-mighty Smirnoff dynasty. He would not be buried with them and nothing would specifically identify his final resting place for nearly sixty years.

It was a sad, odd conclusion for a man who had lived such a loud and flamboyant life, but Vladimir, though he may not have known it, had come full circle. Just before his death, the son of an uneducated serf-turned-wealthy-capitalist had planted the seeds that would win his identity back. Because of Vladimir's perseverance, Pyotr Arsenievich Smirnov would get his legacy back, too. In one of Vladimir's last letters to Kunett, he unveiled his heartfelt emotion and genuine excitement at the prospect of keeping his father's handiwork alive. "Your business is dear to me," he wrote, "because I see reconstruction of our old Smirnov company . . . I look at you with great hope. I am certain of your success."

Vladimir could not have imagined how right he was.

Epilogue

Success did not come swiftly. Kunett, a persistent sales-man, promoted Smirnoff vodka every way he knew how. He oversaw the factory and its output, often wearing a smock to keep his suit from becoming soiled. The problem was, however, convincing Americans to forsake their favored beers, gins, and whiskeys for an unknown Russian alternative was a tougher sell than Kunett had imagined. In his first year in business, he sold just 1,200 cases, each case holding twelve bottles. By the fifth year, he increased sales to roughly 5,000 cases, which accounted for the total amount of vodka produced in America, but it was not nearly enough.[1] By 1939 Kunett was on the brink of bankruptcy.

With little choice, he shopped the vodka brand around, hoping to find not only a buyer but also a partner. Kunett still believed that Smirnoff could win over Americans. He had few takers, though, until he approached John Martin, an affable, bespectacled Englishman running G. F. Heublein & Bros., a family-owned business in nearby Hartford,

Connecticut, that had started up as a producer of pre-mixed drinks. Due to the lingering effects of prohibition, Heublein was also struggling, relying on its one notable food product, A-1 steak sauce, for most of its revenue. Kunett proposed to sell his Smirnoff enterprise to Martin for $50,000, Martin recalled in a videotaped interview. Martin declined, though he was intrigued. He saw something promising and potentially profitable in a neutral-tasting spirit. Martin hammered away at Kunett's offer, agreeing to buy Kunett's equipment and the Smirnoff name for $14,000. He also made Kunett president of a newly formed Smirnoff subsidiary and gave him a 5 percent royalty on each case of vodka sold over the next decade.[2] Financial analysts and company insiders pronounced the purchase foolish, dubbing the agreement Martin's Folly.

Within two years, though, sales of Smirnoff vodka grew to more than 22,660 cases. South Carolina was an especially fruitful market, mainly because a distributor in Columbia came up with an ingenious, highly effective slogan: "Smirnoff White Whiskey—No Smell, No Taste." The distributor was apparently inspired by the cap Heublein used on the first batches of Smirnoff vodka shipped to the state. It read "whiskey" because the company had none that read "vodka."[3] When World War II arrived, the spirit's slow but steady climb stalled, as production of all alcohol was sharply curtailed and Martin went into the U.S. Army. It was not until about 1946 that Smirnoff vodka truly emerged from obscurity in America.

To hear Martin tell it, he and his old friend Jack Morgan can take much of the credit. Morgan was the owner of the Cock 'n Bull restaurant on Sunset Boulevard in Los Angeles, a favorite watering hole for Hollywood starlets. The two friends met one another in New York when Morgan was trying to unload cases of ginger beer and Martin was trying to jumpstart demand for vodka. According to Martin, they came up with a new cocktail that combined Smirnoff vodka with ginger beer and lime.

Served in an engraved copper mug, the drink was called the Moscow Mule. "I imagine [the name] had to do with the kick," said Martin.[4]

To promote the cocktail, Martin used a grassroots marketing strategy reminiscent of his vodka's namesake, Pyotr Arsenievich Smirnov, reportedly used in Russia decades earlier. According to company lore, Martin flew out to Los Angeles with one of the first models of the Polaroid camera. He went into bars and took two photographs of the bartender serving the Moscow Mule. He gave one photo to the bartender as a keepsake and took the other photo to a different bar, highlighting to the next bartender his competition's promotion of Smirnoff vodka and the new cocktail. The ploy worked. Sales of Smirnoff vodka took off, surpassing one million cases annually by 1955.*

Heublein then launched a series of aggressive campaigns showing American consumers how to mix vodka with a variety of liquids, from juices to teas to beef bouillon. Slick print advertisements over the next three decades were eye-catching, too, featuring a parade of such top stars as Woody Allen, Groucho Marx, Eva Gabor, Vincent Price, and Marcel Marceau. In 1962 Smirnoff also began a long, high-profile partnership with the James Bond movie franchise. In the first Bond movie, *Dr. No*, Sean Connery drinks a martini, famously "shaken not stirred," made with Smirnoff vodka. Since then, bottles of Smirnoff have been featured in twenty-one of the twenty-two Bond films.

These marketing drives propelled Smirnoff from a little-known, foreign commodity into a powerhouse brand, eventually outselling all other premium spirits in America. Moreover, it helped vodka surpass gin and bourbon as the top-selling liquor in America, a position it has largely retained since the 1970s. "Americans, you know, were *un*informed about Russia, but they

---

* During the height of the Cold War, the popularity of the Moscow Mule waned. However, in the summer of 2008, Diageo, the largest spirits company in the world, reintroduced the classic cocktail through a multimillion-dollar advertising campaign.

were *mis*informed about vodka," explained Kunett in a 1955 interview with *The New Yorker.*[5] Once Americans were reeducated, though, vodka's upward spiral continued almost without interruption. Today, more than 23 million nine-liter cases of Smirnoff vodka are sold each year in some 130 countries, and Smirnoff, almost 150 years after its founding, is the best-selling premium spirit in the world, outperforming second-place Bacardi by some 4 million cases.[6] As for the brand itself, a 2008 study estimated its worth at $4.7 billion.[7]

As SMIRNOFF SURGED in the West, the political realities of the Soviet state under Josef Stalin took their toll on the Smirnovs and other similarly situated families. The known fates of Smirnov's descendants differed, depending upon how closely tied they were to the fallen vodka empire and the former aristocracy. Arseniy, Pyotr Petrovich's son and the patriarch's grandson, for instance, suffered miserably. According to an interview in the early 1990s with his son, Pyotr,* Arseniy worked as a street cleaner following the revolution. He was arrested and sentenced to death by firing squad in the 1920s because of his family's capitalist background, but Arseniy's wife saved him from execution by giving prison authorities everything the couple had. Still, life continued to be unkind to Arseniy; after divorcing his wife a few years later, he moved to the Volga River region and worked as a cemetery caretaker. He tried to flee Russia but was caught and beaten by soldiers with the Red Army. He later remarried and had three children. The family struggled to make ends meet. In 1943 Arseniy died, buried only in his underwear because his clothes had been sold for food.

Vladimir's son, Vladimir Vladimirovich, also faced difficulties under the Soviet regime. He continued the excellent

---

* Interview with Anton Valdin.

education his father had started, graduating with an advanced degree from the prestigious Plekhanov Institute. He spoke several languages, including English and French. Before World War II he worked as a senior instructor of physical metallurgy at Moscow's Machine Tools Institute. According to archival documents,* Vladimir was arrested on September 10, 1941. The home he shared with his mother, Aleksandra, his wife, and two daughters was searched. Vladimir was accused and convicted of having "anti-Soviet attitudes and to have expressed dissatisfaction with the existing social order of the U.S.S.R."[8] It was noted in his interrogation, during which he denied the charges against him, that he was from a family of first guild merchants.

For his crimes, Vladimir was sentenced to five years at a corrective labor camp. The hope of the authorities was that his anti-Soviet attitudes could be rehabilitated, and that later he might rejoin society in a more productive manner. His mother, Aleksandra, filed a protest, citing his innocence, her poor health and advancing age, and the livelihood of his daughters, as reasons to reopen his case. Justice was slow in coming, but after five years in prison and almost fifteen years after his arrest, Vladimir was cleared in 1956 of the charges against him for "lack of proof."[9] He left Moscow and moved to Tver, where he taught at a local polytechnic institute. He died in 1969 at the age of sixty-seven, just eight years after his mother had died.

The other Aleksandra, Smirnov's rebellious daughter who had married Borisovskiy, died in 1950. At the time, she lived in poverty in a small dark room in a communal apartment.[10] Her son, Vadim, fared better as an accomplished musician who founded a Soviet school for viola players. As for Eugeniya, she spent the last years of her life in a modest nursing home in Nice. Three years before her death in 1961 at the age of ninety-

* Translated archival documents obtained from the Davis Center for Russian Studies, the Smirnoff Vodka Archives Collection in the Fung Library, Harvard University.

two, she signed over to her daughter, Tatiana, her claims to the Smirnov estate. According to Eugeniya's grandson, Boris, his grandmother still held out hope that her rights could one day be restored. "My grandmother gave full power [of attorney] to my mother to do all she could do to prove that she was the sole proprietor of all the [Smirnov] assets," Boris said.[11]

Members of the Bakhrushin side of the family had similarly mixed outcomes. These descendants became noted doctors, scientists, and teachers. Pyotr Bakhrushin, for example, worked in a psychiatric hospital in Moscow. Others, though, were not so lucky. Nina Bakhrushina, a foreign language teacher, married a prominent chemist. They were exiled to Siberia after one of her husband's students accused him of unpatriotic conduct.[12]

It is, again, unlikely that any of the Smirnovs who remained in Russia, with the possible exception of Nikolay, until his death, knew of Vladimir's efforts to revive the family business in Europe or his agreement with Rudolph Kunett. Years later, however, as the Smirnoff brand grew in prestige and notoriety, they, like other descendants of once prominent merchant dynasties, grew curious. They wondered about their roots and tried to piece together their forgotten or hidden heritages. Oleg Sergeyevich Smirnov, Sergey's son and a retired lawyer in Moscow, led the effort in the 1970s for the Smirnovs. Outraged by the way his grandfather's name was being used in the West, he combed through reams of archived information, assembling a three-volume monograph about the patriarch's business history and his far-flung family. He discovered relatives he did not know and a global business giant he had not fathomed. The big question, Oleg began to ponder, was whether the Smirnovs could get it back.

THE FIRST OFFENSIVE was launched in the early 1980s in Cologne, Germany. Plodymex, a joint Russian–East German spirits export company, sued a German importer of Smirnoff. Plody-mex claimed that Smirnoff's labels, which included Cyrillic lettering and images of the awards Smirnov had earned a century earlier, misled consumers about its Russian origin. Relying on Oleg's research, the plaintiff further argued that Vladimir had had no right to sell his family's trademarks and copyrights to Kunett in 1933 because he had already sold his shares in the business to his brother, Pyotr, in 1905. The charge was potentially explosive. Smirnoff's future—and past—might hinge on the actions Vladimir took almost five decades earlier, the same actions that salvaged his father's legacy.

The two companies settled the case in Cologne. Heublein agreed to alter its labels, removing the Cyrillic script and references to Russia or Moscow. In addition, it would make clear that the vodka it was selling was not manufactured in Russia. This settlement, which affected trade only in Germany, was far from the end of the matter. There was a glint of promise in this battle that perhaps there was some merit in the fight. Moreover, Russia was on the brink of dramatic change, just as it had been when Smirnov launched his enterprise in the nineteenth century. Mikhail Gorbachev was coming to power.

Russia in 1985 was in a period of deep stagnation, economically, politically, and socially. Like Tsar Aleksander II following the painful lessons of the Crimean War, Gorbachev realized that key aspects of communism were outdated and ineffective in a globally integrated world. Problems ranging from corruption to alcoholism to apathy were contributing to a sharp decline in industrial productivity and output. He vowed to introduce comprehensive reform through *perestroika* (restructuring) and *glasnost* (openness). These initiatives, Gorbachev hoped, would prompt entrepreneurism, technological innovation, and corporate development.

Gorbachev's first major campaign, however, did not directly target the economy. It targeted alcoholism. Vodka was still an

integral part of life in Russia, and like Witte and others before
him, Gorbachev associated drunkenness with Russia's poor economic and moral condition. Even though the state stood to lose
millions of rubles in revenue from its vodka monopoly, he figured
that if the people's drinking could be controlled, other issues
might be more easily resolved. Gorbachev's government in 1985
announced a "comprehensive program for the prevention and
overcoming of drunkenness and alcoholism."[13] The production
and sale of vodka and other spirits were now limited, and efforts
were made to encourage moderation. Russians reacted much
the same way they always had—with anger and dissatisfaction.
Long lines formed outside liquor shops. It was estimated that
some Muscovites spent an average of up to ninety hours a year
waiting to purchase alcohol.[14] Prices of vodka and other spirits
spiked, and a black market for moonshine flourished. In the end,
Gorbachev's sobriety drive failed, and restrictions were relaxed
after just a few years.

Other initiatives had a more lasting impact. Gorbachev wanted
to transform the old centralized Soviet system into a more robust
market-oriented economy. He believed, as Aleksander II had, that
modernizing the nation's financial infrastructure would ease existing societal pressures. He noted that "it is only the market, in
tandem with the humanistic orientation of all society, that will be
able to satisfy people's needs, ensure just distribution of wealth,
safeguard social rights and guarantees, and consolidate such
values as freedom and democracy."[15] Gorbachev's rhetoric was as
groundbreaking as were the reforms he crafted. Private ownership of profit-oriented businesses and cooperatives was not only
legalized but encouraged. The law also permitted the establishment of corporations. Greater freedom of speech, more independent media, and an increased democratic political process were
also integral parts of Gorbachev's agenda.

These policies, though hailed in the West, were too slow in
coming for most Russians and too restrictive to be effective.

Gorbachev faced the difficult task of balancing his communist roots and devotion to socialism with twentieth-century concepts of capitalism and democracy. Moreover, his economic drive ran headfirst into ingrained prejudices throughout Russian society against Western-style capitalism and its foreign institutions. The economy did not improve and everyday life for most Russians went from bad to worse, as shortages of food and other essentials intensified. Gorbachev was replaced in 1991 by the more radical Boris Yeltsin, but few question that it was Gorbachev's bold reforms that led to the collapse of the Soviet Union by the end of that year. As for the Smirnovs, Gorbachev and his policies also provided the opening they needed.

IN 1985, THE year Gorbachev took office, the Smirnovs held a family reunion at the home of Oleg's brother, Viktor. Cousins descended from several of Smirnov's children were present, some having never met before. At this gathering, according to a book written by several Smirnov descendants, some of the Smirnovs began discussing the possibility of reviving the Smirnov dynasty.[16] Gorbachev promised to be more hospitable to private business ventures, and Russia would likely welcome the chance to reclaim one of its most storied brands. Little progress, though, was made for five years. First, Oleg died in 1986. Second, the tenuousness of Gorbachev's economic and legal reforms made it difficult to formulate a cohesive plan of attack.

By 1991 the possibilities were clearer. Boris Smirnov, the great-grandson of Smirnov's youngest son, Aleksey, and a former KGB officer, led the charge. He registered his family's trademarks in Russia. One was the "Trade House of Pyotr Smirnov and Descendants in Moscow," while another was "P. A. Smirnov and Descendants in Moscow." A month later, Heublein's new owner, International Distillers and Vintners (IDV), now a subsidiary of British liquor giant Diageo, filed papers for its Smirnoff trademark. Both were readying for the repeal of the vodka monopoly in Russia, which took place in 1992 under Yeltsin's hand. Russia's patent office rejected IDV's claims to sell Smirnoff vodka, thus permitting Boris Smirnov to do so.[17]

This decision marked the beginning of what would become a protracted international legal tussle for control of the Smirnoff name. The cases hinged primarily on the same arguments posed in the German case—whether consumers were misled about the origins of Smirnoff vodka, and whether Vladimir had illegally sold his family's name and copyrights after the revolution. Boris and his relative Andrey Smirnov began manufacturing vodka in Krymsk, a small town in southern Russia. They also leased the house by the Cast Iron Bridge in Moscow as their headquarters, partially renovating the grand old residence to its original nineteenth-century condition. Their hope was to revive the traditions of Pyotr Smirnov, profits and all. At first, it looked as though they might succeed. A Russian court in 1995 invalidated IDV's trademarks and barred the company from claiming that its vodka was related to the spirit's original founder.

Although IDV appealed the decision, a bigger showdown was on the horizon. Boris sought access to more than the Russian vodka market. He had designs on the lucrative U.S. market. Boris partnered with Eugeniya's grandson in France, also named Boris, attempting to prove that the French Smirnov had the legal right to the trademark because Eugeniya had bequeathed it to his mother. The Russian Boris then formed the Russian American Spirits Company with an American partner and sued Diageo for fraud and consumer deception in a Delaware court. Smirnoff's label, they claimed, which featured a crown, shield, red shrouds from the Russian Imperial Court, the state coats of arms, and reference to the tsar's purveyor title, caused people to conclude that the American Smirnoff was the same one supplied to tsars before the revolution. Boris additionally argued that he and his partners were owed nearly $1.3 billion, or roughly 2 percent of the profits he figured had been made off Smirnoff vodkas since 1939.[18]

Diageo countered in legal filings that it had purchased the brand in good faith, saving it from almost certain extinction, and had spent more than $700 million promoting Smirnoff since 1939.[19] All Boris and his allies were trying to do, the company argued, was profit from Diageo's sizable investment and decades of hard work. Furthermore, a schism had developed among Smirnov's descendants. More than thirty Smirnovs appeared at a press conference in Moscow, questioning Boris's arguments and charging that his actions threatened the good name of the family.[20]

In 1999 a U.S. court dismissed Boris's claims, and an appellate court affirmed the decision two years later. A British panel also considering the matter concluded much the same. It was during this time, too, when Boris's partner, Andrey, sold his half in their Russian vodka venture to Alfa Group, the giant privately held Russian consortium. Boris was furious and would not recognize the new shareholders. When a new director came to the office at the house by the Cast Iron Bridge in 2000, neither Boris nor a guard would let him in. Representatives from Alfa returned later, this time backed up by armed riot police wearing black masks. Captured on Russian television, the incident resembled something out of an action movie. Police broke through doors and smashed windows while workers inside lobbed bottles of vodka at them. Throughout the melee, Boris refused to leave, according to press accounts, even after his wife suffered a head injury.

Other lawsuits followed over the brand's true ownership until 2006, when Diageo and Alfa reached a pact. They formed a joint venture to sell and distribute liquor in Russia, including Smirnoff vodka and Diageo's stable of other spirits. Diageo paid Alfa $50 million and obtained 75 percent ownership in the venture.[21]

. . . .

VODKA CONTINUES TO hold a pivotal place in Russian society. Vladimir Putin considered resurrecting the vodka monopoly in 2005, not so much to decrease consumption as to fight against the destructive nature of low-quality, illegal alcohol production. Recent official estimates suggest that more than one-third and as much as almost two-thirds of the vodka sold in Russia may come from illegal producers. At a time when the country's population is in decline and life expectancy rates are slipping, alcohol's economic and human toll on Russia's citizens is all the more disheartening. Some thirty-three thousand Russians died in 2006 due to alcohol poisoning, according to the state's most recent data, and many more succumbed to illnesses related to alcohol consumption.[22] Still, Putin's call for another vodka monopoly to replace a hefty excise tax fizzled in 2007, ensuring that the hunt for a lasting solution to this centuries-old conundrum will go on. As it was during the time of the tsars, Russia's current economic, political, and social landscape cannot escape vodka's long shadow.

Resolution, though, in a sense, has come to at least one of the Smirnovs. Vladimir Petrovich Smirnov, the son most responsible for shepherding the family's heritage through the revolution and beyond, has found a measure of justice and peace. In 1993 his granddaughters arrived in Nice from Moscow to find his unmarked grave. They erected a tombstone on the site. The epitaph reads: IN HONOR OF VLADIMIR PETROVICH SMIRNOV 1875– 1934. A VODKA MANUFACTURER, CITIZEN OF RUSSIA. It was, finally, as it should have been.

Acknowledgments

I wrote this book because I had to. There was no choice for me. Once this little corner of nineteenth-century Russia grabbed me, I was lost to it. Many others, however, did have choices and joined me anyway. I will forever be grateful to them. My skillful editor, Ben Loehnen, offered unwavering support from the first moment. He demonstrated superb instincts on every matter that came before him and, even more amazing, he managed to keep my neurosis in check. He also happens to be a very nice guy. Thanks, too, to Matt Inman for his prompt responses to my many queries, and to Richard Ljoenes for his incomparable artistic flair. My unflappable agent, David Black, deserves an abundance of credit for his judgment, loyalty, and relentless drive for editorial excellence. An author could have no better advocate.

The research associated with this book was a massive undertaking. Many wonderful librarians in the United States and Russia offered essential guidance throughout the process, including Carol Leadenham and Molly Molloy at the Hoover Institute; Tanya Chebotarev at Columbia University's Bakhmeteff Archive; Allan Urbanic at UC Berkeley; and Sue Sypko at Harvard's Fung Library. I am also indebted to officials at the Central Historical Archive of Moscow and the State Archive of the Yaroslavl Province, Uglich branch. Experts from a variety of fields played important roles in helping me understand this story's many complexities. In Russia, I would like to thank Olga Bimman, Valentin Skurlov, Vladimir Grechukhin, Andrey Kuzmitchev, Olga Savelyeva, Mikhail Zolotarev, and Andrey Kokorev. In the United States, Patricia Herlihy deserves particular mention for her treasure chest of knowledge, for allowing me to pester her, and for her kind soul. Kate Transchel, Thomas Owen, Stefan Hedlund, and Anita Friedman also lent a much-needed hand.

Given the history, descendants of the Smirnov family were understandably hesitant to participate in this book. Nonetheless, I wish to express my sincere appreciation to Kira Smirnova and Tatiana Fomina for overcoming their misgivings and sharing some of their stories. The book is richer for it. Vadim Maksheyev and Alfonsina Mekhedinskaya, relatives of Tatiana Smirnova-Maksheyeva, should be recognized for their assistance and kind hearts. I am also grateful to the people at Diageo for their help with this book.

Special recognition must go to a handful of individuals whose contributions went well beyond what any reasonable person could have expected. Anton Valdin, an accomplished researcher and genealogist in Moscow, was unfailingly generous with his documents, time, and immense knowledge. Alina Polonskaya worked tirelessly and smartly on behalf of this project, too, unearthing many critical nuggets of information. Then there is Tatiana Glezer, the one person without whom this book could not have been possible. I count my blessings every day that I found such an intelligent, thorough investigator. Tatiana's perseverance, integrity, and natural instincts made her an ideal partner for this endeavor. She began as a researcher thousands of miles away. Now, I am honored to call her my dear friend.

I also owe an enormous debt of gratitude to those nearest me who have endured four years of this odyssey. My friends have been priceless assets, cheering me on through writer's block and worse. I can't possibly mention them all, though they know who they are. Leah Spiro believed in this idea from the start. Betsy Corcoran gave invaluable counsel and encouragement. Alison Ross lent me her considerable brainpower. Julia Flynn Siler generously offered astute insights into this crazy process.

Finally, I cannot conclude without paying tribute to my remarkable family. They have been my greatest champions—and I theirs. I dedicate this book to them, for their unconditional support, inspiration, and love. My sister Lisa read every word I wrote, critiquing and praising as the material warranted. She was a necessary ingredient in this process, a steady, gentle reminder that anything is possible. My brother also never stopped cheering me on. I am thankful for my mother's extraordinary writing genes and for my father's enthusiasm, which was pure and powerful, carrying me past my own, not insignificant doubts. His good humor, when I needed it most, ensured that I remembered to laugh, something for which I am especially thankful. To my wonderful husband, Michael, who selflessly agreed to pack up our two young children and head to Russia with me, thank you is not nearly enough. He has steadfastly backed this project in every way possible, proving in more ways than I could ever count what a wise choice I made in marrying him all those years ago. And to the jewels of my life, my children, who would have preferred their mom write a kid's book about animals with colorful illustrations, thank you for your patience, flexibility, and hearty hugs. You make it all worthwhile.

Endnotes

PROLOGUE

1. "Pokhorony P. A. Smirnova," *Moskovskiy Listok*, Dec. 3, 1898.
2. Ibid.
3. David Christian, *Living Water: Vodka and Russian Society on the Eve of Emancipation* (New York: Oxford University Press, 1990), 27.
4. Ibid., 45.
5. State Archives of the Yaroslavl province, subsidiary in Uglich, Fund 1, Inv. 1, Case 2604, 21.
6. Ibid., Fund 56, Inv. 1, Case 1053, 11/Inv. 1, Case 1076, 25.
7. Central Historical Archives of Moscow, Fund 3, Inv. 3, Case 419 (hereafter CHAM).
8. *Vestnik finansov, promyshlennosti i torgovli, Ukazatel pravitelstvennyh rasporyazheniy po ministerstvu finansov. 1899. Otchyoty kreditnyh uchrezhdeniy, torgovyh i promyshlennyh predpriyatiy* (St. Petersburg: Tipografiya Ministerstva Finansov V. Kirschbauma, 1899), 755.

9. CHAM, Fund 142, Inv. 5, Case 809, 2 and 34–49.

10. "Pokhorony P. A. Smirnova," *Moskovskiy Listok*, Dec. 3, 1898.

11. Patricia Herlihy, *The Alcoholic Empire: Vodka and Politics in Late Imperial Russia* (New York: Oxford University Press, 2002), 7.

12. A. P. Chekhov, *Complete Works* (Moscow-Leningrad: The State Publishing House of Artistic Literature, 1932), vol. 11:194–95.

13. Herlihy, *Alcoholic Empire*, 113.

14. William E. Johnson, *The Liquor Problem in Russia* (Westerville, OH: The American Issue Publishing Co., 1915), 154–57.

15. *Albom uchastnikov vserossiyskoy promyshlennoy i Khudozhestvennoy Vystavki v Nizhnem Novgorode 1896 g.* (St. Petersburg: Tipografiya Ministerstva Putey Soobshcheniya, 1896), Part 2, Dept. "g," 47.

16. Central State Archives of Moscow, Fund 142, Inv. 5, Case 809, 76–77 (hereafter CSAM).

CHAPTER 1: HELLO

1. Roderick E. McGrew, *Russia and the Cholera 1823–1832* (Madison: University of Wisconsin Press, 1965), 51–52.

2. P. Karatygin. *Cholera of 1830-31* (St. Petersburg: M. M. Stasyulevich, 1887), 13.

3. McGrew, *Russia and the Cholera*.

4. F. A. Brocgauz, I. A. Efron. *Entsyklopedicheskiy slovar.* Vol. T.XXV^A (50) (St. Petersburg: tipo-litografiya I.A.Efrona, 1898), 841.

5. *Cholera of 1830. Rasskaz avtora Afoni-Bogatyrya*, (Moscow, 1875), 6.

6. McGrew, *Russia and the Cholera of 1823–1832* (Madison: University of Wisconsin Press, 1965), 111.

7. Ibid., 111–13.

8. M. Sh. Shafeyev, L. M. Zorina, I. K. Khasanova et al., *Especially Dangerous Diseases: Epidemiology and prophylaxis* (Kazan: KGMU, 2001), 26.
9. State Archives of the Yaroslavl province, subsidiary in Uglich, Fund 43, Inv. 1, Case 904, 321.
10. "Litso russkoy natsionalnosti." *Vlast*, Sept. 26, 2005.
11. State Archives of the Yaroslavl province, subsidiary in Uglich, Fund 43, Inv. 1, Case 904, 395-a, 336-a, and 346.
12. V. A. Pushkin and B. A. Kostin, *As a Reason of Unified Love to Motherland* (Moscow: Molodaya Gvardia, 1998), 101, http://militera.lib.ru/bio/pushkin_kostin/index.html.
13. A. A. Galagan, *Istoriya predprinimatelstva rossiyskogo: Ot kuptsa do bankira* (Moscow: Os-89, 1997), 61.
14. State Archive of the Yaroslavl Province, subsidiary in Uglich, Fund 1, Inv. 1, Case 2604. 20.
15. Ibid., 23.
16. Ibid., 22.
17. William L. Blackwell, *The Industrialization of Russia* (Arlington Heights, IL: Harlan Davidson Inc., 1982), 20–23.
18. State Archives of the Yaroslavl province, subsidiary in Uglich, Fund 1, Inv. 1, Case 2672, 37–38.
19. *Russkiye Vedomosti*, no. 105, Saturday, May 19, 1873, 1.

CHAPTER 2: MOSCOW
1. A. G. Rashin, "Population of Russia over 100 years (1811–1913)," in *Statistical essays*, ed. S. F. Strumilin (Moscow, 1956), 124–25.
2. German Shtrumph, *Iz istorii Kanalizatsii Moskvy i Peterburga*, quoted after http://saturday.ng.ru/time/2000-04-08/1_cloakamaxima.html, *Subbotnik* 25 (72), June 30, 2001.
3. Orlando Figes, *Natasha's Dance: A Cultural History of Russia* (New York: Henry Holt & Co., 2002), 27–36.

4. Ibid., 36.
5. Ibid., 144.

CHAPTER 3: THE LAND OF DARKNESS

1. CHAM, Fund 2, Inv. 1, Case 5665, 4.
2. *Federalnaya arkhivnaya sluzhba Rossii. Vserossiyskiy nauchno-issledovatelskiy institut dokumentovedeniya i arkhivnogo dela. Genealogicheskaya informatsiya v gosudarstvennyh arkhivah Rossii.* Spravochnoye posobiye (Moscow, 1996), 126.
3. Dostoevskiy, F. M., "Dnevnik pisatelya za 1876 god." *Complete works in 30 volumes.* (Leningrad: Nauka, 1981), vol. 23, 158.
4. Ibid.
5. Nadezhda von Mekk to P. I. Tchaikovskiy, Belair, Mar. 2, 1887, *Perepiska s N.F. Mekk*, vol. 3, 1882–90 (Moscow-Leningrad: Academia, 1936), 467.
6. CHAM, Fund 2, Inv. 1, Case 5665, 4.
7. V. A. Fyodorov, *The Peasants' Sobriety Movement in 1858–1860s*, vol. 2, *The Revolutionary Situation in Russia 1859–1861* (Moscow, 1962), 110.
8. William E. Johnson, *The Liquor Problem in Russia* (Westerville, OH: American Issue Publishing Company, 1915), 117.
9. Ibid.
10. David Christian, *Living Water: Vodka and Russian Society on the Eve of Emancipation* (New York: Oxford University Press, 1990), 300–302.
11 Ibid., 311.
12. Ibid., 302–3.
13. Fyodorov, *Peasants' Sobriety Movement in 1858–1859*, 122.
14. CHAM, Fund 1264, Inv. 1, Case 29, 4.
15. Ibid., Case 34.
16. Thomas Owen, *Russian Corporate Capitalism from Peter the Great to Perestroika* (New York: Oxford University Press, 1995), 20.

17. N. V. Davydov, *Iz istorii Kanalizatsii Moskvy i Peterburga* (Moscow: Moskovskiy rabochiy, 1964), 22.

18. S. I. Chuprynin, *Moskva i moskvichi v tvorchestve Petra Dmitriyevicha Boborykina // Boborykin P. D., Kitay-gorod* (Moscow, 1985), 6.

CHAPTER 4: THE VODKA MAKER

1. *Moskovskiye Vedomosti*, Jan. 9, 1863, 3.

2. Igor Kurukin and Yelena Nikulina, *Tsar's Pub Business: Essays of Alcohol Politics and Traditions in Russia* (Moscow: Publishing House AST, 2005), 129.

3. David Christian, *Living Water: Vodka and Russian Society on the Eve of Emancipation* (New York: Oxford University Press, 1990), 377–78.

4. I. G. Pryzhov, *History of Beggary, Pub-Keeping and Hysterics in Russia*, Online Source: http://pryzhov.narod.ru/kabak.html.

5. I. G. Pryzhov, *Istoriya kabakov v Rossii v svyazi s istoriyey russkogo naroda* (St. Petersburg-Moscow: M. O. Volf, 1868), 318–19.

6. Ben Eklof, *Russia's Great Reforms, 1855–1881* (Blooming-ton, IN: Indiana University Press, 1994), 200.

7. *Sekrety i nastavleniya vodochnomu torgovtsu po raznopitiyu i vodochnym skladam i sushchestvuyushchiye zakonopolozheniya po semu predmetu* (Moscow, 1876), 67.

8. James L. West and Iurri A. Petrov, *Merchant Moscow: Images of Russia's Vanished Bourgeoisie* (Princeton, NJ: Princeton University Press, 1998), 46.

9. S. V. Bakhrushin, ed. *History of Moscow in Six Volumes* (Moscow: Izdatelstvo Akademii nauk SSSR, 1952–1959), vol. 4, 673.

10. Ibid., 721–22.

11. V. V. Skurlov and A. N. Ivanov, *Postavshchiki vysochaishego dvora* (St. Petersburg, 2002), 10–38.

12. Ibid., 4–8.

13. Russian State Historical Archive, Fund 472, Inv. 23 (253/1269), Case 9, 29–36 (hereafter RSHA).

CHAPTER 5: "DEMAND SMIRNOV VODKA"

1. "K 150-letiyu firmy "Petra Smirnova Synovya" (Iz vospominaniy i rasskazov moyego pokoynogo muzha V. P. Smirnova, umershago v 1934 godu)" Rodniye perezvony, #202, 1969, Bruzzels, 10.

2. James L. West and Iurri A. Petrov, *Merchant Moscow: Images of Russia's Vanished Bourgeoisie* (Princeton, NJ: Princeton University Press, 1998), 63.

3. RSHA, Fund 472, Inv. 23 (253/1269), Case 9, 29–36.

4. Statisticheskiye etudy // *Biblioteka dlya chteniya*, St. Petersburg, 1864, Oct.–Nov., 31.

5. L. Ye. Shepelev, *Tituly, Mundiry, Ordena v Rossiyskoy Imperii* (Moscow: Nauka Publishing House, 1991), 112–142.

6. Alfred J. Rieber, *Merchants and Entrepreneurs in Imperial Russia* (Chapel Hill, NC: University of North Carolina Press, 1982), 124.

7. CHAM, Fund 3, Inv. 2, Case 405, back page, 1.

8. V. Gilyarovskiy, *Moscow and Muskovites* (Moscow: Poligra-fresursy, 1999), http://www.booksite.ru/fulltext/gui/lya/rov/sky/4/index.htm.

9. N. N. Zhukov, *Iz zapisnyh knizhek* (Moscow: Sovetskaya Rossiya, 1976), 131–32.

10. *Ukazatel russkogo otdela venskoy vsemirnoy vystavki 1873 goda* (St. Petersburg, 1873), 50.

11. CHAM, Fund 203, Inv. 764, Case 173, 293–94.

CHAPTER 6: TO VIENNA AND BACK

1. Ye. Trigo, *The Business: A Literary Political Magazine* (St. Petersburg: The Publishing House of V. Toushnov, 1873), 107.

2. *New York Times*, May 30, 1873.

3. Ye. Trigo, *The Business: A Literary Political Magazine*, 119.

4. S. Razgonov, *Honor Before Profit: A Documentary Story about Pyotr Arsenievich Smirnov, a Serf who became a Prince of Russian Vodka and a Hereditary Noble* (Moscow: Inkombuk, 2000), 59.

5. Ye. Trigo, *The Business*, 107.

6. *Russkiye Vedomosti*, #105, May 19, 1873, 1.

7. *New York Times*, Aug. 10, 1873.

8. *Grazhdanin*, Nov. 12, 1873, 1229.

CHAPTER 7: MARIYA

1. Vladimir Smirnov's memoirs as told to his wife Tatiana Smirnova-Maksheyeva, obtained from Columbia University's Bakhmeteff Archive of Russian and East European Culture, translation provided by Bella Gregorian (hereafter noted as Vladimir Smirnov's memoirs).

2. *Svod uzakoneniy o zhenskih institutah vedomstva uchrezhdeniy imperatritsy Marii* (St. Petersburg: Gosudarstvennaya tipografiya, 1903), 9.

3. Moscow State Historical Archive, Fund 3, Inv. 3, Case 419.

4. "K 150-letiyu firmy "Petra Smirnova Synovya" (Iz vospominaniy i rasskazov moyego pokoynogo muzha V. P. Smirnova, umershago v 1934 godu)" Rodniye perezvony, #202, 1969, Bruzzels, 11.

5. CHAM, Fund 46, Inv. 6, Case 26, 21.

6. "K 150-letiyu firmy "Petra Smirnova Synovya" (Iz vospominaniy i rasskazov moyego pokoynogo muzha V. P. Smirnova, umershago v 1934 godu)" Rodniye perezvony, #202, 1969, Bruzzels, 11.

7. James L. West and Iurri A. Petrov, *Merchant Moscow: Images of Russia's Vanished Bourgeoisie* (Princeton, NJ: Princeton University Press, 1998), 142.

8. Pavel A. Buryshkin, *Moskva kupecheskaya* (New York:

Chekhov Publishing Co., 1954), http://museum.micex.ru/annals/02?start=31.

9. *New York Times*, July 9, 1876, 2.

10. *Albom uchastnikov Vserossiyskoy Promyshlennoy i Khudozhestvennoy Vystavski v Nizhnem Novgorode 1896 g* (St. Petersburg: Tipografiya Ministerstva Putey Soobshcheniya, 1896), Part 2, Dept. "g," 47.

11. *Rabocheye Dvizhenie v Rossii v XIX veke* (Moscow-Leningrad: Gosudarstvennoe izdatelstvo politicheskoy literatury, 1951), vol. 2, Part 2, 644–76.

12. A. Sakharov, L. Milov, P. Zyryanov, and A. Bokhanov, *History of Russia from the Beginning of the 18th Century until the End of the 19th Century* (Moscow: AST, 2001).

13. N. Flerovsky, *The Working Class Condition in Russia* (St. Petersburg, 1869).

14. *Rabocheye Dvizhenie v Rossii v XIX veke*, vol. 2, Part 2, 302–3.

15. K 150-letiyu firmy "Petra Smirnova Synovya," 10–11.

16 Moskovskiy fabrichniy okrug. Otchyot za 1884 g.fabrichnogo inspektora moskovskogo okruga professora I. I. Yanzhula. St. Petersburg 1886. Appendices, Tables 1, 7, 9.

17. "K 150-letiyu firmy "Petra Smirnova Synovya" (Iz vospominaniy i rasskazov moyego pokoynogo muzha V. P. Smirnova, umershago v 1934 godu)" Rodniye perezvony, #202, 1969, Bruzzels, 10.

18. Ibid., 11–12.

CHAPTER 8: VODKA WARS

1. Edvard Radzinskiy, *Alexander II: The Last Great Tsar* (New York: Free Press, 2005), xi.

2. Ibid., 410.

3. Ibid., 426.

4. *Otchyot o vserossiyskoy vystavke 1882 goda v Moskve pod redaktsiyey V. P. Bezobrazova* (St. Petersburg: V. Bezobrazov i kompaniya, 1883), vol. 3, class 44 (Napitki), 17.
5. William E. Johnson, *The Liquor Problem in Russia* (Westerville, OH: The American Issue Publishing Co., 1915), 142.
6. R. E. F. Smith and David Christian, *Bread and Salt: A Social and Economic History of Food and Drink in Russia* (Cambridge: Cambridge University Press, 1984), 304.
7. Ibid., 301.
8. *Vestnik Yevropy, Piteynoye delo i kabatskiy vopros v Rossii* (St. Petersburg, Sept. 1876), book 9, 215.
9. *Trudy syezda Vinokurennyh zavodchikov i spirtopromyshlennikov, sostoyavshegosya v Moskve v iyune 1892 goda*, vol. 2 Prilozheniya (St. Petersburg: V. Kirschbaum, 1893), 312.
10. *Otchyot o vserossiyskoy vystavki 1882 goda v Moskve*, vol. 3, Class 37, 21.
11. *Novoye Russkoye Slovo*, #16346, Mar. 30, 1958, 7.
12. *Moscow Gazette*, Dec. 25, 1882.
13. *Russkiy Courier*, 1885, #179, 4.
14. *Novosti Dnya*, 1885, #37, 4.
15. Ibid., 1884, #300, 4.
16. A. P. Chekhov, *Complete Works* (Moscow-Leningrad: The State Publishing House of Artistic Literature, 1932), vol. 11, 194–95.
17. *Trudy syezda*, vol. 2, app., 317.
18. A. P. Chekhov, *Complete Works* (Moscow-Leningrad: The State Publishing House of Artistic Literature, 1932), vol. 11, 194–95.
19. *Oskolki*, #15, April 14, 1884, 5.
20. *Mezhdunarodniy istoricheskiy zhurnal*, #7 (January/February, 2000), (Pervaya monografiya: N. Kh. Bunge: sudba reformatora. Glava III: Ministr-liberal, 3. Kosvenniye nalogi i gerboviye sbory, http://history.machaon.ru/all/number_07/pervajmo/bunge/part3/p3/index.html.

21. Smith and Christian, *Bread and Salt*, 309.

CHAPTER 9: THE VODKA KING

1. RSHA, Fund 472, Inv. 38 (415/1935), Case 42. 1.
2. Ibid., 2.
3. CHAM, Fund 16, Inv. 27, Case 905.
4. Vladimir Smirnov's memoirs.
5. CHAM, Fund 149, Inv. 1, Case 17, 7–8, 21
6. RSHA, Case 472, Inv. 38 (415/1935), Case 42, 5–6.
7. *Moskovskiy Listok*, #352, 1886.

CHAPTER 10: FROM PURSUIT TO PRESERVATION

1. *Ukazatel fabrik i zavodov Yevropeyskoy Rossii i Tsarstva Polskogo. Sostavil po ofitsialnym svedeniyam departamenta torgovli i manufaktur P.A. Orlov. Izdaniye vtoroye, ispravlennoye i znachitelno dopolnennoye* (St. Petersburg: R. Golike's Publishing House, 1887), 563.
2. *Istoriya predprinimatelstva v Rossii*. Online source: http://www.rus-lib.ru/book/35/52/343-416.html.
3. *Alkogolism i borba s nim. Osoboye prilozheniye k Trudam komissii po voprosu alkogolizma, pod redaktsiyey M. N. Nizhegorodtseva*, #1, Izdaniye obschestva "Rossiyskogo obschestva okhraneniya narodnogo zdraviya" (St. Petersburg: P. P. Soykin's publishing house, 1909), 49.
4. Patricia Herlihy, *The Alcoholic Empire: Vodka and Politics in Late Imperial Russia* (New York: Oxford University Press, 2002), 113–14.
5. *Alkogolism i borba s nim*, 58.
6. Boris M. Segal, *Russian Drinking: Use and Abuse of Alcohol in Pre-Revolutionary Russia* (New Brunswick, NJ: Rutgers Center of Alcohol Studies. 1987), 158.
7. CHAM, Fund 3, Inv. 3, Case 419.
8. RSHA, Fund 472, Inv. 23 (253/1269), Case 9, 29–36 (2)
9. *Novoye Russkoye Slovo*, Mar. 30, 1958, 5.

10. Moscow State Historical Archive, Fund 3, Inv. 3, Case 419.
11. G. N. Ulyanova, *Blagotvoritelnost moskovskih predprini-mateley: 1860–1914 gg* (Moscow: Izdatelstvo obyedineniya "Mosgorarhiv," 1999), 164.
12. *Kratkaya Yevreyskaya Entsiklopedia*, vol. 5, Kolonki 472–83.
13. M. I. Fridman, *Vinnaya Monopoliya v Rossii* (Moscow: Ob-schestvo kuptsov i promyshlennikov Rossii, 2005), 159.
14. Ibid., 152.
15. *Trudy syezda Vinokurennyh zavodchikov i spirtopromyshlen-nikov* (St. Petersburg: V. Kirshbaum, 1893), vol. 2, 314.
16. *Perviy godovoy otchyot Moskovskoy gorodskoy sanitarnoy stan-tsii pri Gigiyenicheskom Institute Imperatorskogo Moskovskogo universiteta. Mar. 1891–May 1892*, Pod redaktsiyey F. F. Erismana (Moscow: Gorodskaya tipografiya, 1892), 79.
17. *Trudy syezda*, vol. 2, app., 318.
18. Ibid.
19. Fridman, *Vinnaya Monopoliya*, 144.
20. Ibid., 145.
21. *Otechestvennaya istoriya*, #4 (Moscow: Nauka, 1993), 111.
22. Orlando Figes, *A People's Tragedy: A History of the Russian Revolution* (New York: Penguin Books, 1997), 160.

CHAPTER 11: MONOPOLY CAPITALISM

1. Constantine Pleshakov, *The Tsar's Last Armada: The Epic Jour-ney to the Battle of Tsushima* (New York: Basic Books, 2003), 14.
2. *Russkiy rubl. Dva veka istorii. XIX–XX vv* (Moscow: Prog-ress-Akademiya, 1994), 116–17, Russian State Archives of Literature and Art, Fund 1208, Inv. 24, 1–4.
3. Theodore H. Von Laue, *Sergei Witte and the Industrialization of Russia* (New York: Columbia University Press, 1963), 50.
4. Sidney Harcave, *The Memoirs of Count Witte* (Armonk, NY: M. E. Sharpe Inc., 1990), 187.
5. William E. Johnson, *The Liquor Problem in Russia* (Wester-ville, OH: The American Issue Publishing Co., 1915), 120.

6. L. I. Zaitseva, *Chast I: Kazyonnaya vinnaya monopoliya (1894–1914) / S. Yu. Witte i Rossiya* (Moscow: institut economiki RAN, 2000), 36–37.

7. K. V. Smirnova, G. V. Chinyaeva, V. O. Smirnov, M. I. Gogolashvili, *Vodochniy korol Pyotr Arsenievich Smirnov i yego potomki* (Moscow: OAO Izdatelstvo "Raduga", 1999), 24; letter from Feb. 6, 1896.

8. CHAM, Fund 16, Inv. 235, Case 4361.

9. *Spravochnaya kniga o litsah Sankt-Peterburgskogo kupechestva i drugih zvaniy na 1894 god*, St. Petersburg, 1895, "2-aya guildiya," f549; *Adresnaya kniga g. Sankt-Peterburga na 1893 god*, Dept. 3, 256; na 1895 god, Dept. 2, col. 1268; Dept. 3, 372; *Ves Petersburg na 1894 god*, St. Petersburg, A. S. Suvorin, Dept. 3, 217.

10. Russian State Archives of Ancient Acts, Fund 1468, Inv. 1, Case 496, #57.

11. Power of Attorney from Smirnov to Pyotr Petrovich, from Oleg Smirnov's research, PSC009149.

12. L. Ye. Shepelev, *Aktsionerniye companii v Rossii* (Leningrad: Nauka, 1973) 134–35.

13. CSAM, Fund 16, Inv. 237, Case 19, 47.

14. Vladimir Smirnov's memoirs.

15. Ibid.

16. Ibid.

17. Ibid.

18. Ibid.

19. Index of Russia exhibitors at the exhibition, *Vsemirnaya kolumbova vystavka 1893 goda v Chicago. Ukazatel russkogo otdela* (St. Petersburg: Yevdokimov, 1893), 52.

20. *Albom uchastnikov Vserossiyskoy Promyshlennoy Khudozhest-vennoy Vystavski v Nizhnem Novgorode 1896 g* (St. Petersburg: Tipografiya Ministerstva Putey Soobshcheniya, 1896) Part 2, Dept. "g" 47.

21. *Moskovskiy Listok*, Oct. 17, 1894, 2, col. 4.

22. *New York Times*, Nov. 4, 1894. 1.

23. Harcave, *Memoirs of Count Witte*, 213.
24. R. E. F. Smith and David Christian, *Bread and Salt: A Social and Economic History of Food and Drink in Russia* (Cambridge: Cambridge University Press, 1984), 315.
25. *Prilozheniye k otchetu glavnogo upravleniya neokladnyh sborov i kazyonnoy prodazhi pitey za 1895 god* (St. Petersburg: Yevdokimov, 1897), 155.
26. Johnson, *Liquor Problem in Russia*, 120.
27. David Christian, *Living Water: Vodka and Russian Society on the Eve of Emancipation* (New York: Oxford University Press, 1990), 381.
28. Patricia Herlihy, *The Alcoholic Empire: Vodka and Politics in Late Imperial Russia* (New York: Oxford University Press, 2002), 15.
29. *Vserossiyskaya khudozhestvenno-promyshlennaya vystavka 1896 goda v Nizhnem Novgorode* (St. Petersburg: German Goppe, 1896), 199.
30. Zaitseva, *Chast I: Kazyonnaya vinnaya monopoliya*, 57–59.

CHAPTER 12: THE TSAR AND 3,000 FLASHING BOTTLES

1. James L. West and Iurri A. Petrov, *Merchant Moscow* (Princeton University Press, 1998), 38.
2. Theodore H. Von Laue, *Sergei Witte and the Industrialization of Russia* (New York: Columbia University Press, 1963), 131.
3. *Nizhniy Novgorod 1896, Yarmarka. Vystavka. Putevoditel Nizhnego Novgoroda*, Nizhegorodskiy gumanitarniy tsentr, 1996, from *Vserossiyskaya vystavka 1896 v Nizhnem Novgorode*, 24.
4. *Izvestiya vserossiyskoy promyshlenno-khudozhestvennoy vystavki*, July 12, 1896, 3.
5. *Novosti dnya*, #4705, July 14, 2.
6. *Albom uchastnikov Vserossiyskoy Promyshlennoy Khudozhest-*

vennoy Vystavski v Nizhnem Novgorode 1896 g (St. Petersburg: Tipografiya Ministerstva Putey Soobshcheniya,
1896), Part 2, Dept. "g," 47.

7. Essay on the Imperial Court Ministry's Activities for Celebrations related to the Sacred Coronation of their Imperial Majesties in 1896, vol. 3, 292.

8. Von Laue, *Sergei Witte and the Industrialization of Russia*,
132.

9. *Moskovskiy Listok*, Aug. 26, 1896, 3.

10. Sergey Shumilkin, *Nizhegorodskaya yarmarka* (Nizhniy
Novgorod: Ponedelnik. Volgo-Vyatskoye knizhnoye izdatelstvo, 1996), 174.

CHAPTER 13: TWILIGHT

1. CHAM, Fund 16, Inv. 235, Case 4361, 8.

2. N. A. Varentsov, *Rossiya v memuarah* (Moscow: NLO,
1999), 133.

3. Ibid.

4. Russian State Archive of Ancient Acts, Fund 1468 Inv. 1,
Case 496. Borisovskiy letter Apr. 6, 1896.

5. Ibid., Fund 1468, Inv. 1, #21, Case 497, #24, May 1,
11:45 PM.

6. "P. A. Smirnov (skorbniy list)," *Moskovskiy Listok*, Nov. 30,
1898.

7. *Trudy tehnicheskogo komiteta glavnogo upravleniya neokladnyh
sborov i kazyonnoy prodazhi pitey*, vol. 14, 1901 (St. Petersburg, 1903), 100–102; and Krshizhanovskiy V. Yu. Starshiy
laborant tsentralnoy himicheskoy laboratorii ministerstva
finansov v g. Odesse; *Chistota kazyonnyh pitey, priyomy ih
izgotovleniya i kachestvo osnovnyh materialov (syryo i rektifikat-
sionniye spirty, drevesniy ugol i prochee) pri etom primenyay-
uschihsya* (Tver, 1906), 94–102.

8. Ibid., *Trudy technicheskogo komiteta*, 102

9. Ibid., 100.

10. Vera Grigorieva, *Vodka izvestnaya i neizvestnaya: XIV–XX veka*, from RSHA (St. Petersburg), Fund 476, Inv. 1 Case 2239, vol. 7, 20–22, 40–41, 60–73, 78.

11. *Vserossiyskaya khudozhestvenno-promyshlennaya vystavka 1896 goda v Nizhnem Nogvorode* (St. Petersburg: German Goppe, 1896), 198–200; also, *Albom uchastnikov Vserossiyskoy Promyshlennoy i Khudozhestvennoy Vystavski v Nizhnem Novgorode 1896 g* Tipografiya Ministerstva Putey Soobshcheniya, 1896), (St. Petersburg: Part 2, Dept. "g," 47).

12. CHAM, Fund 51, Inv. 5, Case 122.

13. Ibid.

14. "On the change of the regulations of P. A. Smirnov's Company of the vodka factory of wine and spirit warehouses and of Russian and foreign grape wine in Moscow," *Sobraniye Uzakoneniy i Rasporyazheniy Pravitelstva, izdavaemoe pri pravitelstvuyushchem senate, September 16, 1897. St. Petersburg: Senatskaya tipografiya*, 4096, 1292.

15. CSAM, Fund 16, Inv. 237, Case 19, 17.

16. Russian State Archives of Ancient Acts, Fund 1468, Inv. 1, Case 497, Dec. 3, 1897.

17. Ibid., Fund 1239, Inv. 3, Case 25310.

18. Vladimir Gakov, *Forbes* (Russian ed.), May 2005, 172.

19. Jo Ann Ruckman, *The Moscow Business Elite* (DeKalb, IL: Northern Illinois University Press, 1984), 18.

20. CSAM, Fund 142, Inv. 5, Case 728, 67–71 (translation from the Smirnoff Vodka Archive at Harvard University's Davis Center Collection at the Fung Library).

CHAPTER 14: TWO DEAD BODIES

1. Vladimir Smirnov's memoirs.

2. CSAM, Fund 142, Inv. 5, Case 728, 67–71.

3. Ibid., Case 809, 5.

4. Ibid., Case 809, 76–77.

5. *Moskovskiy Listok*, Mar. 10, 1899, 3.

CHAPTER 15: A NEW CENTURY, A NEW REALITY

1. Gregory Freeze, ed. *Russia: A History* (New York: Oxford University Press, 1997), 206.
2. David Floyd, *Russia in Revolt: 1905: The First Crack in Tsarist Power* (MacDonald & Co., 1968), 37.
3. *Vestnik finansov, promyshlennosti i torgovli. Ukazatel pravitelstvennyh rasporyazheniy po ministerstvu finansov. 1899. Otchyoty kreditnyh uchrezhdeniy, torgovyh i promyshlennyh predpriyatiy* (St. Petersburg: V. Kirschbaum, 1899), 756.
4. Ibid., 755.
5. Andrey Kokorev and Vladimir Rouga, *Moskva povsednevnaya* (Moscow: OLMA-Press, 2005), 39.
6. K. V. Smirnova and T. I. Voznesenskaya, "Semeinaya Khronika podmoskovnoy Shelkovki Smirnovyh," *Russkaya Usadba* #12 [28] (Moscow: Zhiraf, 2006), 239.
7. *Vestnik finansov, promyshlennosti i torgovli,* 755.
8. *Magazine Iskry,* Moscow, 1901, #25, 6, in A. Kokorev and V. Rouga, *Moskva povsednevnaya,* 2005, 39.
9. *Vestnik finansov, promyshlennosti i torgovli* (St. Petersburg: V. Kirschbaum, 1901), 741.
10. CSAM, Fund 16, Inv. 237, Case 19, Magazine of the Moscow Government Administration, 1–4.
11. Vladimir Smirnov's memoirs.
12. CSAM, Fund 16, Inv. 237, Case 19, 23–24.

CHAPTER 16: MONOPOLY MADNESS

1. A. Kokorev and V. Rouga, *Moskva povsednevnaya* (Moscow: OLMA-Press, 2005), 39.
2. *Moskovskiy Listok,* Sept. 5, 1900, 3.
3. Ibid., Sept. 2, 1901, 1.
4. Ibid., app., July 5, 1901, 4.
5. Ibid., July 16, 1901, 1.
6. "K 150-letiyu firmy "Petra Smirnova Synovya" (Iz

vospominaniy i rasskazov moyego pokoynogo muzha V. P. Smirnova, umershago v 1934 godu)" Rodniye perezvony, #202, 1969, Bruzzels, 11.

7. Ibid., 13–14.

8. Ibid., 14.

9. *Vestnik finansov, promyshlennosti i torgovli. Ukazatel pravitelstvennyh rasporyazheniy po ministerstvu finansov, 1902. Otchyoty kreditnyh uchrezhdeniy, torgovyh i promyshlennyh predpriyatiy* (St. Petersburg: V. Kirschbaum, 1902). 1339.

10. "Za nedelyu," *Magazine Iskry*, #25, 1901, 13.

11. Patricia Herlihy, *The Alcoholic Empire: Vodka and Politics in Late Imperial Russia* (New York: Oxford University Press, 2002), 6.

12. Kate Transchel, *Under the Influence: Working-class Drinking, Temperance, and Cultural Revolution in Russia, 1895–1932* (Pittsburgh, PA: University of Pittsburgh Press, 2006), 32.

13. "Russian Liquor Reform," *New York Times*, Feb. 2, 1902.

14. David Christian, *Living Water: Vodka and Russian Society on the Eve of Emancipation* (New York; Oxford University Press, 1990), 390.

15. William E. Johnson, *The Liquor Problem in Russia* (Westerville, OH: The American Issue Publishing Co., 1915).

16. *Kratkiy ocherk pyatidesyatiletiya aktsiznoy sistemy vzimaniya nalogov s krepkih napitkov i pyatidesyatiletiya deyatelnosti uchrezhdeniy zaveduyuschih neokladnymi sborami* (St. Petersburg: V. Kirschbaum, 1913), 38.

17. K. V. Smirnova, G. V. Chinyaeva, V. O. Smirnov, and M. I. Gogolashvili, *Vodochniy korol Pyotr Arsenievich Smirnov i yego potomki* (Moscow: OAO Izdatelstvo "Raduga," 1999), 198–201.

18. CSAM, Fund 16, Inv. 237, Case 19, 4.

19. Ibid., 1–4.

20. Smirnov Vodka Archive at Harvard University's Davis

Center Collection in the Fung Library, research by Oleg Smirnov, PSC009272–PSC009274, 136–38.

21. Ibid., PSC009276-PSC009283, 140–47.

CHAPTER 17: FROM BAD TO BIZARRE

1. Central State Archives of Moscow (CSAM), Fund 16, Inv. 237, 24–25, (hereafter cited in text).
2. *Moskovskiy Listok*, July 31, 1903, 3, in CHAM, Fund 131, Inv. 5, Case 926.
3. Theodore Von Laue, *Sergei Witte and the Industrialization of Russia* (New York: Columbia University Press, 1963), 258.

**CHAPTER 18: A WAR, UPRISINGS,
AND THEN THERE WAS ONE**

1. Gregory Freeze, ed., *Russia: A History* (New York: Oxford University Press, 1997), 212.
2. Boris M. Segal, *Russian Drinking: Use and Abuse of Alcohol in Pre-Revolutionary Russia* (New Brunswick, NJ: Rutgers Center of Alcohol Studies, 1987), 104.
3. Stephen White, *Russia Goes Dry: Alcohol, State, and Society* (Cambridge University Press, 1996), 20–21.
4. Kate Transchel, *Under the Influence: Working-class Drinking, Temperance, and Cultural Revolution in Russia, 1895–1932* (Pittsburgh, PA: University of Pittsburgh Press, 2006), 36.
5. *Russkoye Slovo*, Nov. 7, 1905.
6. David Floyd, *Russia in Revolt: 1905: The First Crack in Tsarist Power* (Macdonald & Co., 1969), 61.
7. Maxim Gorkiy [Aleksey Maksimovich Peshkov], *Complete Works in Thirty Volumes*, (Moscow: GIKhL, 1949–56), vol. 7, http://home.mts-nn.ru/~gorky/TEXTS/OCHST/PRIM/9jan_pr.htm.
8. Irving Werstein, *Ten Days in November: The Russian Revolution* (Philadelphia: Macrae Smith Co., 1967), 76.
9. Vladimir Smirnov's memoirs.

10. Ibid.
11. Ibid.
12. Jo Ann Ruckman, *The Moscow Business Elite* (DeKalb, IL: Northern Illinois Press, 1984), 66–67.
13. *Russkoye Slovo*, Nov. 17, 1905, http://starosti.ru/archive. php?m=11&y=1905.
14. Vladimir Smirnov's memoirs.
15. S. P. Urusov, *Kniga o loshadi* (St. Petersburg: Russkoye knizhnoye tovarischestvo "Deyatel," 1911), 480, http://www. cnshb.ru/AKDiL/0005/base/480.shtm.
16. *Spisok chastnyh konskih zavodov v Rossii* (St. Petersburg: Yu. Ya. Rimana, 1904), 374.
17. Central State Archives of Moscow (CSAM), Fund 16, Inv. 237, Case 19, 56.
18. CHAM, Fund 87, Inv. 2, Case 1037, 27–32 (Oleg Smirnov's research: PSC009083).
19. Ibid. (Oleg Smirnov's research: PSC 009084).
20. Ibid. (Oleg Smirnov's research: PSC 009085).
21. Richard Pipes, *A Concise History of the Russian Revolution* (New York: Alfred Knopf, 1995), 43.

CHAPTER 19: LIFE AND DEATH AND LOVE AND DEATH

1. I. R. Takala, *Veselie Rusi. Istoriya alkogolnoy problemy v Rossii* (St. Petersburg: Zhurnal Neva, 2002), 166.
2. *Kratkiy ocherk pyatidesyatiletiya aktsiznoy sistemy vzimaniya nalogov s krepkih napitkov i pyatidesyatiletiya deyatelnosti uchrezhdeniy zaveduyuschih neokladnymi sborami* (St. Petersburg: V. Kirschbaum, 1913), 38.
3. Kate Transchel, *Under the Influence: Working-class Drinking, Temperance, and Cultural Revolution in Russia, 1895–1932* (Pittsburgh, PA: University of Pittsburgh Press, 2006), 62.
4. "Russian War on Vodka," *New York Times*, Feb. 16, 1908.
5. Boris M. Segal, *Russian Drinking: Use and Abuse of Alcohol*

in Pre-Revolutionary Russia (New Brunswick, NJ: Rutgers Center of Alcohol Studies, 1987), 334.

6. *Vestnik vinnoy, pivovarennoy promyshlennosti i torgovli,* Moscow, #26, Aug. 20, 1911, 5.

7. Ibid., #32, Feb. 25, 1912, 3.

8. Ibid., #10, May 22, 1910, 5.

9. CHAM, Fund 126, Inv. 2, Case 84, 216–17.

10. *Novosti Utra i Vechera,* Apr. 20, 1907, 3.

11. Russkoye slovo, Nov. 17, 1907, 1.

12. Vladimir Smirnov's Memoirs.

13. Central State Archives of Moscow (CSAM), Fund 16, Inventory 237, Case 19, 67–73.

14. Ibid., 67–68.

15. S. P. Urusov, *Kniga o loshadi* (St. Petersburg: Russkoye knizhnoye tovarischestvo "Deyatel," 1911), 480, http://www .cnshb.ru/AKDiL/0005/base/480.shtm.

16. Grigoriy Yaron *O lyubimom zhanre* (Moscow: Iskusstvo, 1960), 29.

17. M. Yankovskiy, *Sovetskiy teatr operetty: Ocherk istorii* (Moscow: Iskusstvo, 1962), 32.

18. Vladimir's Nov. 1, 1910, party menu and entertainment list from the Smirnoff Vodka Archive at Harvard University's Davis Center Collection in the Fung Library.

19. P. P. Isheyev, *Oskolki proshlogo, Vospominaniya 1889–1959* (New York, 142).

20. Yaron, *O lyubimom zhanre,* 40.

21. A. Mendelson, *Itogi prinuditelnoy trezvosti i noviye formy pyanstva. Doklad Protivoalkogolnomu Soveshchaniyu Obshchestva Russkih Vrachey v pamyat N. I.Pirogova v Moskve* (Petrograd: Gosudarstvennaya tipografiya, 1916), 3.

22. Patricia Herlihy, *The Alcoholic Empire: Vodka and Politics in Late Imperial Russia* (New York: Oxford University Press, 2002), 116.

23. L. N. Tolstoy. *Complete Works*, 3rd series, Letters, vol. 80 (Moscow: GIKhL, 1955), 291–92.
24. Transchel, *Under the Influence*, 63.

CHAPTER 20: SUDDEN CHAOS
1. *Moscow Gazette*, Apr. 27, 1910. Article and translation obtained from the Smirnoff Vodka Archive at Harvard University's Davis Center Collection in the Fung Library.
2. *Bulletin of Wine, Vodka, Beer, Eating-house Industry and Grocers*, Year 1, #10, May 22, 1910, from the Smirnoff Vodka Archive at Harvard University's Davis Center Collection in the Fung Library.
3. *Novoye Vremya*, St. Petersburg, #13124, 1912, 3.
4. Ibid., 13113, 1912, 5.
5. Patricia Herlihy, *The Alcoholic Empire: Vodka and Politics in Late Imperial Russia* (New York: Oxford University Press, 2002), 8.
6. Ibid., 117.
7. Testimony, Boris Aleksandrovich Smirnov, Feb. 12, 1998, 163–64, from the Smirnoff Vodka Archive at Harvard University's Davis Center Collection in the Fung Library.
8. Ibid., Feb. 11, 1998, 69.
9. Research compiled by Oleg Smirnov, obtained from the Smirnoff Vodka Archive at Harvard University. Document #PSC009365.
10. L. K. Yezioranskiy, *Fabrichno-zavodskiye predpriyatiya Rossiyskoy Imperii pod nablyudeniyem Redaktsionnogo Komiteta, sostoyashchego iz chlenov Soveta Syezdov Predstaviteley Promyshlennosti i Torgovli*, St. Petersburg, 1909, #7092.
11. *Bulletin of Wine, Vodka, Beer*, Year 11, #28, Oct. 29, 1911.
12. Trading House P. A. Smirnov (Moscow) to Administration of Police, 1st div., Pyatnitskaya district, 1911, from the Smirnoff Vodka Archive, #EC000754.

13. R. Atzhanov, "Povest pro postavshchikov," *Ogonyok*, Moscow, #8, Feb. 25, 2002, http://www.ogoniok.com/archive/2002/4734/08-61-61.

14. *Spisok fabrik i zavodov Rossiyskoy Imperii so vklyucheniyem Sibiri, Sredney Azii i Kavkaza. Sostavleno po ofitsialnym svedeniyam otdela Promyshlennosti Ministerstva Torgovli i Promyshlennosti pod red. V. E. Varzara* (St. Petersburg: V. Kirschbaum, 1912), pt. 2, 205.

15. *Moskovskiy Listok*, Sept. 1, 1912, 201, 4.

16. Research compiled by Oleg Smirnov, obtained from Harvard. Document #PSC008996.

17. CSAM, Fund 83, Inv. 2, Case 1037, 78–79.

18. Ibid.

19. D. A. Zasosov and V. I. Pyzin, *Povsednevnaya zhizn Peterburga na rubezhe XIX–XX vekov* (Moscow: Molodaya gvardiya, 2003).

20. State Archive of the Russian Federation, Fund 102, Inv. 67, Case 42, pt. 1, 51, 54.

21. *Peterburgskaya Gazeta*, Mar. 21, 1912, 4.

22. *Moskovskiy Listok*, Mar. 21, 1912, 3.

23. Boris M. Segal, *Russian Drinking: Use and Abuse of Alcohol in Pre-Revolutionary Russia* (New Brunswick, NJ: Rutgers Center of Alcohol Studies, 1987), 118.

24. William E. Johnson, *The Liquor Problem in Russia* (Westerville, OH: The American Issue Publishing Co., 1915), 191.

CHAPTER 21: REVOLUTION

1. Irving Werstein, *Ten Days in November: The Russian Revolution* (Philadelphia: Macrae Smith Co., 1967), 114.

2. A. Kokorev and V. Rouga, *Voina i moskvichi. Ocherki gorodskogo byta 1914–1917 gg* (Moscow: Olma Media Grupp, 2008), 142.

3. *New York Times*, July 25, 1915.

4. William E. Johnson, *The Liquor Problem in Russia* (Westerville, OH: The American Issue Publishing Co., 1915), 207.

5. *New York Times*, July 25, 1915.

6. Patricia Herlihy, *The Alcoholic Empire: Vodka and Politics in Late Imperial Russia* (New York: Oxford University Press, 2002), 67.

7. *Spisok fabrik i zavodov Rossiyskoy Imperii so vklyucheniyem Sibiri, Sredney Azii i Kavkaza. Sostavleno po ofitsialnym svedeniyam otdela Promyshlennosti Ministerstva Torgovli i Promyshlennosti pod red. V. E. Varzara* (St. Petersburg: V. Kirschbaum, 1912), Part 2, 92.

8. Document #EC 000711, from the Smirnoff Vodka Archive at Harvard University's Davis Center Collection in the Fung Library.

9. Robert Goldston, *The Russian Revolution* (New York: Bobbs-Merrill Co., Inc., 1966), 92.

10. Boris M. Segal, *Russian Drinking: Use and Abuse of Alcohol in Pre-Revolutionary Russia*, (New Brunswick, NJ: Rutgers Center of Alcohol Studies. 1987), 120.

11. Werstein, *Ten Days in November*, 128–29.

12. *Moskovskiy Listok*, Oct. 30, 1915, 3.

13. Werstein, *Ten Days in November*, 122.

14. E. Radzinskiy, Stalin (Moscow: AST, 2006), 99.

15. Werstein, *Ten Days in November*, 156.

16. Vladimir Smirnov's memoirs.

CHAPTER 22: ESCAPE

1. J. N. Westwood, *Russia 1917–1964: A History of Modern Russia from the 1917 Revolution to the Fall of Krushchev* (New York: Harper & Row, 1966), 51.

2. Testimony, Boris Aleksandrovich Smirnoff, Feb. 12, 1998, 160.

3. Kate Transchel, *Under the Influence: Working-class Drinking,*

Temperance, and Cultural Revolution in Russia, 1895–1932 (Pittsburgh, PA: University of Pittsburgh Press, 2006), 75.

4. "Nesvoyevremenniye mysli. Zametki o russkoy revolyutsii i culture," http://antology.igrunov.ru/authors/gorky/mysli. html.

5. Testimony, Boris Aleksandrovich Smirnoff, Feb. 11, 1998, 123.

6. K. V. Smirnova, G. V. Chinyaeva, V. O. Smirnov, and M. I. Gogolashvili, *Vodochniy korol Pyotr Arsenievich Smirnov i yego potomki* (Moscow: OAO Izdatelstvo "Raduga," 1999), 159.

7. Orlando Figes, *Natasha's Dance: A Cultural History of Russia* (New York: Henry Holt & Co., 2002), 437.

8. Document #TH001151, translation from the Smirnoff Vodka Archive at Harvard University's Davis Center Collection in the Fung Library.

9. James L. West and Iurri Petrov, *Merchant Moscow: Images of Russia's Vanished Bourgeoisie* (Princeton, NJ: Princeton University Press, 1998), 176.

10. Testimony, Boris Aleksandrovich Smirnoff, Feb. 12, 1998, 161–63.

11. Vladimir Smirnov's memoirs.

12. *Izvestiya*, Sept. 4, 1918.

13. Vladimir Smirnov's memoirs.

14. Ibid.

15. Orlando Figes, *"A People's Tragedy: A History of the Russian Revolution,"* (New York: Viking, 1996), 645.

16. State Archives of the Russian Federation, P-470, Inv. 1, Case 1, 19–20.

17. *Krasniy terror v gody grazhdanskoy voiny. Po materialam Osoboy sledstvennoy komissii po rassledovaniyu zlodeyaniy bolshevikov. Delo #1. Osobaya komissiya po rassledovaniyu zlodeyaniy bolshevikov, sostoyaschaya pri glavnokomanduyuschem vooruzhennimy silami na Yuge Rossii. Akt rassledovaniya po delu ob areste i ubiystve zalozhnikov v Pyatigorske v oktyabre 1918*

goda. Pod red. Doktorov istoricheskih nauk Yu. G. Feltishinskogo i G.I. Chernyavskogo, State Archives of the Russian Federation, P-470, Inv. 1, Case 2, 230–32.

18. Ibid.
19. Figes, *People's Tragedy*, 648.
20. A. G. Shkuro, *Zapiski belogo partizana*, ch. 19, http://militera.lib.ru/memo/russian/shkuro_ag/19.html.
21. Westwood, *Russia 1917–1964*, 51.

CHAPTER 23: SMIRNOV WITH AN "F"

1. Letter to the editor, *New York Times*, Sept. 23, 1921.
2. Document and translation from the Smirnoff Vodka Archive at Harvard University's Davis Center Collection in the Fung Library.
3. P. P. Isheyev. *Oskolki proshlogo, Vospominaniya 1889–1959*, 139.
4. Ibid., 140.
5. Ibid.
6. K. V. Smirnova et al., *Vodochniy korol Pyotr Arsenievich Smirnov i yego potomki* (Moscow: OAO Izdatelstvo "Raduga"), 77.
7. Documents #PSC009001, PSC009008 from research by Oleg Smirnov.
8. K. V. Smirnova et al., *Vodochniy korol Pyotr Arsenievich Smirnov i yego potomki* (Moscow: OAO Izdatelstvo "Raduga"), 134.
9. K. K. Parchevskiy, *Po russkim uglam* (Moscow: Nasledniki K. K. Parchevskogo. Institut vseobschey istorii RAN, 2002), 176.
10. Vladimir Smirnov's memoirs.
11. Ibid.
12. Testimony, Boris Aleksandrovich Smirnoff, Feb. 11, 1998, 122.
13. Ibid., 91.
14. Ibid., Feb. 12, 1998, 180.

CHAPTER 24: THE END IS A BEGINNING

1. Vladimir Smirnov's memoirs.
2. K. V. Smirnova et al., *Vodochniy korol Pyotr Arsenievich Smirnov i yego potomki* (Moscow: OAO Izdatelstvo "Raduga"), 204–5.
3. *Posledniye Novosti*, Paris, Dec. 10, 1933, 6.
4. Ibid., Dec. 24, 1933, 5.
5. Obituary of Rudolph P. Kunett, *New York Times*, May 6, 1979; "Rudolph Kunett of Heublein Dies," *Hartford Courant*, May 5, 1979.
6. Richard Lemon, "The Talk of the Town," *New Yorker*, Sept. 24, 1955.
7. Agreement between Vladimir Smirnov and Rudolph Kunett, Aug. 21, 1933, 1, Exhibit E from the Smirnoff Vodka Archive at Harvard University's Davis Center Collection in the Fung Library.
8. "Russian Vodka Now Made Here," *Danbury News-Times*, Apr. 19, 1934.
9. Advertisement obtained from the Smirnoff Vodka Archive at Harvard University.
10. K. V. Smirnova et al., *Vodochniy korol*, 202–3.
11. "Russian Vodka Now Made Here," *Danbury News-Times*, Apr. 19, 1934.
12. K. V. Smirnova et al., *Vodochniy korol*, 204–5.
13. Ibid.

EPILOGUE

1. http://www.brandrepublic.com/News/159590/Superbrands-case-studies-Smirnoff.
2. "Smirnoff White Whiskey—No Smell, No Taste," *New York Times*, Feb. 19, 1995.
3. Ibid.
4. John Martin, interview, Smirnoff Heritage Video, n.d.
5. Richard Lemon, "Little Water," *New Yorker*, Sept. 24, 1955.

6. http://www.diageo.com/en-row/ourbrands/ ourglobalbrands/smirnoff, Impact Databank Mar. 2007, ranking of leading premium spirits brands.

7. Millward Brown's Top 100 Most Powerful Brands 2008, 23, http://www.millwardbrown.com/Sites/optimor/Media/ Pdfs/en/BrandZ/BrandZ-2008-Report.pdf.

8. Resolution on the presenting charges against Smirnov Vladimir Vladimirovich, Sept. 18, 1941, in Moscow.

9. Protest in the case of V. V. Smirnov, Aug. 31, 1956.

10. K. V. Smirnova et al., *Vodochniy korol Pyotr Arsenievich Smirnov i yego potomki* (Moscow: OAO Izdatelstvo "Raduga"), 128.

11. Testimony, Boris Aleksandrovich Smirnov, February 12, 1998, 194.

12. N. A. Filatkina, *Pokolennaya rospis moskovskoy vetvi Alekseya Fyodorovicha Bakhrushina* (Moscow: 1997), 262.

13. Stephen White, *Russia Goes Dry: Alcohol, State, and Society* (Cambridge: Cambridge University Press, 1996), 71.

14. Ibid., 140.

15. Thomas C. Owen, *Russian Corporate Capitalism from Peter the Great to Perestroika* (New York: Oxford University Press, 1995), 84.

16. K. V. Smirnova et al., *Vodochniy korol*, 155.

17. A. Sokovnin, "Konflikt vokrug tovarnogo znaka Smirnoff," *Kommersant*, #49 (517), Mar. 19, 1994, http://kommersant .ru/doc.aspx?fromsearch=dfae45ba-5df9-45f6-ad94- 51b2c302aae9&docsid=73940.

18. *Delovaya pressa* 8, May 20, 1999, http://www.businesspress .ru/newspaper/article_mId_44_aId_17227.html.

19. Decision by the U.S. Court of Appeals for the Third Circuit in the matter of The Joint Stock Society, "Trade House of Descendants of Peter Smirnoff, Official Purveyor to the Imperial Court" and the Russian American Spirits Co. v. UDV North America, Inc. and Pierre Smirnoff Company, Sept. 14, 2001.

20. S. Muravyov and F. Pogodin, "Borisa na tsarstvo," *Vlast* 2 (161), Jan. 30, 1996, http://www.kommersant.ru/doc .aspx?DocsID=11970.

21. "Diageo and A-1, an Alfa Group company, create strategic partnership for expansion in Russia," Diageo press release, Feb. 27, 2006.

22. Russian Statistical Annual, 2007. http://www.gks.ru/bgd/ regl/B07_13/IssWWW.exe/Stg/d01/04-27.htm.

Selected Bibliography

Blackwell, William L. *The Industrialization of Russia: An Historical Perspective*. Arlington Heights, IL: Harlan Davidson, Inc., 1970.

Borodkin, L. I., ed. *Ekonomicheskaya istoriya*, "Vekselniye kursy, svyazanniye s Rossiyey, 1814-1914 gg." *Obozrenie* / Issue 11. Moscow: Izdatelstvo Moskovskogo Universiteta, 2005, 84–87.

Christian, David. *Living Water: Vodka and Russian Society on the Eve of Emancipation*. New York: Oxford University Press, 1990.

Daniels, Robert V. *Red October: The Bolshevik Revolution of 1917*. New York: Charles Scribner's Sons, 1967.

Dole, Nathan H. *The Life of Lyof N. Tolstoi*. New York: Charles Scribner's Sons, 1923.

Elkhof, Ben, John Bushnell, and Larissa Zakharova. *Russia's Great Reforms, 1855-1881*. Bloomington: Indiana University Press, 1994.

Erisman, F. F. The First Year Report of the Moscow

Hygiene Station at the Hygiene Institute of the Emperor's Moscow University. Moscow: Gorodskaya Tipografiya, 1892.

Figes, Orlando. *Natasha's Dance: A Cultural History of Russia.* New York: Henry Holt & Co., 2002.

Figes, Orlando. *A People's Tragedy: A History of the Russian Revolution.* New York: Penguin Group, 1996.

Floyd, David. *Russia in Revolt: 1905: The First Crack in Tsarist Power.* Macdonald & Co., 1969.

Freeze, Gregory. *Russia: A History.* New York: Oxford University Press, 1997.

Fridman, M. I. *Wine Monopoly in Russia.* Moscow: Obshchestvo kuptsov i promyshlennikov Rossii, 2005.

Galagan, A. A. *History of Russian Entrepreneurship: From a Merchant to a Banker.* Moscow: Os-89, 1997.

Goldston, Robert. *The Russian Revolution.* New York: The Bobbs-Merrill Co. Inc., 1966.

Grigorieva, V. Z. *Known and Unknown Vodka: 14th–20th Centuries.* Moscow: Enneagon Press, 2007.

Gilyarovskiy, V. *Moscow and Muscovites.* Moscow: Poligrafresursy, 1999.

Harcave, Sidney. *The Memoirs of Count Witte.* Armonk, NY: M. E. Sharpe Inc., 1990.

Herlihy, Patricia. *The Alcoholic Empire: Vodka and Politics in Late Imperial Russia.* New York: Oxford University Press, 2002.

Isheyev, P. P. *Shards of the Past.* New York, 1959.

Johnson, William E. *The Liquor Problem in Russia.* Westerville, OH: The American Issue Publishing Co., 1915.

Kokorev, A. and Rouga, V. *Everyday Moscow.* Moscow: OLMA-Press, 2005.

Krshizhanovskiy, V. Yu. *Purity of the State's Alcohol.* Tver: Tipo-Litografiya N. M. Rodionova, 1906.

Kurukin, I., and E. Nikulina. *The Tsar's Pub Business: Essays on Alcohol Politics and Traditions in Russia.* Moscow: AST, 2005.

McGrew, Roderick E. *Russia and the Cholera 1823–1832.* Madison, WI: University of Wisconsin Press, 1965.

Owen, Thomas C. *Russian Corporate Capitalism from Peter the Great to Perestroika*. New York: Oxford University Press, 1995.

Pipes, Richard. *A Concise History of the Russian Revolution*. New York: Alfred A. Knopf, 1995.

Pokhlebkin, William. *A History of Vodka*. London: Verso, 1991.

Radzinskiy, Edvard. *Alexander II, The Last Great Tsar*. New York: Free Press, 2006.

Rashin, A. G. *Population of Russia during 100 Years (1811–1913) Statistical Essays*. Moscow: Gosudarstvennoe statisticheskoe izdatelstvo, 1956.

Razgonov, S. *Honor Above Profit: A Story about Pyotr Arsenievich Smirnov*. Moscow: Inkombuk, 2000.

Rieber, Alfred J. *Merchants and Entrepreneurs in Imperial Russia*. Chapel Hill, NC: University of North Carolina Press, 1982.

Ruckman, Jo Ann. *The Moscow Business Elite*. DeKalb, IL: Northern Illinois University Press, 1984.

Savelyeva, O. *Living History of Russian Advertising*. Moscow: Gella-print, 2004.

Segal, Boris M., *Russian Drinking: Use and Abuse of Alcohol in Pre-Revolutionary Russia*. New Brunswick, NJ: Rutgers Center of Alcohol Studies, 1987.

Skurlov, V. V., and A. N Ivanov. *Purveyors of the Highest Court*. St Petersburg: 2002.

Slonov, I. A. *From the Moscow Trading Life*. Moscow: Tipografiya Russkogo tovarishchestva pechatnogo i izdatelskogo dela, 1914.

Smirnova, K. V., G. V. Chinyaeva, V. O. Smirnov, and M. I. Gogolashvili. *The Vodka King Pyotr Arsenievich Smirnov and his Descendants*. Moscow: OAO Izdatelstvo "Raduga," 1999.

Smith, Robert, and David Christian. *Bread and Salt: A Social and Economic History of Food and Drink in Russia*. Cambridge: Cambridge University Press, 1984.

Takala, I. *Joy of Russia: History of the Alcohol Problem in Russia*. St Petersburg: Zhurnal Neva, 2002.

Transchel, Kate. *Under the Influence: Working-class Drinking, Temperance, and Cultural Revolution in Russia, 1895–1932.* Pittsburgh: University of Pittsburgh Press, 2006.

Troyat, Henri. *Daily Life in Russia under the Last Tsar.* Stanford, CA: Stanford University Press, 1959.

Ulyanova, G. N. *Sponsorship of Moscow Entrepreneurs: 1860–1914.* Moscow: Izdatelstvo obyedineniya "Mosgorarhiv," 1999.

Villari, Luigi. *Russia, Russia of Today.* Boston: J. B. Millet Co., 1911.

Von Laue, Theodore H. *Sergei Witte and the Industrialization of Russia.* New York: Columbia University Press, 1963.

Von Jurgen, Schneider, hrsg. Wahrungen der Welt: Europaische und nordamerikanische *Devisenkurse 1777-1914.* Stuttgart: Steiner 1., Teilbd. 1., 1991, 320-325.

Werstein, Irving. *Ten Days in November: The Russian Revolution.* Philadelphia: Macrae Smith Co., 1967.

West, James L., and Iurii A. Petrov. *Merchant Moscow: Images of Russia's Vanished Bourgeoisie.* Princeton, NJ: Princeton University Press, 1998.

Westwood, J. N. *Russia 1917–1964: A History of Modern Russia from the 1917 Revolution to the Fall of Krushchev.* New York: Harper & Row, 1966.

White, Stephen. *Russia Goes Dry: Alcohol, State and Society.* New York: Cambridge University Press, 1996.

Williamson, Samuel H. "Six Ways to Compute the Relative Value of a U.S. Dollar Amount, 1774 to present," *Measuring-Worth,* 2008. http://www.measuringworth.com/uscompare/.

Yanzhul, I. I. From the Memoirs and Correspondence of the Factory Inspector. St. Petersburg: AO Brocgauz-Efron, 1907.

Yaron, G. *About the Favorite Genre.* Moscow: Iskusstvo, 1960.

Zaitseva, L. I. *S. Yu. Witte i Rossiya.* Moscow: Institut Economiki RAN, 2000.

Zhukov, N. N. *From the Notes.* Moscow: Sovetskaya Rossiya, 1976.

Index

About the author

About the book

Read on

Insights,
Interviews
& More...

Meet Linda Himelstein

Kristen Sandifer

LINDA HIMELSTEIN began her career in the Washington bureau of the *Wall Street Journal* before working at the *San Francisco Recorder* and the *Legal Times*. In 1993, she joined *BusinessWeek* as a legal affairs editor, writing about a wide array of topics, including the tobacco industry and Wall Street. One of her cover stories helped *BusinessWeek* win the National Magazine Award. Later, as the magazine's Silicon Valley bureau chief, she wrote about the infancies of eBay, Yahoo!, and other companies. She lives with her family in northern California. ❧

On Writing
The King of Vodka

THE QUESTION I HAVE BEEN ASKED the most about this book is what compelled me to write it. It is a terrific question since there is little in my background suggesting that the history of the Smirnoff vodka family was the obvious topic for me. I grew up in Phoenix, Arizona, which then was nothing like the sprawling metropolis it is today. As I recall it, the city was charmingly provincial. I walked to my elementary school, rode my bike around our neighborhood, participated in summer recreation programs, joined the Girl Scouts, and enjoyed what I now identify as the all-American childhood. My exposure to most other cultures was pretty limited. Phoenix had some good ethnic restaurants, Mexican mostly, and a wonderful museum dedicated to Native American crafts. I studied French in high school, which came in handy when I traveled to French-speaking Switzerland between my junior and senior years. And even though I have some ancestors who hailed from Ukraine and Belarus, the closest I ever got to anything Russian was when the national touring company of *Fiddler on the Roof* came to town. What I did know about Russia and its grand history came primarily from the writings of Tolstoy and Dostoevsky.

College in Los Angeles and graduate school in New York City opened up my world immensely. I became enamored with anything new, developing a thirst ▶

> 66 Even though I have some ancestors who hailed from Ukraine and Belarus, the closest I ever got to anything Russian was when the national touring company of *Fiddler on the Roof* came to town. 99

and curiosity that could only be satisfied by a constant parade of novel experiences and encounters with interesting people. Journalism, then, became my vehicle for exploration. I first fell in love with journalism while working in the Washington bureau of the *Wall Street Journal*. I was a lowly news assistant charged with supporting other reporters who were pursuing stories. My assigned tasks ranged from compiling background research to making a fresh pot of coffee.

My big break came out of the tragedy of the *Challenger* explosion. It was January 1986 and the space shuttle had just blown apart shortly after takeoff, instantly killing its seven crew members. Coverage of this horrible accident was being coordinated out of the *Journal*'s Washington bureau. The atmosphere in the office was frantic that day as everyone ran around trying to figure out what had happened and what we were going to write about it. It took all hands to pull together the various stories in the works. It fell to me to research and compile a chart listing NASA's worst accidents. Finally I had my chance to show what I could do. The next day, imbedded in the stories written by other journalists, was my itty-bitty chart. It was a great feeling to see my contribution in print. What's more, the rush I had experienced from being in the thick of an unraveling story—and trying to understand its many moving parts—was intoxicating. To this day, I still get a thrill from chasing a good story.

66 To this day, I still get a thrill from chasing a good story. 99

My journey continued at Columbia University Graduate School
of Journalism in New York. The story
assignments were diverse, to say the least.
I remember one month in particular.
It started off with my covering a fire
in the Bronx. Then I went on a police
ride for a night in Brooklyn, which
included one stop at what appeared to
be an abandoned drug den and another
in an area frequented by prostitutes.
Both visits were educational and, well,
unforgettable. The month ended with
the most delicious highlight of my year
at Columbia: going to dinner at the
swank Café des Artistes to interview the
man who had been named New York's
waiter of the year. After this assignment,
I had no doubt about the wisdom of my
choice to pursue journalism. Little did I
know then that I would return to the
subject of food and drink, albeit some
twenty years later.

After graduating, I was no longer
required to make coffee. But I still had
to pay my journalism dues. So I spent
the next several years doing just that.
I hopped from city to city, covering
everything from local courts in San
Francisco to the federal government
in Washington, D.C. I have always had
a fascination with politics, so being back
in the capital was very appealing. It was
there that I met my husband, another
political junkie and a rare Washington
native. We married and started our new
lives together with yet another move.
This time it was back to New York City, ▶

On Writing *The King of Vodka* *(continued)*

where I had taken a job as the legal affairs editor at *BusinessWeek*.

I loved my beat because it allowed me to get my nose into almost anything. I tackled issues on Wall Street, the tobacco industry, and product liability litigation. As you will read in the next section, "Discovering the Smirnovs," this was also how the all-American girl from Phoenix came to learn and write about vodka makers in nineteenth-century Russia. ◕‿

Discovering the Smirnovs

IT WAS LATE 1995. The Soviet Union had fallen apart; Boris Yeltsin had taken over Russia; and the rule of law, such as it was, was in flux. A man came to see me at my office in midtown. He was a distinguished-looking gentleman by the name of William Walker, and he was on a mission. He represented some of the descendants of Pyotr Smirnov as well as a company that hoped to gain control of the Smirnoff brand in the United States. The reason for Walker's visit was to convince me to write about the lawsuit initiated by some of the Smirnovs against the company that owned the brand. At the time, that company was Connecticut-based Heublein Inc. The descendants made many claims against Heublein, including the charge that their family name (the brand) had been taken from them illegally following the Russian Revolution.

Walker just about had me at hello. How could I not write a story about a ubiquitous, multibillion-dollar brand born during one of the most tumultuous periods in Russian history? As we talked, Walker tantalized me further with stories about the family itself. They had been serfs in tsarist Russia, completely uneducated, totally unconnected. Yet they had achieved great wealth and power in a society that was built to prevent such social advancement. And they made vodka, the only spirit ▶

“ How could I not write a story about a ubiquitous, multibillion-dollar brand born during one of the most tumultuous periods in Russian history? ”

7

Discovering the Smirnovs *(continued)*

I could ever really tolerate. My story ran on January 15, 1996.

A couple of months later I had the opportunity to move to San Francisco with *BusinessWeek*. My husband and I loved New York but, for many reasons, decided to head west. This turned out to be a fortuitous move. Silicon Valley was heading straight into a technology bonanza, as companies like eBay, Yahoo!, and eTrade all made their debuts. I was covering some of these upstarts when I became pregnant with my first child. While on maternity leave, I was offered the job of Silicon Valley bureau chief. I didn't hesitate and enjoyed four years heading up our coverage of what ultimately turned into the dot-com bust.

Despite all the excitement Silicon Valley was serving up, the Smirnovs and their story were always in the back of my mind. They were like a boomerang. No matter how hard I tried to get rid of them, they just kept coming back. The lawsuit was still going on. Beyond that, though, I didn't really know much. So I decided to do some research. With the technology meltdown, I had a little more time on my hands. I had two books translated from Russian into English. They were written by different members of the Smirnov family and revealed two very different perspectives. I also started reading about Russian history—everything from the rise and fall of the tsars to the emancipation of serfs to the country's battle with alcoholism. In addition, I explored the history of vodka. I stayed out of the bars to do this part of the research—at least initially.

I came away with a level of excitement and conviction I had not known before. The Smirnov story was endlessly fascinating to me. The big question was whether anybody else would think so. Plus, given my background, I would be expected to write a straightforward business history. I didn't really want to do that. If I was going to write a book, I wanted it to be dramatic. I wanted it to be accessible to a broader audience. But how? And then I read *Seabiscuit*. This tale of an underdog racehorse who came from nothing to achieve great glory somehow resonated with the Smirnov tale. They were underdogs, too. They achieved glory, too. What's more, *Seabiscuit* captured an era. The author, Laura Hillenbrand, had done a masterful job of enabling readers to touch, smell, and see the moments described in the book. As I thought about it more, *Seabiscuit* was the model for me. I could re-create tsarist Russia. I could read more Tolstoy and Chekhov. I could narrate a tale that was incredible, brilliant, and ultimately heartbreaking. I was going to write a book.

There was still the glaring problem of not knowing the Russian language, however. So many of the documents I would need would be in Russian—most likely located in Russia. It was ▶

Discovering the Smirnovs *(continued)*

clear I would have to sell the project before I could really commit to writing it. Fortunately, I landed an amazing agent and found an enthusiastic editor at HarperCollins. My adventure had begun. I read everything I could get my hands on about the era. I discovered the memoirs of Vladimir Smirnov at Columbia University during a research trip to New York. I found a twenty-five-year-old videotape about the history of the Smirnoff brand. And I made contact with Tania Glezer, the Russian researcher and translator who would become my right hand for the next four-plus years.

A trip to Russia seemed in order. I wanted to meet some of Smirnov's descendants personally, visit a number of sites that were important to the family, and get into some of the archives. In the summer of 2005, I packed up my husband and children and flew to Moscow. Thankfully, they were all as game for this new adventure as I was. I had been to this city once before on a reporting trip in 1990. Mikhail Gorbachev was in power then and the streets were full of talk about *glasnost* and *perestroika*. It was an exciting time. Hope was in the air—despite the long lines of Russians waiting for their rations of cheese or sugar.

Circumstances had shifted dramatically in fifteen years. Moscow was now a city of plenty. Russians had access to the same things New Yorkers and Londoners did, and they would tell you, if you dared to ask, that their lives

66 In the summer of 2005, I packed up my husband and children and flew to Moscow. 99

overall were much better. Moreover, both the economy and government were stable, which had certainly not been the case in the '90s. Still, upon landing in the Russian capital, I couldn't help feeling that something was missing. After a few days, I identified the missing element as the hopeful spirit that had permeated so many of the days following the collapse of the Soviet Union. To me, Muscovites now looked almost complacent, as if they had given up wanting more because it hurt too much.

That might explain why the people I met during my visit fell largely into two categories. First were the extraordinarily generous Russians. Upon hearing about my book project, they were filled with national pride. They were truly touched that an American would be interested in bringing an aspect of their history to a Western audience and wanted to do whatever they could to further the process. They were warm, intelligent, and utterly selfless. The second group stood in sharp contrast to the first. They resented my foreignness and took offense with my assumption that I could accurately tell a story that belonged to them. Sadly, the Smirnovs I contacted fell into the latter category, and I ended up with only snippets of cooperation from them.

Still, while my husband ventured out with the kids to places like Gorky Park and a local chocolate factory, I trudged on with Tania to the historical archives. ▶

Discovering the Smirnovs *(continued)*

When you walk into an archival library, you begin to wonder what it must be like to drown. The information overload is just that daunting. The archivist will bring out boxes of material that you sift through hoping to uncover some never-before-seen historical nugget— or at least something relevant to the task at hand. Sometimes we were lucky, discovering everything from some of the Smirnov passports to extensive business records to marriage and birth certificates. Unexpected bonuses surfaced, too. For instance, while looking for Vladimir Smirnov's passport, we accidentally came across his application for a gun permit. As the seeds of the revolution were being sowed, we discovered, he had wisely sought some extra protection.

Even better was when I learned, almost halfway into my project, that Harvard University had been given a treasure trove of Smirnov documents. Yes, you read that right. It hadn't even been catalogued yet. I managed to get myself to Boston within days and, due to the kindness of a librarian, was able to peruse the documents there. Imagine my surprise and overwhelming joy when I not only came across incredible information pertaining to the Smirnovs' lives after the revolution, but also discovered that most of these documents had already been translated into English. It doesn't get much better than that.

Of course, there were plenty of frustrating days, too, from both research and writing standpoints. These times

66 When you walk into an archival library, you begin to wonder what it must be like to drown. 99

were especially tough when I had expected certain kinds of information to be readily available, and it wasn't. The weather is one such example. I knew from newspaper articles that it had snowed on the day of Smirnov's funeral, but not whether it had been cold enough for the snow to stick on the ground. Because of the dearth of available data, it took about a month to track down enough information to conclude that the snow had indeed blanketed Moscow that day.

I have often wondered if, had I known at the start of this project what I knew at the end, I still would have done it. Did I really understand how difficult it would be to put together a book when much of the research was written in a language I did not know? Did I appreciate the great distance between San Francisco and Moscow—both in miles and in culture? Or how I would feel about the descendants not embracing my project? The truth is, I would do it all over again. I am not one of those journalists who always had a burning desire to write a book. In fact, I had never seriously thought about it—until the Smirnovs came along. From that first day in my office in New York to the day I submitted my manuscript, I was in love. I was in love with the history. I was in love with the story. And in a strange way, I was also in love with the people. Theirs was a story worth telling. ⌒

Vodka Tastings

CONTRARY TO POPULAR WISDOM,
vodkas are not all created equal.
They are made from a wide variety
of organic ingredients, from grains to
beets to potatoes to grapes to molasses.
They deliver various flavors, smells,
textures, and aftertastes. And vodkas
often reflect the regions and cultures
from which they come. This truth was
readily apparent during my visit to
Russia. Traditionally, Russians drink
their vodka in one gulp. It is served
very cold and followed by chasers,
such as black bread or some kind
of salty treat. Drinking vodka with
Russians on their own turf is very
different from drinking with friends
during girls' night out. I found with
my Russian friends I wanted to relate
to the experience the way they did—
all in the name of research, of course.
This meant I had to understand not
only what I was tasting, but how to
taste it. So with the help of master
mixologist Kenji Jesse, here are a
few tips to help you become a
more discerning vodka drinker.

Many of the techniques used to
taste wine can be applied to vodka.
You need to start with a cleansed palate.
You can achieve this a number of ways,
by drinking chilled water or eating plain
crackers, for example. In addition, Kenji
recommends smelling the back of your
hand before each tasting to allow for a
purer olfactory experience. He also adds
a splash of mineral water to each vodka

to "open up any hidden sugars." You then smell the vodka as you would smell wine. Your nose can pick up on ingredients as well as flavors.

The tasting itself will reveal more than anything. The first sip you take of vodka is a throwaway. It should be small and swallowed quickly. Or, like me, you can just spit it out. The second sip is the main event. You should be on the lookout for the four Fs: fragrance, flavor, feel, and finish. Allow the vodka to roll over your tongue and sit in your mouth for a moment. Try to identify the flavors and sensations you experience. You might notice a whiff of fruit or a hint of nuts. Once you swallow, pay attention to the aftereffects. Does the vodka burn, or is it smooth? In all vodkas, you are looking for a lack of acidity, roughness, or burn.

Admittedly, it is often difficult to distinguish one from another, because vodka is meant to be a neutral, water-based spirit. That is, of course, why vodkas make such an ideal base for cocktails. But if you are really attentive, it is amazing the differences you will quickly notice. I'm no connoisseur, but even I can now tell Smirnoff from Grey Goose or Ketel One. They are very distinct from one another.

For a fun evening, invite some friends over and see if you can tell the difference between vodkas made from a variety of ingredients. Here are some suggestions of brands you may want to test. This list is by no means definitive, but at least it gives you a place to start. ▶

Vodka Tastings *(continued)*

Brand(s)	Made From
Chopin or Blue Ice	Potatoes
Cîroc	Grapes
Finlandia	Barley
Smirnoff	Grains
Ketel One/Absolut/Stoli/ Grey Goose	Wheat

Cheers! ∾